CW01082480

EXTRA-TERRESTRIAL FRIENDS AND FOES

George C. Andrews

1993
ILLUMINET PRESS

Copyright © 1993 by George C. Andrews
All rights reserved.

First Edition, 1993

No part of this publication may be reproduced or transmitted in any form or by
any means, electronic or mechanical, including photocopy, recording, or any information storage and retrieval system now known or to be invented, without permission in writing from the publisher, except by a reviewer who wishes to quote brief
passages in connection with a review written for inclusion in a magazine, newspaper or broadcast.

Library Of Congress Cataloging in Publication Data

Andrews, George C. (George Clinton), 1926—
    Extra-terrestrial Friends and Foes / by George C. Andrews. — 1st
IllumiNet Press ed.
        p.   cm.
    Includes index.
    ISBN: 0-9626534-8-9 : $14.95
    1. Unidentified flying objects — Sightings and encounters.
    2. Life on other planets.
    3. Conspiracies   I. Title.

TL789.3.A53   1993
001.9'42—dc20   93-3037

Cover Art by James Koehnline

IllumiNet Press
Division of I-Net Group, Ltd.
P.O. Box 2808
Lilburn, GA 30226

10 9 8 7 6 5 4 3 2

Printed in the United States of America

I wish to thank Tatiana Andrews, Bob and Barbara Bartholic, Olga Anderson, Larry Bogart, Larry Bryant, Tina Choate, Scott Corrales, Jacquie Dersin, Janet Flett, J.F. Gille, Judith Gomez, Geoff Graff, Dr. Oscar Guerra, Jimmy and Claudia Guieu, Lars Hansson, Ida Kannenberg, Pat Kephart, Eugenia Macer-Story, Jacques Maniez, Jean-Claude Massa, Anna Mitchell-Hedges, Bryan Myers, Floyd and Kate Sandberg Olden, Cat Powers, Louise Randolph, Alain Ranguis, Tom and Elaine Richards, Lucille de Saint-Andre, Frank and Maureen Scherer, Dr. Berthold E. Schwarz, Marjorie Sherrill, Jerry Sheppard, Barbara Sowell, Lee Spence, Shirley Starke, Michael Tetu, Alice Thompson, Walter and Mary Jo Uphoff, Simon Vinkenoog, Rene Voarino and the C.E.O.F., Ron and Kay West, Thomas S. Woodruff, Nell Zajac, and Lionel Ziprin for their help.

"You have been always, and before you nothing has been. There is nothing to pray to but you. The star nations all over the universe are yours, and yours are the grasses of the Earth. Day in, day out, you are the life of things."

—From one of Black Elk's prayers to the Great Spirit

Contents

1

The Stonewalling of High Strangeness

A large crack appeared in the stonewalling of high strangeness on October 14, 1988. On that date, there was a semi-official admission of extra-terrestrial intervention in human affairs, in the guise of a two-hour TV special entitled UFO COVER-UP?...LIVE! Participation by U.S. and Soviet officials was so extensive that the broadcast could not have occurred without the consent of both governments.

The program was presented to the public simultaneously in the United States and the Soviet Union, the first time in history that any TV program has received such preferential treatment. However, in spite of this clearly implied U.S. - U.S.S.R. seal of approval (or perhaps because of it?), the program contained a clever mix of information and disinformation.

The valid information was that we are not alone, and that the government has made a hitherto secret agreement with short gray humanoids (the "Grays") who say they are from Zeta Reticuli.

Although it was not specifically stated that the Grays were the only E.T. group our government has made contact with, that implication was made. To the extent that implication was made, it was a falsehood.

The statement that the Grays nourish themselves on vegetables was an outright lie, to which the recent cattle mutilations (not even mentioned on the program) bear unequivocal testimony (see the "Mysterious Mutilations" chapter of my *Extra-Terrestrials Among Us* [Llewellyn, 1986]). Linda Moulton Howe's brilliant master-work, *An Alien Harvest* (published by LMH Productions, P.O. Box 538, Huntingdon Valley, PA 19006) presents irrefutable photographic and documentary evidence that these mutilations have occurred on an enormous scale and are still occurring.

The complex question of what the nourishment of the Grays consist of is investigated in detail in what you are about to read, as is the relationship between this subject and the epidemic of abductions we presently face. The 1988 TV program admitted the existence of these abductions, but implied that the motivations of the Grays are benign — another falsehood.

The TV audience heard that the Grays are the guests of the U.S. government and have been given a base in Nevada. Nothing was said about the other bases our government has given the Grays, or about the activities being carried on in those underground bases. The conditions of the agreement made between our government and the Grays were not mentioned. What those conditions consisted of, and what kind of relationship our government really has with the Grays, are examined at length in this book.

UFO COVER-UP?...LIVE!, hosted by Mike Farrell, implied that Uncle Sam had made a smart deal. However, the truth of the matter is that this deal was the most disastrous mistake, not only in the history of our nation, but in the history of our entire civilization. There were other E.T. groups that we could have made incomparably better arrangements with. Although this scandal is similar in nature to the Iran-Contra deal, it is a tragedy on a scale of such unprecedented magnitude that in comparison Iran-Contra seems like very small change indeed.

The case of contactee Edouard "Billy" Meier in Switzerland, which Mike Farrell stigmatized as "an obvious hoax," is not without its ambiguities, absurdities and contradictions. Nevertheless, the physical evidence is so strong that this is one of the best-substantiated cases on record. Dr. James Deardorff has speculated that the E.T.s may be making deliberate use of absurdity as a form of strategic camouflage, in order to ensure gradual rather than sudden realization of their presence. By cloaking their activities in an aura of absurdity, they repel serious investigation and make people hesitate to endorse the reality of the phenomena, keeping it all borderline and marginal, which distracts human attention from their presence.

If this is the game that is going on, the E.T.s may be feeding Meier a mixture of truth and falsehood, which he relays to the public in the sincere belief that it is all true.

For example, Meier believes himself to be the only genuine UFO contactee, an obvious absurdity, because there have been thousands of genuine human/alien contact cases during recent years. He also states that the many thousands of abduction and crop circle incidents reported during recent years were all hoaxes, another obvious absurdity. I concur with Deardorff that Meier is sincere in his beliefs, but that he is being fed information mixed with disinformation.

One of the most curious aspects of the Meier case is the veritable obsession displayed by the government's plainclothes media agents (such as William Moore, who has publicly admitted his links with government agencies) in over-zealous attempts to discredit the evidence. An all-out media vendetta has been waged against the Meier case that seems totally out of proportion with the investigation of any one single UFO case. Is this because Meier's contact was not with the Zeta Grays but with a rival E.T. group that in appearance is almost indistinguishable from us, and which shares a common ancestry with us, known among researchers as the Blonds or Swedes? This is the same group that was known in antiquity to the Scandinavians as the Aesir, to the Irish as the Tuatha Te Danaan, and by other names in other cultures. One of the modern Soviet cases mentioned on the Mike Farrell program, in which the UFO opened up like a flower, was an encounter with the Blonds, a group with whom I think we could work out a valid alliance.

Dr. Jean Mundy is a Professor Emeritus in Psychology at Long Island University and has been in private practice in psychotherapy and hypnotherapy for over twenty years. She is a member of a long list of professional and honorary societies, and she has published articles on a wide variety of subjects in both the academic and the popular press. During recent years, she has focused her expertise on the subject of UFO phenomena. Dr. Mundy has written the following analysis of the public reaction to the 1988 TV program especially for this book:

The most astonishing UFO TV documentary aired to date, on October 14, 1988, with Mike Farrell as the host, had all the ingredients of a blockbuster. Note just some of the cast of characters: 1) A Russian scientist, revealing that aliens have landed in Russia and contacted their military personnel. 2) Two CIA agents, identities disguised, revealing that extra-terrestrial aliens are now the 'guests of the U.S. Government.' 3) About a hundred residents of Gulf Breeze, Florida, who have witnessed and photographed the extensive UFO activity in their home town. 4) Abductees telling their own stories under hypnosis. 5) Expert witnesses from the military saying that sightings they reported while in service 'disappeared' from the records. 6) A psychiatrist reporting that abductees she has treated were sane and suffering from trauma as a result of their contact with aliens. 7) Evidence by investigators of crashed UFO sites. 8) Testimony from Budd Hopkins, who has investigated hundreds of abductee cases for over 12 years, that genetic experiments are being performed by aliens on humans on a large scale. 9) Other witnesses, each expert in his/her own field, testifying to the validity of photographic or other tangible documentation of UFOs. 10) Paintings of aliens drawn by artists from the testimony of witnesses.

Surely, even by Hollywood standards, here are all the ingredients of a box-office hit. Was it a hit? Well, during the two-hour show, 75,000 viewers did pay one dollar each to have their phone-in vote about their belief in human-alien contact recorded. What other signs of success made the front page? Not a one! The show was a flop in terms of arousing public interest. How can this be? How could such a carefully concocted combination of ingredients, culminating in the most newsworthy disclosure in history, not elicit a bang, nor even a whimper?

I played a videotape of the show to my adult education class on alien-human contact. I watched the reactions of my class members. Thanks to the review/playback capability, I was able to conduct some experiments.

The adult students who signed up for this course were believers in the possibility of human-alien contact. Some even had personal experience of contact, yet after the screening they were more doubtful than before! I then recognized that UFO COVER-UP?...LIVE! made brilliant use of the best propaganda techniques. If you have a tape of the show, watch it again, and listen carefully to the soundtrack. Look at the painted backdrops and, most important, look at Mike Farrell's reactions.

You will see and hear some interesting contradictions. The astute viewer cannot dismiss these contradictions as sloppy production. The production had a huge budget and was planned many months in advance. In fact, Budd Hopkins reported to me that each witness was interviewed at length before the show, then certain words of that interview were selected to be used. The words were put on cue cards, and on the night of the show, the witnesses were allowed to say only what was on the cards. UFO COVER-UP?...LIVE! was carefully rehearsed. Reading from cue cards, unless one is experienced in doing so, gives words a stilted sound that many listeners take as phony. Score one for not believing the witnesses.

Score two: when words are spoken over background music, the music makes an unconscious impression that flavors the emotional impact of the words. For example, the relentless "approach," louder and louder in intensity, of the orchestration of the *Jaws* soundtrack as the shark nears its victim builds up a feeling of dread even before any action takes place. The background music for UFO COVER-UP?...LIVE! is light, pleasant dance music. While the Russian is speaking of terrifying abductions, the music is a rousing polka!

Score three: when the Russian says, "The aliens communicated with the terrified soldiers by mental telepathy," Mike Farrell responds, "Oh, they used music, just like in the movie *Close Encounters*." We depend very much on the reaction of others to set our own reaction. Obviously, if someone tells you a story and they are laughing, you think the story is funny. If they are in a panic state while telling it to you, you think of it as tragic. Throughout the entire show, Mike Farrell reacted to all the UFO information with puzzlement, but in an amused and light-hearted manner. So, for the most part, the audience did too.

Score four: through the skillful but unobtrusive use of another media technique, the painted backdrop against which the alien Grays are portrayed is a bright sunny room overlooking a garden! Nothing to take seriously there, certainly nothing to worry about.

Also the depictions of the Grays were idealized and did not conform to witness descriptions, giving the impression of benign Disneyesque animated characters.

Score five: Another powerful media technique is to trivialize something important by focusing on a tiny detail. For example, telling the audience that the aliens "prefer strawberry ice cream" reduces these mysterious life forms to a childish format.

Score six: we are so accustomed to Hollywood movies that we are entertained by a "historical" film, but never for a moment truly believe that the "action" taking place on the screen is real. We know it is rehearsed and played by actors. When Mike Farrell puts the UFO reports in the same category as the movie *Close Encounters,* the audience automatically thinks of the TV documentary UFO COVER-UP?...LIVE! as just another Hollywood movie. No one writes a letter to the editor of their local newspaper or phones their Congressman to demand action about a crime committed in a Hollywood movie.

There is more. One of the women presented in the documentary who has been abducted by aliens is an acquaintance of mine. Her entire life has been affected by her terrifying alien contact. The one and only comment highlighted on the cue card for her to use on the supposedly "LIVE!" Mike Farrell show was, "Oh, he's so ugly." When my students heard this, they giggled! They took it to be comical.

Neither my students nor the majority of the viewing audience took the UFO COVER-UP?...LIVE! program seriously. That is why there was no audience response. One of my students said he thought, "The man portraying the Russian couldn't have been a real Russian, because he spoke English too well." No doubt he was trying to account for why the show did not have the ring of truth to it.

The question remains: were the producers of the show, whoever they really are, *pleased* that their show was a "flop," in that few viewers took the reality of alien-human contact (or invasion) seriously? Or were they disappointed by the lack of audience response? What, indeed, was the real purpose of this carefully staged show? The format in which UFO COVER-UP?...LIVE! was presented tranquilized the general public, as did the movies *E.T.* and *Close Encounters of the Third Kind*, in the comfortable belief that there is absolutely nothing to worry about, as far as any reports of alleged "aliens" are concerned.

As Dr. Mundy has pointed out, this comfortable belief system — so assiduously maintained by the authorities through their constant insistence on relegating the subject of alien intervention in human affairs to the realm of media trivia — relies for its support on some very thin ice indeed.

This ice is so thin that it can be shattered by featherweight random events, such as the arrival in my mailbox of a letter from Rev. John E. Schroeder of the UFO Study Group of Greater St. Louis, saying: "You mentioned William Moore's TV program hosted by Mike Farrell. Is it any surprise that the November 1989 issue of prestigious *Millimeter* magazine for film and TV producers listed the CIA as paying producer for that show? I wonder what happened to the response requests? Who effectively collected whose paying phone numbers? Why? How are they to be used? Was any data ever given congressional members? The plot thickens!"

The plot does indeed thicken. A search of the November 1989 issue of *Millimeter* magazine did not locate the item which Rev. Schroeder is nevertheless sure that he and his wife saw in *Millimeter*, though he may have been mistaken as to the issue. This does not necessarily mean that the item does not exist, but as we go to press the question remains unresolved. In spite of this uncertainty, the item seems worth retaining, because both the possibility and the questions raised by Rev. Schroeder remain relevant, even if neither confirmed nor invalidated.

The ability to face phenomena of high strangeness with an open mind is a rare trait, not shared by the vast majority of contemporary humanity. The average person feels threatened or terrified by any unprecedented divergence from conventionally accepted norms of reality, and may react with dangerous violence.

Let us consider the case of Herbert Schirmer, who in 1967 held the distinction of being the youngest Chief of Police in Nebraska, and who was one of the most prominent citizens in his home town of Ashland, Nebraska. One night while on duty in his patrol car, he encountered a large disc-shaped UFO, which had landed not far from the highway. When a glowing humanoid figure appeared in his headlights, he tried to draw his gun, but found himself inexplicably paralyzed. When the humanoid opened the door of his car, Schirmer felt a cold hard instrument being applied to the back of his neck, and he blacked out. Upon regaining consciousness, he drove straight back to the police station and reported the incident to his fellow officers, who noticed that he was unable to account for about half an hour. There was an unusual welt on the back of his neck, which later left a permanent scar. A qualified hypnotist, Dr. Leo Sprinkle, was brought in to regress him back to the period of missing time. Under hypnosis, the regression indicated that he had been taken aboard the UFO and had communicated with a group of alien humanoids during the period of missing time. A search of the location where the incident occurred revealed physical landing traces.

How did Chief of Police Schirmer's old friends react to his adventure? By firing him from his job, dynamiting his car, and hanging and burning him in effigy in the town square. His wife divorced him, and he was driven out of town. He has since moved frequently, contacting various UFO investigators, trying to make sense of his dilemma.

There is a remarkable resemblance between Herbert Schirmer's ordeal and the Jeff Greenhaw case. In 1973, Jeff Greenhaw was the youngest Chief of Police in Alabama, and was one of the most prominent citizens in his home town of Falkville, Alabama. One night he received an anonymous phone call from a woman who said that a UFO had just landed in a field not far from town. Greenhaw got into his patrol car and drove toward that area. As he approached the field, he encountered a humanoid about six feet tall, covered from head to foot in metallic clothing, standing in the middle of the road. Greenhaw pulled up near him and said: "Howdy, stranger." There was no response. Greenhaw reached for a Polaroid camera he happened to have with him and took four pictures. Then he turned on the flashing blue light on the top of his patrol car. The humanoid began to run, but not in normal fashion, moving sideways instead of forward, taking large leaps of about 10 feet at a time very quickly, traveling at extraordinary speed. Greenhaw began to pursue him, but his patrol car suddenly went out of control and into a spin as he reached 45 miles per hour, obliging him to give up the chase. He returned to town and reported the incident.

How did Chief of Police Greenhaw's old friends react to his adventure? By firing him from his job, dynamiting his car, and burning down the trailer in which he lived. His wife divorced him, and he was driven out of town. He has since disappeared.

These two cases are not isolated. One could easily fill a book with the many cases of UFO contactees who have been obliged to leave their homes and change their names because of hostile social pressures. As our history clearly indicates, such witch hunts are nothing new. The average citizen's tolerance of diversity has increased only minimally since medieval times. What sets the Schirmer and Greenhaw cases apart from the hundreds, if not thousands, of other cases of contactee harassment is the secure social position they both enjoyed, until they reported their UFO encounters.

Being the Chief of Police in a small town one has grown up in implies widespread respect and trust from a closely knit group of people who have known you since childhood, and is about as secure a social position in the hierarchy of the American system as it is possible to attain. The fact that one encounter with the unknown could in one day transform the role model for an entire community into a despised outcast demonstrates the extreme extent to which the average citizen feels insecure, and therefore fears the unknown.

This is true on the national level as well as on the individual level. The thousands of documents that the government has been obliged to release under the Freedom of Information Act demonstrate that its internal policy concerning UFOs and extra-terrestrials is extremely different from its publicly stated policy. To put it bluntly, our government has been lying to its citizens about UFOs and extra-terrestrials for over 40 years.

To point out merely one example of this duplicity: Air Force Regulation 200-2, JANAP-146 provides a penalty of 10 years in prison plus a $10,000 fine and a forfeiture of pay and pension for any member of the Armed Forces who makes an unauthorized statement about UFOs. If you write to the Library of Congress and ask for a copy of this regulation, you will get an answer stating that no such regulation exists. Air Force spokesmen blandly deny that any such regulation exists. However, if you write to the Library of Congress and ask for a copy of The UFO Enigma by Marcia Smith and David Havas, which was published by none other than the Library of Congress itself in 1983, you will find in it a statement that Major Donald Keyhoe was the first to make public reference to the previously secret JANAP-146.

Further details are to be found in a book by a well-known French researcher, Aime Michel, published in 1969. The preface to a previous book by Michel was written by General L. M. Chassin, General Air Defense Coordinator, Allied Air Forces, Central Europe, NATO. General Chassin commends Michel's ability and integrity in strong terms. The statement Michel made in 1969 translates as follows: "However, if it is so certain that for the American authorities this subject is no more than crazy stories that are completely without interest, how does one explain the extraordinary precautions in Air Force Regulation 200-2, and the 10 years in prison plus

$10,000 fine of JANAP-146, all of which are still being enforced 15 years later, and more vigorously than ever?"

Since Michel stated in 1969 that the regulation had been enforced for fifteen years, it must have originated in 1954, which just happens to have been a year during which an exceptional amount of UFO activity took place.

According to Ralph and Judy Blum, who received assistance from government sources while compiling their excellent book *Beyond Earth* (Bantam, 1974), the text of JANAP-146 is contained in an official publication of the Joint Chiefs of Staff, entitled Canadian-United States Communications Instructions for Reporting Vital Intelligence Sightings (CIRVIS/MERINT, JANAP 146).

I'd now like to describe how the covert censorship of the news media works. Most newspapers and TV or radio newscasters depend largely on the major wire services for their material. The major wire services, which are few in number, do not carry UFO stories unless the incidents are on such a scale that it is impossible to ignore them. When a UFO incident on this scale occurs, the typical treatment is to truncate the story, arbitrarily selecting one detail of a complex event and presenting it in a facetious manner, as if it was the whole story.

For example, the complex series of events that occurred in Brazil on May 19, 1986, was reduced by the wire services to a brief, tongue-in-cheek reference to "flying ping-pong balls." As I was able to obtain translations of some of the articles that appeared in the Brazilian press immediately following the incidents, I had access to details that the wire services neglected to mention. I described the events in the Appendix to my previous book, but further information has reached me since the publication of *Extra-Terrestrials Among Us*, so here is an updated version of them:

Ozires Silva is the president of Embrair, the largest manufacturer of aircraft in Brazil, and is also president of Petrobas, the government-owned oil company. Being at the head of both of these important corporations, he is one of the most influential men in Brazil. San Jose de Campos is the high-tech center of Brazil's military-industrial complex. On May 19, 1986, Mr. Silva had a conference with the President of Brazil, Jose Sarney, at Brazilia, at which the Minister of Aviation, Brigadier General Octavio Moreira Lima, was also present. Mr. Silva then took his private jet to San Jose de Campos. At 9 p.m., the pilot of Mr. Silva's jet had begun his descent to land, when the control tower informed him that three UFOs were in his flight path. The pilot canceled his approach and, with the permission of Mr. Silva, attempted to pursue the objects. He gave up after 13 minutes, as the UFOs were traveling at such high speed that he was unable to catch up with them. The pilot saw two of the objects, and described them as very bright red lights, which could not be confused with stars or known types of aircraft. Three jet fighters were scrambled. One of these picked up the three UFOs on radar at 9:45 p.m. and pursued them for half an hour, after which he gave up further pursuit because his fuel was running low. At that time, ground radar at several different air bases reported UFOs. Air traffic controllers found themselves confronted with the impossible task of keeping track of 21 different UFOs simultaneously for over three hours. The objects were seen on 50 different radar sets belonging to the Brazilian government, over an area covering three states. The pilots sent up to intercept the objects, who reported both visual and radar contact while being outdistanced at every turn by the objects, were among the best in the Brazilian Air Force. The statements made by the pilots on their return were all similar and unequivocal.

Three more jets were scrambled. Some of the pursuers found themselves being pursued. According to a dispatch from one of the major wire services, about which I'll have more to say later on, one jet reported being chased by objects that were very small, approximately the size of ping-pong balls. The 13 objects temporarily paced the jet, taking positions near its right and left wings. They were intensely luminous, red and white and green, traveling at speeds estimated by the military jet pilot as varying between 160 and 1,350 miles per hour.

Three days previously, on May 16, a civilian pilot flying near Brazilia had reported having been followed for 460 miles by small luminous objects. Two days after the incident, on May 21 at Ceara, Brazil, many people witnessed a large cigar-shaped mother ship, from which many smaller UFOs emerged. On May 22, sightings continued to be reported from different regions of Brazil. Minister of Aviation Lima confirmed that the events of May 19 had actually taken place, specifically stating that "radar scopes in Sao Paolo became saturated with an enormous number of targets characterizing an invasion of Brazilian airspace." General Lima ordered an official investigation of the incidents. This was a historic moment, an unprecedented new development: for the first time, a government was obliged to officially acknowledge the reality of UFO phenomena.

The U.S. government explained the events of May 19, 1986, at San Jose de Campos as "lenticular clouds," a blatant absurdity dutifully repeated by the news media, but so utterly ridiculous that it is unworthy of refutation.

Just as is the case with Easter Island, there are strong magnetic anomalies in the vicinity of San Jose de Campos, particularly on the ocean floor.

So you see, there is quite a difference between an in-depth coverage of such events and the snide superficial version provided by the major wire services.

At the time I wrote this account, I was not aware of a matter of considerable importance, which Willy Smith of the UNICAT Project has now pointed out. Willy Smith developed the UNICAT Project in association with the late Dr. J. Allen Hynek, and since Dr. Hynek's death has continued the work with a team of 60 colleagues. I now quote from a Letter to the Editor that Willy Smith wrote, which appeared in *Pursuit* (P.O. Box 265, Little Silver, NJ 07739), Fourth Quarter, 1986:

> Your collaborator...writing about the penetration of the Brazilian airspace in the night of May 19, 1986, refers to the lights that played with the fighter planes for about three hours as 'colored ping-pong balls,' and quotes his source for this statement as a UPI dispatch dated May 24, 1986. The interesting thing is that the label 'ping-pong balls' was created by the wire services, and not even immediately after the incident, as the date of the dispatch shows...I consulted almost a hundred clippings from Brazilian newspapers and in none of them could I find any reference to ping-pong balls. Moreover, there are no words in the original Portuguese that could erroneously be translated as 'ping-pong balls.' On the other hand, the term appears ad nauseam in clippings from Europe and other South American countries, where indeed it was picked up from the wire services...Was it a deliberate effort to discredit the sightings a few days after the events? If one adds to this the fact that a large number of dubious 'cases' — and in many instances bogus cases — happened to occur in the following days, it seems as if someone were orchestrating a debunking symphony.

What we learn from this is that the wire services will not only truncate UFO stories to make them seem ridiculous, but are so utterly unscrupulous that they will deliberately invent false details, in order to reduce an important UFO story to absurdity.

As the vast majority of UFO incidents get coverage only in local newspapers, if they even get that, there is no general awareness of the persistent UFO activity occurring in other parts of the country and other parts of the world. Some stories in the media even state that UFO activity is now almost non-existent and was just a passing fad of the 50s and 60s, when the truth is that there are just as many incidents as there ever were, but that the covert censorship is being enforced more effectively.

Major wire services operate in collusion with governmental intelligence agencies in perpetrating this devious form of camouflaged censorship for one basic reason, as clearly expressed by nuclear physicist Stanton Friedman: "No government on Earth would want its citizens to pledge allegiance to the planet rather than to itself, and to think of themselves first as Earthlings, rather than as Americans, Canadians, Russians, etc."

On pages 188-191 of *Extra-Terrestrials Among Us,* I described the adventures of an officer using the pseudonym of "Toulinet," who had been assigned to write an analysis of the top secret "Grudge 13" report, after which he had been summarily discharged from military service. During the summer of 1989, this man took the courageous step of publicly identifying himself as former Captain William English of the Green Berets, who had been working at the RAF Security Services Command, RAF Chicksands, England, at the time that he was assigned to write the analysis of "Grudge 13." I have been unable to either confirm or invalidate the rumor that no sooner had he publicly identified himself than his residence was firebombed, as had been the residences of police chiefs Schirmer and Greenhaw in 1967 and 1973.

Attempts have been made to destroy English's credibility, such as the U.S. Army stating that it has no military records concerning him. However, it is standard operating procedure for military commanders to delete, either partially or in totality, the service records of subordinate personnel who have become security risks, as is exemplified in "The Cutolo Affidavit," published in *Erase and Forget* by Paragon Research, P.O. Box 981, Orlando FL 32802, in 1991.

Records are also systematically destroyed by the highly paid defense contractors engaged by the Pentagon for secret projects. In November 1989, physicist Robert Lazar went public with disclosures concerning alien disks and related activities at Area 51 of the Nevada Test Site. From one day to the next, all records of his previous employment, his education, and even of his birth, vanished as if by magic. This would have effectively destroyed his credibility, if there had not been certain items that survived the onslaught of the modern Inquisitors. For example, Lazar stated that he had worked as physicist for Los Alamos National Laboratories, whose representatives denied that he had ever been employed by them. However, independent investigators found a copy of the telephone directory issued by the Los Alamos Lab in 1982, which listed Robert Lazar among the scientists employed by them. An article in the Los Alamos paper during that same year, 1982, described Lazar's interest in jet cars, mentioning his employment at the Los Alamos Lab as a physicist. Finding themselves unable to destroy Lazar's credibility in any other way, the authorities resorted to a crude but time-tested technique and tarnished his reputation with a sex scandal, which Lazar's lifestyle unfortunately made possible.

Some people have taken issue with my statement that we are about to experience direct confrontation with non-human intelligent beings from elsewhere in the cosmos in the near future, pointing out that UFO intervention in human affairs has been minimal during the last 40 years, so why shouldn't that pattern continue indefinitely? I have answered that question at length in my previous book, but would like to extend my response by describing some major incidents that occurred since its publication, which clearly indicate that we have entered a new phase of UFO activity, a phase characterized by deliberate and ostentatious UFO displays over heavily populated areas on an unprecedented scale.

There was a flurry of significant UFO activity both before and after August 12, 1986, but it was on the night of August 12 to 13 that the climax of the first incident occurred. During that night, reports came flooding in from Lake Huron to Nova Scotia in Canada, and in the United States from Maine, New York, Michigan, Indiana, Illinois, Arkansas, Louisiana, Kentucky, Pennsylvania, South Carolina, and Florida, as well as from the town of Leongatha in the province of Victoria in Australia. There had also been multi-witness sightings of a large UFO in Pennsylvania. Both of the Pennsylvania sightings appeared to involve the same object, described as bright silver and elliptical, the size of three buses in length. On the night of August 12 - 13, the reports from Arkansas, Louisiana, and Kentucky described a large cloud-like ball of fire. In Clark County, Kentucky, the appearance of an enormous ball of fire that lit up the whole sky was accompanied by a sonic boom that made houses shake, along with an odor described as similar to gunpowder. From Illinois, Indiana, Michigan, and Ontario came a flood of reports about "a spiral cloud with a star-like object beside it." An air traffic controller at Syracuse, New York, reported a UFO with red, white, and green lights that were flashing on and off, and that had "a spiraling rooster tail effect." It hovered and darted about. The air traffic controller, Tim Jones, saw it both visually and on his radar screen, and stated that the way it was behaving was unlike any aircraft he had ever seen. On that same night in Leongatha, Victoria Province, Australia, an English teacher and a science teacher at the local high school reported that a UFO with flashing lights had hovered and maneuvered above them for about 40 minutes.

On the following day, the scramble for explanations began. Both NASA and NORAD denied any involvement in the phenomena, and further specified that it did not correspond with any known Soviet space activity. Speculation that a new Japanese satellite might have exploded was squelched by a statement from Japan's Tanageshima Space Center that their satellite was functioning normally.

At this point, as it usually does whenever a UFO incident occurs that is difficult to explain away in conventional terms, the U.S. government brought NASA expert (or establishment hatchet man, according to your point of view) James Oberg into the controversy to make a statement. Mr. Oberg stated authoritatively that what everyone had seen was fuel being dumped from a rocket on the Japanese satellite, as the rocket boosted the satellite into orbit, and that was that. Although this explanation left many questions unanswered (in particular, concerning the incidents in Clark County, Kentucky, and Syracuse, New York), it was accepted tamely without protest by the entire news media of this great nation as the final solution to the mystery of that night.

A lady named Lorraine Whitaker in Lanesboro, Pennsylvania, got a clear photograph of what had been visible in the sky over her area on the night of August 12, which depicts a sharply defined, intensely bright cigar shape, emitting a swirling cloud of luminous gas.

Paul Oles, who is the Planetarium Director at the Buhl Science Center in Pittsburgh, made the following statement: "We know what it wasn't, but we have no idea what it was. Our most logical explanations have been totally ruled out. It now falls into the category of an unidentified sighting." However, only one newspaper even mentioned the statement by Mr. Oles. Every other newspaper nationwide that carried the story featured the statement by Mr. Oberg of NASA as definitive.

On the night of August 15, 1986, three days after the incidents I have just described, Angelo and Grazia Ricci of Verona, Italy, were abducted while on a summer vacation camping trip near Belluno, Italy. They were taken aboard a UFO by two humanoids, each about 6'6" tall, who were dressed in gray coveralls that left only their heads exposed. Their heads were long and hairless and had very pale skin. Their eyes were phosphorescent. They had pointed ears, a normal nose, and a narrow slit where the mouth should be. Mr. and Mrs. Ricci were subjected to medical examinations and various tests for about three hours before being released.

A series of events comparable in importance to those of August 12 occurred on September 23, 1986. They began at daybreak, when two brothers fishing on a lake near Daventry, England, reported that shortly after dawn they had seen six UFOs flying in formation behind a large UFO. Within the next few hours, thousands of people (including police) reported UFOs flying in formation and performing maneuvers, during which they left behind multi-colored vapor trails over West Germany, Holland, Belgium, Luxembourg, and France. In Paris, whole crowds of people driving to work during the morning rush witnessed a fleet of fifteen UFOs flying in formation. Simultaneously a ball of fire was seen over Amsterdam; what was described as a "flying machine" was reported by a staff member of the Royal Observatory in Belgium; "a very luminous object, shaped like a rocket, three times as large as an airplane" as well as "a cluster of five or six luminous green objects" were reported from Luxembourg; and "a bright flying object with a luminous tail" was reported from West Germany. There were also similar reports from Derbyshire and Leicestershire in England.

The fifteen UFOs seen over the Montreuil region of Paris were described as silver-colored, but over the Chatelet region of Paris witnesses perceived them as intensely luminous green and turquoise blue, some of them emitting green flame. Over Paris they were traveling at a leisurely pace, about the speed of an airplane during an air show.

The nearly simultaneous occurrence of such phenomena over six of the nations of Western Europe on the morning of September 23, 1986, has all the characteristics of a carefully orchestrated and deliberately ostentatious display, obviously intended to bring about widespread recognition of the reality represented by UFOs among the intelligent citizens of these key countries.

What was the result?

It is hard to know whether to laugh or cry over the incorrigible hypocrisy with which the news media handled this story. How did the journalists deal with this unprecedented manifestation of high strangeness in the skies of Europe? They understandably requested an explanation from NORAD. However, when NORAD explained that what everyone had seen was debris from a Soviet booster rocket, an explanation that was directly contradicted by the observations the journalists had themselves recorded, this implausible explanation was instantly and uncritically accepted by the news media, which abdicated all pretense of independent reasoning and parroted it ad nauseam as the only rational solution to the enigma of what had happened that morning throughout six nations of Western Europe.

The next example of a deliberate and ostentatious UFO display did not occur over a heavily populated area, but northeastern Alaska is certainly a sensitive military zone. The report did not reach the U.S. news media until January 1, 1987, though the incident happened on November 17, 1986. The time lag between the date of the incident and the date the report was made public supports the hypothesis of covert censorship of the news media.

This case bears a remarkable resemblance to the case officially announced by the Soviet Academy of Sciences in 1985, in which a Soviet airliner was followed by a UFO for approximately 800 miles. I described that case on the third and fourth pages of my previous book.

The case of November 17, 1986, involved the pilot, co-pilot, and flight engineer of a Japan Air Lines cargo jet that was making a return trip from Iceland to Anchorage, Alaska. The crew members first became aware of the three UFOs in the vicinity of their jet while over northeastern Alaska. Two of the UFOs were small, but the third was enormous, twice the size of an aircraft carrier. The UFOs followed the cargo jet for about 400 miles, during nearly an hour. They emitted flashing amber, green, and yellow lights. They played games with the jet: disappearing, reappearing, moving at incredible speeds, and hovering. At one point, the two smaller UFOs maintained positions directly in front of the cockpit of the cargo jet at close range, pacing the jet for several minutes at a distance of only a few feet in front of the cockpit, although the jet was traveling at 570 miles per hour at the time.

The large object appeared on the radar screens of Federal Aviation Administration flight controllers, who gave the Japan Air Lines pilot permission to attempt evasive action. Veteran pilot Captain Terauchi carried out evasive maneuvers, but was not able to shake off his pursuers. The UFOs later abandoned the pursuit of their own accord, without having taken any hostile action.

FAA officials interviewed the crew members upon their arrival at Anchorage and issued a statement saying that the crew was "normal, professional, rational, and had no drug or alcohol involvement."

At first the FAA confirmed the sighting, then a few days later decided that one air traffic controller had mistakenly interpreted a split image of the cargo plane as a separate object. Establishment hatchet man Phil Klass was then called in to kill the story by announcing that Captain Terauchi, despite 29 years of experience as a pilot and a hitherto impeccable record, had mistaken the planet Jupiter for a UFO. The fact that the large UFO had been witnessed not only visually by all crew members, but also on the jet's radar screen, and that neither Jupiter nor any other planet appears on radar screens, was ignored by Philip Klass. Hal Bernton, a reporter for the *Daily News* of Anchorage, Alaska, conducted an interview with the air traffic controller in question, Sam Rich, which was printed on Jan. 9, 1987. Sam Rich's testimony contradicted the FAA's version of the event in several important ways.

Rich, who has worked with the FAA for over a decade, denied categorically that he was the only air traffic controller to have seen the radar track of the UFO. The two other controllers who were working that shift also saw it. The track was not very strong, but neither he nor his two colleagues thought that it could be a split image, a possibility they considered at the time. Right after spotting the track, Rich phoned the Military Regional Operations Control Center, and "they informed me that they had the same radar track."

Rich confirmed that double images often occur on the FAA radar screen but said the JAL plane was not in the area where these split images usually occur. Also, over the past decade there have been about half a dozen reports by pilots of unidentified lights in the region where the JAL plane sighted the UFOs.

To all this, I can now add the fact that there have been several sightings from the area of the JAL encounter since the incident took place, reported both by airplane pilots and by people on the ground.

So who are we to believe — the air traffic controller who was actually on the job at the time of the incident, or the professional disinformation agents?

Another interesting aspect of the Japan Air Lines story is that although the incident occurred over Alaska on November 17, 1986, no U.S. media coverage of it took place until January 1987. When this six-week delay in making the story public was investigated, it turned out that the story never would have been made public at all in the United States if a family member of one of the JAL crew had not leaked the news to journalists in Japan. Once the story had entered the public domain in Japan, the U.S. authorities could no longer pretend that nothing had happened

Yet another major development in the story of this case, which apparently just refuses to die, occurred at the end of August 1987 when MUFON researcher T. Scott Crain, Jr. revealed (in an article entitled "New JAL Sighting Information," *California UFO*, vol. 2, no. 3) that there were indications that the images on the radar tapes had been tampered with. The FAA officials in Anchorage, Alaska, had sent the radar tapes to the main FAA office in Washington, D.C. — but they had not sent them directly. The tapes had traveled an indirect route, making an unexplained detour via the FAA Technical Center at Atlantic City, New Jersey. Researchers suspect that it was during this brief sojourn at the FAA Technical Center that the images on the tapes were altered. The Freedom of Information Act request that Mr. Crain sent to the FAA Technical Center was answered evasively.

So once again, the story of the way this case has been handled by the authorities provides a detailed demonstration of how the covert censorship enforces the UFO cover-up.

What this prolonged series of deliberate ostentatious displays appears to add up to is a reinforcement schedule, discreetly but firmly making the presence of extra-terrestrials undeniably obvious, puncturing the balloon of the big lie that has been foisted on U.S. citizens and the world for over 40 years, deflating it gradually in a manner that is calculated to oblige public recognition while avoiding public panic.

Another important case that just refuses to die is that of the "Westchester Wing," which was described in the Appendix of my previous book and which continues to be persistently reported. A major incident occurred on March 17, 1988, when hundreds of reports came in from northern New Jersey, New York City, and up the Hudson River Valley past Ossining to Mahopac, NY. As usual, the same old implausible explanation was spewed forth by the authorities: pranksters in ultralight aircraft. Attempts have been made, presumably by the authorities, to bolster the acceptability of this nonsense by sending up a fleet of ultralights now and then to imitate the Westchester Wing, but the imitations are so obviously different from the genuine sightings that this desperate ploy has been a complete flop.

Scientists at the Jet Propulsion Laboratory in Pasadena, California, who examined a videotape of the Westchester Wing made in 1984, gave their "unofficial" opinion in the form of a letter that the lights are on a single, solid object — thereby ruling out formations of ultralight aircraft. They would not, of course, go on record with an official opinion, being employees of the same authorities who continue to maintain, despite overwhelming evidence to the contrary, that what huge numbers of people in greater New York have been seeing for the last ten years is pranksters in ultralight aircraft. This unprecedented series of sightings over the same area, the first of which took place on December 31, 1982, remains ongoing as we go to press with this book, just as it was when we went to press with my previous book in the fall of 1986.

Substantial evidence of the covert censorship of UFO news coverage can be demonstrated by making a list of all the sightings described in Lucius Farish's indispensable UFO Newsclipping Service (Route 1 Box 220, Plumerville, AR 72127) for a time period such as from the beginning of July 1987 to the end of June 1988, including in the Credits section of this book the names and locations of all the newspapers that the articles were taken from, as well as the dates on which the articles appeared. If, after reading the following list, you will turn to the Credits section at the end of this book, you will see that nearly all of the reports, with only rare exceptions, are from small local newspapers in the areas where the incidents occurred. Hardly ever are these small local newspapers aware of UFO incidents going on elsewhere. Without the presence of Lucius Farish, regularly making an end run around the covert censorship for us, we researchers would have no way of estimating the extent and pervasiveness of the phenomena. In the following list, I have numbered the dates of the incidents, so that they correspond with the numbers given to the newspa-

pers in the Credits section, in order to facilitate cross-referencing.
1. During the first week of July 1987, there were multiple UFO sightings with many witnesses in the vicinity of Washingtonville, Pennsylvania.
2. July 13-15, multiple sightings with many witnesses in Screven County, Georgia.
3. July 14, sighting by a woman in Stoughton and by police officers in Waunakee, Wisconsin.
4. July 26, sighting near Roswell, New Mexico, associated with the deaths of many sheep.
5. Aug. 4, sighting at Exmouth, England.
6. Aug. 11, sighting at Brick Town, New Jersey.
7. Aug. 16 (the "Harmonic Convergence" announced by Jose Arguelles), sighting in Vancouver, B.C., Canada, then again on Aug. 19, another witnessed by police on Sept. 6, ongoing through Sept. 13. There were also sightings in Derby and in Luton, England, on Aug. 16. There was a flood of reports from Derby during the week preceding Aug. 20.
8. Aug. 25, sighting at Fairbanks, Alaska.
9. Aug. 27, sighting in Victoria province of Australia. Also on the same date in Gwent, England.
10. Between the beginning of September 1987 and the beginning of January 1988, there were over 2,000 sightings reported from Wythe County and surrounding areas in Virginia.
11. Sept. 1, sighting at Fountain Mesa, Colorado.
12. Sept. 3, sighting at Detroit Lakes, Minnesota.
13. Sept. 14, flood of reports from Midlands, England.
14. Sept. 15, sighting at Lewistown, Montana.
15. Sept. 22, sighting at Cornwall, England.
16. Sept. 25, sighting at Amery, Wisconsin.
17. Sept. 27, sighting at Framlingham, England.
18. Sept. 28, and days immediately preceding and following, a cluster of sightings in Devon, England.
19. Sept. 30 and Oct. 5, sightings in Haifa, Israel.
20. From the beginning of October through Feb. 19, 1988, there were 124 reports from the West Midlands, England. Same time span during previous year: 31; year before that: 18.
21. Oct. 4, sighting at Salisbury, England.
22. Oct. 5, sighting at Staffordshire, England.
23. Oct. 6 and 8, sightings at Worthing, England.
24. Oct. 8, 16 and 18, sightings at Delmont, Pennsylvania.
25. Oct. 19, sightings at Maidstone, England.

26. Oct. 22, sighting at Bennington, New Hampshire.
27. Oct. 26, sighting at Little Fork, Minnesota.
28. Oct. 28, sighting at Staffordshire, England.
29. Nov. 2, sighting at Chichester, England.
30. Nov. 9, sighting at Edgerton, Wisconsin.
31. Nov. 10, sighting at Simi Valley, California.
32. Nov. 11, Gulf Breeze, Florida. On this date, massive multi-witness UFO manifestations began to occur in the area of Gulf Breeze, which have yielded photographic evidence of extraordinary quality. Some investigators have doubts as to the authenticity of this case, suspecting it to be an elaborate hoax, arranged with super-sophisticated equipment. However, multi-witness sightings continue to be reported as we go to press. It seems beyond coincidence that just as Foreman, Arkansas, is in the vicinity of the Red River Arsenal, so Gulf Breeze is in the vicinity of Eglin Air Force Base. The UFO manifestations at Foreman began on Jan. 19, 1988. On the same date that the Gulf Breeze manifestations began (Nov. 11, 1987), there was a sighting in the general area of Bismarck, North Dakota, followed by sightings on Nov. 14, Dec. 4, Dec. 9, and Feb. 26.
33. Nov. 16, sighting at Blackpool, England.
34. Nov. 23 and preceding week, a flood of reports from Wolverhampton, England.
35. Nov. 24 and preceding weeks, multiple reports from Bluefield, West Virginia.
36. Dec. 12 and 15, sightings at Monticello, Kentucky.
37. Dec. 14, in Tasmania, an incident occurred similar in nature to the widely publicized Mundrabilla incident in Australia on Jan. 20, 1988. The Mundrabilla incident is described in detail in the second chapter of this book. All that has been publicly released about the Tasmanian incident is that an eggcup-shaped UFO touched down on the roof of a businessman's white Mercedes, leaving a soot-like deposit all over it and damaging its electric system.
38. Dec. 22, sighting at Hawley, Pennsylvania.
39. Dec. 30, sighting at Qatar, Persian Gulf, and also at Kuwait. On Feb. 7, 1988, another sighting at Qatar.
40. Jan. 1, 1988, through Jan. 27. There were 72 sightings reported from the north of England during this period.
41. Jan. 3, sighting at London, England.
42. Jan. 6, sighting at Bolton, Lancashire, England.
43. Jan. 7 and preceding week, many reports from Yorkshire, England. Also many reports from Essex, England, during this same period of

time.
44. Jan. 7 and following days, a cluster of reports from Binghamton, New York.
45. Jan. 11, sighting at Ashley, North Dakota.
46. Jan. 15, sighting at Cannon Falls, Minnesota. Also on this date, sighting at Seaford, Sussex, England. This incident is remarkable not so much for the sighting itself, which is like thousands of others already on record, but for the explanation given to account for it, and the position of the person giving the explanation. I'll first quote from an article by Sue Baird in the *Seaford Gazette* of Jan. 20, 1988, then add my comments:

> A mysterious unidentified flying object was spotted silently hovering above Seaford Head just before 9 pm and reported to Seaford police.
> A display of red, blue, green and white lights apparently gave way to five red lights the size of footballs traveling just above house height....
> Jenny Randles, director of investigations (for the British UFO Research Association), explained that in the past two or three months, there had been similar sightings to the one seen in Seaford last week.
> In fact, they turned out to be military exercises. A lot of NATO exercises, including aircraft refueling, have been taking place at night, she explained.
> But often sightings turn out to be more amusing or bizarre in reality. At this time of the year, we sometimes get sightings which are geese flying south for the winter. The lights from street lamps reflect on their underbellies and make them look mysterious. One sighting turned out to be a phosphorescent owl that had eaten diseased fungi which was giving it a strange color.

I'll begin my comments by pointing out that NATO aircraft do not hover silently, nor do they display the type of lights described, nor do they perform refueling operations at an altitude that is just above house height. Street lights reflecting on the underbellies of geese are totally irrelevant to the phenomena described. The old chestnut about the phosphorescent owl had already lost its credibility in Charles Fort's time. I venture to suggest that if Charles Fort were alive today, he would have found this statement by Jenny Randles utterly hilarious.
What is at first glance puzzling about all this is that Jenny Randles is an

intelligent person, as is obvious from her published work and her position in the hierarchy of highly respected BUFORA, the British equivalent of the American MUFON, by far the largest civilian research group in England, supposedly impartial and open-minded.

I am not the first person to suspect that the hierarchies of the major civilian research groups have been so heavily infiltrated by government agents posing as independent researchers that it is not realistic to expect any significant new information to get out to the public through the filtering process imposed by the hierarchies of these organizations. It certainly seems remarkable to find the director of investigations of a supposedly unbiased and independent research group ignoring the facts of the case on which attention has been focused, in order to divert attention from the recorded facts with implausible red-herring statements of the type that are exactly what the government wants to hear.

47. Jan. 16, sighting at Christchurch, New Zealand.
48. Jan. 17, sighting at Omaha, Nebraska.
49. Jan. 19, The magnitude and extent of the incidents that began to be reported on this date from Little River County, Arkansas, and that continued into 1989, are on a scale that goes beyond anything else that occurred during 1988. They erupted just as the series of incidents in Virginia (see the entry for the beginning of September) were tapering off, as if the E.T.s had for some reason shifted the focus of their activities from southwest Virginia to the southwest corner of Arkansas, centering on the region between the towns of Foreman and Ashdown, near the Texas border. A few sporadic sightings had occurred in previous months, including a low-altitude sighting of a UFO as large as a football field in November, but the witnesses did not dare to speak out for fear of ridicule. The local population tends to be quite conservative, and the first witnesses to go public after a UFO chased three women in a car at terrifyingly close range on Jan. 19 were subjected to persistent harassment and ostracism, until hundreds of citizens began seeing the phenomena simultaneously and its reality became undeniable. There were also Bigfoot sightings in the region around this time.

A typical report described "a ball of light that was as big as a hay wagon at first, but which got smaller when as many as 100 people gathered to look at it. The object changed color from red to green to blue. It was first seen near ground level, then flew high into the sky. It got under the moon and it looked just like a star up there until everyone went away, then it came back down. When it was up off the ground, lights were flashing, and you had to see it to believe it."

Witnesses included an astronomer, an Air Force veteran who had been a navigator on a B-52 with 1,800 hours of flying time, a science teacher who had been selected as a finalist for the NASA "teacher in space" program, and a design engineer familiar with propulsion systems. Photos were taken that neither the Arkansas Sky Observatory, NORAD, or NASA were able to give plausible explanations for. Clay Sherrod, the Director of the Arkansas Sky Observatory, succeeded in insulting everyone's intelligence by maintaining that the extremely mobile metallic objects with multicolored flashing lights being perceived simultaneously by whole crowds of people, hovering at low altitude then suddenly rising straight up at incredible speed, performing maneuvers such as no aircraft known to man can perform, were misidentifications of the planet Venus or "moonlight reflecting off the bellies of white snow geese flying overhead." Local journalists on the staff of the *Little River News* and the *Northwest Arkansas Times* did a brilliant job of describing the strange series of events in an unbiased fashion. The excellent articles by William Macomber, Jim Williamson, Jeanne Jackson, and Steve Mitchell deserve to constitute the nucleus of a book of their own. Although newspaper coverage of the incidents ceased on March 27, the incidents continued for about a year, but were no longer considered newsworthy, having been persistently disparaged by the authorities and by the major news media, which has been content to parrot the "planet Venus" and "moonlight reflecting off the bellies of snow geese" explanations by the Director of the Arkansas Sky Observatory, seated hundreds of miles away from the scene of the action in his comfortable office in Little Rock.

Barbara Sowell of FLAME (Foundation of Light and Metaphysical Education, 1004 Live Oak, Arlington, TX 76012) conducted an independent investigation into the Foreman sightings right after they began and published the results in a brochure entitled "Ashdown-Foreman Arkansas Sightings," from which the following excerpt from an interview with witnesses who wish to remain anonymous is taken:

H. asked us about animal mutilations. We didn't bring it up. H. said, 'There's a lot of cattle mutilations around.' H. and V. also brought up the fact they would soon be very, very rich because they had been told that their land was now worth twice its value. It seems that a Swiss national with mega-bucks has bought up several thousand acres across the Red River with the intention of turning the area into a highly exclusive resort. They said that the TV in Little Rock did a special story on it and they said that 'Only 3% of the world's population would be rich enough to go to that resort.' There will be many facilities, including an air strip. The area is very close to the Red River Arsenal. They gave the name of a local architect who has a bid in for the project who might know more.

This is indeed an intriguing constellation of circumstances. We find that cattle mutilations are rampant in the region, though no mention is being made of this by the authorities or the news media. The Red River Arsenal is a major U.S. Army base. The area of land between the Red River Arsenal and Foreman has suddenly doubled in value. The story about the Swiss millionaire intending to build a luxury resort seems quite implausible, as neither the climate nor the landscape are suitable for a resort of that nature. If the U.S. government wanted to take over the land to extend the Red River Arsenal, all it would have to do would be to say so, taking it over by right of eminent domain, paying the ranchers no more than the current market value. So who is really offering the ranchers double the current market value?

Is the mysterious Swiss millionaire a front man for the aliens, a human agent of the aliens? Any such agent would be able to amass vast wealth by applying minor aspects of the advanced alien technology to our contemporary industrial procedures.

Because the region between Foreman and the Red River Arsenal is more suited to cattle ranching than an exclusive luxury resort, could this land purchase be designed to resolve the cattle mutilation problem by giving the aliens their own ranch, where they could raise their own herds of cattle?

Ranchers all over the nation would heave a sigh of relief if this turned out to be what is happening. It is a possibility, but we must beware of wishful thinking and jumping to conclusions. An examination of all the available evidence indicates that this is not the only time that strange goings-on have been reported in close proximity to a major U.S. Army base. For example, in 1974 and in 1976 there were outbreaks of bizarre phenomena very similar in nature to the Foreman incidents in the immediate vicinity of the U.S. Army's Picatinny Arsenal, near the town of White Meadow in northwestern New Jersey. White Meadow residents persistently reported UFO and Bigfoot sightings in 1974, then again in 1976. There was an incident in October 1976 that understandably outraged the local citizens: the body parts of dozens of dismembered cattle, including severed heads and entrails, were strewn along over a mile of public highway, that just happened to adjoin the entrance gate into the Picatinny Arsenal. Local residents also reported hearing strange sounds resembling "underground construction work" and "subterranean machinery."

Valdamar Valerian published some relevant remarks in his *Nevada Ae-*

rial Research Newsletter (P.O. Box 81407, Las Vegas, NV 89180):

> After purchasing Aeromagnetic and Gravitational Anomaly maps from the United States Geological Survey, it became evident that there was indeed a valid connection between these areas and UFOs to Mr. Lew Tery, who gave a public lecture about this relationship in Arizona. He was subsequently harassed by the FBI and ceased to give public lectures on this subject.
>
> Both the Aeromagnetic and Gravitational (Bougier Gravity) maps indicate basic field strength, as well as areas of high and low field strength. Interestingly enough, the areas of maximum and minimum field strength have the following:
>
> All have frequent UFO sightings.
>
> All are either on Indian reservations, government land, or the government is trying to buy up the land.
>
> Many of them, especially where several are clustered together, are suspected base areas, and/or areas where mutilations and abductions have historically taken place.

In these observations, Mr. Tery has gone far, but he has gone a little further in noting that there are times when the UFOs are seen in these areas. Through painstaking research, Mr. Tery found that the sightings, as well as many abductions and mutilations, occur:

> On the New Moon or within two days before the New Moon.
>
> On the Full Moon or within two days before the Full Moon.
>
> At the Perihelion (Moon closest to Earth) or within two days before the Perihelion.

50. Jan. 20, the Mundrabilla incident occurred in Australia, which is described in detail in the second chapter of this book.
51. Jan. 21, sighting at Idabel, Oklahoma, which is near Foreman, Arkansas. On that same day, there was a sighting at Oak Harbor, Washington.
52. Jan. 22, sighting at Waco, Texas.
53. Jan. 23 and days preceding, a cluster of reports from Wolverhampton, England.
54. Jan. 27, sighting at Swansea, Wales.
55. Jan. 29, sighting at Wenatchee, Washington.
56. Beginning of February, many reports from Barrow-in-Furness, Lancashire, England.

57. Feb. 2, many reports from Sheffield area, south Yorkshire, England. On that same date, also sightings at Narbonne, Saint-Jean-du-Pin and Alberes in France.
58. Feb. 3, sighting at Cerdagne in France.
59. Feb. 5, sighting at Mansfield, England.
60. Feb. 7, sighting at Fabreques, France.
61. Feb. 9, sighting at Bogota, Colombia. On that same date, a sighting at Saint-Didier, Vaucluse, France.
62. Feb. 11, a sighting at Beira, Mozambique.
63. Feb. 18 and days preceding, a flood of reports from the West Midlands, England.
64. Feb. 19, sighting at Bedfordshire, England.
65. Feb. 21, sighting at Bucks County, Pennsylvania.
66. Feb. 23 and week preceding, continuing on through March 8, a cluster of reports from Battletown, Kentucky.
67. Feb. 25 and preceding weeks, a cluster of reports from Doncaster, Yorkshire, England.
68. Feb. 26, sighting at Hull, England.
69. Feb. 28, sighting at Bury, England.
70. Feb. 29, sighting at Lichfield, England. On that same date, sighting at Bangor Naval Base, Bremerton, Washington.
71. March 1 and 2, sightings at Egg Harbor, New Jersey.
72. March 3, sighting at Amsterdam, Holland.
73. March 4, sighting at Bay City, Wisconsin.
74. March 7, sighting at Surrey, England.
75. March 10 and weeks preceding, sightings at Conway, Wales.
76. March 11 and week preceding, sightings at Wallsall, Staffordshire, England.
77. During the middle of March, there were 24 sightings at Annapolis, Maryland, followed by five more at the beginning of April.
78. March 16 and weeks preceding, cluster of sightings in Hertfordshire, England.
79. March 17, the major Westchester Wing sighting in New York's Hudson River Valley, described just before the beginning of this list.
80. March 18, sighting in Beijing, China.
81. March 24, 90 sightings in the past month in the area of Cannock Chase, England.
82. March 23 through 26 and weeks preceding, a cluster of reports at Staunton, Virginia.
83. March 25, sighting at Idabel, Oklahoma (see Jan. 21).
84. March 26. On this date there was a repeat performance on a slightly

smaller scale of the events that occurred on Aug. 12, 1986, described earlier in this chapter. Luminous phenomena in the nocturnal sky over Texas on March 25 were explained as Soviet rocket debris by Air Defense Command officials. A fireball that passed over Ohio and Michigan on the evening of March 27 was explained as "probably a meteor" by the Scientific Event Alert Network of the Smithsonian Institute. The light it emitted was bright enough to cast shadows. However, none of the authorities were able to offer any sort of explanation whatsoever for the phenomena witnessed by multitudes over Indiana, Kentucky, and Tennessee on the night of March 26. In some areas what was described was silently moving bright white light. In other areas the light was accompanied by loud crashing noises. In yet other areas the reports were of a UFO "bigger than three football fields." As on the night of Aug. 12, 1986, on March 26, 1988, there were also inexplicable explosions in Kentucky.

85. March 30, sighting at Birmingham, England.
86. March 31, sighting at Bluefield, West Virginia (see Nov. 24).
87. April 7, sighting at Westleigh, Lancashire, England.
88. April 9, 10 and 25, sightings at Norfolk, Virginia.
89. April 10, sighting at Morris, Illinois. Also on that same date, sighting in Oxford, England.
90. April 11, sighting at Stevenage, England.
91. April 13, sighting at Guernsey, England.
92. April 14, sighting in Essex, England.
93. April 15 at Godmanschester, Cambridgeshire, England. A small black UFO with a nauseating odor came within 15 feet of schoolgirl Pauline Emerson, who went into a state of shock that required medical treatment. Her mother, Barbara Emerson, said their house was shaking and she felt as if the oxygen was being sucked out of it.
94. April 16, sighting at Frejus, France.
95. April 17, a sighting of the Westchester Wing at Egremont, Massachusetts, apparently left behind some physical evidence.
96. April 20, sighting at Broomhill, Yorkshire, England.
97. April 22, sighting at Ellsworth, Wisconsin.
98. April 22 and 23, sightings at Huelva, Spain. On April 23, sightings at Madrid, Spain, which were so widespread that they caused huge traffic jams, as motorists got out of their cars to get a better view.
99. April 24, sighting at Birmingham, England.
100. April 25 and preceding two weeks, dozens of reports from Pennsylvania.
101. April 28 and days preceding, sightings at Aberdare, South Wales.

102. April 29, sighting at River Falls, Wisconsin.
103. May 3, sighting at Lewis, Wisconsin.
104. May 5 and 6, sightings at Aberdare, South Wales.
105. May 8, sighting at Kent, England.
106. May 15, sighting at Bookham, Surrey, England.
107. May 16 at Fernwood, Stafford, England. Mrs. Eileen Ballard, a statistical officer with the Staffordshire police, who had previously served for four years in the RAF, described what she had seen in the presence of four other witnesses: "We were standing in the garden when two spotlights came through the sky towards us so that we couldn't see anything else. They banked over and went into side by side formation, one above the other, and slowly flew across the sky without any noise at all. They flew very close together and were triangular in shape, too high for micro light aircraft and too low for normal aircraft. There were a lot of lights underneath, red and green, around the edge and within that lots of others." Besides the group with Mrs. Ballard, other witnesses independently described the objects as silent and flying very low with a lot of very bright lights. Reports came in on that same evening from as far away as Wolverhampton. Jenny Randles, Director of Investigations for BUFORA, said it sounded like top secret Stealth aircraft. "We've had quite a spate of these in the Midlands, about a dozen since December. Of course, there is a veil of official secrecy, but we think there may be a small squadron secretly based in Britain at RAF Alconbury." Jenny Randles seems blissfully unaware of the implausibility of testing top secret aircraft that are lit up like Christmas trees at low altitude over heavily populated areas.
108. May 17, sightings at Leicestershire, England.
109. May 19 and weeks preceding, multiple Bigfoot sightings near Jonesboro, Arkansas.
110. May 23, sighting in King, North Carolina.
111. May 24, sighting in Simi Valley, California (see Nov. 10).
112. June 6, Norfolk and Suffolk, England. UFO sightings accompanied by strange rumbling noises were reported by many people. The noises were registered on seismic equipment operated by the University of East Anglia, but the results of the analysis have not been released. On that same date, there was a sighting at West Point, Tennessee.

As the year ended, sightings were again reported from the Pennsylvania region that is the first item on this list.

Until Oct. 10, 1989, the major wire services had been unanimous in covering up every UFO incident they were unable to ignore with a blanket of ridicule. However, this unanimity was broken by the Soviet news agency Tass on that date, when it reported a UFO landing in the city of Voronezh, about 300 miles south of Moscow. Despite attempts by the other major news agencies to dismiss this report in their usual jocular fashion, Tass insisted that it was no joke, that the landing had in fact occurred in a park of that city, and that three-eyed aliens with small heads, nine to thirteen feet tall, had not only been seen by but had interacted with some of the inhabitants of Voronezh, among other things causing a 16-year-old boy to disappear and then reappear. There had been three landings between Sept. 23 and Sept. 29. The story was carried in the *New York Times* on Oct. 11 under the headline, "U.F.O. Landing is Fact, Not Fantasy, Russians Insist."

As this book approached completion, I circulated copies of the manuscript among friends whose opinions I respected, requesting feedback from them. Some of the responses were so perceptive that I decided to include them in the text of the book. The following remarks were made by Rosemary Decker:

In pointing out that the vast majority of contemporary humanity feels threatened or terrified by any unprecedented divergence from conventionally accepted norms of reality, you are presenting a powerful argument in favor of governmental silence and media low-profiling. In view of the fact that government agencies are already acutely aware of the fear problem, we should be willing to see that some degree of reserve and silence is appropriate. There is no good reason why everyone should be entitled to know all there is to know on an immediate and widespread scale, as most of the population could not handle it, though it would be unwise to try to tell them so directly.

The behavior patterns of our visitors indicate that they also must be aware of the dangers of sudden wide-spread publicity concerning their presence. Otherwise why would they consistently manifest in waves within specific limited areas for specific periods of time, build gradually to peaks, and then withdraw from these areas for long periods?

Discriminating reserve and caution on the part of officialdom are appropriate. However, blatant lying, deceit, and silencing of witnesses by ridicule or personal threats are deplorable. Such tactics are undermining both national and international security. The population of the entire world has by now received absurd explanations and outright lies from their respective governments for so many years that distrust of governments has reached epidemic proportions on a global scale.

If, during the 1940s or early 1950s, the official agencies had agreed among themselves on a policy of gradual and cautious, but honest presentation of the facts known to them, with the humility to be able to say 'We don't know' at times, the situation would not have gotten so completely out of hand, as it now is. Ever since 1947, officialdom has suffered from disagreements between agencies, between individuals within a given agency, and from differences in direction as key UFO policy personnel were toppled from office and replaced. Part of the problem of inconsistency in policy has been due to varying degrees of fear of public reaction, but is also due to the individual fears of those in office, as office-holders. What government wants to admit that it does not know everything? Researchers who have been studying this subject full-time for as long as forty years admit that they don't know everything about it, and that there are frequently extreme differences of opinion between even the best informed of the experts.

What government wants to admit there is something vitally important going on that is completely beyond its control? Our visitors flit blithely about with total disregard for national borders and 'restricted areas.'

What government wants its citizens to begin to think of themselves as citizens of the planet rather than as French, Russian, American, etc.? To give their allegiance primarily to the planet and only secondarily to the nation to which they belong? With every year that passes, many more millions of people all over the world are becoming aware that we Earth-folk are being visited from elsewhere, irrespective of our national borders.

What I would like to say in response to Rosemary Decker is that since sightings and abductions have escalated to unprecedented and ever-increasing levels, the situation is now completely out of control. The lid of secrecy imposed on the subject by the government for over 40 years is about to blow, no matter how desperately the government may attempt to continue to stonewall the high strangeness. The most effective way to avoid a sudden explosion, traumatic for all concerned, is to decrease the pressure by releasing as much information as possible in forms that the public can assimilate without being excessively traumatized, such as through this and other books and unbiased media coverage, so that there is no longer such a gross disparity between what the public has been conditioned to believe and what is actually going on.

A major development in the release of previously secret information has been the publication of the briefing papers for President Eisenhower by William Moore, Stanton Friedman, and Jaime Shandera in the spring of 1987. There has been considerable debate over the authenticity of these documents, which describe the circumstances under which President Truman created the top secret Majestic-12 group in order to investigate the national security implications of UFO phenomena. One of the original members of MJ-12 was Admiral Roscoe Hillenkoetter, who was head of the CIA at the time that the incoming Eisenhower administration was installed, and whose signature was appended to one of the controversial documents, dated Nov. 18, 1952.

Critics bent on disparaging the authenticity of the documents were dealt a major blow when Dr. Roger W. Westcott announced the result of his in-depth study on the basis of stylistic analysis. Dr. Westcott graduated from Princeton Summa Cum Laude and is Director of the Linguistics Department at Drew University. He has published 40 books on Linguistics, approximately 400 articles, and is considered the most eminent authority on this subject in the United States. Dr. Westcott compared the signature on the controversial document with the signatures on 27 other documents signed by Admiral Hillenkoetter, the authenticity of which is not in question, and with 1,200 pages of personal correspondence and memoranda written by Hillenkoetter. Dr. Westcott concluded that Admiral Hillenkoetter's signature on the controversial document is authentic.

It would seem that such a verdict, combined with the information content of the document whose authenticity was thus confirmed — concerning a crashed UFO and the recovery of four small alien bodies — should be sufficient to deal a final death blow to the credibility of our government's publicly stated official attitude towards UFOs. However, as any psychologist will tell you, deeply entrenched, long held, rigidly assumed, conventionally accepted, blind and fanatical belief systems do not die easily. They tend to be thick-skinned to the point of being almost impervious to logic. I stress that "almost," as it is our only hope of at last achieving a sane and rational approach to the subject.

Edward Mazur made some very relevant remarks about the MJ-12 controversy in the July/August 1989 issue of the *Arkansas MUFON Newsletter*:

> The unauthorized disclosure of a highly classified document is a serious federal crime. The forging of a classified document purported to come from the highest levels of government is perhaps an even more serious crime. Yet in the five years or so since the documents surfaced, there have been no arrests or prosecutions by the Department of Justice. Why?
>
> According to this writer's logic, the FBI could have easily determined, through the issuing agency, whether the document was authentic or forged. If it was a forgery, there wouldn't be great difficulty in finding the forger, prosecuting him, and setting an example.

This action would also discredit and ridicule the gullible UFO community who had 'bought' MJ-12. Why didn't the FBI take advantage of this opportunity if the document was phony? Or wasn't it? But if the document was genuine, what would the government gain by apprehending its leaker? Prosecution would be a public admission that MJ-12 was authentic and would reveal the very fact that the document's high and sensitive classification was designed to suppress. It would be far better to treat the matter with benign neglect, as is the case now, and to work behind the scenes to thwart any progress that might be made by UFO researchers while undermining their activity wherever possible.

The fact that there have been no indications of any investigations, arrests, or prosecutions in the past five years in the matter of these documents is of great significance.

According to the *Nevada Aerial Research Newsletter*, P.O. Box 81407, Las Vegas NV 89180, the black-uniformed elite Delta Special Forces, which carry out their missions in black unmarked helicopters and which act as security for the U.S. government alien-related projects, are selected almost exclusively from soldiers who grew up as orphans or have no close family ties.

Is this because the enemy they are trained to fight is the citizens of the United States? And we are paying for this with our own tax dollars?

The publication of the U.S. edition of *Above Top Secret* by British researcher Timothy Good (Morrow, 1988) was a landmark event that from here on out puts the critics who persist in denying the reality of UFO phenomena on the defensive. Timothy Good employs a similar technique to that of Barry Greenwood and Lawrence Fawcett in their *Clear Intent* (Prentice-Hall, 1984), using contradictions within government documents to demonstrate that the government is perpetrating a cover-up. However, *Clear Intent* was focused mainly on the devious activities of the intelligence community within the United States. The scope of *Above Top Secret* is world-wide. Timothy Good also deals with the United States, bringing up much material that was not included in *Clear Intent*, but the main thrust of his book is a meticulously detailed investigation of what went on concerning UFOs within the intelligence communities and officialdom of England, Canada, Australia, Russia, China, France, Italy, Portugal, and Spain. It is particularly illuminating to compare the information contained in *Above Top Secret* with information contained in *Clear Intent*, as they supplement each other in remarkable fashion, and the correlations provide powerful confirmation of their basic hypotheses. Both books are focused primarily on unidentified flying objects as aircraft, dealing only marginally with the subject of UFO occupants, which is of course the subject that my own books have been devoted to investigating. The publication of *Clear Intent* put the cynics who maintain that UFO sightings are all explicable in terms of weather balloons, the planet Venus, swamp gas, mass hysteria, or flocks of geese in a difficult position. The publication of the worldwide evidence presented with such concise, conservatively understated, devastating effectiveness in *Above Top Secret* puts these same cynics in an impossible situation, from which there is no way they can recover their lost credibility.

Let us now turn our attention to the aborted attempt to bring the subject of UFOs to the attention of the United Nations.

A highly important figure in this series of events was Major Colman Von Keviczky, whose background was summarized in the following terms by his colleague and long-time research associate, J. Antonio Huneeus, in the *New York City Tribune* of May 19, 1988:

> Von Keviczky received his Master of Military Science and Engineering (MMSE) at the historical Ludovica University in Budapest. As a Captain and then Major with the Royal Hungarian Army, he created the Audio-Visual Department of the Hungarian General Staff before World War II. After the war he worked for the U.S. occupation forces in Germany and emigrated to the United States in 1952, the year his interest in UFOs began. Von Keviczky is a member of the American Institute of Aeronautics & Astronautics (AIAA) and his biography appears in *Who's Who in Aviation & Aerospace*.
>
> In the mid-60s, Von Keviczky worked with the United Nations staff audio-visual department, where he became involved in a controversy over UFOs and the U.N. In 1966, Von Keviczky was actually commissioned by Secretary General U Thant to work on a preliminary memo on how the UFO problem could be inserted in the U.N. agenda. However, the Major found he no longer had a job at the U.N. after he leaked news of this assignment to the press. Yet U Thant confided around that time that 'he considers UFOs the most important problem facing the U.N. next to the war in Vietnam,' as reported in Drew Pearson's syndicated column.

While Von Keviczky was employed as a staff member of the United Nations Secretariat's Office of Public Information, the UFO wave of 1952 over Washington, D.C., occurred. Being an expert in photography, Von Keviczky realized that the photographs were genuine, and became interested in the subject. Private discussions with diplomats, scientists, and old friends who were still military officers convinced him of the subject's importance. In 1966, he undertook the initiative that destroyed his career, which will now be described in his own words:

In February 1966, after a long-scrutinized military study of the UFOs' global operation, as Staff Member of the United Nations Secretariat, I addressed THE FIRST UFO MEMORANDUM to my Secretary General U Thant. Seizing on his constitutional duty regarding the endangered international security, Thant assigned me to elaborate the FIRST U.N.-UFO PROJECT. This project referred to:

1. A coordinated cooperation amongst the nations to control the UFOs' global operation and activities.

2. Immediate STOP to any HOSTILE CONFRONTATION, which at any time could trigger a fatal Space War.

3. Seek OFFICIAL CONTACT AND COMMUNICATION with the exploring UFO forces, assisted by UNESCO, and by the governments' respective UFO organizations.

4. Declare the 550-mile belt around our Celestial Body under the PROTECTION and JURISDICTION of the United Nations.

Thant's common sense and constitutional duty on the alarming worldwide UFO fever is demonstrated by his remark within the diplomatic corps and his cabinet that: "UFOS ARE THE MOST IMPORTANT PROBLEM FACING THE UNITED NATIONS AFTER THE WAR IN VIETNAM." The Pentagon and the U.S. diplomacy were immediately alerted to stop him!

During the next month, in March, to thwart Thant's U.N.-UFO Project, the Air Force Scientific Research Board "AD HOC PANEL" was mobilized in haste to find a suitable University to study the UFO phenomena. Evidence: CONDON REPORT, preface, pages 7-9 written by the Vice President of the Colorado University.

Thant was totally silenced! A "mysterious" diplomatic power constrained him to violate the U.N. Constitution, and confess also toward the public that his interest in UFOs was only "purely academic and personal."

According to the Associated Press, Ambassador Trofimirovich Fedorenko of the U.S.S.R. comforted him thus: "UFOs are only the nightmares of the imperialist and capitalist countries." But against this, on the other side of the token...

"For my honorarily-accepted U.N.-UFO Project, I became the No. 1 ENEMY OF THE UNITED STATES UFO POLICY. I was awarded with the notorious SECURITY RISK for scientists! This governmental denunciation over my lifetime prevented me from having any career job at reputable firms in the United States...."

United Nations Secretary General U Thant, and the Member Nations in 1966, were convinced that the Colorado University SCIENTIFIC STUDY OF UFOS had been established to supervise the Pentagon UFO file trustworthiness and credibility, which would liquidate the media-generated UFO fever.

Only three years later, the Report's preface, written by the University's vice president Thurston E. Manning, exposed how he was hoodwinked in 1966, because the Committee was assigned to study the UFO phenomena "WHOLLY OUTSIDE THE JURISDICTION OF THE AIR FORCE." Namely, "outside the jurisdiction" meant the scientific study of the hundreds of UFO weekend clubs and news clipping collector hobbyists, thereby discrediting the respected NICAP and APRO valuable public research. Evidence:

On February 20, 1967, before the Committee started, the CIA gave Dr. Edward U. Condon, Committee Director, the necessary guideline and instruction. THE MEETING WAS SECRET. No comments on the masterly delusion and deception of the nations!

Well, in UFO research all roads lead to the USA's Rome — as we have learned — THE OMNISCIENT AND OMNIPOTENT C! I! A!

The climax of the struggle over whether or not the subject of UFOs should be placed on the agenda of the United Nations will now be briefly described.

It is a matter of historic record that Dr. J. Allen Hynek and Dr. Jacques Vallee prevented Von Keviczky from presenting his evidence that UFOs are space-craft of extra-terrestrial origin before the Special Political Committee of the United Nations, by threatening to boycott the Committee if Von Keviczky was allowed to testify. The other three experts were Dr. David Saunders, Dr. Claude Poher, and astronaut Gordon Cooper. Only Gordon Cooper, who held the rank of Colonel in the U.S. Air Force and was therefore under obligation to obey orders, supported Hynek and Vallee on this issue. Due to the pressure that Hynek and Vallee exerted, Von Keviczky's invitation to testify was canceled.

In documents concerning the Robertson Panel that was convened by the CIA in 1953 to deal with the subject of UFOs, Dr. Hynek was listed not only as an Air Force Project Bluebook consultant, but also as an "OSI" consultant. "OSI" is an abbreviation for the Office of Scientific Intelligence, which is a sub-section of the CIA. According to a public statement made by Dr. Hynek, he was not invited to attend all the sessions of the

Robertson Panel. However, this statement is contradicted by an official document dated Jan. 27, 1953, and declassified in 1977, which stated that Hynek "sat in on all the sessions after the first day," but did not sign the report as an official group member. Hynek was already an OSI consultant before he became a consultant to Project Bluebook. Did he remain an OSI consultant for the rest of his life? Was he assigned to play the part of the maverick scientist in revolt against the authorities, when the authorities realized that explanations such as "swamp gas" were no longer credible, in order to more effectively acquire information from and control over the genuinely independent researchers?

Jacques Vallee began his UFO research career in the 1960s as the assistant of Dr. Hynek. Considering this in combination with the result of his close collaboration with Dr. Hynek at the United Nations, is Dr. Vallee also an OSI consultant?

On Nov. 27, 1978, Dr. Vallee stated to the Special Political Committee of the United Nations, which had been convened to decide whether or not to place the subject of UFOs on the U.N. agenda, that: "although the UFO phenomenon is real and appears to be caused by an unknown physical stimulus, I have so far failed to discover any evidence that it represents the arrival of visitors from outer space." Having said that, he skipped briefly over the physical manifestations of the phenomenon, saying only they should be studied. He then stressed the importance of studying the psycho-physiological effects on witnesses, carefully pointing out that: "I do not believe it is within the province or the budget of the United Nations to address such effects directly..." He continued by insisting at length on the importance of studying the social belief systems generated by the phenomenon, as well as the emotional factors involved — aspects of the phenomenon so clearly outside the province and budget of the United Nations that it was not necessary for him to repeat this a second time. Thus with a few deft strokes, he effectively sabotaged the placing of the subject of the UFO phenomenon on the agenda of the United Nations, which was exactly what the CIA wanted to prevent. If Von Keviczky had been allowed to present his evidence, there is a strong probability that the Committee would have decided to place the subject on the U.N. agenda, after which the cover-up would have been impossible to maintain.

I salute the example set by Major Colman Von Keviczky, as I consider him a genuine modern hero. The four propositions he suggested to Secretary General U Thant should be implemented by the United Nations without further delay, since they are as valid now as they were in 1966.

I was recently asked to define the type of UFO research program I would set in motion, if a benefactor provided substantial funds for that purpose, with no strings attached except to get results that would bring the amorphous ambiguity of the hitherto mysterious phenomena into clear and accurate focus, so we would at last know precisely what we are dealing with.

As the hypothetical benefactor has not yet materialized, I offer the following ideas in the hope that it may be possible to implement them.

A truly scientific approach would not place preconceived limits on areas to be investigated, such as declaring lights in the sky and reports of physical craft to be acceptable subjects for study, but contact and abduction reports to be unworthy of serious attention. True science would approach the subject in an all-inclusive manner, without neglecting any aspect of it. Instead of minimizing or deprecating aspects of the subject matter which are in the "high strangeness" category, it would pay particular attention to them, carefully making note of all their characteristics and the circumstances under which they occurred, cataloguing them for future reference if no immediate correlations could be found.

Veterans of the psychedelic movement might be able to interpret material in the "high strangeness" category in ways that academics with conventional backgrounds would not think of. The research team should consist not only of scientists and academics of different disciplines, but also of artists, musicians, psychics, dowsers, telepaths, and a variety of practitioners with "wild talents," selected on the basis of past performance, having demonstrated successful practice of their respective specialties.

Of course, it is necessary to have a solid data base concerning the physical manifestations as a foundation to start from. This has already been compiled and computerized by the major research groups, and undoubtedly by the government. However, the major research groups are about as forthcoming with material from their information banks as a miser gloating over his hoard of Krugerrands. It is almost as difficult for an independent researcher to pry loose information from the major research groups as it is to obtain it from the government. Unless it is possible to persuade the major research groups to pool their respective reservoirs of information, and to make it reasonably accessible to the public, the only alternative would be to form yet another research group, which would be an unnecessary duplication of effort. It would save a tremendous amount of time and energy if the major research groups would agree to cooperate on such a venture. If such an agreement can not be reached, it will be necessary to painstakingly re-do work that has already been done, to take the trouble of assembling the most complete physical data base possible, in such a way that the public can have reasonable access to it.

In my opinion, the close encounter and abduction cases constitute the spearhead of UFO research. Of course, it is essential to distinguish between genuine and fraudulent cases, and this is not always easy to do. However, with patient, open-minded, persistent and alert attention, it can be done. The analogy of sorting out batches of gemstone rough is relevant here. There are ways of detecting whether one is in the presence of the real thing or an imitation.

The genuine contact and abduction cases are the interface between terrestrial humanity and the UFO phenomenon. There are literally thousands of such case histories on record, and perhaps tens or hundreds of thousands, or more, which have not been reported. I would suggest that about two-thirds of the hypothetical budget be allocated to investigating as thoroughly as possible the thousands of case histories already on record: evaluating them for authenticity, conducting follow-up interviews and hypnotic regression sessions when appropriate, and feeding all the information obtained into computers.

The data bank derived from the review of contact and abduction cases should then be correlated with the data bank derived from the lights-in-the-sky and physical nuts-and-bolts manifestations.

If project funds are still available after this procedure has been completed, we should start interviewing the oceanic multitude of contactees and abductees whose stories have only recently begun to surface and are not yet on record. These interviews would be conducted and tabulated along the same lines as those case histories already on record.

From these myriad correlations, certain major patterns should emerge. What I would consider to be of prime importance would be the patterns indicating the characteristics of the different types of extra-terrestrial and/or inter-dimensional humanoids, human-appearing beings, and extremely dissimilar alien entities involved in these manifestations, to which we have been applying the catch-all UFO label. The information derived from such profiles would include not only the physical characteristics and types of craft most frequently used, but also the behavioral characteristics. Typical ways of interacting with us would contain clues as to motivations for making contact with us, as well as to psychological traits and the extent to which communication may be possible. Such questions as superiority, inferiority, or equality of intelligence between them and us would be explored, as well as unusual aspects of their intelligence. Indications of the relative benevolence, malevolence, or neutrality of the various types would show up clearly in such profiles, as well as of their friendliness or hostility to each other. As abductee Ida Kannenberg (whose story is to be found in the final chapter of my previous book) has so perceptively pointed out: "There are so many different types of extra-terrestrials that it is not possible to make statements that are valid for all of them. Many types are as alien to each other as they are to us."

By establishing reliable profiles of the different types most persistently reported, we would at least know what we are dealing with and be in a far better position to communicate meaningfully.

If there was a war in heaven that is still going on, in which who we give our allegiance to may be a matter of importance, though Earth may be no more than a single sector of a multi-galactic battle zone, at least we would be able to make an informed choice concerning which group we enter an alliance with. That would certainly be preferable to making a decision of such importance in our present state of blind ignorance.

If, on the other hand, peace and harmony reign supreme over the inhabitants of outer space, and it is we humans who must learn to transcend our aggressive bellicose natures in order to become eligible for galactic citizenship, we still need to know who we are dealing with, and be able to communicate with them.

Those who are still arguing about whether or not UFOs are real will continue to do so, until obliged to face the facts with their own eyes. For those of us who are already aware that UFOs are real, the question becomes: What types of beings are piloting them, and what is their motivation for keeping us under surveillance and clandestinely interacting with us?

It is a matter of extreme urgency that an all-out effort be made to find out as much as possible about the different types of non-human intelligent life-forms at present hovering above us and among us. We can no longer continue to pretend that we are dealing with misidentifications of weather balloons, the planet Venus, flocks of geese or swamp gas, and retain our position as the dominant life-form on planet Earth. It is time to face the fact that outer space is inhabited, and that ever since we exploded the first atomic bombs its inhabitants have been watching us very closely. It is obvious that in comparison to a number of already existing alien civilizations, our space technology is in the kindergarten stage. We must establish open alliance with the groups we can work out mutually beneficial relationships with, and take appropriate measures to defend ourselves against the predatory activities of the groups who have come here to exploit us. It is imperative that we learn to distinguish between extra-terrestrial friends and foes. What is at stake is our survival, not only as individuals, but as a freely evolving species.

2

The Martyrdom of Wilhelm Reich

Dr. Wilhelm Reich was a brilliant and original thinker who was martyred by our government for telling the truth as he saw it, just as Giordano Bruno was martyred by the Inquisition for maintaining that the Earth turns around the Sun and that inhabitants of other worlds exist. Reich's colleagues and fellow scientists, instead of coming to his defense, collaborated in destroying his reputation and his research.

One of the most specious and odious methods used in this attack was to assume that because Reich was seriously investigating UFO phenomena, he was therefore insane. This persecution culminated in his being sent to die in a federal penitentiary at age 60. All of his published work that government agents were able to get their hands on was burned. They smashed his research equipment with an ax. Not a single murmur of protest came from his fellow scientists as this outrage was perpetrated.

However, his genius is now more widely appreciated than it ever was during his lifetime, and most of his work has been republished. The opinions of the scientific community have evolved to the point where many scientists will now freely admit that Wilhelm Reich was unjustly persecuted.

The last book Reich wrote before being railroaded into the penitentiary, *Contact With Space*, was about his UFO research. Trevor James Constable wrote about it in *The Cosmic Pulse of Life*, published by Merlin Press in 1976:

Those who want to study Dr. Reich's own account of events will find this in *Contact With Space*, a Record Appendix to Petitioner's Reply Brief, U.S. Court of Appeals for the First Circuit, No. 5160, Wilhelm Reich et al., Defendants-Appellants versus the U.S.A. *Contact With Space* is the Record Appendix to Briefs for Appellants, Volume 5, Secret and Suppressed Evidence, OROP Desert Ea 1954-55. 'OROP' is a contraction for orgone energy operation, and 'Ea' is Dr. Reich's term for what is generally known as UFOs. Close to the core of things as usual, Dr. Reich's term is accurate and drawn from experience: 'E' stands for energy and 'a' is for alpha — primordial. We are indeed dealing with primary energy in the UFO field. Dr. Reich was right in this as in so much else.

Upon reading this, I remembered that Ea was also a god in the Babylonian pantheon. I decided to investigate his attributes, to see if they correlated in any way with Reich's choice of this name for what everyone else has been calling "UFO."

There is good reason to think that the early Babylonian god Ea was a prototype for the much later Hebrew god Jehovah. Ea had an even earlier prototype: the Sumerian god Enki. Although there are significant differences, Enki, Ea, and Jehovah do have some important points in common: all three were specifically designated by the cultures they represented as the creators of humanity and the founders of human civilization. Both Enki and Ea were described as having come from the "Apsu" or primordial abyss — and what is outer space if not the primordial abyss? In the earliest known Mesopotamian version of the Creation myth (the Sumerian), Enki came to Earth from the primordial abyss in a ship. Before proceeding to the area between the Tigris and the Euphrates, Enki made his base on the paradise island of Dilmoun, described as a place of purity and clarity in which there was no disease, menstruation, birth, or lamentation, in which the lion did not kill and the wolf did not attack the lamb.

The first detailed description of the creation of humanity is found in the *Enouma Elish*, the epic poem on which the religion of Babylon was based. According to this fundamental text, which was sacred to the inhabitants of Babylon, when Ea decided to create humanity in order to serve the gods and to make plants and animals grow in abundance, these were secondary motives. The primary motive was to punish one of the immortal gods who had revolted against Ea and the other gods and had been vanquished. Ea created mortal humanity from the body of the rebellious immortal, who was thereby fragmented and obliged to endure the ignominy of dying over and over again innumerable times, while continuously undergoing birth into yet more bodies doomed to die; thus, the rebel was punished, but the immortality of the gods remained intact. To transpose this Babylonian legend into Biblical terminology, it is as if Jehovah had created Adam and Eve directly from the body of the fallen angel Lucifer as a punishment for his rebellion, transforming what had been a unique immortal into innumerable mortal forms that were being endlessly reborn.

Gray Barker, a pioneer UFO researcher, first heard of Wilhelm Reich in the spring of 1957, when he received "a puzzling phone call. A woman with a husky, commanding voice told me her name was Dr. Eva Reich and pleaded that I might be able to help her father, who had been unjustly imprisoned because of his studies of flying saucers. She desperately wanted to know what Bender had found out and who silenced him. I had never heard anything about Reich's work at that time and unfortunately I remember little of what his daughter told me. What memory is left indicates that I probably classified the conversation as a crank call and got off the phone as quickly as I could. I will always regret not having heard her out more completely....Peter Mills, the prosecuting attorney for the Government, was originally the attorney for the Wilhelm Reich Foundation, the Orgone Institute, as well as being Reich's personal attorney at the time. Having had access to the inside of Reich's operations, including many confidential details, he had a distinct advantage over any lawyer in prosecuting this case. I don't know the ethics involved here, or trial procedures at the time, but his selection as prosecutor in this case would seem to have been improper."

Wilhelm Reich died on Nov. 3, 1957, but even that did not put an end to the Food and Drug Administration's harassment. The ultimate insult occurred when his daughter, Eva Reich, came to the penitentiary to claim his body. She discovered that they had opened up his body to perform an autopsy and had removed his internal organs, but had not bothered to replace them.

Was that merely an insult to his memory? Or was it to dispose of evidence that he had been murdered just as he was about to be paroled? Were the guts of Wilhelm Reich required for an operation of ceremonial black magic? As these possibilities are not mutually exclusive, all three of them could be true.

I find the relevance of Reich's *Contact With Space* to our contemporary circumstances staggering. Over 30 years ago, he was warning of the devastating consequences of what we now call "acid rain," such as the wholesale death of the forests and other ecological disasters. He described most eloquently and precisely how green fertile land is transformed into barren and then desert land, and how these cycles relate to our human emotional barrenness, as well as to Ea (UFO) discharge of noxious exhaust from their vehicles into Earth's atmosphere. He thought that the Ea entities were conducting an insidious, noiseless, emaciating war of attrition: "Drawing off life energy from a planet covered with green, seething with living beings." It was his opinion that the Ea vehicles ride the waves of the cosmic ocean of positively oriented life-giving energy, which he termed "orgone" or "OR." Under certain circumstances, the OR energy dies. It then becomes DOR, the death-dealing negative orgone energy, the opposite of the positive life-giving OR energy. DOR manifests in forms such as acid rain, smog, cancer, industrial waste, vehicle exhausts, excrement, etc.

Reich frequently referred to a concentrated form of DOR, which he called Melanor. He associated Melanor with Ea activity and specifically stated that it was a by-product of the Ea propulsion system. Melanor was a black powder-like substance that came down from above after UFOs had passed over his laboratory and "made us miserable with thirst, cyanosis, nausea, pains of all sorts."

A startling example of synchronicity occurred as I was at work on this chapter. Friends sent newspaper articles about a UFO close encounter that occurred in Australia on Jan. 20, 1988. Two different groups of people had reported nearly simultaneous close encounters. In both groups, speech became distorted during the incident. One group was the crew of a tuna fishing boat. The other group was about 50 miles from the boat, and consisted of a mother and her three sons, two of whom were adults. Mrs. Faye Knowles and her sons were driving in their family car, near Mundrabilla on the Nullarbor Plain, when they noticed that they were being approached by a luminous flying object shaped somewhat like an egg-cup, which picked their car up off the road, shook it violently, and then slammed the car back down on the road with such force that it blew out one of the tires. The car was covered both externally and internally by a black powdery ash-like substance that, according to Mrs. Knowles and her sons, "smelled like dead bodies."

Mrs. Knowles and her sons were taken to Dandenong Valley Private Hospital, where the doctor who examined them made a public statement that they were fine, but told their relatives that it could take as long as six months for them to recover from what they had been through. The contradiction inherent in this sterling example of medical double-talk was not noticed by the reporters covering the case, who lost no time in finding an "expert" capable of dreaming up a conventionally acceptable explanation. The unfortunate lady and her sons "could have been hit by a large carbonous meteorite shower," according to Charles Morgan of the Sydney Observatory, who apparently managed to keep a straight face while proposing this ridiculous suggestion.

Besides the crew of the fishing boat, the crew of a second fishing boat and other independent witnesses had seen the UFO. The occupants of four other vehicles on the same stretch of highway had also seen it. Furthermore, it had been seen again on the following night. And on Dec. 14, 1987, a similar incident had happened to a businessman in Tasmania, including the deposit of a soot-like substance all over his white Mercedes.

The Australian police had already dismissed the possibility of a hoax, so what was a poor reporter to do, but to fish up yet another "expert," who explained the black powdery ash-like substance — that covered the car both externally and internally, that smelled like dead bodies, and that resembled so remarkably the Melanor described by Dr. Reich over 30 years ago — as "dust from brake linings."

Graham Henley, a professional truck driver with over 30 years of experience, was one of the independent witnesses and one of the first people on the scene to talk with the family and look at the car. His testimony was straightforward and unequivocal: "The whole car smelt like bakelite or just like as if you'd blown a fuse...A soot was all over the car and there were four dents as if the car had been picked up by a magnet...I felt the sooty material on the roof of the car and it was not brake dust. I've been around the car-racing scene and I know what brake dust is like. This stuff was a fine, silicon-type material. It was like powdered glass; it had an incredible feel to it. Brake dust only gets on the wheels, not on the roof, and the brakes weren't even hot." Mr. Henley's statement was printed in an article about the Mundrabilla incident by Walt Andrus in the March 1988 issue of *MUFON UFO Journal.*

The results of the scientific analysis of this dust were not made public until Nov. 26, 1988, when *The Australasian Post* ran an article stating that:

> The Victorian UFO Research Society, the largest in the Southern Hemisphere and third largest in the world, has released a 300-page research report on its investigation into the Knowles incident.
>
> Scientists from Melbourne's Monash University have confirmed that the 'UFO dust,' although made of potassium chloride, looks like nothing they have ever seen before.
>
> Victorian UFO research society member John Auchettl, who led the Knowles investigation, said that under an electron microscope scientists found the enlarged dust particles to be 'unusual.'
>
> 'The particles were made of potassium chloride, but instead of being a crystal formation, which is usual, they were velocity particles,' Mr. Auchettl said.
>
> 'This means that the dust must have been forced out of something at a great velocity.'

Scientists said that under enlargement the dust molecule looked as though it might have come from a space shuttle blast. 'The UFO society theory is that the dust came from the UFO,' Mr. Auchettl said.

'In fact the dust had such a dense amount of chloride in it, scientists thought it might have come from a swimming pool, which wasn't possible. The dust backs up the Knowles' claim. The UFO society was on the scene as soon as we heard about the incident and we went through their car with a fine-tooth comb. This time, we were leaving nothing to chance.'

Although the Mundrabilla incident received world-wide media attention at the time that it occurred, the release of the physical evidence analysis results was almost totally ignored. Here at last was the long-sought scientifically verifiable physical evidence that the skeptics have been demanding for over 40 years as a prerequisite for taking the subject of UFOs seriously, yet when it was finally produced and made available for inspection, the dust was basically swept under the rug and covered with a blanket of silence as far as the world news media was concerned.

A Melanor-like substance also turns up in a report by a British police officer. In 1980, John Heymer attended the scene of a "rather unusual death fire." Here is how he described what he saw:

I am a retired Scenes of Crime Officer who served 25 years in the Gwent Police. My job involved attending the scenes of serious crimes and sudden deaths to gather evidence for forensic examination. As a result, I am both familiar with death and a trained witness.

On 6 January 1980, I was called to a council house in Gwent, to the scene of what I was told was a rather unusual death by fire.

The house was located on top of a hill and the weather was bitterly cold. On entering the house I was struck by the pleasant warmth. There was no sign of central heating or any other form of heating. The uniformed officers who had requested my presence told me that the fire had occurred in the living room.

I opened the door and stepped into a cooling oven. There was a steamy, sauna-like heat, and the room was bathed in a garish, orange radiance. The orange light emanated from a bare light bulb which was coated on a sticky, orange substance, as was the window. The temperature of the room had recently been extremely high. The walls were radiating heat. Condensation was running down the window. Heat had cracked one of the window panes.

The light bulb was bare because the plastic lampshade had melted, oozed down over the bulb and fallen to the floor. The walls, ceiling and all surfaces were coated with a greasy black soot.

In one wall was an open grate, which contained the dead ashes of a coal fire. The hearth was tidy; there were no signs of any coals having fallen from the fire.

On the floor, about one meter from the hearth, was a pile of ashes. On the perimeter of the ashes, furthest from the hearth, was a partially burnt armchair. Emerging from the ashes were a pair of human feet clothed in socks. The feet were attached to short lengths of lower leg, encased in trouser leg bottoms. The feet and socks were undamaged. Protruding from what was left of the trousers were calcined leg bones which merged into the ashes. The ashes were the incinerated remains of a man.

Of the torso and arms nothing remained but ash. Opposite the feet was a blackened skull. Though the rug and carpet below the ashes were charred, the damage did not extend more than a few centimeters beyond the perimeter of the ashes. Less than a meter away, a settee, fitted with loose covers, was not even scorched. Plastic tiles which covered the floor beneath the carpet were undamaged.

Although extremely high temperatures had developed in the room, nothing had burnt that had not been in contact with the body while it was being consumed. Reason told me that the scene I was viewing was impossible. Everyone at the scene experienced the same sensation of incredulity: a strong urge to deny the evidence of their senses.

One brief statement that Paul Bennewitz makes is directly relevant to the subject of Melanor. The following quotation is from *The Matrix: Understanding Aspects of Covert Interaction With Alien Culture, Technology and Planetary Power*, by Valdamar Valerian, published by Arcturus in 1988, which contains much information of high importance that supplements and confirms the information contained in this book. While discussing personally experienced UFO sightings, Bennewitz states that: "They can be seen in the clouds. They go into the cumulus clouds and produce nitrogen nitride. I assume or speculate it is this. You will see black spots in the cloud. They eat holes in the cloud. If you can see black spots in a cloud, then you can tell that a vehicle is in there."

In *Contact With Space*, Reich stated that the OR/DOR cycle can be reversed, and described how he and his equipment, with a small team of devoted assistants, got grass to grow knee-high in the Arizona desert, where it had never grown before within living memory. All of Reich's activities were carried on under the constant harassment of what he called "Higs" (Hoodlums In Government). When Reich discovered that the "cloudbuster" he had invented also had the capability of being used effectively as a "spacegun" that made UFOs fade out from the sky, he scrupulously informed the U.S. Air Force of this development and gave the U.S. Air Force his equations concerning gravity and anti-gravity free of charge. He was puzzled when the Weather Bureau failed to mention the rainfall that had occurred for the first time in 25 years in the desert region where he had been working. He was puzzled as the Higs hounded him to his death, in the Land of Freedom he had emigrated to from Nazi Germany.

It seems fitting to close this chapter with a brief excerpt from *Contact With Space*, which gives an idea of the train of thought that Reich was pursuing:

> Am I a Spaceman? Do I belong to a new race on earth, bred by men from outer space in embraces with earth women? Are my children offspring of the first interplanetary race? Has the melting-pot of interplanetary society already been created on our planet, as the melting-pot of all earth nations was established in the U.S.A. 190 years ago? Or does this thought relate to things to come in the future? I request my right and privilege to have such thoughts and to ask such questions without being threatened to be jailed by any administrative agency of society....In face of a rigid, doctrinaire, self-appointed, ready-to-kill hierarchy of scientific censorship it appears foolish to publish such thoughts. Anyone malignant enough could do anything with them. Still the right to be wrong has to be maintained. We should not fear to enter a forest because there are wildcats around in the trees. We should not yield our right to well-controlled speculation. It is certain questions entailed in such speculation which the administrators of established knowledge fear....But in entering the cosmic age we should certainly insist on the right to ask new, even silly questions without being molested.

3

Hitler's Alien Alliance

*O*ne of the many puzzling questions that keeps turning up in UFO research, and about which there has been considerable speculation, is whether the Nazis had any UFO contact.

Several references in the literature are at least marginally relevant to this matter. The first two references describe incidents when automobiles suddenly and inexplicably died. Then, after a period of time, they resumed normal functioning without any adjustments having been made. This is a well-known side-effect of many UFO encounters. Although UFOs were not reported in relation to these incidents, that does not necessarily mean they were not involved. I realize that these are slender threads, but slender threads may lead to more substantial evidence.

The first incident, described by Charles Fort in his book *Wild Talents*, took place Oct. 25, 1930. About 40 automobiles had stalled, for an hour, on the road between Risa and Wurzen.

The Nazis were not yet in power in 1930. However, the surge in popularity which brought them to power in 1933 began to reach overwhelming proportions in 1930, when they first became the largest political party in Germany. At that time, Hitler had many wealthy followers who owned large estates. Was there contact between members of the Nazi inner circle and a certain type of UFO occupant on Oct. 25, 1930? Was this incident a demonstration of power, intended to impress influential people? Did the incident have the desired effect?

The second reference describes incidents from 1938, when the Nazis were firmly in control of Germany. The following quotation is from *Hitler's Secret Sciences* by Nigel Pennick, published by Neville Spearman in London in 1981. As the title suggests, the book deals with different types of secret research the Nazis conducted:

> In connection with this high-energy research, various mysterious 'transmitters' were erected at several 'key points' in the Reich. In 1938, the Brocken, a celebrated peak in the Harz mountains, was the site of feverish construction work. Holy mountain of the goddess Freyja, the Brocken is best known for the curious optical phenomenon known as the 'Brocken Spectre,' which occurs when the shadow of a person on the summit is cast by the rays of the sun onto a cloud below...
> This 'transmitter' was a strange contraption, a tower surrounded by an array of posts with pear-shaped knobs on top. At the same time, a similar system was erected on the peak of the Feldberg near Frankfurt. When it began operation, there were soon reports of strange phenomena in the vicinity of the Brocken tower. Cars travelling along the mountain roads would suddenly have engine failure. A Lutwaffe sentry would soon spot the stranded car, and tell the puzzled motorist that it was no use trying to get the car started at present. After a while, the sentry would tell the driver that the engine would work again now, and the car would then start up and drive away.

If the Nazis had developed a device capable of stalling engines at a distance in 1938, it is remarkable that they never used it in the war years that followed. However, if cars stalled when a UFO was hovering over the transmitter device they had constructed, this particular piece of the puzzle fits in with the other pieces.

The third reference may amount to no more than deliberate disinformation, but sometimes disinformation contains a clue that indicates the nature of what is being covered up. By this, I do not mean to imply that *Brighter Than a Thousand Suns* by Robert Jungk, which was published by Harcourt Brace in 1956, is not a serious scholarly study of the development of nuclear energy by a qualified expert. Jungk's scholarship is of high quality, but anyone associated that closely with top-secret governmental projects would unhesitatingly follow intelligence agency guidelines when making public disclosures. This is the quotation from his book:

> The indifference of Hitler and those about him to research in natural science amounted to positive hostility. The only exception to the lack of interest shown by authority was constituted by the Air Ministry. The Air Force research workers were in a peculiar posi-

tion. They produced interesting new types of aircraft such as the Delta (triangular) and 'flying discs.' The first of these 'flying saucers,' as they were later called — circular in shape, with a diameter of some 45 yards — were built by the specialists Schreiver, Habermohl and Miethe. They were first airborne on February 14, 1945, over Prague and reached in three minutes a height of nearly eight miles. They had a flying speed of 1,250 m.p.h. which was doubled in subsequent tests. It is believed that after the war Habermohl fell into the hands of the Russians. Miethe developed at a later date similar 'flying saucers' at A.V. Roe and Company for the United States.

First, Jungk neglects to mention that the so-called "flying saucer" developed by Miethe for A. V. Roe and Company did not fly and it never even got off the ground. By 1956, when Jungk's book was published, the CIA disinformation campaign about UFOs was in full swing. A convenient way of discrediting the extra-terrestrial hypothesis would be to present an at least superficially plausible explanation of UFOs as advanced aircraft manufactured by Germans, Russians, or Americans. I think that this is what Mr. Jungk was obediently attempting to do. However, in 1956 the abundant evidence of UFO sightings previous to World War II, as well as to World War I and the first flight of the Wright brothers in their crude airplane, was nowhere near as firmly established as it is today. The hypothesis that UFOs were invented by the Nazis during World War II no longer has even superficial plausibility. However, if the Nazis were in contact with a certain type of UFO entity, it makes sense that they would have had models or prototypes of disc-shaped aircraft, some of which might have become nearly functional by the end of the war.

It is on record (in *The Morning of the Magicians* by Louis Pauwels and Jacques Bergier, Stein & Day, New York, 1960) that Hitler made these remarks to his aide-de-camp, Von Rauschening:

What will the social order of the future be like? Comrades, I will tell you. There will be a class of overlords, and after them the rank and file of the Party Members in hierarchical order, and then the great mass of anonymous followers, servants and workers in perpetuity, and beneath them, again all the conquered foreign races, the modern slaves. And over and above all these will reign a new and exalted nobility of whom I cannot speak....But of all these plans the ordinary militant members will know nothing....The new man is living amongst us now! He is here! Isn't that enough for you? I will tell you a secret. I have seen the new man. He is intrepid and cruel. I was afraid of him.

Von Rauschening also described how Hitler habitually suffered from devastating nightmares from which he would awaken in panic terror, screaming incoherently about entities that were invisible and incomprehensible to his aide-de-camp, as well as to everyone else in his entourage.

Hitler's terror of the new class of overlords he had made a pact with so closely resembles the "body terror" described by Whitley Strieber and other Gray abductees that it is a clear indication of which type of E.T. Hitler was in contact with. The subtle emanations from the physical bodies of the Grays are so alien to the type of energy field the human aura is composed of that close range interaction with them is almost inevitably traumatic.

The concentration camps may have been designed specifically to provide the Grays with nourishment they required, just as the Aztec ritualized mass murders were structured for that purpose. All it would take would be for the President of the United States to go on TV and announce a State of Emergency for our normal civil liberties to be replaced by martial law, enforced not by local law authorities but by the black-uniformed Delta Special Forces, the resurrected Gestapo, for it to happen all over again in our time.

Among the mail I received after the release of *Extra-Terrestrials Among Us* was a letter that led to a witness of a UFO incident closely associated with Hitler:

Diane Duurland lives in Amsterdam. She spent her childhood in the town of Beveren, which is now named Roeselare, in Belgium. During the winter of 1944, when she was about 11 years old, Hitler used to visit Beveren frequently, and she would see him being driven by in an automobile.

During that winter her mother was sick, so she had to do all the errands. She had to work very hard, as she was the oldest of her mother's five children. In the darkness of the winter evenings, one of her chores was to walk to the farm of the Sommers family to get milk. While walking in this direction on the road from her house (Grafee Road), she saw strange swift movement behind the hedge of the Belgian cemetery, which is next to the German cemetery. Something zoomed as it passed by her. Her first thought was that Hitler had gotten a new car, but it didn't have any wheels. It had red-blue-yellow-green-white-violet colored lights that kept changing. There were people inside it. It made a strange zooming sound, not at all like an automobile engine. It hovered about a meter (three feet) above the ground. When she realized what a strange thing she was seeing, she became so frightened that she jumped into a patch of tall stinging nettles.

As she watched it, the thing seemed to dissolve. She thought it might have gone over to a field on the Wallekamp farm, but she didn't see it again. It was no longer to be seen. Instead of continuing on her way to get the milk, she returned home and told her mother what had happened. Her mother did not believe her and boxed her ears for telling such a fantastic story. Her mother did take a look outside, but it was unfortunately no longer to be seen. Although she was very frightened, she was sent out again to get the milk.

When she reached the farm of the Sommers family, she told Mrs. Sommers what had happened. Mrs. Sommers said that there were a lot of these flying saucers around, but it was important to keep one's mouth shut, because if the Germans found out anyone had seen this, the person would be shot or sent away to the camps.

What Diane Duurland saw on that winter evening in 1944 was circular and saucer-shaped, something like an umbrella with an edge on it that kept turning. The edge that kept turning was white. The red-blue-yellow-green-violet lights that kept changing came from the dome-shaped part of it. The object itself was a silvery metallic color, about as large as an automobile. It was opaque or semi-transparent. It was a strange and wonderful sight that she will always remember.

When I mentioned to Diane Duurland that the term "flying saucer" was supposedly first invented by a journalist after the Kenneth Arnold sighting of 1947, she pointed out that the shape of the object so closely resembled a type of plate in common use in every household that it was natural to use that name.

According to an article by Bill Lawren in *Omni*, October 1987, there is now substantial evidence that the corpse identified as Hitler's by the Russians was not Hitler's. Lawren asks:

Did Adolf Hitler really die a suicide in his underground bunker near the Berlin Chancellery? The Russians, who captured the bunker, maintain that he did, saying that they discovered a charred corpse whose teeth precisely matched descriptions of Hitler's mouth based upon the written records of the Fuhrer's dentist. But a new and exhaustive investigation by a Canadian forensic dental expert casts doubt on the authenticity of the corpse, reviving speculation that the Nazi leader may have escaped.

Dr. Robert Dorion, Director of Forensic Dentistry for the Ministry of the Solicitor General of Quebec in Montreal, has compared photographs of the corpse's teeth with thousands of openmouthed closeup photos of the Fuhrer himself. Dorion found a number of glaring discrepancies. The pattern of gaps between the teeth was different; Hitler had a root canal and porcelain tooth that did not show up in the corpse; and the corpse had different lower bridgework from what Hitler is alleged to have had.

Is the Hitler corpse a fraud? Did the Fuhrer make it off to Argentina?

The question may not be so much whether Hitler made it to Argentina, as whether a specific type of UFO entity took him to a base where he was placed in suspended animation, to be turned loose on an unsuspecting world during some time of crisis.

It is my opinion that through the ceremonial black magic practiced by the innermost elite core of the Nazi party, the Black Order (which now appears to be at the innermost core of our CIA — see the "Strange Suicides" chapter of *Extra-Terrestrials Among Us*), contact was established with the type of E.T. that we at present call the Grays. This contact was sporadic and elusive, following the pattern that has since been repeated so persistently with other contact groups. Having gotten all the mileage they could out of the Nazis, in terms of abundant provisions of the substances the Grays are now known to feed upon, the Grays followed their standard operating procedure of double-crossing their no longer useful devotees, discarding them like the rind of an orange that has been pulped.

One of the allegations concerning the Grays is that, besides being themselves emotionally and sexually atrophied, they derive a second-hand gratification from intense human emotion of any kind, whether ecstasy or agony. It is, unfortunately, easier to induce agony than ecstasy. Another persistent allegation concerning the Grays is that although they do not feed on flesh, they have more than a passing interest in blood and guts, as has been demonstrated by the cattle mutilations in the United States and elsewhere (see the "Mysterious Mutilations" chapter of *Extra-Terrestrials Among Us* and Linda Moulton Howe's *An Alien Harvest*). The condition that the cattle cadavers were constantly found in made it clear that the mutilations were perpetrated in order to harvest glandular extracts from the entrails and to collect blood, literally every drop of blood that the bodies contained. There may have been other motivations also, but the evidence indicates that these were the primary purposes.

It could well be that the Nazi obsession with breeding a tall blond Master Race was fostered and encouraged by the Grays in order to acquire access to a reservoir of genetic material that would resemble their hereditary enemies as closely as possible, yet would be subservient to them. The Grays would then have no longer needed to be exclusively dependent on prisoners of war and the unsatisfactory clones and hybrids as sources of supply for beings of this type, willing to take orders from them.

It is obvious from the historical record that World War II need never have occurred, if it had not been for the actions of one man, Adolf Hitler, who almost single-handedly brought about the situation that made World War II inevitable. Hitler, the human (at least in appearance) instrument of the Grays, provided them with a feast of unprecedented magnitude at the expense of humanity. Hitler furnished the secret masters he lived in fear of, the "new overlords," with even more tremendous amounts of blood and guts than the Aztecs had, but the always devious Grays either would not or could not bestow any enduring victory upon him. The victories he temporarily enjoyed turned out to be like the folk tales about devil's gold, which on the following day turns into excrement.

If it is indeed true that the U.S. government, in exchange for technology, has made a clandestine agreement with the Grays permitting them to mutilate animals, abduct humans, and install themselves in underground bases, that would be a devil's bargain if there ever was one.

Just as they appear to have been doing with the contemporary U.S. government, the Grays gave the Nazis bits and pieces of advanced technology, but never anything that could be put together to actually work well enough to decisively dominate their enemies. If at any time before the collapse of Berlin, the Nazis had even temporary access to one single flying disc that actually worked, they could have wiped out the entire Allied Air Forces in next to no time with that one disc, and within a few hours transformed defeat into victory. The fact that this did not occur is proof that the Nazis did not have access to even one flying disc that was operational, though they had models on the drawing boards and under experimentation. Some of the Nazis who had potential for long-term usefulness to the Grays may have been taken to already existing Gray underground or undersea bases in the Antarctic or elsewhere at the time of the Nazi collapse, but would not have been in control of those bases.

Undeniably, the Nazi party is now not only alive and well, but thriving. Thanks to the intervention of the CIA, the Nazi party has been for many years in open control of Chile, though the Pinochet dictatorship is now so universally detested that it is on its way out. Thinly disguised Fascist fronts constitute powerful minorities or even majorities in Argentina and many other Latin American countries, as well as elsewhere in the world, including Germany, Austria, South Africa, Japan, and our own country. The special relationship between Standard Oil and I.G. Farben is a thing of the past, but similar special relationships undoubtedly exist between contemporary cartels, such as those belonging to or associated with the Trilateral Commission and the Bilderberger group. Under the Reagan and Bush administrations, money and weapons have been distributed on an enormous scale to neo-Nazi groups worldwide. By brandishing the bugaboo of national security, Mrs. Thatcher succeeded in abolishing the freedom of the press in England.

It is also true that the Spear of Destiny (*The Spear of Destiny* by Trevor Ravenscroft was published by Neville Spearman, Ltd. in London in 1973), which General Patton was the only high-ranking U.S. officer to recognize the profound significance of, and which General Eisenhower (who outranked Patton) insisted on returning to the museum in Vienna from which it had been taken by Hitler, is now in the custody of Kurt Waldheim.

How could Hitler have lost the war, if he had a working relationship with technologically advanced extra-terrestrials, while the leaders of the Allies were not even aware of the possibility of such a thing?

The political and military leaders of the Allies may not have been aware of such a possibility, but the Nazis did not have a monopoly on the art of invoking and communicating with other-dimensional and/or extra-terrestrial entities through ritual magic. There were highly developed adepts in England and elsewhere who were also masters of this art, and who opposed the objectives of the Nazis. These adepts may not have been in positions of political or military power, but that would not have prevented their ceremonial workings from exerting an influence on the course of events.

Just because an entity is extra-terrestrial does not necessarily mean that it is omniscient or omnipotent or even truthful. If the type of E.T. the Nazis were in contact with occupied a rather low position in the hierarchy of the cosmic totem pole, and was itself under surveillance by more highly evolved and powerful groups, it would be obliged to operate within certain parameters.

For example, predatory activity by a low-level E.T. group on terrestrial humanity might be permitted by higher echelons of the hierarchy only to the extent that humanity is responsible for polluting and destroying the fragile biosphere of planet Earth. Adepts capable of contacting higher echelons of the cosmic hierarchy might be able to restrict or neutralize the activities of a low-level group of E.T.s.

These are the birth-dates of the most successful world-conquering warriors known to our history:

Alexander	—	356 B.C.
Julius Caesar	—	101

Attila the Hun	—	395 A.D.
Mohammed	—	569
Charlemagne	—	742
Genghis Khan	—	1162
Tamerlane	—	1336
Pizarro	—	1475
Cortez	—	1485
Napoleon	—	1769
Bismarck	—	1815
Hitler	—	1889

It is as if every few hundred years, a leading character is released on the world stage who inexorably brings about massive blood-letting. Although frequently camouflaged by philosophical, patriotic, or religious doctrines, the bottom-line net result of these meteoric careers is human sacrifice on an enormous scale, comparable to a harvest of the human herd. Some of these irresistible warriors were relatively enlightened, and did make some positive contributions to the development of humanity, while others were unequivocally demonic personifications of destruction.

Tamerlane, who struck terror into the hearts of the entire known world of his time, was born in Samarkand and died on his way to invade China in 1405. The resemblances between his life story and Hitler's are so remarkable that they raise the question of whether Hitler was his reincarnation. Tamerlane conquered most of the Arab world and invaded Christian Europe, occupying Moscow for a year. Having overcome Russia, Turkey, and Egypt, he turned his attention to India, conquering and plundering it. He was among the cruelest of the many cruel tyrants recorded in human history. One of his favorite pastimes was to slaughter every single inhabitant of a city he had just conquered and to build a tower with their severed heads. Before traveling on, he systematically destroyed any ancient monuments and sacred places.

Less than two centuries before Tamerlane terrorized the known world, Genghis Khan employed similar tactics in subduing an empire that extended from Central Europe to the China Sea. Genghis Khan obtained from a source that remains a mystery weaponry more sophisticated than that of his contemporaries: rockets that spread terror through the ranks of opposing armies before the battle had been joined. He also somehow acquired a propaganda ploy worthy of Goebbels. His excuse for invading one neighbor after another was that he wished to plant fruit trees throughout their territories. While persistently presenting this seemingly altruistic and idealistic goal for his activities to the public, he diligently perpetrated the most horrifying abominations imaginable, resulting in mass human sacrifice on a scale comparable to the Aztecs in ancient Mexico and to that of the CIA against the populations of the Third World in modern times. Who or what was pulling his strings? What periodically activates these marionettes to go forth upon the world stage and harvest the human herd?

Let us consider two legendary incidents that illustrate how magic may exert a substantial influence on political and military events. At the time of the Spanish Armada, the witches of England raised for England a cone of power that caused a tempest so tremendous that it shattered and scattered the otherwise invincible Armada. A different but related legend concerns the cone of power that the British witches raised after the Battle of Dunkerque, when England was prostrate in defeat and defenseless against invasion by the seemingly invincible Nazis. On that occasion, the cone of power was aimed directly at the mind of Hitler, in the form of telepathic hypnosis that caused him to keep delaying the invasion of England from one day to the next by stimulating his interest in other projects, culminating in his fatally flawed decision to embark on the project of invading Russia before having completely secured his otherwise total control of Europe by the conquest of England.

A coalition of free-thinking liberty-loving people defeated Hitler once, and if necessary could do it again, as the rigid caste system he was trying to impose is not suited to terrestrial humanity at its present stage of development. However, we need to be alert and prepared for danger rather than smug complacent couch potatoes, hypnotized and subliminally programmed by the boob tube. It is also imperative to recognize and renew the ancient alliance with the type of E.T. that is ancestral to us, in the sense of having been the progenitors of Cro-Magnon man.

4

Lethal Lakes and Disappearing Children

*L*ake Whitney is a beautiful vacation spot near the Dallas/Fort Worth area. Thousands of tourists go there every weekend. With only rare exceptions, they return home safely. Things go wrong occasionally at any large resort frequented by crowds of temporary visitors. However, when things go wrong at Lake Whitney, there are indications on some occasions of an unknown factor in the equation, a force in action that is not publicly recognized.

Local residents are reluctant to discuss the matter because the well-being of their community depends on the tourist trade. I do not wish to disturb the well-being of their community by frightening away tourists, but feel that for the well-being of all concerned (which includes residents, visitors and the whole wide world) the bizarre nature of some of these anomalous incidents should be investigated in order to bring this unknown factor into clear focus. It can then be dealt with in the light of conscious awareness instead of being repressed and continuing to lurk hidden in the depths, unrecognized and therefore able to literally get away with murder.

In order to give an idea of the kinds of incidents I am referring to, I now quote from an article by Glenn Guzzo, which appeared in the Fort Worth *Star-Telegram* of February 15th, 1976, entitled:

Whitney Triangle? Lake Deaths Still Baffling

Lake Whitney — The Texas Parks and Wildlife Department may have to conduct a seance to get any meaningful citizen input on how to keep motorists from driving off a boat ramp here and ending up on the bottom of the lake.

It's not that the citizenry is unconcerned about three bodies discovered at the same location in a recent 20-month span. They just haven't been able to solve the mystery.

Nor do they have answers to assorted drownings, airplane crashes and other unusual events that seem to be more in keeping with a science fiction novel than a casual recreation site in Bosque County.

"There's something weird going on out there in that lake," says a not-so-salty dog who has done his fishing in Lake Whitney for 15 years. "But if you say I said that, I'm going to come looking for you."

Investigators from Warr Acres, Oklahoma came looking at Lake Whitney in 1971, hoping to find traces — possibly the bodies — of two Warr Acres women who disappeared in 1963.

Authorities thought they had a major break in the case with the discovery of a black and white 1963 Cadillac like the one Mrs. Margery Elston, 41, and her daughter Melinda, 18, were driving when they vanished.

The empty Cadillac turned out to be the wrong car.

But while they were at it, divers found two almost-identical cars nearby.

During that same year, in the same area, divers found another dozen autos, all empty.

Instead of solving a puzzle, the discoveries only led to more mysteries and the Oklahoma case remains unsolved....

Citizens of the small towns that dot the lake's perimeter and the fisherman who doesn't want his name associated with superstitions aren't the only ones without explanations for numerous mysterious incidents at the lake.

County officials are equally baffled, as are regional and state departments.

Parks and Wildlife personnel in Austin say they want to hear public opinion before taking steps to remedy whatever hazards they can identify at the lake.

They may have to do without it, unless they can contact the spirits of those who have died strangely on or near Lake Whitney.

As expected, the lake has had its share of drownings. Small boats have sunk, fishermen have gone overboard, swimmers have gone down for the last time and drunks have turned an innocent dock into a pirate's plank.

But there also have been unusual deaths caused by such occurrences as cars going off the end of a short road into 10 feet of water and airplanes falling into the lake.

What makes the events so intriguing is that conditions that would be considered unusual in just a single accident have been repeated several times....

When Robert and Dan Mutto of Cleburne dragged the area near the boat ramp in Lakeside Village January 3, they were looking for the body and car of their father, 47-year old Robert Alton Hutto. They found them. But they also found the body of Bobby Webb of Weatherford, whose sunken auto was near Hutto's. Hutto had been missing since New Year's Eve, but Webb, 46, had not been seen for 13 months. Webb, who had suffered a massive heart attack four months before he disappeared and was recovering slowly, was discovered nine feet below the surface.

Hundreds, maybe thousands, of small boats had passed over Webb's car while launching and docking at the popular boat ramp without anyone noticing its presence.

A mobile home park close to the water houses the population of Lakeside Village, listed in the 1970 census as 226. Several park residents and weekend visitors swear that the Webb and Hutto cars were pulled from Lake Whitney front first, as if they had entered the lake backwards.

None of the residents tries to explain it.

Sheriff Baxter denies the reported position of the cars, but he confirms another village tale: the automatic transmissions of both cars were in park.

"No one will ever know why they were in park," Baxter said.

Rex Broome, who manages the marina between the mobile home park and the water, suggested the drivers, discovering their dilemma too late, may have shifted into park as a last resort to keep from entering the lake.

However, there were no skid marks on the boat ramp showing signs of sudden efforts to stop. And fishermen who look for bass, catfish and trout in that part of the lake say they like the rough surface of the boat ramp because it's not slippery.

The Hutto and Webb bodies were only the second and third found recently off the boat ramp.

On April 27, 1974, the body of Howard Wane Jackson, 33, of Waco floated out of an open window of a car found 60 feet from the ramp. In that instance, too, there were no skid marks.

Less than a mile from the boat ramp, easily within sight, is the spot where four people were killed July 20 when a plane crashed about 300 yards from the shoreline.

Vernon K. Carter, 54, and his wife Lois of Fort Worth and their two sons died in the crash.

The Carter crash is similar to a two-fatality plane crash on the opposite side of the lake in Hill County five years before.

Steve Bowman, 20, and his wife Sammie, 18, both University of Texas students, died Oct. 4, 1970, when their plane plunged into 20 feet of water 200 feet offshore and sank.

In both accidents the pilots reportedly were flying at very low altitudes — less than 100 feet above the water. When the pilots tried to climb suddenly, the engines stalled and the planes fell into the water.

Coincidentally, both accidents were witnessed by people who knew the victims well.

Seven family members, including Bowman's parents, and a friend watched the UT couple crash after the plane had flown only 20 feet above the water.

A close friend of the Carters told investigators he waved to the family, then watched as the plane wagged its wings, flew about a quarter-mile, then nose-dived 100 feet into the water.

National Transportation Safety Board records indicate the pilots erred in both accidents by flying too low.

However, it never was established why 24-year-old Roland Carter, a flight engineer and co-pilot for Alaska Airlines, was flying his Cherokee 180 so low or exactly what caused the plane to crash.

Residents of Lakeside Village say you have to be "spooked" to believe a mysterious force drew the planes to their destruction.

But the same residents and visitors talk about the highly unlikely string of events.

"Whenever you get four of five people together they're going to talk about it." marina manager Broome said....

But not everyone from the area likes to discuss the matter.

"It's taboo," said a fisherman who refused to give his name, "You don't talk about things like that. It's a jinx."

Is it a jinx, or is the unknown factor in the equation to be defined in other terms? An aspect of the situation that Mr. Guzzo did not consider in his otherwise excellent article is that there have been many UFO sightings in the Lake Whitney area over the years, and sightings continue to be reported. There was intense UFO activity in the area of Calvert, Texas, about 60 miles southeast of Lake Whitney in 1973-4, the time period during which many of the incidents described in Mr. Guzzo's article occurred. There have been two UFO landings near Lake Whitney, which left physical evidence in the form of burn marks. This is how a woman, who wishes to remain anonymous, described the sinking of her boat in 1984:

It all happened in less than three minutes. It was late in the afternoon on what had been a beautiful day. There were some storm clouds building far in the distance, about thirty miles to the south, on the rim of the horizon. Otherwise the sky was clear and blue, except for one small gray cloud that was almost directly above us. The lake was calm. There was not even a breeze. There were no waves at all. Then from one second to the next, out of nowhere came a wind of hurricane force. It did not come in gusts, it was like a wall of wind. Huge waves sprang up and pounded our boat, which was a 1980 model Baretta that was flotation-insulated to stay at least partially afloat, even if completely filled with water. The boat began to spin like a top, turning around and around in counterclockwise circles. Then suddenly the bow went up and the stern went down, and it sank dead straight vertically like a stone. Fortunately we were able to jump clear in time and to swim to shore. Later on, the insurance company sent a scuba diver down to locate the sunken boat, but he was not able to find it.

Several weeks after the sinking of the boat, a sweat lodge ceremony was performed on Serenity Point (a peninsula extending into Lake Whitney) for the specific purpose of making contact with extra-terrestrials. When the participants came out of the sweat lodge, a UFO was clearly visible in the sky and a photograph of it was taken.

Divers have disappeared. Diving instructors warn their students that Lake Whitney is dangerous, that although it is a contained lake which should not have an undertow, sometimes there is a powerful undertow. Here is what one student had to say:

When we went to do our scuba certification, the school took us to another lake. Our instructor told us a story about the last time he ever took a class to Lake Whitney. The diving spot they had used for a long time was about eighty feet deep and completely pitch black. There was no light at that depth. There was a tree he would tie equipment to at the bottom. He went down first to check things out. It was pitch black and he couldn't see his hands. Suddenly two small red lights about the size of nickels flashed on and blinked. He shot up a few feet and then started thinking: 'There must be some light reflecting on something down here. It must be my angle.' So he went back down. Pitch black again. Suddenly the two red lights came on again, and began to blink faster and faster. He shot to the surface: to hell with the bends! He never brought another class to

Whitney.

The woman who described what the diving instructor had told her, but who wishes to remain anonymous, says she has also heard that similar types of strange events are occurring at a lake in Mexico. However, her informant was not able to specify which lake it was.

Lake Whitney may not be the only miniature Bermuda Triangle within the boundaries of the United States. Apparently there have been whole series of bizarre fish and bird kills, animal mutilations, and human disappearances in the vicinity of Lake Tahoe since early 1987.

According to this correspondent, who also demands anonymity, media coverage of the incidents is very different from the real story. Some sort of mysterious illness is spreading among animals, birds, and humans in the area. There have been scores of animal mutilations — which are never reported in the media as Lake Tahoe is heavily dependent on tourism — and the mutilations have coincided with an epidemic of "missing persons." Media coverage attributes the massive fish kills to pollutants or salinity, but something else is responsible, which biologists involved in the investigations refuse to discuss. Quite a few horses have been among the animals mutilated. During the same time (January-April 1987), numerous animal mutilations occurred near Kingman, Arizona, which were systematically ignored by the news media.

Another disturbing reference to Lake Tahoe surfaced in an article by Hillary Johnson in the July 16, 1987, issue of *Rolling Stone*, entitled "Journey Into Fear: The Growing Nightmare of Epstein-Barr Virus." Some researchers consider chronic Epstein-Barr virus syndrome (CEBV) even more dangerous than AIDS. Where did the first outbreak of this disease occur? At Incline Village, which is on the shore of Lake Tahoe, in 1984. Like AIDS, CEBV attacks the immune system, and there is no known cure.

Although CEBV is not now considered fatal, it destroys its victims both physically and mentally (middle-aged people develop symptoms similar to Alzheimer's), ruining careers and marriages as well as healthy normal functioning. CEBV is so difficult to detect and diagnose in the early stages that a doctor has compared it to the Stealth Bomber. There is disagreement among researchers as to whether the high levels of Epstein-Barr virus that accompany the disease are its cause, or merely a symptom. Dr. Robert Gallo of the National Institutes of Health, who discovered the AIDS virus, has discovered a virus called HBLV that many researchers think is more likely to be the real cause. Epstein-Barr virus has been well-known to the medical community for many years, but the HBLV virus, which is of astounding and unprecedented virulence, appears to be a newcomer on the scene. Hillary Johnson brings up this point in her interview with Dr. Paul Cheney, who treated the first wave of cases at Incline Village and alerted the medical community to the danger:

> What's crucial, of course, is whether Gallo's virus is new to the planet, or the human race, or simply an old virus newly discovered. 'If I find out that the virus is 3,000 years old,' Cheney said, 'I'll do this.' He sighed with relief. 'After all. it's been around for that long, and we're still here. But if it's new, then no one knows what it can do. Can we handle it immunologically? Only time will tell. One thing — it's difficult to imagine an old virus could suddenly cause an outbreak.'

If Gallo's virus is new to this planet and to the human race, just like the AIDS virus that it resembles in so many ways, including the time frame of its inception, then we must at least consider the possibility that these two previously unknown viruses came to this planet from elsewhere.

Yet another indication of intervention from elsewhere is to be found in the following brief article, released by the Associated Press on May 28, 1987:

Death Bolt Strikes Top Attorney

Bossier City, La. — Prominent attorney Graves Thompson stood on his new boat, raised his hands, looked skyward and declared, "Here I am."

Then a lightning bolt struck him dead.

There was no thunder, lightning or sign of lightning before the killer bolt struck.

Thomas, 40, died of electrocution on Memorial Day.

It was not immediately determined why Thomas gestured toward the sky just before he was killed.

"He just got the boat last week, and he's been out with it just about every night after work," said Lisa Hester, the lawyer's secretary.

Thomas came from a family of prominent Louisiana judges and lawyers, and his cases regularly made headlines.

All of this brings to mind the bizarre story of the "exploding lake" in the small African nation of Cameroon in August 1986, which was never satisfactorily explained and in which there was very heavy loss of life. Tom Adams of Project Stigma summarized the little that is publicly known about this mysterious incident in the 1987 issue of *Crux* (P.O. Box 1094,

Paris, TX 75460):

> World scientists disagree still on the cause of the death of over 1,700 people in the African nation of Cameroon in August 1986. The deaths of people and animals were attributed to a cloud of toxic gases emanating from the volcanic Lake Nios' (Why? is the matter in dispute). A moderate-length *Associated Press* article on the incident appeared in the first edition of the *Kansas City Star* of August 26, 1986. The second edition that day included the identical story but with the omission of this one paragraph:

> The French news agency Agence France-Presse quoted the Rev. Fred Tern Horn, a Catholic missionary, as saying, 'It was as if a neutron bomb had exploded, destroying nothing but killing all life. In the first village we went through, we saw men, women and animals stretched out dead on the ground, sometimes in front of their huts or on their beds, sometimes on the path.'

Could it be that this paragraph was omitted because it hints that these massive unexplained deaths may have had an artificial rather than a natural cause?

Approximately three months before this massacre, on May 13, 1986, there was an apparition of the Virgin Mary in a jungle area of Cameroon, not far from the little village of Nsimalen. (*Liberation*, Paris, France, July 31, 1986.) The nearest town of any size is Yaounde. The apparition was visible at the top of a tree continuously for several weeks and was accompanied by other types of paranormal luminous phenomena, such as the sun appearing to dance and stars appearing to come down from the sky. Thousands of pilgrims from all over the nation flocked to see it, and did so, returning to their homes with vivid descriptions of what they had seen. Many healings were reported. What the relationship may be between this unusually long-sustained apparition, witnessed by such large crowds of people, and the large-scale tragedy that occurred less than three months later is difficult to determine. Some of the possibilities will be investigated at length and in detail in the next chapter of this book.

In the special issue of *Critique* devoted to the subject of Evil (P.O. Box 11368, Santa Rosa, CA 95406), a horrifying hypothesis was suggested: that the massacre at Lake Nios had indeed been a neutron bomb test, prearranged with the Cameroon government by the U.S. government through the intermediary of Israel. Until we know more about the matter, let us keep our minds open and continue to investigate all of the possibilities.*

Although its relevance may be only marginal, it seems appropriate at this point to quote the hypothesis proposed a quarter of a century ago by William Burroughs in his *Nova Express* (Evergreen Press, New York, 1964):

> Let me explain how we make an arrest — Nova Criminals are not three-dimensional organisms — (though they are quite definite organisms as we shall see) but they need three-dimensional human agents to operate — The point at which the criminal controller intersects a three-dimensional human agent is known as 'a coordinate point' — And if there is one thing that carries over from one human host to another and establishes identity of the controller it is habit: idiosyncrasies, vices, food preferences ... a gesture, a certain smile, a special look, that is to say the style of the controller — A chain smoker will always operate through chain smokers, an addict through addicts — Now a single controller can operate through thousands of human agents, but he must have a line of coordinate points — Some move on junk lines through addicts of the earth, others move on lines of certain sexual practices and so forth — It is only when we can block the controller out of all coordinate points available to him and flush him out from host cover that we can make a definitive arrest — Otherwise the criminal escapes to other coordinates ... Virus defined as the three-dimensional coordinate point of a controller — Transparent sheets with virus perforations like punch cards passed through the host on the soft machine feeling

---

* A remarkable example of synchronicity occurred just as this book was about to go to press. I was invited to a gathering of friends in the south of France. Among the guests was Lt. Col. Roger Vanni of the French Army. During our conversation, it developed that he had been stationed for many years in Cameroon. I asked him what he knew about the tragedy of Lake Nios, and was staggered when he replied that he had been among the first to arrive on the scene afterwards, and had been in charge of burying the cadavers. It was he who wrote the report, before the team of international scientists took over. In addition to his military career, he has also served with the Paris Fire Department, so he has extensive professional experience in identifying causes of death of cadavers found under a wide variety of circumstances. The cadavers he found and buried near Lake Nios displayed symptoms characteristic of asphyxiation by carbon dioxide. Other symptoms indicated the presence of SO_4. He not only discussed the matter at length with me, but later provided me with a whole stack of reports that describe down to the most minute details everything known or reported by witnesses about the tragedy. The evidence that the cause was in fact an eruption of volcanic gas is precisely detailed, massive and irrefutable.

for a point of intersection — The virus attack is primarily directed against affective animal life — Virus of rage hate fear ugliness swirling round you waiting for a point of intersection and once in immediately perpetrates in your name some ugly noxious or disgusting act sharply photographed and recorded becomes now part of the virus sheets constantly presented and represented before your mind screen to produce more virus word and image around and around it's all around you the invisible hail of bring down word and image — What does virus do wherever it can dissolve a hole and find traction? — It starts eating — And what does it do with what it eats? — It makes exact copies of itself that start eating to make more copies that start eating and so forth to the virus power the fear hate virus slowly replaces the host with virus copies — Program empty body ... The classic case presented to first year students is the Oxygen Impasse: Life Form A arrives on alien planet from crippled space craft — Life Form A breathes 'oxygen' — There is no 'oxygen' in the atmosphere of alien planet but by invading and occupying Life Form B native to alien planet they can convert the 'oxygen' they need from the blood stream of Life Form B — The occupying Life Form A directs all the behavior and energies of Host Life Form B into channels calculated to elicit the highest yield of 'oxygen' — Health and interest of the host is disregarded — Development of the host to space stage is arrested since such development would deprive the invaders by necessity of their 'oxygen' supply — For many years Life Form A remains invisible to Life Form B by a simple operation scanning out areas of perception where another life form can be seen — However an emergency a shocking emergency quite unlooked-for has arisen — Life Form B sees Life Form A — (Watching you have they thought debarred) and brings action in The Biologic Courts alleging unspeakable indignities, mental and physical cruelty, deterioration of mind body and soul over thousands of years, demanding summary removal of the alien parasite — To which Life Form A replies at the First Hearing: 'It was a question of food supply — of absolute need — Everything followed from that:' Iron claws of pain and pleasure squeezing a planet to keep the host in body prison working our 'oxygen' plants — Knowing that if he ever saw even for an instant who we are and what we are doing — (Switched our way is doomed in a few seconds) — And now he sees us planning to use the host as a diving suit back to our medium where of course Life Form B would be destroyed by alien conditions — Alternative proposed by the aroused partisans fumbling closer and closer to the switch that could lock us out of Life Form B and cut our 'oxygen' lines — So what else could we do under the circumstances? The life form we invaded was totally alien and detestable to us — We do not have what they call 'emotions' — soft spots in the host marked for invasion and manipulation — The Oxygen Impasse is a basic statement in the algebra of absolute need — 'Oxygen' interchangeable factor representing primary biologic need of a given life form.

The research accomplished by Ted Holiday during the final years of his life contains some extremely valuable insights, which are eloquently expressed in *The Goblin Universe* (Llewellyn, 1986). Colin Wilson's brilliant introduction sets the stage for an unforgettable journey through a multi-dimensional hall of mirrors.

Ted Holiday was no ordinary researcher. He was involved in a quest on the heroic scale, and his life was at stake. His investigations led him into areas of forbidden knowledge, guarded by entities at whose nature he could only guess. Holiday's book basically records the cycle of events that culminated in his own death.

The first evening he spent on the shore of Loch Ness, he had a feeling of foreboding "hard to define and impossible to explain," that "Loch Ness was better left alone." Yet he would not, could not, leave it alone. He was drawn back to it again and again, as if by a powerful magnetism, haunted to the point of obsession by the mystery of its depths.

Strange signals from the remote and recent past clustered around his activities, weaving a web of synchronicities in which the Elizabethan Magus, Dr. John Dee, Aleister Crowley, and the Fairy Folk made their presence felt. UFO activity erupted around him, as he penetrated more deeply into the labyrinth. Although I am not always in agreement with the theories he proposes to explain UFO phenomena, the case histories he presents are fascinating and provide a welcome supplement to my own work.

If neither UFOs nor dragon-like lake monsters are psychic projections, but are in fact as physically real as meteors (which eminent scientists of the not-too-distant past indignantly denied existed), some unacknowledged hidden variables are indeed at work, which will disrupt the neat and tidy academically approved version of reality each time they surface.

Ted Holiday accumulated strong evidence that creatures of the "phantom menagerie" — such as dragon-like lake monsters, Bigfoot, and certain anomalous large cats and dogs — do not follow the rules obeyed by normal terrestrial animals. They appear in areas where the available food supply is not sufficient to sustain animals of that size. They leave behind no excrement or skeletal remains. They are able to materialize and dematerialize, just as UFOs do. They are capable of provoking amnesia, hypnotic somnolence, or sudden blind panic, which may be so intense as to result in suicide or sudden death.

We tend to automatically assume that the triggering of such a state of panic would be an act of diabolical malevolence, but we should at least consider the possibility that from the point of view of the anomalous creature, it may simply be self-defense. It is not so long ago that human warriors, such as the Japanese Samurai and the American Indians, used war cries before going into battle that were intended to magically strike their adversaries with panic or paralysis. The anomalous animals associated with UFOs may use some sort of ultra-sound to exert a similar effect.

Some American Indian shamans believe that the same entity which manifests as Bigfoot can also manifest as an aquatic monster or a panther. In Scandinavian mythology, Loki was a shape-shifting trickster, a malevolent renegade among the gods. Case histories of UFO abductees indicate the existence of a renegade category among extra-terrestrials. Certain types of E.T.s may use such anomalous animals to explore or act as sentinels in terrestrial or aquatic environments. Certain types of renegade humans may invoke their materialization in order to communicate with them and obtain power from them, as is indicated by the grimoires of black magic.

Perhaps it was this deeply entrenched, ancient, and tremendously potent negative force that Ted Holiday confronted when he collaborated with a Christian priest in an attempt to exorcise Loch Ness. The experienced exorcist was not harmed, but the semi-skeptical Holiday was vulnerable to the backlash, as he lacked the single-pointed concentration necessary for self-protection under such circumstances, no matter what the religious framework.

The day after the exorcism, Holiday was discussing with friends whether he should investigate the scene of a UFO landing near the Loch. He was advised not to go and accepted that advice. At the moment he decided not to go, there was a sound like a tornado, followed by several loud thuds, and "a pyramid-shaped column of blackish smoke about eight feet high revolving in a frenzy. Part of it was involved in a rosebush, which looked as it were being ripped out of the ground." A beam of white light focused on Holiday's forehead, and the phenomena ceased as suddenly as it had started.

The next morning, he woke early and went for a walk before breakfast, during which he met a man dressed entirely in black, including gloves, helmet, and mask, who disappeared inexplicably.

One year later, Ted Holiday had his first heart attack on the precise spot where he had encountered this man in black. Upon recovering from it, he completed the manuscript of *The Goblin Universe*. Five years after that first heart attack, he had his second heart attack, which killed him.

Tim Dinsdale, a down-to-earth 62-year-old engineer, has picked up the trail Ted Holiday left. In an interview with Alison Leigh-Jones of *Titbits* (London, England, March 1987), Mr. Dinsdale said, "There's much more to the place than the monster. It's a very peculiar region indeed." Although he was unwilling to discuss the many peculiarities of the area in full, he did refer to the place as "magical" and was willing to share some of his information. Near the Loch is a rock formation known as the Rock of Curses, where witches' covens have met nocturnally since prehistoric times. The late Aleister Crowley believed that energy emanating from a nearby mountain, named Mealfuorvonie, was helpful to his progress in black magic, and that the whole area of the Loch was propitious for his activities. Mr. Dinsdale mentioned unexplained nocturnal lights and human disappearances. If anything, the exorcism of the Loch mentioned earlier appears to have made matters worse. Similar paranormal phenomena occur at the nearby Loch Morar, which is the deepest lake in Britain. Mr. Dinsdale discreetly continues his investigations. He would not be surprised if the Loch Ness monster turned out to be somehow linked with UFOs.

More interesting material comes from an article entitled "Aliens and You," by Rev. Lynn Johnson and published in *The Mind Science Journal*, Box 1302, Mill Valley, CA 94941.

As everyone knows, in recent years there has been an unprecedented epidemic of children mysteriously disappearing. The standard explanation is human kidnapers or sexual deviates, and this is certainly valid for many of the cases. However, some law enforcement officials and criminal psychologists have pointed out that the number of such cases is too great to be attributed entirely to kidnappers and sexual deviates. Edmond Cunningham, Ph.D., is one of our most esteemed criminal psychologists, and he recently made this statement: 'The numbers are far too great for that many kidnappers to be that cunning. Human behavior is such that the conscience either eventually overtakes the criminal and he starts making major mistakes in his actions, thereby revealing his identity, or he simply kills the kidnap victim and a body usually shows up. The vast majority of the children whose pictures are currently being displayed on milk cartons, grocery bags, posters and TV have vanished without any ransom being demanded or any corpse being found.'

I don't know of any evidence directly linking UFOs to the current epidemic of missing children, and one must be careful not to jump to conclusions in such matters. However, neither should we ignore the possibility that there may be some sort of UFO involvement. All we can do at this point is to keep an open mind and our attention alert, carefully examining each case history for clues as it comes in.

Two newspaper reports that have arrived from Australia provide support for this frightening hypothesis. The first is from the *Sunday Mail* of Adelaide, S.A., Australia, on March 29, 1987:

> Perth: Weird lights and strange phenomena have surrounded the area where two young boys have gone missing near the Gibson Desert. Two men have reported lights, which looked like a big bus or a convoy of trucks in an area where there are no roads, and which seemed to follow them near where teenagers Simon Amos, 17, and James Annetta, 16, went missing.

The article goes on to describe unusual lights, loud noises and circular burn marks in shrubbery reported by four local "level-headed businessmen," who were reluctant to discuss their findings. The large semi-trailer truck in which two of them were driving was followed by a UFO for approximately 50 miles. They had a camera with them, and got a clear picture of the saucer-shaped object. All the reports concerned the area in which the two youths had disappeared.

The second newspaper article appeared in the *Sunday Territorian* of Darwin, N.T., Australia, on April 12, 1987:

> A 23-year-old Casuarina man has brushed aside fears of being labelled a 'nut case' to give his account of the night he was followed by an unidentified flying object near Kununnurra.
>
> Damien Monck came forward with his account after newspaper reports last month that three men travelling from Lake Gregory station to Kununnurra saw mysterious lights in the area where two teenagers disappeared in December.
>
> Mr. Monck said he saw a strange light about 90 km. from the area one month before this sighting.
>
> "He said he was with two passengers driving along the main Darwin to Broome highway and was 70 km. from Kununnurra on a clear November night when a bright light followed his car. He said it travelled with the car for about 40 km. and appeared to be coming from a round object travelling at the same speed as his car but at

least 4 km. away. It was first spotted by seven-year-old passenger James Newton, who pointed it out to his mother Karen. Mr. Monck ignored Ms. Newton's pleas to turn back and look for the light after it disappeared over a hill 30 km. outside Kununnurra.

It seems appropriate at this point to quote a passage from *UFO Contact From Reticulum* by Wendelle C. Stevens and William J. Herrmann, which was privately published by Lt. -Col. Stevens in 1981. Mr. Herrmann has just been abducted for the second time and has established friendly relations with the short humanoid captain of the spacecraft, who is showing him around the ship:

> I looked at the instruments and the checker-board lit up and grew bright...the occupants in the room moved back and forth in an organized pattern... Again the leader spoke.
> 'Our velocity is now decreased from 2,000 to 60. You will notice the people below have pulled over and stopped their cars to observe. Our visor scans will bring the facial expressions with five foot scanning.'
> The screen showed a Pinto station-wagon in front and a Buick Electra directly behind it. Both cars were pulled off the road. A lady was standing at the driver's side of the Pinto, and a man was standing on the driver's side of the Buick. The screen then moved up to a close-up picture. I felt less than five feet away! The looks on their faces will be with me for a long time. The leader spoke,
> 'Do you recall such wonder expressed? We will move forward. Observe the woman get into her car. The man will do likewise.'
> Even though inside the object, I couldn't detect motion. Sure enough, the woman ran around the passenger side and jumped in, locking her door. The man calmly opened his door and got in, locking the door. At the same time the leader spoke,
> 'A two-foot scanning will show her holding the lock down...The man will just sit and watch. A useless gesture on their part if we wished to direct observe, but this is not our purpose...we will now continue on our way.'

The following is from *Intruders* by Budd Hopkins, published by Random House in 1987:

> Lucille F. wrote that this alien society seemed to be 'millions of years old, of outstanding technology and intellect but not much indi-

viduality or warmth.' She had the sense that 'the society was dying, that children were being born and living to a certain age, perhaps preadolescence and then dying.' There was 'a desperate need to survive, to continue their race. It is a culture without touching, feeling, nurturing... basically intellectual. Something has gone wrong genetically. Whatever their bodies are now, they have evolved from something else. My impression is that they wanted to somehow share their history and achievement and their present difficulties in survival...I saw a child about four feet tall, gray, totally their race, waving its arms... it was in pain and dying. I was told that this is what is happening now.'.... In this unexpected scenario the UFO occupants — despite their obvious technological superiority — are desperate for both human genetic material and the ability to feel human emotions — particularly maternal emotions. Unlikely though it may seem, it is possible that the very survival of these extra-terrestrials depends upon their success in absorbing chemical and psychological properties received from human abductees.

Don Ecker is the MUFON state section director for Idaho. The following quotation is taken from his article entitled "Report on Human Mutilations," which was published in the July/August 1989 issue of *UFO* magazine (Box 355, 1800 S. Robertson Blvd., Los Angeles, CA 90035):

According to a recent report just received from Westchester County, NY, researchers have discovered that in a small area of the county, which has been the site of numerous UFO overflights and reported human abductions, over 3,000 missing children reports have surfaced. After extensive investigation by local police departments, these children have not yet been found at centers for young runaways or in red light districts. Researchers and law enforcement officials are baffled.

Le Monde Diplomatique (5 rue Antoine-Bourdelle, 75501 Paris) is a French monthly of the highest quality, featuring sophisticated analysis of political events world-wide, and is remarkably free from bias. In its issue of August 1992, it carried an article by Maite Pinero on abductions of children, not by aliens, but by humans motivated by financial greed, who then sell the kidneys and other body parts of these children that they have either kidnapped or "adopted." There is an enormous traffic in such organs, particularly in impoverished regions of South America, much of it flowing in the direction of the United States. The article covers a whole series of scandals concerning this traffic that have erupted throughout South America since 1985, and documents a number of occasions when direct or indirect pressure from the U.S. government was used to silence local protests, routinely attributing the incidents to Soviet or Cuban propaganda. One of the recent cases, in February 1992, involved an American lawyer, Patrick Gagel, who was responsible for having exported three thousand children in thirty months from Peru for "adoption," which then disappeared without a trace. Yet when the Peruvian police arrested Gagel, pressure from on high obliged them to release him. Who applied that pressure from on high? The U.S. Embassy? Gagel's operation was but one of many, merely the tip of the iceberg, according to Defense of Children International. Throughout South America, each time local police have made an arrest, the Gagel scenario has been repeated over and over again. Pressure from on high has been exerted, on a number of occasions openly by the U.S. government, and those arrested have been released. The number of children involved is far greater than the number of sick people wealthy enough to pay black market prices for both the transplanted organ and a clandestine transplant operation. Is this type of abominable activity related to the secret treaty with the Grays?

5

Clues Contained in Traditional Mythologies

*B*esides modern indications that the language of at least one type of UFO occupant resembles Sanskrit, we have unequivocal statements from ancient India that Sanskrit was in fact the language of the "Devas," which translates into English as "the gods."

The Devas were indeed, and still are, the gods of the Hindu pantheon. Our word "deity" is derived from the Sanskrit word "Deva." The four Vedas are the literary foundation-stones on which the entire civilization of India is based, equivalent in importance to the Bible in the development of European civilization. According to Hindu tradition, the four Vedas were not composed by inspired humans; they were written in Sanskrit directly by the Devas, who gave them to the Hindus, in order to maintain a mutually beneficial relationship between terrestrial humanity in India and the celestial Devas.

One of the most striking characteristics of the social structure prescribed by the Devas was the system of dividing the population into castes. It need hardly be pointed out that this is the antithesis of the modern democratic system, and one of the main reasons why the religion based on the Vedas finds such minimal acceptance outside of India. Indeed, even within India, some of the most highly revered holy men (such as Gautama the Buddha and Ramakrishna) have found it necessary to speak out against the caste system.

The Devas possessed aerial vehicles, which rendered them invincible in battle. Like the Greek gods who gathered on the summit of Mount Olympus, they were in many respects quite human. Just as the Greek Olympians cherished the beverage they called "ambrosia" and indulged in love affairs with mortal humans, so the Himalayan Devas cherished the beverage they called "soma" and at times became involved in amorous adventures with mortal humans.

It is extremely difficult, but not impossible, for a human to become more powerful than the Devas. As a yogi approached supreme enlightenment, he would be tempted by the Devas, who would send celestial enchantresses and magical inebriants toward him in an attempt to thwart the breakthrough that would render him superior to the Devas. It is only possible to attain supreme enlightenment during a human incarnation in which one is fully exposed to both pain and pleasure. The Devas are so thoroughly involved in pleasurable activities that supreme enlightenment eludes them. The inhabitants of the various hell worlds are so wrapped up in the pain they are experiencing that supreme enlightenment eludes them also. The Devas have much longer life-spans then humans do, but nevertheless must die eventually, and there is no guarantee of becoming a Deva again in one's next incarnation. As the yogi who has obtained supreme enlightenment no longer needs to reincarnate, he has conquered death forever.

According to Hindu tradition, between the Devas and terrestrial humanity exist another type of beings, called the "Asuras." The literal meaning of "Asura" is "not-god," so the Asuras are definitely not gods. However, they travel in celestial chariots and have other abilities that terrestrial humans do not have.

During the early period of Hindu civilization, the Asuras were considered to be basically benevolent, just as the Devas were. However, at a certain point they began to be described as the enemies of the Devas, as proud malevolent demons motivated by insatiable titanic lust for power. The hostility between the Greek Olympians and the Titans is comparable to the hostility between the Hindu Devas and Asuras and may be a mythological description of the same series of events, recorded through a different tradition.

What this historic rupture appears to indicate is the outbreak of warfare between different types of celestial beings, which in modern terminology we would describe as races from outer space, or UFO occupants.

In ancient Persia, this celestial conflict was also reflected in the scriptures of the Mazdean religion founded by Zoroaster, whose sacred beverage "haoma" bears an obvious resemblance to the Hindu "soma." However, according to the Zoroastrian version of the legend, it is the Devas who are the demons and the Asuras who are angelic. Yet in India, according to both the Hindu and Buddhist scriptures, it is the Devas who are angelic and the Asuras who are demonic.

If you think this difference of opinion is unimportant for us today consider that if the Devas and Asuras do in fact correspond to rival types of extra-terrestrial humanoids, still at war with each other and still active in our environment, resolving this enigma becomes a matter of extreme urgency. By comparing the records from antiquity with our modern abduction and close encounter reports, we can learn to deal effectively with phenomena that would otherwise be incomprehensible and terrifying.

One such record from antiquity, which I interpret as a highly significant and detailed description of an intervention by a specific type of extra-terrestrial in human affairs, is contained in the Homeric "Hymn to Demeter." In preparing this summary and brief direct quotation, I have made use of the translation by Danny Staples in *The Road to Eleusis: Unveiling the Secret of the Mysteries* by R. Gordon Wasson, Carl A.P. Ruck, and Albert Hofmann, published by Harcourt Brace Jovanovich in 1978:

Demeter's daughter, Persephone, had been abducted by Hades, brother of Zeus and Lord of the Underworld. Persephone was carried off into the Underworld, where her marriage to Hades was consummated. Meanwhile Demeter, who had found out what had happened but who was unable to rescue her daughter (since it had been the will of Zeus to bestow Persephone on his brother Hades), was heart-broken and furious. She left the assembly of the gods and disguised herself as a mortal, wandering incognito among terrestrial humans. She came to the town of Eleusis, and sat weeping by the Virgin's Well, in appearance like an old woman long past the age of child-bearing. The daughters of the Lord of that city noticed her as they came to draw water from the well and took pity on her, mentioning that their mother had recently given birth to a son and needed a suitable nurse to help take care of him. So the goddess in disguise became a servant in the palace of the Lord of Eleusis, the nursemaid of his son the prince, who flourished in her care. Demeter only pretended to feed him the food of mortals, and secretly fed him on ambrosia, the food of the gods. At night, when everyone was asleep, Demeter would perform a magical rite in which she placed the child in the fire on the hearth without harming him at all, in order to gradually remove what was mortal in his substance and replace it with an immortal substance, such as the gods have. However, one night the child's mother happened to enter the room while Demeter was performing this magical operation and screamed in horror, accusing the servant of murdering the child. Demeter took the child out of the fire and dropped him unharmed on the floor, then furiously reproached the mother for having interrupted the boy's transformation from mortality to immortality, which now could no longer be completed. After having ordered the mother to build a temple to Demeter in which the rites of the Eleusinian Mysteries were to be performed, the withered old hag who had been living in the palace as a servant threw off her disguise:

"As she said that, the goddess was transformed, as if a wind had blown off her old age and left but her glorious beauty: her robes exhaled sweet perfumes, her skin radiated the aura of the immortals, and her golden hair covered her shoulders. The palace was filled with a brilliance such as the brilliance lightning gives. Then she turned and walked out of the hall."

As Demeter continued to boycott the assembly of the gods, and was herself the goddess of agriculture, the fields lay barren and there were no harvests. Famine decimated the human population, and even the immortal gods, who had become accustomed to being propitiated with abundant offerings that were no longer forthcoming, became uneasy. The wily Zeus finally resolved the problem by making a shrewd bargain: Persephone could spend half of each year with her mother on the surface of the Earth or in the heavens, but must spend the other half with her husband, Lord Hades, in the underworld. This took the edge off of Demeter's wrath, and with her beloved daughter once again by her side, she returned to the assembly of the gods.

The transformation scene in which the old crone who is a servant throws off her disguise gives us a glimpse of the type of extra-terrestrial described further on in this book as the tall Blonds. As Greek and other mythologies demonstrate, the individuals who belong to this group are not altruistic, unsexed, or emotionless. Although in antiquity they were considered deities, they had all of our human weaknesses as well as our strong points, so much so that the relationship between gods and humans had the characteristics of a family relationship. The poet Pindar wrote: "Men and gods are of the same family; we owe the breath of life to the same mother." Misunderstandings sometimes occurred, but basically gods and humans understood each other's ways and respected the differences between them, so that relationships were more frequently harmonious than not.

However, it should be remembered that relationships between humanity and the gods were at their most harmonious before Zeus seized power in the heavens from his father, Cronos, and became the supreme Olympian deity. At that time men and gods had lived together peacefully under the rulership of the Titans in the Golden Age. Vanquished by the thunderbolts of the rebellious Zeus, the Titans were banished by him to Tartarus, which is located deep within the Earth. There were only twelve of them in all, but they were immortal and were the primordial deities until they were dethroned by one of their own children. Prometheus, who stole the fire of the gods to bestow it on humanity, and was therefore chained by Zeus to Mount Caucasus, where an eagle fed on his liver every night, yet every day it was renewed because he was an immortal. Doomed by Zeus to endless torment for his deed, Prometheus was like Zeus a son of the Titans. It was only after Zeus dethroned Cronos that humanity came under the rule of gods that commanded adoration and sacrificial offerings.

Such myths give highly condensed outlines of periods of prehistoric development, in which vast cycles of time are summed up in a few words.

The Orphic/Pythagorean tradition, which was so important to the historic development of our civilization, and which continues right down to the present, was hostile to the Giants, but was in alliance with the Titans, and did not recognize the divinity of the Olympians.

If aeons ago immortal beings were chained deep within the Earth, they may be there yet. By this time, they may have out-lived their chains. Do we have unexpected allies, whose existence we have not been aware of?

Arise, Osiris! Be thy mouth given unto thee! Triumphant, shout: my heart, my mother! My heart, my coming forth from darkness! The word of a hundred letters resounds in the tomb. The mummy wakes like a bear from its winter sleep.

As Yeats put it in "All Souls Night":

> I have mummy truths to tell,
> whereat the living mock,
> though not for sober ear,
> for maybe all that hear
> should laugh and weep an hour upon the clock.

The Druse religion was founded by Caliph Hakim of Egypt, who began his reign in 996 A.D. He proclaimed himself to be an incarnation of the divine intelligence in the main mosque of Cairo in 1016 A.D., and disappeared mysteriously (abducted?) in 1021 A.D. The Druse believe that he will return in triumph, in similar fashion to the Christian belief in the Second Coming of Christ. Little is known about the doctrine that the Druse belief system is based on, because they do not accept converts to their religion. The only way to become a Druse is to be born into a Druse family, whose ancestors accepted Caliph Hakim as a divine incarnation during the quarter-century of his reign.

Some Druse families have emigrated to the United States, and to varying degrees their children have become Americanized in the process. What I now recount is no more than a statement made by one of these youngsters to a friend of his family, who also happens to be a friend of mine, and who relayed it to me. The twelve-year-old boy said that his father had told him that at a certain point in time, the Druse would all come down from the Syrian and Lebanese mountain areas that are their traditional homelands, as well as coming from other areas of the world, and would gather at the Great Pyramid in Egypt, where extra-terrestrials would come and take them away to a kingdom not of this world, on another planet. The boy said his father had told him that this long-awaited event would take place within his lifetime.

Besides the "coincidence" or synchronicity through which I happened to know a friend of a friend of a Druse family, another synchronicity in my life concerns the Druse. About 30 years ago, I was living in France and felt a strong affinity for certain parts of the work of Gerard de Nerval, who had among other things written a book entitled *Voyages en Orient*, published in Paris in 1854. One particular portion of this book aroused intense interest in me: "L'Histoire du Calife Hakim," a rambling Lebanese folk tale that Nerval had heard during his travels, probably while sitting around a waterpipe in a Lebanese tea-house. I had never heard of the Druse religion, and had no idea of who Caliph Hakim was, but I was fascinated by the story. I felt impelled to do a very free-form translation, taking considerable liberties with the text, smoking Lebanese hashish non-stop as I condensed the long folk tale down to three paragraphs, which were as follows:

The Beggar King

Once upon a time, there was a prince in the land of Egypt. It came to pass that the king, his father, lay dying, and called him in to tell him the secrets of ruling the kingdom. One of the secrets was that he should not believe what his ministers told him, but should slip out of the palace by a secret door every night disguised as a beggar, and wander through the streets of the city to see for himself how things were. After the death of the king, the new king followed the instructions of his father. Every night he wandered through the city in disguise, returning to his palace at dawn through the secret door.

During the reign of his father, both wine and hashish had been forbidden in the land of Egypt. One night the king disguised as a beggar came to a place where people had gathered to smoke hashish. They offered him a pipe. He smoked it, and another, and another. He stayed there all night, returning to the palace at dawn through the secret door. The next night, instead of wandering around the city as usual, he went straight back to the same place, and again stayed all night. He did the same thing every night. Several months went by. One night he was sitting there, smoking with his friends, when the place was raided by the royal guards. The king disguised as a beggar tried to explain to the officer of the guards that he was the king, but the officer gave him a kick in the pants and said: "You smoke too much! Get into the wagon with the rest of them."

As the beggar kept insisting that he was the king, instead of being put in jail he was put in the insane asylum. Meanwhile one of his ministers, who knew the king went out in disguise and what had happened to him, told everyone that the king had gone off alone into the desert to meditate, leaving the power in his hands. So there was the king, unarmed and helpless, starving in the insane asylum while a usurper ruled from his throne. But because he really was the king, he organized the lunatics into an army. This army first of all broke out of the insane asylum. Then the army of lunatics, led by the hashish-smoking king, still dressed as a beggar, faced and defeated the royal army in the field of battle. So the king returned to his palace by the front door, not the secret door.

Gerard de Nerval hung himself in a Paris doorway during a midwinter night in 1855. The friend who came to claim his body, Theophile Gautier (a fellow writer and member of the Club des Haschichins), found a manuscript entitled "Aurelia" in Nerval's pocket, which contains the following passage:

> I said to myself: 'If electricity, which is the magnetism of physical bodies, can be directed according to laws, then there is all the more reason to believe that hostile and tyrannical spirits can enslave minds and make use of their divided forces to dominate. It is thus that the old gods were conquered and enslaved by the new gods.' As I consulted my memories of the distant past, I said again to myself: 'It is thus that the necromancers dominated entire nations, whose generations succeeded each other in captivity under their endless dynasties. O horror! Death itself could not free them! For

we live in our sons as we have lived in our fathers, and the merciless science of our enemies knows how to recognize us everywhere. The hour of our birth, the place on the Earth where we first appear, the first gesture, the name, the room — and all those ceremonies, all those rites that are imposed on us.'

Salvador Freixedo sent me a copy of his most recent book, *La Granja Humana*, Plaza and Janes Editores, Barcelona, Spain, 1989. The title translates as "The Human Farm," and the subtitle as, "Are we the guinea pigs of the gods?" Although my Spanish is far from fluent, I was particularly struck by the contents of one chapter in this book of high importance, which I have summarized as follows:

The Case of Doctor Torralba

Let us begin our presentation of cases with one about which there can be no doubt, since it is part of the history of Spain's Century of Gold (between the fifteenth and sixteenth centuries). No less an authority than Cervantes mentions Doctor Torralba and the extraordinary events in which he was involved. However, the discourse on this doctor's adventures, which Cervantes expressed through the character of Don Quixote, contains considerable exaggeration and poetic license, in comparison to the lesser-known but more soberly factual account of the historian, Marcelino Menendez y Pelayo, in his *Historia de los heterodoxos espanoles*.

Zequiel appeared to Doctor Torralba much as Mephistopheles did to Faust: in the form of a vigorous youth with a pale complexion and very blond hair, dressed in red and black, offering to be at the doctor's service for the duration of his life. After this initial overture, visits became frequent, with conversations carried on in Latin or Italian. Zequiel never said anything contrary to the Christian faith or morality, and appeared to be of good character. As a result of this association, the doctor stopped indulging in certain minor vices, such as greed in demanding excessive fees for his services.

The two most striking characteristics of Zequiel's appearance were his very pale white complexion and his very blond hair, because of which he was sometimes referred to as "El Rubio" ("The Blond"). He taught the doctor things about herbs and animals which enabled the doctor to perform exceptional works of healing. When the doctor was in need of money, Zequiel brought it to him. Behind-the-scenes political secrets of the State were revealed to the doctor, who then used this knowledge to gain access to the highest levels of the aristocracy. Future events began to be foretold by the doctor, who in private audience with Cardinal Cisneros delivered predictions about the deaths of political leaders, both in Spain and abroad.

Cisneros wanted to become directly acquainted with the mysterious person responsible for these remarkably accurate predictions, but Dr. Torralba was not able to arrange a meeting between the Cardinal and the youth he knew only as Zequiel, or by the nickname El Rubio. For some unexpressed reason, Zequiel was not willing to cooperate in the arrangement of any meeting with Cardinal Cisneros.

Besides becoming famous for his medical cures, Dr. Torralba began to be widely acclaimed for his discourses on theology. Although Torralba had received no scholastic training in this subject, he was suddenly able to debate fine points of complex doctrine with the greatest experts, who had devoted their lives to the study of this subject.

Zequiel gave the doctor instruction in all sorts of things. There was even a friend of the doctor named Camilio Ruffini, who wanted to learn how to win consistently at gambling games, and became a wealthy man by using the formula of Cabalistic letters that Zequiel gave him.

Torralba's fame spread from Madrid to Rome. Torralba traveled to Rome long enough to get to know the city well, and to establish friendly relationships with ten of the existing Cardinals. Several of these Cardinals did not hesitate to ask Torralba to ask Zequiel to do certain favors for them.

A curious detail in all of this is that Zequiel persistently took back from Torralba much of the money that the doctor received, to the point that the doctor frequently found himself short of funds and began to hide portions of the money that came in, so as not to be obliged to share it with Zequiel.

As the years went by, Torralba began to become blasé about Zequiel's strange powers. While in these moods, Torralba became less careful about keeping certain aspects of their relationship secret. Perhaps because of his powerful connections, he did not seem particularly concerned about the fact that the Inquisition had developed an intense interest in the young man named Zequiel.

For years now, Torralba had been making predictions about important political developments that consistently turned out to be accurate. At that time, it normally took about three weeks for news to travel from Madrid to Rome, or vice versa.

On May 6, 1527, Torralba described the Sack of Rome, and the complex series of far-reaching events that accompanied it, to a group of high-ranking members of the Spanish royal court. Three weeks later, messengers confirmed the complete accuracy of this description, down to the most minor details. The Sack of Rome had taken place on the exact same day that Torralba had delivered his prediction.

Several months later, upon an occasion when Torralba was asked yet again the by-now routine question of how he had been able to do this, he made the mistake that cost him his life. Instead of gravely pronouncing some pious platitude that left no one the wiser, he indiscreetly answered that he had been to Rome, and had himself witnessed the events that he described. Further questioning elicited a statement that he had, with the help of Zequiel, traveled to Rome by air, and had returned within a few hours to Madrid, on the morning of the day in question.

This indiscreet statement, comprehensible to his contemporaries only in terms of diabolical magic, was sufficient to provide the Inquisition with the grounds to arrest Torralba, to seize his belongings, and to systematically question him under torture. The Inquisitors were, however, unable to capture the elusive Zequiel. The transcript of the testimony extracted from Torralba under torture still exists, and bears many resemblances to modern contactee reports.

Approximately one year before the Inquisition arrested Torralba, the Inquisitors had arrested 29 women in the province of Navarre, accusing them of witchcraft, specifically demonstrated by "flying through the air." Numerous witnesses testified that these women had not only flown through the air with marvelous ease, but that some of them had remained aloft for as long as three days, after which they had been seen to come down out of the sky in a field that was near the field from which they had been seen to go up into the sky. This indicates that these 29 women accused of witchcraft were what we would today call abductees.

The historic record also contains numerous descriptions of Catholic nuns and monks who surprised their respective communities by flying through the air in miraculous fashion, but who were nominated for sainthood instead of being tortured and then burned at the stake.

There are indications of E.T. involvement in the belief system of the Gypsies, but they are elusive and difficult to pin down. A few of the more substantial of the tantalizingly vague hints are to be found in *L'Enigme des Gitans* by Jean-Claude Frere, Maison Mame, Paris, 1973, from which I have translated these brief quotations:

> The opinion which has prevailed is that the appearance of the Gypsies in the Occident goes back to the year 1417....In 1417 a group of Gypsies suddenly appeared near the mouth of the river Elbe, near the North Sea. No one had seen where they came from.
>
> 'We were already old when humanity was born, for it is the gods who taught us how to walk.'
>
> 'We come from a land that no longer exists, and we travel toward a land that does not yet exist.'

About 20 years ago, when I was living in England, I met a Gypsy in Glastonbury, who told me that during the olden days, when his family was constantly on the move, they knew of eleven other zodiacal circles in Britain besides the Glastonbury Zodiac. They would spend one month traveling each of the zodiacal circles, and if their timing was correct, they would periodically encounter UFOs. Such contacts were one of the main reasons for their constant traveling.

There are the ruins of prehistoric forts on hilltops in Scotland and Ireland that were vitrified in deep antiquity. The upper layers of the stones they were built of were subjected to such intense heat coming from above (the upper layers having been vitrified far more completely than the lower layers) that the stone was transformed into glass. The conventional explanation is that this was done by enemy forces to destroy the forts with immense bonfires. However, no fire built of wood can attain a temperature sufficient to vitrify stone, to transform stone into glass. The inference is obvious: the forts were indeed destroyed by enemy action, but not with bonfires. What the evidence indicates is aerial attack, perhaps from laser weapons positioned directly overhead.

Frederick Mitchell-Hedges was a British explorer who was fascinated by the legends of Atlantis and was searching for a link between the Mayan culture and Atlantis. In 1919, he was deep in the jungle of what was then British Honduras, now Belize. He discovered the ruins of a major Mayan ceremonial center, which he named "Lubantuun," a Mayan word meaning "City of Fallen Stones."

The main ruin was an enormous collapsed temple, covering an area of about eight acres. He was granted a seven-year license to carry out archaeological excavations. His adopted daughter, Anna Mitchell-Hedges, was one of the members of the team that accompanied him during these seven years. Toward the end of 1923 Anna, who was 16 at the time, noticed something glistening in the stone rubble of the main temple in direct sunlight, too far down between the stones to reach. She reported it to her father, who went to work with his assistants. It took them several weeks to clear away the rubble. What he found when he reached the glistening object was a transparent skull, made from one huge block of clear quartz crystal.

As soon as he lifted it up for everyone to see, his Mayan assistants went wild with joy. They wept over it and built an altar for it. Indians from different tribes came from many miles around to see it. As he recognized that it was part of their religion, Frederick Mitchell-Hedges gave it to his Mayan friends and renounced all claim to it. Several weeks later, the jaw that goes with the skull was found, also of clear quartz crystal, articulated so accurately that it was a perfect fit. Neither of the two pieces had been at all damaged by the collapse of the temple, except for one small chip out of one of the teeth of the Crystal Skull.

Several years later the day came when his permit to dig expired, and Frederick Mitchell-Hedges prepared to leave. He had been a good friend to the local tribe of Indians, sharing food and medicine, giving them tools, helping out in any way he could. There were many tears shed at his departure. At the last minute, just as he and his team were about to leave, the Indians made the ultimate gesture and gave him their most valued possession, the Crystal Skull.

Upon his return to London, it was examined by all the top experts, a process that has continued for over half a century. It was studied intensively for several years by Hewlett-Packard Laboratories, but it remains an unsolved mystery. It would be impossible to duplicate today, even with our present technological resources. The internal lenses, light pipes, and prisms are of a stunning sophistication. It is anatomically accurate down to the most minute details. There are no instrumental markings on it, yet it was somehow shaped with total disregard for the axis of the crystal. Analysis established that the jaw was made from the same block of clear quartz crystal as the skull. The Crystal Skull weighs 11 lb. 7 oz., is 5 inches tall and wide, and 7 inches long. Since its discovery, other skulls made from crystal have been found in Central America, but without exception the workmanship is crude in comparison to the Mitchell-Hedges Crystal Skull, of which they appear to be clumsy imitations.

All of these details are fascinating, but the Mitchell-Hedges Crystal Skull also has other qualities of even greater importance. Paranormal phenomena persistently occur in its vicinity. Anomalous images appear within it. As these phenomena tend to be subjective, subtle, and elusive, it is not possible to describe them satisfactorily in scientific terms, except to say that phenomena such as clairvoyance, clairaudience, precognition, healing, telepathy, and anomalous lights and sounds and odors have been reported. I have been fortunate enough to have the privilege of spending a substantial amount of time in its presence and have had first-hand experience of some of these paranormal properties.

Among the items that Frederick Mitchell-Hedges found in the vicinity of the Crystal Skull, and that are now gathering dust somewhere in the basement of the British Museum, was an item which he described as "a mummy of a deformed child with a skull structure hitherto unknown." I suspect this to be the mummy of an extra-terrestrial. I think that the Crystal Skull was an extra-terrestrial artifact, used as a communication device between the Mayan high priests and other worlds. I also think it quite likely that the Mayan high priests inherited it from Atlantean high priests, and that if we could figure out the correct way to use it, we could use it to communicate with extra-terrestrials today.

Forensic analysis by independent experts has established that the Crystal Skull was modeled from the skull of a woman who was short in stature and died during early maturity. What was so special about this particular young woman?

I will now for a moment shrug off the shackles of rational linear thinking and soar off into the stratosphere of uninhibited speculation. My wild guess is that this particular young woman may have been the original ancestor of all the different varieties of Homo sapiens, the one and only Great Mother of us all, remembered in the Judaeo-Christian tradition as Eve, and by other names in other traditions. I further speculate that after having given birth to children in a difficult environment, upon her death the extra-terrestrials who had created her, or brought her here from elsewhere, made a model of her skull in an imperishable substance which was itself alive, in quartz crystal, to be kept as a testimony, a talisman and a communications device with the entities known as the Elohim, by her innumerable descendants.

Returning now to earth, and placing my feet once again firmly on the ground, I feel I should mention the fact that one of the major puzzles in Central American archaeology is what became of the Mayan high civilization, as their great temple cities were suddenly abandoned for no apparent reason. Were their high priests and initiated leaders lifted off in UFOs shortly before the high civilizations of Mexico were overwhelmed by a tidal wave of barbaric and bloodthirsty Aztecs, followed soon after by a second tidal wave of bigoted and bloodthirsty Conquistadors?

R.L. Dione presented a perceptive analysis of the relationship between apparitions of the Virgin Mary and UFO phenomena in his *God Drives a Flying Saucer*, which was published by Bantam in 1973. Here is a brief summary of some of the main points that he made:

> The first of the well-known and authentic apparitions of the Virgin occurred in Guadalupe, Mexico, on Dec. 9, 1531. Since then, most of the apparitions have taken place in remote Catholic villages. Those contacted by the Virgin have consistently been children or child-like adults, who would never question how a miracle occurred. Prophecies of war and famine if humanity does not accept conversion to the Catholic Church, building shrines to the Virgin in the places where she has appeared, are delivered at each manifestation. The message is persistently the same. The pattern repeats over and over again, in different places at different times. The person contacted first sees a light of indescribable brilliance, out of which the Virgin materializes. This usually occurs on a cloudy or rainy day and is frequently accompanied by a persistent insectile buzzing sound. The famines and wars predicted do come to pass, but we should not overlook the possibility that they may be deliberately brought about by other-worldly entities for control purposes. During the two years preceding the Fatima miracle, the three children involved had a series of contacts, the first three of which were with an entity who announced himself as the Angel of Peace, after having approached them in a ball of light, while they were tending their flocks of sheep in an isolated area. The entity was human in appearance, but luminous. He taught them a prayer and then departed. The sequence of events during the second contact was similar. On the third and final time that he came, he brought a chalice from which he told two of the children to drink: Francisco and Jacinta, ages eight and six, respectively. He did not offer the chalice to Lucia, age nine. Lucia later said that as Francisco and Jacinta drank, all three of them knew that the two who drank would soon die. Both Francisco and Jacinta died about a year and a half after the main appearance of the Virgin. Dione suggests that the Spanish influenza they died of, which was the plague that was dominant during that period of history, may have spread from the gathering of the 70,000 witnesses of the miracle at Fatima, who had come from all over the

world, and could have been inoculated with the virus. Before suc-
cumbing to the influenza, Jacinta had developed another major medical problem: the malignant tumor which appeared on her chest and
kept her constantly in severe pain.

Dr. Jean Mundy has also studied the apparitions at Fatima, and has had
access to information that was not available at the time when R.L. Dione
was at work on his book. She has been so kind as to permit me to include
her study in this book:

The Miracle of Fatima Documented!
Secret Prophecy Revealed?

As a teenager, raised from the cradle into Catholicism, I fully accepted
that three children, Lucia, Jacinta, and Francisco, and approximately 70,000
adults, saw the Blessed Mother of Jesus appear at Fatima, Portugal in 1917.
In high school, I would have felt it impertinent to ask the good Nuns for
newspaper reports of those strange events or for interviews with eye
witnesses. I had cried through "Song of Bernadette" about another child in
Lourdes, France, with another vision of Our Lady. The last message to
appear on the screen was imprinted on my brain like the whirling sun. "For
those that believe, no explanation is necessary. For those that do not believe, no explanation is possible." I was a confirmed believer, feeling most
smug about not being a doubting Thomas.

However, not long after my diploma arrived certifying a Ph.D. from
Catholic University, I fell directly into the limbo of lapsed souls called
"Ex-Catholics." Ironically, my training in science made me smug about
taking nothing for granted and always asking for proof. So it came to be
that my eye caught a tiny listing in an old Video Exchange catalogue.
There it was after all these years, the test of my faith, "The Miracle of
Fatima: Documentation."

Three of the eye witnesses, interviewed and filmed years after the
event, were Carolina and Maria Dos Santos, sisters of Lucia, and a brother
of Jacinta. They spoke with fervor as if the experience was fresh in their
minds. The translator for Carolina said:

"A miracle! A miracle for everyone to see. It seemed the sun was saying good-bye to the sky and coming down like a saucer singing and working, and coming down, and stopped only when it almost reached the
ground. We thought we would die. We saw a shadow and it was like lightning. Everyone kneeled down and was screaming, '*Miracle! Miracle!*'"

Jacinta's brother's statements were translated:

"The sun, like a disk in the sky, trembled, and made brusque movements unprecedented and outside of all cosmic law. The sun has danced!"

The local newspaper, *O Seculo,* reported: "The sun zigzagged for twelve minutes, and then plunged down, almost to the ground, and then it suddenly reversed itself. It was seen by witnesses as far away as 40 kilometers. Certainly beyond all cosmic laws, were the sudden trembling movements of the sun, and dancing as it were, before the astonished multitude who gazed in awe, with spectators crying 'Miracle! Miracle!'"

"Other witnesses saw something 'Unworldly,' '*A second sun.*'" Many witnesses saw the second sun spin in much the same way that a firecracker wheel spins. It gave off fiery fingers of light that extended across the sky."

Estimates of the crowd varied in the reports from 50,000 to 70,000. The crowd was certainly astonished by the falling disk of light, but I was more astonished to find that in all the reports only one child, Lucia, reported seeing a bright light in the form of a young woman in white, who said she would reveal her identity at a later time. Lucia concluded it was the Blessed Virgin. The other two children did not see the figure, nor did anyone in the crowd.

It is most curious that in the crowd of devoted Catholics, who had come to this place repeatedly over two months expecting to see the Virgin, eager for a religious manifestation of Divinity, told that they would see the Virgin, praying for a glimpse of her, yet no one, except Lucia, saw her. This is no case of mass hysteria, or hypnotic suggestion, or hallucinations.

Here is Lucia's report, as she wrote herself, in her memoirs in 1935 from the Convent of the Sisters of St. Dorothy in Tuy, Spain, where she took vows, which she maintained to her death.

"Opening her hands, she made them reflect on the sun, and as she ascended, the reflection of her own light continued to be projected on the sun itself....I wanted to call the attention of the crowd to the sun. I was moved to do so under the guidance of an interior impulse." (Mental telepathy?)

"After our Lady had disappeared into the immense distance of the firmament, we beheld St. Joseph with the Child Jesus and Our Lady robed in white with a blue mantle, beside the sun. St. Joseph and the Christ Jesus appeared to bless the world, for they traced the sign of the Cross with their hands. Then I saw our Lord and our Lady, then it was our Lady of Dolors. Then our Lord blessed the world. This apparition also vanished and I saw our Lady once more resemble Our Lady of Carmel."

Lucia, as a religious, took the name, "Sister Maria das Dolores" — Mary of Sorrows. While in the convent of the Discalced Carmelites, among the most strict of Catholic orders, Sister Mary of Sorrows reported many more visions. In December 1925 she saw the Christ Child in the arms of the Holy Mother. Again, the Holy Mother spoke to her, pointed to the thorns around her heart and expressed gratitude that Sister Mary was trying to console the Mother of God.

Now, as a professional psychologist, I know that the mind can play tricks on us, and I have been trained to respect physical reactions more than verbal reports. So I look for signs of behavior changes, rather than memory recall, and whenever I hear the news of fiery disks making 180 degree angle turns in the sky, I begin to look for signs of post-trauma stress syndrome.

Using Bullard's model of the typical (alas!) abduction, I compared the on-the-scene reports of the miracle at Fatima with the contemporary alien abduction scenario. Bullard has evidence gleaned from over 300 cases to demonstrate that there is a standard order in the procedures for all cases, all cases go through the procedure in rigid order. In my work during the past year, I have confirmed Bullard's model in my own analysis of on-going psychotherapy cases. Budd Hopkins, also, has commented on "the clip-board mentality of aliens, doing their job, checking off each step."

The abduction stages are: 1. Capture (alien intrusion). 2. Zone of Strangeness. 3. Time Lapse. 4. Procurement. 5. Examination. 6. Conference. 7. Tour. 8. Other-worldly Journey. 9. Religious Experience. 10. Return. 11. Aftermath.

In the following comparisons, all quotations about the Miracle at Fatima are taken from *Secret Prophecy of Fatima Revealed!!* by Arthur Crockett (Global Communications, 1982).

1. Capture. Capture is typically in one's bedroom or in open country. "They were hard at work keeping the sheep bunched up and running after strays."
    Alien Intrusion. Either a UFO is spotted, or a ball, or beam of light is suddenly thrust into the presence of the witness. "Suddenly, there were two flashes of lightning...on a cloudless day...was frightening...it brought the children's attention up sharply...They saw a globe of light...Eventually, Lucia could make out the figure of a woman...they were frozen with fright."
    Temporary paralysis is routinely reported in abduction cases, early in the procedure.
2. Zone of strangeness. The witness enters a twilight zone of strange events. The natural laws seem to lapse, the witness feels isolated from people who might observe or help. The witness enters an environment he or she can neither understand or control..."The apparition did not identify herself."
    But the Lady did ask the three children to return to the same spot on

the 13th of every month until October. She said she would reveal her identity. She urged the children to keep her presence a secret. (This secret motif is also something I find routinely in my work. For example, couples who were abducted together do not discuss what happened, even with each other.)

3. Time Lapse. The witness's memory of the abduction blanks out, and the witness suffers paralysis/lethargy/or uncharacteristic behavior. Although we have no evidence for or against a missing time period, in which the subject cannot recall anything without hypnosis, we do read in Crockett that "Lucia did not reveal many details of the Lady's request for ten years."

Jacinta, characteristically an obedient child, disobeyed her parents' injunction not to return to the grotto. She returned often, neglecting her flock of sheep, even in stormy weather, in spite of being threatened with hell fire by the parish priest, and beaten, and even jailed by the local authorities. In contemporary cases, this compulsive-like return to the scene is prevalent in abduction cases. (Although one may also find a phobic avoidance of the location in some cases.)

Francisco also showed a major change in behavior. Before the visitation, he was "a boy of few words. He preferred to go apart and hide, even from his sisters." Yet afterwards, "He set out with his sisters through such large crowds that he could advance only with difficulty." He seemed to enjoy his role as an "instant celebrity."

4. Procurement. Procurement has a pattern of its own. After a beam of light strikes the witness, and captures the total attention of the person, a drawing force pulls the human being into a one-on-one meeting. (Some of my cases describe two forces, one pulling forward and one pushing from behind, or two "Grays" who carry out this maneuver.) In all cases, the beings who appear then begin instructing and controlling the witness. Commonly, there is mental telepathy, reassurance, and verbal or physical pacification. He or she is often escorted or floated to an examination room.

5. Examination. The children do not report being taken anywhere, or being examined. Perhaps they skipped this stage, or having been physically beaten by their caretakers for "lying" they neglected to mention this part of the experience. Also, I have found that amnesia routinely sets in just as the person is transported, and is lifted upon return.

If I may be allowed a bit of speculation, furthermore, it seems to me that there are at least two major abduction programs. A) The genetic breeding program, well documented by Budd Hopkins and others, and

B) The Messenger program. This is my term to offer a tentative explanation as to why some people are not subjected to a medical exam when captured by aliens, and subsequently re-captured again and again. I find people who are certain that they have been given a message which they are to reveal to others at a preordained time and place. Furthermore, the Messengers are least likely to come to a professional for help, as they do not feel traumatized.

6. Conference. Crockett tells us, "Then the woman said, 'Do not be afraid. I will not harm you. Say your rosary every day. Lucia will have to remain on Earth to spread the message of the Immaculate Heart of Mary."

Bullard comments that, even as the mood of the abduction changes from fear to friendliness, and the captive is allowed to ask questions, "One characteristic stands out—the replies are invariably absurd."

Probably it didn't strike Lucia as absurd, but she heard the Lady say, "Continue to pray the rosary in order to obtain the end of the war. In October Our Lord will come, as well as Our Lady of Dolors and Our Lady of Carmel. Saint Joseph will appear with the Child Jesus to bless the world. God is pleased with your sacrifices. He does not want you to sleep with the rope on, but only to wear it during the daytime."

7-8. Otherworldly Journey and Theophany. Surely, it was a religious experience for the children. Francisco and Jacinta led large numbers of people to worship at the shrine which they caused to be constructed at the site, and Lucia attributes her lifetime of service as a nun directly to the visitations.

9-10. Return and Aftermath. Again, to quote Bullard, "Abductions seldom end when the spaceship sails off into the night, and may leave the witness literally and figuratively scarred for life." These children, and, no doubt, the lives of most of the thousands of witnesses to the "second sun" dancing in the sky on that plain in Portugal in 1917 were permanently altered.

I feel certain that those who interpreted the events as a sign from the Mother of God never became lapse in the practice of their religion.

The majority of those witnesses left no written records. We do have a full written testimony of Lucia, as Sister Maria of the Sorrows.

The Last Secret of Fatima

Sister Maria continued to have visions of Jesus Christ. This too is typical of those who have endured the modern alien encounter. Contactees, as we call them now, appear to have been magnetized by contact with other forces in the cosmos and subsequently attract all sorts of paranormal phenomena. Sister Maria reported, to use modern words, pre-cognition, forecasting deaths and world events (which were essentially correct but the events were slower to occur than she predicted). And she claimed that she had "the mystery of the Most Holy Trinity revealed to her, but was not allowed to share this with others."

What little Lucia was told to share were three secrets. The first two were revealed as a plea for people to turn away from sin, and thereby save the world from destruction. Sister Maria warned, "Many nations will disappear from the face of the Earth."

The third secret was to be held, unopened, until 1960, and then to be given by the Bishop of Fatima to the reigning Pope. Again, we turn to an eye-witness report, which is quoted by Jacques Vallee in his investigation of Fatima.

"A man whose word I trust received an interesting report from one of the Pope's secretaries, who introduced the highest men in the Church into the presence of John XXIII for the opening of the secret part of the Fatima prophecy in 1960. Although the solemn event took place behind closed doors, the secretary had the opportunity to see the cardinals as they left the Pope's office; 'They had a look of deep horror on their faces.' He got up from behind his desk and tried to speak to one of them whom he knew intimately, but the prelate pushed him aside and walked on with the expression of someone who has seen a ghost.'"

The Cardinals decided *not* to reveal the secret to the faithful. Rumor has it that Pope John Paul I took it upon himself to reveal the final secret of Fatima and announced the date he would do so. However he died suddenly, alone in his room, the night before he was to make the final revelation. The cause of his death may be a secret kept even longer than the final secret of Fatima. He had been in good health. The College of Cardinals denied the request for an autopsy. [ed.: Several books have been written about the circumstantial evidence for murder: One of the best is *In God's Name* by David Yallop, which also recounts Pope John Paul I's intention to expose the nefarious dealings of Vatican officials and the Italian Secret Service P2, along with a host of other swindlers, in the massive illegal manipulations of the Vatican Bank and the Banco Ambrosiano of Milan. This story, in fact, forms the basis of the third in the trilogy of *Godfather* films by Francis Ford Coppola.]

No other Cardinal has taken it upon himself to come forth with a new date to tell us the final secret.

Conclusion

Examination of the eye-witness reports of the Miracle of Fatima forced me to change a conclusion I had held for all my school years: The Mother of God did not appear to thousands of devout Catholics in 1917 in Portugal. Only little Lucia Dos Santos saw the Blessed Virgin Mary appear at Fatima. Some 50,000 to 70,000 others saw a fiery disk in the sky moving contrary to all known physical laws.

What did happen to the children of Fatima? By comparing selected reports from Lucia and other witnesses one can find a startling similarity between those marvelous events, and the profound changes brought into their lives, and the contemporary alien visitor experience.

If it is logical to conclude that what happened out there was an elaborate staged demonstration by aliens, the next question is "Why?" and especially, "Why this incredibly complex 20-year plan to bring secret messages to the Cardinals of the Catholic Church?"

Here, having endured the lapse from my first faith in the Church, I will voluntarily lapse from my second faith: a Ph.D. in Science. I no longer believe that one can answer all questions by sticking to the facts. I am going to indulge in wild speculation:

What could cause the look of horror on the faces of the Cardinals when they learned the final secret of Fatima? Not the threat of war, or even nuclear disaster. We are strangely accustomed to large scale dying. Death, collectively, is banal. Besides, the first two prophecies were about war and no one squelched the message or the messenger.

I believe that stark horror is a complete disruption of your belief system. Something or someone you have held sacred for a long time, and based your life on, turns out not to be so. Betrayal is horrible. Men who became priests because they believed that the one true Church is the Roman Catholic Church and it was established by Jesus Christ, the Son of God, would be horrified to learn that Jesus Christ was another kind of human being, an alien.

As long as I have climbed out so far on the limb of speculation, I may as well saw it off even as I sit. Why would aliens bother to send this disruptive message? Could it be a part of the huge cultural-conditioning program that we are parcel to, involuntarily, or voluntarily? The point is — and it may well take eons — to have many races of aliens live comfortably on this planet Earth with us. I wonder if the Miracle of Fatima in 1917 was staged and the revelation in 1960 was to give credit to those who staged it. In acknowledging the "Producers" we were supposed to switch our allegiance from Jesus Christ to the aliens. (We saw something similar in the careful de-throning of Hirohito from Emperor-God to ordinary man after World War II, which made it possible for the Japanese nation to accept defeat and a new alien government.)

But the best laid plans of mice and men often go astray, and so it seems, of aliens. In spite of intensive study of the human race, they miscalculated. The year of the supposed revelation was to be 1960 A.D. Maybe in 2060, or 2160, or 3160, or when we no longer set our calendars by the death of Christ, we humans will be ready to admit that there are other races of human beings, and that Jesus Christ, son of man, came to save not just Earthlings, but the *entire* rainbow of human races.

I feel I should point out to Dr. Mundy that humanity may not be given another century or two in which to awaken from its blissful ignorance concerning the reality of extra-terrestrial presences on our planet. I doubt that we will be given as long as another decade. It looks to me as if the tempo of events is such that E.T. intervention in human affairs is likely to reach the stage of paroxysmic climax within five years, and probably sooner. I hope with all my heart that the aliens responsible for the cultural conditioning program we know as Christianity wish to share this planet peacefully with us, themselves living up to the ethical standards of the religion they have promulgated. However, many of the experiences being reported by abductees do not correlate with this type of benign intervention. These cases consistently appear to indicate that at least one group of aliens intends to *replace* humanity as the dominant species on this planet, rather than to peacefully share our living space. It is of the utmost importance to explore as thoroughly as possible these contradictions between the religious doctrines supposedly promulgated by E.T.s and the actual behavior of E.T.s being reported by present-day abductees in order to distinguish what is real from what is imitation. If what we are confronted with is different groups of aliens with extensive camouflage capabilities, who have been involved in a "war in heaven" since deep antiquity and which persists, it is literally a matter of life and death for us to distinguish what is genuine from what is imitation. It should be realized that just because there are imitations, this does not necessarily mean that there is no true Virgin Mary. The problem is to distinguish the real thing from the imitation.

There have been many other recent apparitions of the Virgin Mary. There was one in Cameroon, which had numerous indications of UFO involvement, only about three months before the bizarre "exploding lake" incident in that country, described in chapter 4 of this book. However, the most persistent and well-known of these manifestations have occurred in the little village of Medjugorje in Yugoslavia, where six young people, aged between 10 and 17, began to have contacts with the Virgin in 1981, contacts which are still ongoing. The apparitions and the messages delivered follow the same pattern that Dione described in his masterful analysis of Fatima, down to the detail that one of these six young people now has a cyst on her brain. There is some question as to whether or not the growth is malignant, but there is no doubt that it does cause severe pain. The girl has persistently refused the medical treatment that might cure the condition, stating that the Virgin wants her to offer this suffering to God. The Medjugorje phenomena resemble what occurred at Fatima in other respects as well. The following is from an article by Ann Rodgers-Melnick in the *Fort Myers News-Press* of Aug. 7, 1987, about a group of pilgrims from Florida who had gone to Medjugorje:

> Kay Manglitz, a member of the Church of the Resurrection in south Fort Myers, visited Medjugorje last fall to give thanks because her 30-year-old son had been healed of a spinal disease during a visit to Medjugorje several months earlier, she said ...
> Manglitz said she witnessed the miracle of the sun — when it appears to change color and spin in the sky — two days in a row.
> 'It came down out of the sky. The center of it was like a white host circled with gold and a path led down to us,' Manglitz said. On the second day the path appeared to lead to the church, she said. Although people stared at it for 30 minutes, she said, their eyes were not harmed.

The Rev. Arthur Venzia, spiritual director of St. Vincent de Paul Seminary in Boynton Beach, returned from Medjugorje, also having seen the sun appear to dance in the sky. Along with several other people, he saw a grayish disc, slightly smaller than the circumference of the sun, appear to draw near to the earth, pulsate, spin, and change to hues of pink, blue and gold, he said.

It seems to me that the occupants of that grayish disc must have become over-confident of the gullibility of the spectators they were performing for, and to have neglected to align the disc correctly between the sun and the spectators. A single sloppy maneuver can destroy the effect of a whole series of impeccable performances, in this case allowing a witness to perceive and describe what had been so long and carefully camouflaged.

Mary Craig is an open-minded, free-thinking British lady who wrote a book about her visit to Medjugorje entitled *Spark From Heaven*, published in 1988 by Ave Maria Press, Notre Dame, Indiana 46556. She brings to light a disturbing fact that is certainly a significant piece of the puzzle, though how it fits together with the other pieces of the puzzle is not yet clear. As far as I know, it has never been mentioned in any of the accounts of the Medjugorje apparitions written by devout Catholics, though it certainly seems to be an essential part of the background information necessary to understand the phenomena.

Long before Yugoslavia became a nation, a struggle for dominance went on between Catholic and Orthodox Christians in the Balkans. The Croatians are mostly Catholic, and the Serbians are mostly Orthodox. During the early part of the Second World War, as was the case in Spain, in the Balkans the influence of the Catholic Church was unequivocally aligned with the Fascists. The towns of Medjugorje, Zitomislic, and Surmanci are all within a few miles of each other. On June 21, 1941, Croatian Fascists took seven monks out of the Orthodox Monastery at Zitomislic, including the Father Superior and the youngest novice, then rounded up over seven hundred Orthodox women and children whose menfolk had left to join the Serbian army, and forced them all to enter a large pit at the nearby town of Surmanci, in which they were all buried alive. Forty years after this inhuman atrocity, on June 21, 1981, a plaque in commemoration of that day of horror was erected in the Orthodox Monastery at Zitomislic. It was just three days later, on June 24, 1981, that the first apparition of the Virgin Mary occurred at Medjugorje.

In 1992, eleven years after the original apparition of the weeping Virgin at Medjugorje, in a nightmare reversal it was the Serbs who turned Fascist, while the Croats remained Fascist, both sides perpetrating the most abominable atrocities on each other and their Moslem neighbors, reviving the Nazi death camps in the name of "ethnic purity." Instead of being numbered in the hundreds, the sacrificial victims numbered in the hundreds of thousands and perhaps millions, with no end to the killing in sight, unless it be the total genocide of one group or the other. In the midst of this nightmare holocaust, the apparitions of the Virgin continue to occur.

Although Mary Craig is an unbiased witness who describes her impressions in scrupulously fair fashion, she is apparently not aware of the reality of UFO manifestations and therefore does not even consider the possibility of E.T. intervention in the following account:

> A sudden flash of light and tremor of excitement in the crowd made me turn and look in the direction of the sun. Almost to my horror, I witnessed what so many have called the 'dance of the sun' — the sun moving back and forth as though on a yo-yo string, its

central incandescent white disc surrounded by spinning circles of yellow, green, and red light, for all the world like a Catherine-wheel firework. 'My God,' said an American to his wife, 'it's a Mediterranean sun that I've been staring into. Yet I'm not even dazzled when I look away.' Startled by the thought that I too had been staring into that sun for about ten minutes, I hastily looked away. I didn't even have spots in front of the eyes...All around us, people were on their knees praying. To my regret, I felt no such impulse. Why, I don't know, but I had no sense of the numinous, only of the passing strange...I felt that somewhere there must be a rational explanation.

A similar story surfaced in the *Washington Times*, of July 10, 1987, according to which:

Miracle Seekers Getting a Warning From Eye Doctor

Opelousas, La. (AP) - Ophthalmologists are warning Roman Catholics here that they may harm their eyes if they stare at the sun in hopes of seeing a religious phenomenon.

Some Catholics have been staring at the setting sun for 15 minutes or more in the past few weeks, hoping to see 'the miracle of the sun' or 'the dancing sun.' They were told to stare at the sun by a group of southern Louisianians who returned June 21 from a pilgrimage to Medjugorje, Yugoslavia, where the Virgin Mary is said to have appeared to some children.

The travelers said they saw the miracle at Medjugorje. They reported that the sun changed colors and discs moved and covered the face of the sun, according to Joyce Prejean, director of home health care at Opelousas General Hospital, who was one of the people who made the trip.

'They were able to look at the sun without pain or damage to their eyes, just as though they were looking at a picture,' Mrs. Prejean said.

The Australian edition of *People* magazine recently featured an article about Melbourne millionaire Leon Le Grand, who took his VHS video camera to Medjugorje and captured on film "an immense green disc obscuring the sun, then pulsing as it floods the sky with bands of colored light."

In a book entitled *Medjugorje: Where the Cock Crows and the Birds Sing*, by John O'Connor (Marian Promotions, Galway, Ireland, 1986),

Marinko Ivancovik describes one of the early apparitions:

> One evening about twenty days after the first apparition, the Madonna told the children to go to the hill later in the evening, about 11:00, to the place where she'd appeared. Then the children invited me to go with them, me and some other believers from the village, about thirty or forty all together. As soon as we got there, we started to pray. Then I looked up and it seemed that the sky had opened with a very bright light, maybe fifteen feet across, and something was coming towards us. Everyone saw it and said at the same time: 'Look! See the bright light!'
>
> We were standing in a circle around the hole where people had dug up the ground and taken it home with them, when the Madonna appeared. There was a wooden cross in the hole, and it seemed as if a large globe of light was bursting from the cross into thousands of bright stars. The light was too bright for me to look at, while all this was happening, so I can't tell you exactly what happened. Later we talked this over among ourselves, and no one else can say exactly what happened.

From this same book, we also learn that two of the six children, Vicka and Marija, have unusual cycles of illness and attacks, for which they persistently refuse medical help, having been told by the Virgin to offer their suffering to God. The mothers of Jakov and Ivanka have died since the apparitions began, but it is not clear whether there is any connection.

At the time of the Council of Nicea (325 A.D.), all references to extra-terrestrials and to reincarnation were systematically deleted from the Bible, which was rewritten, edited, and tampered with to such an extent that its reliability has ever since been at best questionable. However, we can compare its text with the texts of the scriptures of other traditions and see what they have in common. There is strong evidence for mutually beneficial E.T./human contact during certain periods of deep antiquity, clustering around names like Imhotep and Merlin and Padma Sambhava and Quetzalcoatl. Thrice-great Hermes-Thoth, and one-eyed Odin who knew the secrets of magic flight, and Lugh of the Long Hand with his helmet of silver and invincible sword and ship that flew over land as well as water, and Demeter who brought seeds from other worlds to this one, and all their ilk and kin, are also part of it. Extra-terrestrials, other-dimensionals, and terrestrial humans have been getting together for various purposes ever since the earliest shaman found a way to pass through the barrier to the

Other World. This is nothing new. It is a game that has been going on far longer than our recorded history. Our mythologies are loaded with legends that are actually condensed histories of real events involving extra-terrestrial or inter-dimensional contact. The Olympians of Greek mythology are to be found under other names in other traditions, but the legends concerning them give a remarkably clear description of one type of extra-terrestrial which helped us on our way to civilization, but whose characters frequently had flaws quite similar to our own, so similar that they may be ancestral traits which have been passed down to us. Their habitat and way of life was different from that of humans, but their ways were understandable to humans and usually in harmony with human ways of life. Their blood was also different than that of humans, a clear liquid for which the Greek name was "ichor." This is yet another indication of a link between ancient mythology and the Blonds, whose lymphatic system is over-developed by terrestrial human standards while their blood circulatory system seems underdeveloped. Upon being wounded their predominant body fluid gushing forth would therefore be lymph, which is clear and yellowish, rather than blood. The tall type of E.T. that closely resembles humans corresponds with the Greek Olympians, the Hindu Devas, the Mexican Quetzalcoatl, and the Peruvian Viracocha; the short gray humanoids with the Hindu Asuras and their equivalents in other mythologies.

This item was given to me by Guy Tarade, a well-known author of many books on the paranormal in France. It consists of documentation concerning the Templars and the Ark of the Covenant. It is unfortunately impossible to verify the validity of the information, as the original documents have disappeared. It can only be traced back with certainty to 1937 when a Catholic priest, the Abbot Corriol, submitted a manuscript entitled "Recueil des Actes du Clergé Regulier et Seculier de la Haute Provence" to a publisher named M. Reynaud in the city of Forcalquier. The publisher never published the manuscript, but in 1972 showed it to some friends who had expressed interest. The portion of the namuscript that is of interest to us purports to be the transcription of notes taken by an Inquisitor of statements made by a Templar who was being submitted to torture for the fourth time on February 13, 1310. The Templar, Brother Arnold, has just told the inquisitor, whose name is not given, that his castle contained, besides ordinary furniture, clay tablets and ceremonial objects.

Inquisitor: Do you know what was written on the tablets?
Templar: I don't know. The parchment scrolls and clay tablets were kept among the archives in the office of our commander.

Inquisitor: What was in the chest?

Templar: I already told you.

Inquisitor: Nothing else?

Templar: There was a smaller chest that no one had the right to approach. The guardian of it was Brother Hély.

Inquisitor: What was this chest used for?

Templar: It was kept near the chapel of the castle. When Brothers were received into our Order, the Commander told Brother Hély to show it to us. Brother Hély spoke to the chest, which seemed to answer him in a language unknown to me. Then a bust of an old man came out of the chest.

Inquisitor: Was it an idol?

Templar: No, Brother Blacas told me it represented Moses, the guardian of the Tables of the Law.

Inquisitor: Is he a prophet?

Templar: Yes, the prophet of the chosen people of the Holy Scriptures.

Inquisitor: Is it him that you worship?

Templar: No, it is Our Lady and her Son.

Inquisitor: What did this chest look like? Where did it come from?

Templar: It was built of a metal unknown to me. Brother Blacas told me it was the Ark of the Covenant, which was brought back from Jerusalem in 1127 and then deposited at the Abbey of Senanque, at the demand of Saint Bernard and of Saint Malachi.

Inquisitor: When was this chest brought to the castle of Greols?

Templar: I don't know.

Unfortunately, at this point Father Corriol stopped transcribing the notes directly, giving as his reason that the Templar had been driven insane by pain. He talked of such things as traveling through time, and in the sky in flying chariots that spat fire, of the Kingdom of the Swan, of a deep well of darkness lost in the sky through which one could attain immortality, reach unknown stars and empires. He spoke of the Apocalypse, of celestial warfare between the powers of light and darkness and of warfare in unknown celestial worlds.

If this document is authentic, what this Templar on the point of death in 1310 described as "a deep well of darkness lost in the sky" would seem to be what we now call a Black Hole.

Author George C. Andrews with the Mitchell-Hedges Crystal Skull *(Brian Myers).*

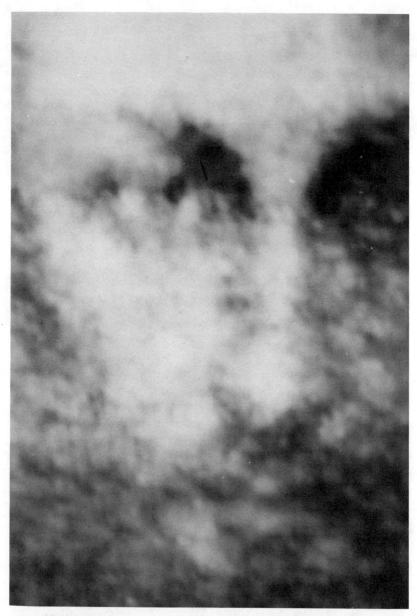

Maurizio Cavallo, an abductee who has had contact with the Blonds, took this photograph immediately following the departure of the aliens. He was suddenly moved to photograph a section of a blank wall in his studio. When the film was developed, this image appeared on the frame that seemed to have been wasted on a section of plain blank wall. *(Maurizio Cavallo, Centro Ricerche Clarion, C.P. 45, 13100 Vercelli, Italy)*

Although Dr. Wilhelm Reich suspected that he was himself of extra-terrestrial ancestry, a certain type of UFO occupant was clearly hostile to his research into the subtle workings of life-energy, and just as clearly had allies within high levels of the U.S. government, who deliberately engineered Reich's professional disgrace and premature death. It is also remarkable that during the short period of time that Reich was actively involved in UFO research, he discovered a simple, inexpensive and effective weapon that could make UFOs fade out from the sky. What began as a cloudbuster turned out to be also a spacegun. It was after he made this discovery that the U.S. government sent him to his death, and burned all of his work its agents could get their hands on.

Was Reich's extra-terrestrial ancestry from a different group of extraterrestrials, hereditary enemies of the group our government has made a deal with? Was that why he was able to discover the spacegun ability of the cloudbuster in such a short span of research time, and why he had to be silenced at all costs?

In the Biblical accounts, as well as in accounts from other traditions, it is not always clear which group of extra-terrestrials is involved, particularly when one realizes that some types have the ability to disguise themselves as other types, or as humans.

The contrast in character between the wrathful jealous Jehovah and the gentle peace-loving Jesus has often been noticed. One of the Gnostic heresies, which William Blake revived in his prophetic poems, was that Jesus had not been sent to fulfill the laws of Jehovah, that Jesus had really been sent to save humanity from Jehovah.

There is a strong element of Gnosticism in the messages transmitted to Swiss farmer Billy Meier by his blond visitors from the Pleiades. A comprehensive investigation of this aspect of the Meier contact case has now been made by an academic with impressive credentials.

Dr. James Deardorff's career was in atmospheric research. He obtained his doctorate at the University of Washington in 1959, and in 1962 joined the National Center for Atmospheric Research in Boulder, Colorado, where as a senior scientist he engaged in laboratory and computer modeling studies of the turbulent air motions in the atmosphere's lowest kilometer. In 1978, he became a professor at Oregon State University in Corvallis, Oregon, in their Department of Atmospheric Sciences, where he continued this research and taught a few courses for eight years before retiring emeritus in 1986 in order to devote full attention to various aspects of ufology. Out of this came over 100 research papers in peer-reviewed journals which, however, does not qualify one for ufological research any more than any number of other backgrounds would. Of greatest importance is to hold an open mind, especially with regards to the possible capabilities of UFO-intelligences standing an unknown number of millennia ahead of us in technology and evolution.

After beginning to switch fields in the early 1980s, Deardorff has concentrated on advancing the hypothesis that UFO aliens likely have various strategies of dealing with us, other than treating us like ants, and that we should not ignore this likelihood merely because it would mean they are somewhat more intelligent and much more experienced than we are. He finds that one of the more evident parts of their strategy is to keep the skeptics deceived, so that the fraction of humanity unable to accept the possibility of their presence in earth's vicinity, both now and in past millennia, will not be forced to accept it, while others may learn at their own rates. This is judged to be a form of ethics. The deception involves not only leaving no accessible UFO evidence behind that would satisfy skeptical scientists, but in feeding contactees and abductees messages often containing absurdities or contradictions that repel scientists. The Meier contactee case has been of special interest to Deardorff because of its unique characteristics, which qualify Meier as a prime contactee within the constraints of the deception hypothesis.

Dr. Deardorff's book is entitled *Celestial Teachings*, (Blue Water Publishing, P.O. Box 230893, Tigard, OR, 97224.) At my request, he was kind enough to summarize its contents for inclusion in this book, in the following synopsis:

Around 1970 Edouard Meier, a Swiss citizen who claims to be the primary contactee of extra-terrestrials based in the Pleiades star cluster, received a translation of part of a document called the Talmud Jmmanuel (TJ) from an ex-priest friend, a Lebanese who understood the Aramaic language. This translation, in German, appears to represent the true testament of Jesus, known in the document as Jmmanuel (spelled with a J instead of an I), and to be the document which led to the Gospel of Matthew. Its first version was written during Jmmanuel's ministry but the scripts were stolen by Pharisees at an early stage of its writing. Some years later it was written over again in a complete form by the same author, one of the twelve disciples, and still later, around the end of the first century, two or possibly more copies of this were delivered to the Palestine area. One of these copies of the TJ, encased in resin, was left secreted under a stone in a tomb near Jerusalem where it remained until Meier's Lebanese friend was prompted to unearth it in 1963. Another copy reached the early Church, and the indirect evidence studied here indicates that it was drastically altered by an early Christian compiler in forming the Gospel of Matthew. Soon thereafter the scripts which had been stolen and had been acquired by the apostle Peter, or by Mark, were apparently augmented with the aid of Matthew's gospel to form the Gospel of Mark. The point in the TJ where the theft is mentioned corresponds to the point in Matthew's gospel where its sequence of events from there on is replicated in Mark's gospel.

In 1975 Meier's main contacts with the Pleiadians began, and in the first contact he was told of the importance of this document, and that he should distribute it to interested persons. So in 1978 he had the German version of the TJ printed in booklet form, and started distributing it. However, as of this writing neither the general public nor biblical scholars are aware of its existence. The document indicates that Jmmanuel's teachings derived in large part from what he had been taught by the Pleiadians during the well known period of forty days and nights. The TJ portrays Jmmanuel as an even greater prophet than does the New Testament, and a teacher of the power of the individual spirit, after one's spirit has become knowledgeable through lifetimes of experience and learning. J's healing ability was made manifest through the purposeful action of his own great spiritual power.

These celestial teachings remain heretical even for the modern-day biblical scholar, as they depict Jmmanuel having survived the crucifixion, and having taught reincarnation, not resurrection. For this reason, and because of its connection to a controversial UFO case, Western scholars cannot be made interested in examining the many points of genuineness of the TJ. If its original Aramaic scripts were still in existence this might not be true, but they were lost or destroyed as the translator and his family were fleeing from an Israeli raid on a Lebanese concentration camp in 1974. This was before he had worked his way through much more than the first quarter of the document. Moreover, he was later killed, in 1976, because of his efforts. As a result, the question of the authenticity of the TJ can only be answered tentatively on a personal basis after studying it thoroughly for oneself.

The TJ answers a large number of outstanding New Testament problems. Among these are the sudden growth of Gnosticism in the early second century, and the appearance of the 'logia of the Lord' in Aramaic writing out of which Matthew compiled his gospel, according to one interpretation of what a second century bishop by the name of Papias wrote. The TJ appears to constitute these 'logia.' The virgin-birth problem does not arise in the TJ where the genetic intervention of Gabriel is what occurs; Gabriel was an extra-terrestrial, not an 'angel.' The 'star' of Bethlehem and the 'spirit descending like a dove' at the nativity and baptism scenes, respectively, and the Ascension, are seen to be explained by the actions of Gabriel's UFO-like vehicle.

The 'angel' at the tomb after the crucifixion turns out to be another extra-terrestrial, and the strange behavior of the guards at the tomb, in Matthew's account, is caused by this extra-terrestrial. The problem of what could have caused Judas Iscariot's betrayal of his teacher, as expressed in all four New Testament gospels, is resolved in a unique manner which seems much too creative for any hoaxer to have invented. With the TJ, all the various bits of evidence which point to Jesus having lived in Syria for a while after the crucifixion, and then having traveled eastward through Pakistan to Kashmir, India, and having died there many decades later, can be examined in a new light.

It is quite evident that, if all this represents truth, the custodians of Christian literature around the end of the first century could not have made use of the TJ's writings except in a highly edited form. This is precisely what one interpretation of Papias' classic statement suggests. The TJ supports the theory that Matthew thoroughly Judaized his source materials in forming his gospel, and that Mark de-Judaized it to a considerable extent while adding on to his short gospel, the stolen scripts, from Matthew's gospel.

The peruser of this synopsis may of course be highly skeptical because at this point in history all this may seem to represent the utmost in sensationalism. For this reason, Part II of the book undertakes a rather detailed comparison of verses in Matthew's gospel which scholars have argued are non-genuine against verses of the TJ which often parallel them. It is found that one scholar, whose comprehensive book analyzing Matthew first appeared in 1981, three years after the TJ, makes some 159 objections to Matthew which do not apply to the TJ. Yet, for about half of these objections the TJ does have parallel verses that are somewhat different. Some 36 of these objections are quite abstruse or are original with that scholar, and 22 of the 36 have TJ parallels, or cognates. One can find some 34 additional criticisms of other Matthean passages by other New Testament scholars which do not apply to the TJ even though 19 of these passages do have TJ cognates. With the benefit of hindsight, this writer noted 66 further logical criticisms of Matthean passages which do not apply to the TJ although it has cognates to 44 of the 66. It is this ability of the TJ to overcome even the most abstruse of criticisms — logical criticisms that plague the gospels — which most strongly dispels the hoax theory.

A further analysis shows, using the TJ as the standard, that the scholar whose textbook was most utilized here was surprisingly capable of detecting as non-genuine those whole verses which are inserts and substitutions within Matthew. He was less able to detect non-genuineness in those Matthean verses which show some correlation with TJ verses. He was least able to detect non-genuineness within those of Matthean verses whose words and meanings correlate more highly with those of TJ verses. This sequence of results is to be expected if the TJ is genuine and the scholar was capable.

In the end, however, it is apparent that only a person who is receptive to the essence of New Age teachings will be receptive to the celestial teachings presented in my book. The interested reader is invited to learn this story of what lies behind the New Testament gospels, and form his or her own opinion as to its reasonableness and genuineness.

The Talmud of Jmmanuel has recently become available from Wild Flower Press. Although in my opinion Deardorff's scholarly analysis of the text remains valid, the book is liberally sprinkled with absurdities, some obvious, some not so obvious. I shall deal only with what seems to me the three most flagrant examples here.

When Pontius Pilate asks the crowd to choose between releasing Jmmanuel or Barrabas, and the crowd chooses Barrabas, before washing his hands of the matter Pilate protests in these words: "He only taught a new doctrine, and for this he shall suffer death? Where then is the freedom of speech, thought and opinion?"

Those are the words of a citizen of a modern democracy, not of a Roman Procurator of antiquity, speaking to his foreign subjects upon whom he would himself impose the death penalty if any of them dared to speak out against Caesar or Roman rule.

The incident of Saul on the road to Damascus is reduced to burlesque slapstick comedy. Jmmanuel sets off fireworks in the path of Saul and his companions, then while they are dazzled with the flares and suffocated by the smoke, calls out to them, slipping away before they see him. Even if Saul was temporarily blinded, his companions would have noticed the debris left behind by the fireworks. Gunpowder had not yet been invented. Other inflammable substances had been used in warfare and their properties were known. The probability of such a childish trick being successful is zero. It is the type of idea that might be dreamed up by a relatively unsophisticated Swiss farmer.

The third absurdity is contained in one of Jmmanuel's prophecies: "So it will prove true in two thousand years, when mankind has become knowing and thinking, that my actual unfalsified teaching will be revealed anew. The new prophet of that distant future will not possess so much strength and power over evil and sickness, but his knowledge will be above mine..." In other words, if one accepts *The Talmud of Jmmanuel* literally at face value, as fundamentalists do the Bible, Edouard "Billy" Meier's knowledge is superior to that of Jmmanuel/Jesus. This, in my opinion, is clearly not the case. Besides the absurdities, there are some implications of a far more sinister nature that must be addressed. Adam is stated to be "the father of the white human race." God is stated to have created only two other races besides the Semites: the Nordics and the Hindus. All other human races are relegated to limbo, as having been created by other E.T. "gods." Is this an aberration due to the limited thought processes of a Swiss farmer, or does it also represent the point of view of his Pleiadian visitors?

How have extra-terrestrial and/or other-dimensional entities (our absentee landlords) controlled humanity throughout the ages? Through our collective belief systems, which maintain certain patterns of behavior far more effectively than armed forces can, though the belief systems and armed forces usually operate in conjunction. This is not necessarily bad, as a firm reliable structure is necessary for development and growth. It only becomes bad when law enforcement becomes rigid and constricting, no longer sufficiently supple and elastic to provide enough freedom for healthy growth, including the development of original thinkers with new ways of doing things. Law enforcement in a totalitarian dictatorship is the intellectual equivalent of rigor mortis. Modern democracies constantly make all kinds of errors, and far too seldom correct them, but democracy remains the best system we have so far devised to maintain the necessary order in our environment, while interfering to the minimum with our individual liberties.

The obvious way to shatter the structure of today's democratic governments would be to revive the racism that was so rampant its dominance was almost unquestioned until only a few decades ago, and which has now once again reached epidemic proportions. Those conspiring to replace democracy with dictatorship, or a restoration of autocratic royalty (the same system under a different name), would do everything possible to fan the smouldering embers and outright flames of race hate, of both racial and religious hatred. That would be the quickest and surest way to transform the United States into another Yugoslavia. Having reduced the country to chaos, they could then seize totalitarian power with an iron hand. The first two steps in the process of replacing democracy with dictatorship would be to deprive law-abiding citizens of their right to bear arms, and to suspend the Constitution through Presidential proclamation of a State of Emergency, using race riots triggered by *agents provocateurs* as a precipitating factor.

The Meier case presents us with an interesting sequence of events, of which the publication of *The Talmud Jmmanuel* is apparently the culmination. I don't think the material it contains should be automatically dismissed because it is sprinkled with absurdities, or indications of concealed intentions of a sinister nature. That is all the more reason to study it seriously in all its ramifications. We should also remain open to the possibility that the text contains truths as well as falsehoods. I have no problem with, for example, the concept of the angel Gabriel as an extra-terrestrial. However, that concept is not original with Meier, but can be traced at least as far back as the 13th century Islamic classic, *The Mathnawi*, by Jalulul-Din Rumi. Even further back, the references in the Dead Sea Scrolls to "the Watchers" are supportive of this point of view.

Among the various possibilities to be considered is the possibility that a rough translation of a genuinely ancient text did come into Meier's hands. Many of the Dead Sea Scrolls that were found by the Bedouins never reached the official investigators, so it is not implausible that one of them could have surfaced in a Palestinian refugee camp in Lebanon, and that a rough translation of some fragments could have been relayed to Meier. Perhaps believing himself to be divinely inspired, Meier might then have filled in the gaps between the fragments in order to make it more publicly presentable, or taken other liberties with the text, inserting his own ideas by rewriting it. That, of course, is exactly what the bishops of the early Church did at the Council of Nicea in 325 A.D. to the collection of ancient texts (at the time, between two and three centuries old) that had come into their hands, now known as the New Testament. Comparison with the Dead Sea Scrolls reveals just how extensive the liberties taken in rewriting the original texts on that occasion were. It is remarkable that the cover-up of the real contents of the Dead Sea Scrolls has lasted almost exactly the same length of time as has the UFO cover-up.

We do know that Meier's Pleiadians are not the only group of extra-terrestrials interacting with us, nor are they the only group of Blonds. It is interesting that the Pleiadians have conditioned Meier to believe that he is the only genuine abductee, and all the others are hoaxes. It is when someone who believes himself to be divinely inspired starts to think that he also has a monopoly on the truth that he becomes a danger to human well-being, prepared to perpetrate atrocities in the name of his fanatical belief system. It is healthy to feel oneself divinely inspired, but a symptom of mental illness to think one has a monopoly on the truth. We would be doing certain of our absentee landlords an immense favor by dismissing *The Talmud Jmmanuel* as trash unworthy of serious investigation, and disposing of it in the garbage without further ado.

It is beyond coincidence that the day after I finished writing the above remarks about the ramifications of the Meier case, I received a book in the mail, loaned to me by a friend who thought I should read it, which turned out to be literally a gold mine of relevant information: *Hitler, l'elu du Dragon,* by Jean Robin (Guy Tredaniel Editeur, 76 rue Claude-Bernard, 75005 Paris, 1987.)

I'll begin my highly condensed summary with a few paragraphs I translated, that may be directly relevant to *The Talmud Jmmanuel.* To put the paragraphs into context, I now abbreviate in telegraphic terms some essentials of the background.

Italy, 1908. Young man befriends old hermit. Old hermit gives him ancient manuscripts, one of which describes a method of divination. Consulting the oracle requires a complex procedure, and the young man does not attempt to do anything with it, because he is not able to understand it. Ten years go by. In 1918, enter friend of young man, immediately enthusiastic when told of divination manuscript, and studies it intensely. The instructions involve a strange kind of arithmetic. The purpose of the calculations is communication with the Little Lights of the Orient, also known as the Three Wise Men, and as the Three Kings of Agarttha: Brahatma, Mahatma and Mahanga. Using this method, they make contact with the hermit, who is now in a Himalayan monastery. Having given you at least a glimpse of the background, here are the paragraphs:

> On April 8, 1930, Father Julian announced that he was about to go through the Gates of Light, being on the point of death. After his death, Cesare Accomani, and Mario Fille continued to receive instructions through this same type of telepathic and arithmetical telegraph system, concerning the goals and ceremonies of a new society they were to create, to be called the Polar Society.*

---

*   Elsewhere in the book, Robin states that the goals were to secretly stage-manage the

The instructions emphasized that the adepts of this group, after having passed the tests required, would receive an initiation and would know great secrets. The oracle indicated that some of the documents, containing a portion of the secrets, were written in German and had been buried in Palestine. The hiding-place would become known at the right time.

Could *The Talmud Jmmanuel* be one of these documents?

The oracle then proceeded to instruct the young men to also form an "Iron Cohort" in France, along the lines of the Iron Guard of the Roumanian Fascist Codreanu. The young men started the Polar Society, which thrived for a few years, then began having chiefs who seemed mentally disturbed to the point of discrediting the Society, which apparently fell apart and ceased to exist. I say apparently, because Jean Robin thinks that this was a cover operation, staged for the occasion, and that what really happened at that point was that the Polar Society went underground, from overt to covert, and became a secret society, which is still very much in active existence today.

Robin is also of the opinion that there has been much confusion concerning the real power sources of the Nazi occult connection. He considers the following sources, usually considered to be of major importance, to be relatively insignificant minor groups, often used to screen and distract attention from the real power sources. The red herrings: Adam Weishaupt and the Bavarian Illuminati, the Mannerbunde, the Order of Teutonic Knights, Goering and the Edelweiss Group, Rudolf Hess and "the Watchers," and the Prussian Masonic lodges — with one exception, which brings us to the real power sources.

That exception was a Rosicrucian lodge founded in Vienna during the 18th century, named "Initiated Brothers of Asia." It was considered a renegade lodge by the other Rosicrucian and Masonic lodges of the period, who repudiated it and were repudiated by it. The mutual hostility was open. The tradition the renegade lodge was based on went back nearly two centuries, to when Charles of Hesse was host in his castle at Gottorp not only to the Count of Saint-Germain, but also to Heinrich von Ecker und Eckoffen, who had been initiated into a Buddhist sect. The symbol used to recognize each

---

Apocalypse, thereby gaining control over the Mahapralaya, the Time of Great Destruction, as well as over the era that is to emerge from the ruins afterwards. The only way to prepare a good future was to be as evil as possible in the present, thus speeding up the approach of Mahapralaya.

other by the members of the sect was the Swastika. It appears to have been a branch of the Dugpa sect of Tibetan Buddhism. The initiation which von Ecker und Eckoffen transmitted to Charles of Hesse included access to a spirit guide, an invisible entity capable of manifesting in paranormal ways.

I suspect that this was the original contact with the Grays, leading up to the Nazi contact, which was then passed on to the CIA.

Besides the Initiated Brothers of Asia, according to Jean Robin, the real Nazi power sources were: Sebottendorf and the Thule Group, which derived from the Bektashi Dervishes in Turkey; Haushofer and the Green Dragon Society in Japan; and the Golden Dawn. Sebottendorf knew and corresponded with MacGregor Mathers, Bram Stoker and Aleister Crowley, visiting them when in London. The Golden Dawn's only link to its Secret Chiefs was through the German woman, Anna Sprengel.

I again quote Robin directly: "As Rene Alleau so rightly said, Sebottendorf's central idea (or rather, of those who inspired him) was to give a racist movement, still embryonic and veiled by its political structure, the internal coherence of a Prophet with militant followers, forming a sect of devotees comparable in more than one respect with the Ismailian 'fedayeen' guided by their spiritual leader, the Old Man of the Mountain. In other words, the idea was to form *a racist order of initiates, with a military and religious structure centered around a leader believed to be divine.*"

The Initiated Brothers of Asia had a Superior College of 72 members, which directed their group, and perhaps a great deal more.

The first Jewish victim of the Nazis was Walter Rathenau, at the time Minister of Foreign Affairs for the German government, who was shot down on June 24, 1922. As Rathenau lay dying, with his last words he designated the group that had ordered his murder: "The 72 who control the world..."

French Intelligence was investigating the 72. According to Robin, they were so alarmed by their findings that they leaked some of their information in the form of fiction: *Les Sept Tetes Du Dragon Vert* by Teddy Legrand (a pen-name), published by Berger-Levraut in Paris in 1933.

Here is how Legrand describes his close encounter in Berlin with one of the 72:

At last we were in the presence of one of those we had been searching for so relentlessly for over six months!

No, the living Buddha of Ourga could not have had a more hieratic and majestic look — or a look more simultaneously cruel, piercing and astute, than the idol we saw seated on a sort of throne, at the back of a raised recess in the room. In the half-light, his sacerdotal ornaments flickered like flames, and scintillated like a reliquary.

But in this whole scene, first of all I saw only one detail: the phosphorescent elbow-length green gloves which shimmered like fireflies.

The Man with the Green Gloves had achieved complete mastery of his reflexes, down to the least of them, but at the price of what prodigiously painful training? When he spoke to us, not a muscle of his face moved. His lips did not even open at all. I had the disagreeable impression that a human voice was coming from the interior of a painted statue. And his eyes were as immobile as if they were made of enamel, not even looking down at us, always looking off into the distance. However, his speech was clear, spoken in excellent Oxford English.

'Whoever you may be, gentlemen, though neither one of you is of my race, the green hand is extended to you, since you bring the keys that open the hundred and ten doors of the secret kingdom of Agarttha.'

So we now had directly in front of us one of those who is leading Europe into chaos by occult methods. We were right in front of one of those famous Greens, whose existence we confirm, in spite of the incredulous pleasantries of government officials. One of those who activated or terminated, turn by turn, Archduke Franciois-Ferdinand, the famous Staretz Rasputin, the last of the Czars: Nicolas II, the Israelite Rathenau, the Oceumenic Patriarch Basil III, General Koutiepoff, the financier Ivar Kreuger ... and how many others of lesser importance?

Let us remember that it might be as irrational to blame the other branches of Tibetan Buddhism for what goes on within the Dugpa sect, as it would be to blame the other Rosicrucian and Masonic lodges of the period for what went on in the lodge of the Initiated Brothers of Asia, or to blame the Protestant clergy for what goes on in the Vatican. Robin states that one of the Nazi power sources has a belief that there are only 72 "True Men" in each generation, but does not say if it is a belief of the Dugpas, of the Bektashi Dervishes, or of the Green Dragon Society in Japan.

Hitler said of himself that he had "the certitude of a sleep-walker," and many astute observers noted that he seemed to be taken over suddenly by something of tremendous power. Could Hitler have been a physical vehicle used by a Tulpa of the Dugpas?

The Hungarian Trebitsch-Lincoln, a Jew who concealed his ancestry, was one of the founding members of the Nazi party, and had a strong influence on Hitler during the 1920s. After traveling to Tibet for an initiation in 1930, Trebitsch-Lincoln became Chao Kung. During his subsequent extensive travels, he always seemed to go from one trouble spot to another, tending to arrive and then depart shortly *before* the trouble broke out.

Rasputin took his orders from telegrams signed "Le Vert," that had been sent from Sweden. In 1929, a Scandinavian link to the 72 appears to have been Baron Otto von Pautenas, an official of the Lithuanian government, who was also second-in-command of a Fascist group called "Wolves of Steel." He was associated with Ivar Kreuger, whose suicide caused international economic upheavals. Other suspected links with the 72 are O. Aschberg and the Nya Bank of Stockholm, which financed both the Nazis and the Bolsheviks — as did also a small group of U.S. millionaires, prominent among them Prescott Bush, the father of President George Bush.

Are we living in the middle of a cosmic battlefield, without even being aware that there is a war going on? Angelic warfare, in which divine and demonic forces manifest through a variety of disguises in a ritual combat that has been going on for thousands of years, and is now about to reach its climax?

There is ample evidence of sporadic UFO activity before 1947, but that year was nevertheless a landmark year, a turning point, as from then on UFOs have been reported on a hitherto unprecedented scale world-wide. The first major wave occurred shortly after the first explosions of the atom bomb, and Dr. Albert Hofmann's hard-to-explain error in laboratory procedure that resulted in the discovery of the unique properties of LSD-25.

What else was going on within that time frame?

John Whiteside Parsons was a government scientist who worked on jet propulsion techniques. He blew himself to pieces in a laboratory accident in 1952. The government honored him posthumously by naming one of the mountains on the moon after him. According to Kenneth Grant, in *Outside the Circles of Time* (Frederick Muller, Ltd., London, 1980), from which most of the information in the rest of this chapter is summarized, during 1945 and 1946 Parsons was involved in a special project with one partner: L. Ron Hubbard, who later founded Scientology. This special project, which was carried out in the California desert, was a series of magical ceremonies, known as the "Babalon Working," designed by Aleister Crowley, who died in 1947. Readers of my previous book will remember the correlation I made between the 1904-1905 "Winter of Weirdness" in England, and the battle being fought during that time between magicians

Crowley and MacGregor Mathers.

The purpose of the series of ceremonies performed by Parsons and Hubbard was to unseal an inter-dimensional gateway that had been sealed in deep antiquity, thereby allowing other-dimensional entities known as "the Old Ones" access to our space/time continuum. The culmination of the ceremonies was described as having successfully resulted in extra-terrestrial contact. As Grant puts it: "Parsons opened a door and something flew in; he supposed it was Babalon and the fourth chapter of the Book of the Law; others have supposed other things but all are in agreement that something unusual, something inexplicable by mundane laws, occurred around that time."

Crowley left behind a drawing of one of his invisible mentors or, as he and others called them, "Secret Chiefs," entitled "LAM." This entity has a very large head on a small body, a pointed chin, a little slit of a mouth. Lam's eyes are smaller than those of the short gray humanoids so persistently reported in modern UFO incidents, but it is said that if one meditates on the portrait the eyes become larger. Lam's nose is slightly more pronounced than the noses of the short Grays, but aside from that, the resemblance is remarkable.

In the same book, Grant describes a cannibalistic ritual called "The Feast of the Hive," dedicated to the Spider Queen of Space in the Obeah system of Voodoo, in which the only parts of the body of the human victim that are eaten by the participants are the glands, which are eaten raw. This correlates so precisely with the cattle mutilations and other known activities of the Grays as to be beyond coincidence, and the very name of the ritual is reminiscent of the collective hive mentality of the Grays.

Something else seems remarkable: the same government that posthumously honored John Whiteside Parsons by naming a mountain on the Moon after him had its agents burn all of Wilhelm Reich's work they could get their hands on, and did everything possible to deface and delete his memory. Both Parsons and Reich were sincere scientists doing their best to make further contributions to the advancement of science, over and beyond the contributions they had already made. Why were their honestly-arrived-at research results so rewarded in one case, and so drastically punished in the other?

"Parsons opened a door and something flew in." Let us consider the possibility that the something which flew in might have been the small gray type of humanoid that so closely resembles Crowley's portrait of Lam. This type previously had occasional access to our time-space continuum, but now had continuously open free access.

The Pentagon would have lost no time in following up on Parson's E.T.

contact. It appears that a deal was made, a deal which our leaders at that time sincerely believed to be in the best interests of the United States, unaware of how insidious and treacherous these new-found allies could be. If Wilhelm Reich was of extra-terrestrial ancestry, but of a different lineage, and was therefore aware of the real motivations of the Grays, his presence here was a major threat to the plans of the Grays. After Reich discovered the spacegun capability of the cloudbuster, thereby causing two UFOs to fade out from the sky, the Grays would have been able to formulate a plaint against Reich in terms comprehensible to their contacts in the government: this man had without provocation damaged (or destroyed) two of their vehicles, along with accompanying crew members. Such a chain of events would be one of the possible explanations for the otherwise puzzling gross disparity in the government's treatment of Parson's and Reich's research results.

Kenneth Grant makes the point repeatedly in his book that the rituals of a modern group which frankly described itself as "a lodge gone black" were persistently accompanied by an insectile buzzing sound, such as is often reported during UFO incidents, and that there was a sudden sharp increase in UFO sightings in the area where the ceremonies were taking place during the same approximate time span. He also mentions that the original Arabic title of the Necronomicon grimoire has the meaning of "a nocturnal sound made by insects."

We have just seen how closely buzzing insectile sounds have been associated with apparitions of the Virgin Mary, along with other indications that such apparitions may be UFO-related, or even directly staged by UFO occupants from start to finish.

Is the same group of extra-terrestrials that manifests to devout Catholics as the Virgin Mary, manifesting to devout Satanists as the Old Ones whose return is imminent? Have they been cynically playing both sides of the conflict, like international bankers who loan money to both sides in a war, or deliberately bring about a war so that both nations or groups of nations will be obliged to ask for loans? The large-headed short gray humanoids are an ancient race. Are the Grays the Old Ones whose return was predicted?

Let's see how these various possibilities are reflected in a statement made by my good friend Bix Chandler:

> I know they're real and they're here. What I'm working on is who belongs to which tribe, and what their game is.
>
> I've had several encounters with the Blonds and the Grays. I've discovered that if a human focuses his attention on them, they pick

up on it in a hurry.

There is one area of data which seldom surfaces in any of these contacts. I've also noticed that almost without exception, the channeled entities gloss over it, if they mention it at all.

L. Ron Hubbard's technical assistants ran thousands of people through recall processes of their past lives over a 25 year period. As the statistics emerged from the methodical comparison of these thousands of past-life confessions, Hubbard came to the conclusion that aliens are quietly invading our sphere of influence. He discovered that they use, and have used for millions of years, forms of painful inculcation, which are sometimes thinly disguised as therapy, and are at other times carefully sugar-coated with religious significance.

The Blonds may have gotten away from these methods of control, but the Grays use them exclusively, along with thought-form projectors, reverse-vector radionics, zapping beams and a vast panoply of other devices. The mental implants can create short-term or long-term amnesia. By long-term, I mean thousands of years, amnesia that perpetuates itself from lifetime to lifetime. It is rigged so that if the concept is mentioned to the person who has an implant, the person will not believe it, and will automatically reject the possibility that it might be true, or even forget that it was mentioned.

But when those slimy reptiles start getting into the genes of our red-blooded all-American girls, that makes my blood boil! The cream of American motherhood being creamed by a bunch of (expletives deleted) really galls me. What a mess! To think that our government propitiated the Grays and gave them access to our people!

I'm surprised at the CIA/NSA/Air Intel boys. They can't be that short-sighted. They should have hooked up with the Swedes, then they wouldn't have needed any technology. By the way, not all Blonds are blond. They include black, brown, auburn and red heads. Their federation is called the Interdimensional Alliance of Free Worlds. The Gray federation is called the Imperial Alliance of (self) Righteous Worlds.

The Grays take human prisoners and milk them periodically, like ants milk aphids, for their vital energies. The type of energy emitted by admiration is the rarest in the universe, and is the most valuable to the Grays, because they are unable to create any of it themselves, so they trick or manipulate humans into providing them with it.

Hubbard called the Grays 'Markabs,' from the Hebrew

'Merkabah.' L & L Research's Ra channel referred to them as the Orion Crusaders. I and most of my fellow researchers are bored to tears with the Grays. Even the Grays are tired of all the publicity they've been getting. You'll never comprehend how much I despise these loathsome shades, these spawned-of-hell manipulators, but they are the gods that humanity has chosen, representing the degradation that our mass-consciousness has identified with. The Grays symbolize humanity's future self, if we remain on the negative path of separation from the rest of nature, headed toward nuclear oblivion. On the other hand, the Pleiadians and Essasanians represent what we could become. We are standing at the crossroads, and the time for decision is now. In the words of the immortal Howland Owl, in Walt Kelly's *Pogo*: 'We have met the enemy and he is us.'

All anyone can ever offer to anyone else in the way of communication is a point of view, for no one can ever prove anything to you but you yourself. Some of the aliens are here to bring man the light. We are sleeping giants hell-bent on our own destruction, and they're simply trying to wake us up, but so loud do we snore in our cocoons of unreason that we fail to hear their knock or the key of freedom rattling in the lock.

I sure as hell would never trust a government dedicated to 'smashing our enemies' to evaluate the UFO data, since they would perceive anyone with more power than they have as an enemy. Perhaps the space jockeys are more benign than we think, if Earth is a lunatic bin for fallen angels. Maybe we're the rebel forces that have been taken off the game-board and locked down on a time-track. It might be a case of we're so bad off that to be good slaves they have got to get us up a notch or two. It could be that they need us to defend this area from marauders from Saint Elsewhere, but we're so screwed up we wouldn't even make good cannon fodder. I like the scenario that says that Earth is the last psychic cesspool in the omniverse, and everyone is standing in line outside of Earth to experience what it's like to mud-wrestle before the old nut-house is torn down.

The history of the universe may not be linear history at all, but simply games within games, played across planes, boards, dimensions, for the lack of something better to do, endlessly. They may all belong to the same chess club and pair off to play games. For what? Who knows? Maybe they play for territory, for sensations, for souls — or even for marbles, such as our big blue marble, Mother Earth.

Implanting has been in use since time immemorial in this and other galaxies. It is a simple field expedient for removing players from the board of play, erasing their memories or disabling them in some way we don't comprehend, parking them in a fixed space/time continuum where they won't come back to haunt you or interfere with your game for a spell. We humans also have games like that, which we call 'prison' and 'the funny farm.'

The Grays have learned that you can't kill beings, that they can never die. You knock off a moonbase somewhere and the spirits zoom on back home and pick up some bodies or droids, get hold of a new cruiser, then come back and blow you off the map. So they hit on this method for taking 'Gods' out of 'the game' and turning them into helpless broken pieces (slaves). As long as the victims never find out, you're safe. But bodies die, so every time they die you give the spirit a command to report back to heaven, where it gets a fresh implant. After that, it gets a new body and doesn't remember anything. It's an automatic assembly-line solution to the problem of what to do with political prisoners.

But recently on this world, beings began to remember what they were supposed to forget.

The only solution I've found personally is for each individual to learn all he or she can in order to acquire multi-dimensional awareness, thereby co-creating an ideal reality and transcending all of this negative crap. Of course, that is precisely what the teams of Grays doing the implants are doing everything possible to prevent.

The Essasani are a hybrid species that resemble Budd Hopkins' space kids, because they are a combination of Zeta-Grays and Earth Humans. Although the experiment is happening now in our present time, certain members of that species have traveled backward in time from the future, in order to thank us for our gift of our genes, and to share what they have learned. One of the reasons they have returned here is to help the Pleiadians guide us into space, for we in our future will become as highly evolved spiritually as the Essasani. You saw them in *Close Encounters of the Third Kind*. They are real. That was a government-sponsored film to introduce the Grays to the public, but it backfired when the Grays double-crossed the U.S. government. Even the mother-ship was modeled on the real one, except that it doesn't have all those stalks and lights sticking out.

Truthfully we've made a lot of headway during the past 47 years. We'll solve the mystery if we (all ufologists) work together as a team, and stop the incessant back-biting and one-upmanship.

When the human mancells realize that all of them are parts of spiritual man, who is one being, and that we are merely fighting ourselves, then we can fully trust each other, and there will be peace on earth.

There is too much fear among researchers at the present time, because of all the negative information that is surfacing and must be faced. However, there is also a lot of light in what is transpiring, if you look into the black hole and out the other end instead of at the toroid doughnut. Building saucers isn't the solution to research efforts. The solution is knowing that we don't need the saucers to travel inter-dimensionally. They're merely symbols to show us that we can do it naturally. The 'Light' Gentry are trying to tell us that once we develop the technology for wormhole navigation, we will no longer need it. Machines are merely teaching devices to show us that we can do it without the machines. Once you learn to ride the bike, the training wheels come off.

There are many beings walking around out there and among us who know totally what is going on, far more than you'd ever dream was possible. They wouldn't go near a UFO convention, but they are in continuous contact with someone elsewhere. Some have the ability to pull up answers to anything at will, but they don't say anything. They read, watch, learn, and their every thought is recorded on big mother-ships. I've been out there. I've seen them. It's wild, man! I can hardly wait to finish up doing my time here and get off of this dirt ball. I'd rather be an android janitor there, than be the wealthiest billionaire on Earth. It's like living in constant joy that never wears thin.

It's the state of awareness known as Christ-consciousness. All the New Agers are working to get there. Belief structures of every kind abound. The 'Aquarian Conspiracy' is simply to raise the mass-consciousness to the level of Christ-consciousness, thereby rendering the Grays invalid and forcing them away, repelled by the Light we shall radiate all together as one Entity composed of many points of Light.

Thank you, Bix, for a most memorably inspired, impeccably phrased, and electrifyingly elegant solo performance.

6

Some Astute Perceptions and Informed Opinions

ABDUCTION: WAS IT ALL A DREAM?
by Dr. Jean Mundy

A woman who reported that she and her brother watched a UFO land, and also had two other close sightings a few years later, wondered if she had a missing time experience. Evaluating an abduction requires psychological detective work. Clues to a possible abduction can be found in one's dreams. Anita (not her real name) reported the following dream: "I was hovering above a hilltop about 100 feet or so above the ground. It was probably lower as I was below the tree tops. I was floating along observing the hilltop, when up over the brow of the hill came a military helicopter, then another, then another. They were noisy and scary. I wondered if they could see me. Obviously they could as they chased me around the hillside. I have no idea where I was or if I was inside some sort of vehicle." Anita continued: "I have had a recent dream that a male entity, who is intent on sexual intercourse, tickled me and made me laugh and remember good memories and brought me strawberries and ice cream."

Another person, a mature man with a lifelong series of 17 alien contacts (consciously recalled) said, "I had a dream that I was telling someone, 'Do you want to see a UFO? Come on, there is one just outside the window'. I see the door, a circle, and two little puppy faces. Like cloth dogs, they had little round ears, like characters of dogs. Two of them in a circle, again, it was only the heads. All I see of any of these people are the heads. They were right close together, facing one another. The UFOs were out in the front yard, he came in the kitchen door somehow."

Which one of these people — based on dream analysis — could have been abducted? Surprisingly, neither dream indicates an abduction of the Fourth Kind, a physical abduction, but it still indicates a different kind of abduction.

All human beings dream, although only a few are remembered. A dream is composed of the actual experiences you have had (technically called "day residue") and your thoughts and feelings about those experiences. The dreamer uses all his or her "memory banks" (all past experiences) to find the appropriate symbols to express not only what happened, but exactly how the dreamer feels about the event. So a person who has actually been abducted would, most likely, dream about it, and dreaming about it will actually be therapeutic in helping to mitigate one's feelings and allay one's fears.

However, another person who has only heard about the experience, or seen a movie, or even just thought about it, could also dream about being abducted. So how can we learn about abductions from the dream? What can we learn about the dreamer? There are certain rules of dream interpretation that can be followed, and one in particular would be helpful to ascertain if a real abduction has taken place, but one must be on guard for peculiar complications.

The main complication is that we have few completely studied cases for comparison. I believe it may take several dozen hours of careful analysis to make an absolutely positive determination of the reality of the abduction experience. I have worked in many psychological settings, such as crisis clinics, psychiatric hospitals, and in private practice, where my principle duty was diagnostic evaluations. Yet here is a new psychological condition, trauma due to contact with a UFO. Not only is it a new problem, but it is probably the most difficult diagnostic problem I have ever grappled with because of two almost insurmountable problems, one internal and one external. Externally, the UFO doesn't hang around for us to examine it. We must work from circumstantial evidence, for even when collaborating witnesses were actually on the scene, they are strangely silent. We must rely very heavily on the witness's own confused report. The witness is understandably confused by the strangeness and terrifying nature of the event. There is even a possibility that the aliens are adding to the confusion by causing memory blocks, using hypnotic suggestions, misdirection, and other techniques of mind control.

The first question is, given this most extraordinary event, is this person a reliable witness? In coming to trust the reporter, one must rule out psychosis, neurosis, brain damage, or any possible source of hallucinations, (e.g., psychedelic drugs). One must watch out for the pathological liar, people that are hyper-suggestible, the psychopathic hoaxer, and just plain criminals who will do anything for profit or fame.

In addition, there is an internal problem (inside the subject) that does not exist in any other psychological evaluation. It is true that trauma victims — such as those in nearly fatal car accidents, major surgery, or military fighting in the front lines — frequently have amnesia for part of the event, and so it is quite understandable that the abduction victim has missing time memory loss. But, in this alien scenario, when the person does finally recall the abduction, they may not be able to accept it as fact. This wanting to disbelieve is found in incest survivors, and in those examining the possibility of incest. But abduction by aliens is an even more startling revelation! They may plead with the therapist, "Tell me it didn't happen" or "Maybe it was all a dream." This may be compounded by a therapist also being unwilling to say it was a physical reality, it can't *really* happen, but was the result of x.y.z. Taking into account these complications, however, there are still ways to sort out what is reality and what is a dream.

Let's look at a recurring childhood nightmare. A man, who we will call "Bob," cheerily called his neighbor to come and look out the window to see a UFO. Bob told me that when he was about three years old he had a terrifying nightmare that "something would come out of the wall at night, right through the wall." The sequel to his nightmare was that he could not go to sleep, for many years, facing any wall. Hypnosis was used to explore this nightmare and the following details of the dream came to his mind. "Some guys on motorcycles, 1927, that guy, wallpaper with big trees on it, and some guy was chasing me on the motorcycle. Only one motorcycle, an old fashioned motorcycle, black jackets, black helmet, black goggles, I can't imagine what they want with me. Menacing, I was frightened. He is chasing me around the trees. They are coming to rob the stagecoach, I get in the way, and they kill me, stab me, and shoot me, several times." This dream, with variations, was repeated until he was about 12 years old.

This nightmare, in spite of the fact that it does not include any mention of UFOs, does actually indicate that an abduction could have taken place.

It is possible, in dream theory, that his recurrent nightmare is actually a symbolic version of his earliest abduction experiences. Bob had a sudden insight, in describing the "motorcycle" men who came through the wall of his early childhood and were pursuing him through the trees. When he took a closer look at them, they were wearing large, black, wrap-around goggles, quite similar to the eyes of the cover of *Communion*. Symbolism is a fascinating study but is never reliable enough to draw final conclusions.

What makes this dream indicate that the abduction could have taken place is seen in the verbs, as the Noun-Verb rule of dream interpretation is a reliable tool of dissection. Bob, in telling of his most recent contact with aliens, calmly reported that, "They came right through the wall of my bedroom." The rule is that the actions in the dream are actions that have actually taken place in the person's daily life. The abduction actions, which we know from well-documented cases, include pursuit, capture, examination, and near-death stresses. These elements are all in Bob's dream, but totally missing in the "hovering," "tickling" dream of Anita, where she is served ice cream. Hovering, tickling, and being served are not actions in the physical abduction cases that have years of documented study. (See *Missing Time* and *Intruders*, by Budd Hopkins and the classic case of *The Interrupted Journey* by John Fuller.)

By repeated dreaming over the years (as well as by conscious work), Bob has overcome his fear and, on recent visits, has tried to engage the aliens in conversation. Also, he has spent considerable time trying to work out a way to know when visits would recur and asks that if anyone else has a way to foretell visits, would they please share it? Write "Bob" in care of Dr. Mundy, 33 Windward, East Hampton, NY 11937.

Incidentally, his family doctor of many years, his close-knit family, and my own interviews all establish that he is a sane person, a loving father, and a genuinely good, honest person.

At first glance, one might think that if a UFO is in the dream, it must be based on seeing a UFO. Not so. Everything we experience or read or hear about can be worked into the dream. Dreaming of UFOs is not necessarily an indication of physical contact with a physical UFO. The Noun-Verb rule has an axiom. The objects seen in the dream (nouns) are *always* symbols, and cannot be taken literally. But still, the dream can be relied on for important information about the character of the dreamer, i.e., a person who dreams of knives and guns is more aggressive in make-up than one who dreams of puppies.

How to know if the report of an abduction was "only a dream?" The basic rule is that reality has continuity, while in a dream one is instantly in a new setting. For example, only in a dream can one be in a New York apartment one second and in Europe the next. A secondary rule, which we will explore here, is that one does not, in daily life, act on the emotions in the dream. That rule may not seem valid at first glance, but it does work. One reacts in the dream, but it is a very watered-down version of what one would feel in the same situation if awake. One can, while dreaming, appear nude at the office and be completely unconcerned. In a dream, one can witness, or even perform, murder without skipping a heartbeat. If there is strong emotional feeling in the dream, it wakes up the sleeper. As in the nightmare, it is the very feeling of terror that awakens one (one ceases to dream) and, with a sigh of relief, knows that one was asleep. In the normal sexual dream there is a bit of feeling, nothing like the total physiological changes that take place in reality. The real abduction experience has pain, heat, cold, nausea, eye pain, headaches, etc., and leaves psychological and/or physical scars. By contrast, again, if one dreams of giving birth, there are no labor pains. So to discriminate the abduction dream from an abduction experience, check out the level of anxiety, fear, awe, and other feelings.

The Noun-Verb rule is useful because verbs appearing in genuine dream reports are very rarely distorted, and they do tell how the person behaves in everyday life and what they have experienced. The verbs tell what the person is capable of doing, or has already done, with the noun symbols in the dream. One must remember that the nouns are not literal but are symbolic. To illustrate: In the first dream, above, Anita reports "hovering, floating, observing, wondering, and tickling." The application of the Verb rule makes it safe to assume that these verbs are indicative of ways she behaves. But it is not trees and helicopters (nouns) that she hovers over and observes or tickles, as trees and helicopters are symbols with many meanings. We are not sure of the individual meaning to her, but it could be that trees represent all of living things and helicopters all man-made things, and she is an astute observer of both the natural and man-made worlds, which she likes to "rise above" and enjoy in a playful manner.

Bob, with his life-time of alien contact, in the first dream, has these action verbs, "telling," "facing," "chasing." Therefore he is the kind of person who faces (confronts), tells others about his experiences (and invites them to share it, as the neighbor in the dream) and is forever "chasing" (pursuing) all manner of things. But it is not the noun *motorcycles* he pursues, but whatever motorcycles might stand for in his lexicon of personal symbols. Incidentally, proof that he wants to share his experience was given by him, in his request that other readers write to him.

So to evaluate the dream as a sign of abduction versus no abduction, separate the verbs and the nouns. Dreaming of an object (noun), a UFO, doesn't mean a thing (or more correctly, we can't be sure of the personal symbolic value of a UFO to that dreamer), but dreaming the action verb of pursuit and capture and probing (abduction actions) *does* indicate that an actual abduction could have taken place. It doesn't matter if those actions are (in the dream) in a totally dissimilar (non-UFO) setting. One could be pursued and captured by any number of things, nouns, that are symbols for how one feels about UFOs. Being captured by an army of ants represents a different feeling than being captured by beautiful Arctarians. But dreaming of abduction actions is a positive sign that an actual abduction could have taken place. By examination of what happened next in the dream, one could find a match or non-match to the established abduction sequence.

Consider the dream of a well-known person, Debbie Tormey (the Kathie Davis of *Intruders*), Debbie revealed this dream at a conference in North Haven and stated that she had the dream while in the hospital recovering from a back problem.

In a field with a hill and there had been something flying over and it was shattered in a million pieces and I went over to it. The area, and there were little tiny pieces of clay and little pieces of stones and slabs of little tiny pieces of road clay with marks on them, embedded in the dirt. I guess from the explosion.

And I was picking this stuff up and saving it. I thought, 'This is great', and I backed into this thing and it was really tall and it didn't move and it didn't have a face and when I backed into it I took off in the other direction, running, I was scared to death, so to speak, and looked back, and it was just standing there, like it didn't even know I was there.

The verbs are: flying, shattered, picking up (the pieces), scared, backed up, didn't move, just standing, didn't know, took off running. The actions in these verbs are all compatible with events in the alien abduction experience. One is confused, picked up, paralyzed, terrified, and released. In addition to lending credence to her alien encounter, the dream also tells us that Debbie is the kind of person who thinks it is great to pick up the pieces, that is, when she has a shattering experience, she goes right to work trying to put it all back together again. Not only did she do this in the several years of working with Budd Hopkins on the published account of her experience, but she put herself in the hospital to repair a back problem.

What do the nouns tell us? "Road clay," "Stones," "Dirt," "A field," "A hill," "Slabs of little tiny pieces." Again, one can never be sure of symbolic value, as the meaning of symbols is based on the dreamer's personal experience with those things, but we speculate: These items are all "earthy." Debbie is a down-to-earth, well-grounded, stable person, open like a field, with some up-and-down hills she has climbed to develop her strong character.

"Was it all a dream?" is a valid question concerning abduction by alien beings. I would like to postulate that abductions follow the same scheme as Dr. Hynek's *Close Encounters*.

Alien Abductions

CE I - Sighting of Space Craft
Human action:
Photographs taken, drawings, other reporting by witnesses.
Sighting of Human's Aura
Alien actions:
Energy beam sent to specific selected human.

CE II - Physical Traces on Earth
Human actions:
Measuring instruments used.
Geiger counters, yard sticks, bio-chemical analysis of soil,
plant life, animal autopsies.
Physical traces in humans.
Alien actions:
Brain wave patterns altered.
Metabolism affected, trance states, hallucinations and dreams induced.

CE III - Close Sighting of Aliens
Human actions:
Evasive action or captured, voluntary or involuntary surrender to
alien action.
Close sighting of humans
Alien actions:
Cooperation elicited by intimidation, force, or mind control techniques.

CE IV - Physical Contact between Humans and Aliens.
Messages exchanged by mental telepathy, gestures, hieroglyphics, video
screens, or books. Medical examination or operations, removal or exchange
of genetic materials, tracking device installed or removed. On some occasions, artifacts may be exchanged. These are either taken away before de-
parting, or they mysteriously disappear later.

Psychological Theory

Because of the strange and dramatic interaction (exchange) of physical
material and mental phenomena, in all these types of encounters, be it I, II,
III, or IV, an intense psychological bonding of the human to the alien is
more or less permanently established. This bonding is evidenced by preoc-
cupation with all aspects of UFOs, gathering and dissemination of informa-

tion about the spacecraft and the occupants, and with others who are so bonded (including choosing a mate who shares one's views of UFOs - I know of two such marriages), and altering one's lifestyle in accord with the meaning one assigns to the gathered information.

This is my psychological theory. It is not fact, but it is based on psychological fact. As with any theory, I will modify it later, or even discard it completely, when more data becomes available. As a psychologist, my basic data is the psychological make-up and behavior of the contactee. Every contactee is a gold mine of resource material. Fortunately, more witnesses now feel safe in presenting their experiences. Now the tools of psychology can be used to dissect the abductee dream and the abductee experience. One tool is dream interpretation (others are protective techniques, analysis of drawings, hypnosis, in-depth interviewing, and psychotherapy).

This article, "Abduction: Was it all a Dream?" shows the application and usefulness of just one of dozens of rules of dream interpretation: The Noun-Verb rule, which is: *nouns must be interpreted as symbols, while verbs are valid indications of life's actions.* Using this rule, and the chart above, one can ascertain whether the reported abduction was a Close Encounter of the I, II, III, or IV, type. If no encounter is indicated, then, by process of elimination, we can chalk up the report to imagination, mental disturbance, or lying skills. Perhaps the latter type are Close Encounters of a No-kind?

In the first dream presented here, Anita who has had CE I, the sighting of a UFO, dreams of a CE I sighting. In Bob's case, who has frequently had aliens around (over 17 contacts) he dreams, "They are right outside the window" and can be shown to others in many CE IIs. Bob's nightmare, given here, indicates CE III, while Debbie's dream indicates her life was shattered by a CE IV, and she proceeded to put it all together again. All the dreamers, by their life-style, indicate some degree of bonding.

A series of abduction or UFO dreams can be evidence of remote or close encounters. Indeed, close enough for the aliens to see the whites of our eyes, and us humankind to see the blacks of theirs. The psychological bonding that occurs from any UFO contact, no matter how remote, can dramatically affect our waking and dreaming states.

So ends the statement by Dr. Jean Mundy.

Rosemary Decker wished to make the following comments:

There are many people whose close encounters and contacts have been vastly different in nature from those so abundantly reported during recent years with the alleged Reticulan beings. I say alleged, because we have to take their word for it that Zeta Reticuli is their home base. My own experiences, and those of other people I have known or investigated during 40 years of research, have been distinctly different.

From the descriptions given by the abductees of these small, gray-skinned, large-headed types, I have gradually gained the impression that perhaps many, though not all, are based in a parallel universe that is not physical as we know it and could as easily be "from" the Earth's vicinity as from far off in outer space. There are probably some in both categories. Some of the many creatures that inhabit the universe are native to the physical dimensions we are familiar with, the chemical universe studied by science and perceptible to our senses. Other creatures inhabit paraphysical realms, usually alluded to as "etheric." These realms still consist of physical matter, but in forms that are less dense, more malleable, and more durable than the matter in the chemical universe. The inhabitants of the mental and creative planes rarely use forms of any kind. These interpenetrating universes have been recognized for millennia world-wide by the esoteric traditions of every major religion and school of thought.

The fairy tales of our childhood represent only a small fraction of the folk tales passed down by our ancestors in Europe and elsewhere about the activities of large-headed 'little folk' and their occasional visibility. The apparent increase in both visibility of and interaction with inhabitants of a parallel universe since UFOs erupted into public consciousness in 1947 may be and probably is an actual increase. However, I believe that at least some of the apparent increase is due to the fact that in our contemporary society it is more permissible to describe paranormal events. People today are more able to find safe places to tell of their experiences, with less risk of ridicule or rejection, if not accusation of insanity or actual commitment to an asylum.

If the alleged Reticulans are in fact doing all the things to and with humans that these abduction reports describe, some of their practices are not ethically acceptable under Universal Law.

If they need terrestrial human genetic material to increase their own hardihood, they are obviously by their own admission a weakened race. Their attempts at exploitation have probably been effectively repulsed by more highly-developed human or humanoid races elsewhere in the cosmos, who are more capable of preventing such parasitic experimentation than is terrestrial humanity in its present stage of development.

Most humans on this planet are so mentally and emotionally primitive that they do not yet know how to use more than 3 to 5 percent of their brains and, furthermore, do not want to know. The vast majority of contemporary humanity prefers not to develop their higher potentialities, which are a gift from the extra-terrestrials who hybridized our race many thousands of years ago in the first place, because such development requires sustained disciplined work and self-responsibility. Because self-responsibility is the last thing that the majority of humanity is willing to accept, rulership by tyranny in all sectors of society — religion, politics, finance, science, and education — has been the norm in most civilizations during most of humanity's recorded history.

Because the emotional level of most of humanity's leaders is so infantile — characterized by greed, territorial posturing, and temper tantrums — at present the blind are leading the blind toward and over the brink of the abyss. Humanity's technological development has so far outstripped its ethical development that it not only has the ability to destroy itself, but all other life-forms on our beautiful planet. The ever-increasing pollution of our air and water and earth is irreversibly bringing about our own destruction. Our civilization is repeating the mistake that brought about the destruction of the primeval civilization on Mars, whose monumental ruins we have only recently become aware of. We have not yet polluted the space beyond our planet's stratosphere, nor will we be allowed to. Our vehicles will not be allowed to land again on the Moon if they are carrying weaponry of any kind. The Earth beneath our feet, the home star that is the only one we have, whose well-being we are responsible for, is already convulsing in its death throes, because of our abusive greed and neglect, taking everything from it but giving nothing in return, insanely murdering the Great Mother from which we come because we have even lost the awareness that Mother Earth is alive. We make pious speeches and resolutions about ecology, but continue to clear-cut the forests on which our oxygen supply depends at the rate of several thousand acres every hour, to say nothing of our many other cosmic crimes.

If the Reticulans at present consider the Earth to be "part of the Reticulan system," that expression does not indicate ownership or even control. According to the map brought back from her abduction experience by Betty Hill, our solar system is on one of their regular trade routes. That is fair enough. However, if they are taking over human bodies by extracting the human souls and replacing them with their own, that is possession, which has been considered an illicit procedure by every great spiritual teacher known to our culture. It is one thing to invite knowledge and counsel from those who are more experienced: allowing an alien entity to take over the steering wheel of one's life-vehicle is quite another.

The following three cases describe contact rather than abduction. They are included because of the high quality of the perceptions of the individuals involved.

Virgil Armstrong was one of the original Green Berets, with whom he served for 10 years. This was followed by a long career in the CIA and Army Intelligence. Although one must always wonder just how "former" a former Intelligence agent may be, the experiences he has described in his book are very interesting. These brief excerpts from *The Armstrong Report*: "They Need Us, We Don't Need Them," privately published from P.O. Box 20174, Village of Oak Creek, AZ 86341, give a sample of the adventures and philosophy it contains. His subtitle is a reference to the E.T. group I have been calling the Grays:

In these most difficult and subtle times, there is only one way to avoid involvement with elements adversarial and negative in nature. To do this we need to continuously think, walk and live in love, light and balance....

The day finally came when I was to make my move so I proceeded. I was receiving all information telepathically including directions as to my appointed place of entry. Still in doubt as to how to proceed or where to enter, I waited and watched. Two hawks emerged suddenly from the grass approximately 300 yards distance and spiraled skyward in ascending circles. After reaching a height of about 500 feet they peeled off in a power dive and disappeared in the branches of a huge oak tree to my left front.

This was apparently the desired entry point and I proceeded accordingly. When I arrived under the tree, I found a hawk wing feather, but there were no hawks where previously there had been two. Where did they go? I know not but accepted all as divine and proceeded up the hill opposite the tree. The initial going, due to thick undergrowth, was difficult but eventually I broke out into a clearing which seemed totally void of any type of life. In fact it was eerie, for there was nothing, no birds and their accompanying chirps or song, but, most significant, no insects. It was totally sterile.

As I stood absorbing this unusual experience, I thought I faintly heard a summer locust. I kept turning my head trying to locate the source when I suddenly realized it wasn't a locust at all. I was standing in the force field of a spacecraft and it had some sort of power or energy source in operation. This was not something I could normally see from my nighttime vantage point so I was not prepared for a spacecraft emitting tons of radiation.

Realizing the danger I uttered some very sacred words and quickly removed myself from the danger, all the while blessing, in a not too gentle way, those who were responsible. I don't exactly recall what it was that I said but I'm sure it was in the neighborhood of: When you get home I hope your mother comes out from under the porch and bites you on the leg.

Having recovered from the shock of my experience and realizing I could in time be seriously affected, I spent the remainder of the day reconnoitering the area and marking a to-scale map, particularly that side which faced the vantage point. This later helped immeasurably in authenticating the ships and their locations.

I returned to town for a dinner engagement with Rick and some friends. Midway through the dinner my right side began to burn as though I had a bad sunburn. Perplexed, I excused myself, went to the men's room, and pulled up my shirt to examine the source of my discomfort. As I looked in the mirror at my right side, it was beet red from the waist to my arm pit, as was the area over my liver. Immediately I associated it with the spacecraft incident and knew I had radiation burns. That night during meditation I communicated to the mother ship and informed them that I was not very happy about the whole affair. I said to them, "You turkeys invite me into your domain and then zap me. For what? And what kind of guys are you?"

My answer was quick. I was informed that the incident had been an accident and they would assume full responsibility for my recovery. They should! The radiation affected my liver function, which had already experienced great stress from a previous ailment. The source of my communication also informed me that the occupants of the spacecraft on the ground were robotoids and could and would only respond to commands from the mother ship. Obviously somebody up there was remiss in deactivating both the ship and the robotoid. The robotoid explanation also explained why, while in that area, I had the sense and feeling of being observed, but the observer was completely amoral and insensitive. One had the feeling that upon command they would eat you alive! My liver progressively became worse and by the time I returned to my home base in Phoenix, a month or so later, it was distended and sore. I began to doubt whether or not they would keep their word.

Now, at the time I was living with my very special lady named Jane, the same lady mentioned in my other ET experience. One evening Jane and I had retired for the night and I remarked to her, "I hope they will, as promised, do something about my liver, soon."

The following morning I arose and as I did so I felt as though I had been kicked in the right mid-section by a mule. I looked down at my side and noticed there was a neat incision over my liver. Upon further examination I discovered that the probe was quite deep and had obviously reached the liver. Immediately, I went to Jane and showed her the incision. She, of course, asked where it came from. My reply was quick and to the point: obviously my space friends heard me last night and had kept their word. They operated on my liver while I was asleep. I never felt a thing.

I was very proud of the incident and was quick to pull up my shirt and show the incision to friends. This didn't last long. A few days later it was completely healed and there was only the scar. I marveled at having it and, when appropriate, planned to show others the neat handiwork of our space brothers. This was short lived. Within a few days even the scar had disappeared....

My dealings with them were strictly impersonal. I was accepted, tolerated, and guardedly protected. The information they gave me was not just handed to me but offered only when I asked for it. Sometimes the waiting was interminable. Many times I asked why I couldn't have it now. In retrospect I guess my initial expectations of them were faulty, for based on books I read, the channels I heard, and other influences over the years, I expected them to respond with profuse love. None of this was forthcoming.... I ask the reader to compare my personal experiences with those of abductees. Notice the distinction in treatment, the non-violation of free will. The good guys did not try to convince me they were good, or bad. Notice also that when the good guys make a mistake, and you are threatened, they assume responsibility and make restoration. Case in point, my radiation burns and the curing of my liver. This is not the case with ETs who are responsible for abductions....

On another occasion:

In fact the ETs had helped themselves without our permission. I was highly indignant about that. I challenged what they were doing for I knew there was a universal law that states you cannot interfere, morally and/or legally, with another planet's commerce or well-being without the express permission of either the planetary government and/or the actual government involved. I later learned from this alien group that there was another proviso: that if a planet was on a path of self-destruction then others could, while time permitted, help themselves....

One must exercise great discernment when dealing with UFOs and ETs. The best rule of thumb to determine whether they are good or bad is to observe what happens to the solar plexus upon initial contact. If your solar plexus registers uneasiness, or contraction, get out of there, for they are not good....If you think and act in love and light and spirituality, you will be divinely linked and protected....Such comportment is your protective armor.

* * * * * * * * * *

The following poem is by Barbara Sowell.

Dancing with the Star Man

The limbs of my soul
Felt the pull of an undertow
And even the burning eyes
Of my angry guard
(Who had finally discovered my whereabouts),
Could not stem my ebbing tide.

Then my gaze fell on this incredible being
I was bathed in the smoke
Of his glacier eyes
That burned beyond my soul.
To be sure, it was not human!
Cold, cold fire froze my mind.

His body flickered and glowed
With each pulsating beat
Of the music pounding in my ears.
And he led me to a place —
A space in the crowd —

To the dance floor he seemed to illuminate.

And the beat grew stronger,
As he swayed back and forth,
Till what sounded like celestial music
Poured out of his every cell.

How oddly severe he seemed?
His thin arms waited at his side,
As he swayed a silent invitation.

He knew.
Then his hair burst into golden flames,
And his face shot out moon beams
That brushed my waiting canvas.

It was me who took that first step and nodded.
Slowly we moved together;
Closer, closer,
With each undulating vibration,
We slithered round each other,
Until we were plied and molded,
Like some sculptor's living dream.
He pasted me with a collage of sound.
And he painted me with the growing thrusts of his art,
Till I glowed as unearthly as him.
And I flashed,
And we thundered,
And he rained such wonderful instruction,
Which my parched soul could not contain.
This ocean submerged my very being.
The waves pounded us one into the other.

When the music stopped,
He dropped my hand
And handed me a mirror that he pulled out of air.
I wore a garment of rainbows!

Almost forgetting his fading presence,
I stepped back to admire my colors.
And when, at last, I looked back,

I saw him standing quite limp.
His garish hair was matted to his skull.
His eyes were sunken inward.
Without expression, he rose and dissipated
Like West Texas heat waving above a scorched highway.

* * * * * * * * * *

Once Upon the End of Day
by Shirley Starke
(from *Voices of the Trees*, Raven Publishing, Route 2 Box 230, Valley
City, ND 58072; 1989)

O, once upon the end of day,
The sunlight's rays were red above,
And soft among the shadows green
I walked between the trees I love.

And then, because my heart was full,
I stopped a while and danced alone:
With leaves below and leaves above
I danced for love of things unknown.

And towers tall and banners bright
I saw that night, and lighted ships:
And roses red and lilies wan
Unfolded on my fingertips.

Then down I lay with arms outstretched,
Embracing earth and grass and stone:
With leaves below and leaves above
I lay for love of things unknown.

And long I lay for love until
The night grew chill and rose the breeze;
And when I rose, the gods of old
Stood still and bold among the trees.

"O, leaves and lights and flaming flowers
And sundry powers around you lie:
So shall it be forever more

If you to shores of ours will fly."

Said I, "My birth is of the Earth,
And so your mirth I share in bloom,
But far beyond my duty lies,
My paradise, my ever-doom."

Though long I search by day and night
And grey twilight, the dream is flown:
With leaves below and leaves above
I sigh for love of things unknown.

* * * * * * * * *

Some astutely perceptive remarks were made by J. Alison, in an article entitled "Alien Allegiance Recognition Foundation," which appeared in the May 1989 issue of the *Nevada Aerial Research Newsletter*, P.O. Box 81407, Las Vegas, NV 89180:

> ... The most important thing to understand is that all beings of higher intelligence fall into two simple categories. They are either working for the "free choice" system or the domination-reflection system. As beings of "reflection," they are in an exact opposite to the reality of the Creator's choice system. Higher-level entities who rule most of Earth's domination-oriented systems are cut off from even understanding or recognizing the choice system of the Creator. While in these other dimensions, these higher-level beings actually feel they are the creators of the Earth and feel humanity should give them allegiance.
>
> When humans lose their physical bodies, they often wind up in the mentally created heavens and worlds, where the leaders bleed their energies. This energy theft allows these higher-level entities to remain strong and powerful, even though they are cut off from the Creator's reality and perfection. Many of the religious books on the planet touch on some of this in allegorical ways.
>
> The entity referred to as "Satan" and 44 other entities associated with him are a fact of life on the astral planes. What brings confusion is when many alien visitors come to this planet without higher intelligence levels. They have a high knowledge level within their particular species or group awareness. Their minds are like human minds, insofar as they aren't aware of knowledge levels outside

their own. A dog doesn't try to understand or even duplicate a cat's knowledge. They couldn't understand it if they wanted to; the connection with their essence keeps their instincts and awareness in a pure state. This is a vital concept to be taken into consideration when you hear of beings that are abducted. No higher-level alien operating under the creator's free-choice system would ever infringe on the free will or choice of any intelligent life form. Only the lower-level or ignorant entities would do this. Only the domination forces of Earth would do so in full knowledge of their actions.

If ever confronted by any alien life form originating from any dimension, the most important thing you can do for your protection is to challenge them and let them know that you know your rights. Insist that they do not abridge your choice and freedom.

If you are embracing domination principles yourself, you will not be in a position to put up powerful walls and exert your full defense potential. If you have chosen to reject the domination system, you will soon be able to stand up to any forces on any dimension. You will have a vast amount of power.

7

A Tentative Taxonomy of Extra-terrestrial Humanoids

*T*he information in this chapter was given to me by a lady who has experienced multiple abductions by both types of entities described, and who insists upon retaining her anonymity. I realize that some of her statements are extremely controversial, and that the prudent course would be to refrain from relaying such explosive material to the public, because it is based entirely on unverifiable statements made by one person. However, I have now shared this with a considerable number of other abductees, many of whom feel that it correlates significantly with their own experiences, and that the information it contains is of such potential importance that it deserves a public hearing, which would be the quickest and most effective way to either confirm or invalidate it.

This is a preliminary and exploratory attempt to establish a taxonomy of extra-terrestrial humanoids. As I don't have any hard evidence to back up my statements, they must therefore be considered as speculation, though they are based on anecdotal evidence that is in my opinion sincere and truthful. The two types I am about to describe represent only a small fraction of the many types, both short and tall and of medium height, who are at present hovering above us or among us.

The first explosions of our nuclear weapons at the end of World War II sent out a signal that brought in a veritable traffic jam of entities from many different regions of this galaxy and of neighboring galaxies, as well as from many other dimensions. Besides this swarm of newcomers, we have been visited by a wide variety of extra-terrestrial and inter-dimensional life forms throughout our history and prehistoric times. However, the following two types have not only been interacting with us since deep antiquity, but are engaged in long-enduring celestial warfare, that is also being carried out on Earth. Our allegiance in this battle is a key factor.

The first type is the short gray humanoids with the large heads, which resemble embryos and average about four and half feet in height. They are from a solar system that revolves around Rigel. Rigel is a double bluish-white star on the left foot of Orion, about 800 light years from Earth. They have problems with their glands, particularly with their sebaceous glands, that make digesting food difficult. These glandular problems were caused mainly by exposure to radioactivity during a nuclear war fought in the distant past, many thousands of years ago.

This type of humanoid is performing most of the animal mutilations and human abductions, has made a secret deal with our government, and was in contact with Hitler. They derive nourishment — absorbed through their pores — from the glandular secretions and the enzymes extracted from the animals they mutilate. Our government permits such activities partially because of its acute fear of these beings, and partially because it is under the delusion that they will give us technical information enabling us to attain military superiority over the Russians in exchange for our permitting the mutilations and abductions.

The Stealth Bomber and Star Wars technologies are being obtained from them. However, our government does not appear to realize that when push comes to shove, this technology will not work as it is supposed to. It is not in these aliens' interest to give us decisive military superiority over the Russians, or vice versa. It is in their interest to keep us in a state of unresolved conflict with each other, the old game of divide and conquer.

If no animals were available, they could subsist upon gland extracts derived from humans. As a rule they do not use humans in this fashion, but they could and would in an emergency. Their attitude toward humans is to tolerate us to the extent that we are useful in raising the animals necessary for their nourishment. Despite many attempts, none of our terrestrial animals (nor their frozen sperm or ovum or embryos) have survived the long journey back to their planet.

They would not attack us with nuclear weaponry, as nuclear war would irrevocably poison or totally destroy this planet's entire biosphere, including any hypothetical human or animal survivors, who would inevitably suffer from glandular problems similar in nature to those already afflicting the aliens. They do have the ability to throw this planet off its axis.

Rigelian technology is more advanced than ours, but that is the only way in which they are more advanced than we are. They manipulate us through our laziness and ignorance.

Working under the instructions of the humanoids from Rigel, CIA and former Nazi scientists have developed and deployed malignant strains of bacteria and viruses, including AIDS. The rationale from the fascist point of view is to exterminate portions of the population considered to be undesirable. The rationale from the Rigelian point of view is to decimate the human population to such an extent that the survivors would accept open control by the Rigelians.

The Rigelians are almost entirely devoid of emotions, but can obtain a second-hand "high" by telepathically tuning in to different kinds of intense human emotion, such as ecstasy or agony. This is not done for the purpose of sadistic gratification, as most of them are oblivious to the difference between positive and negative mental states. It is a biochemical as well as a psychological process, used as a mood-elevator.

Certain types of unusual sexual practices attract these entities like flies. It was Aleister Crowley's sexual pursuits rather than anything else that attracted these entities to him to absorb the energies released. Crowley was more effective as a medium than as a magician. Some of his diatribes about trampling the weak were caused by telepathic linkage with entities who were obtaining a vicarious "high" from the intense emotion involved in such diatribes.

The humanoids that have been nicknamed "Swedes" or "Blonds" are on the average between six and six and a half feet tall. They are from a solar system that revolves around Procyon, a binary yellowish-white and yellow star system that rises before Sirius in Canis Minoris (in the body of the Lesser Dog), about 11.4 light years from Earth. They are from the fourth planet in orbit around the Procyon double star system. The tall blond humanoids from Procyon and the short gray humanoids from Rigel have been enemies for many thousands of years.

The tall Blonds from Procyon have a benign attitude toward humanity, except for their strong disapproval of our inhumanity to each other. This strong disapproval is further intensified by our government having made a secret alliance with their hereditary enemies, in order to obtain even more destructive weapons systems than those already in existence. Our government is not interested in negotiating with the Procyonians, as they would not provide us with weapons systems.

The tall blond humanoids carried out experiments that involved both artificial insemination and interbreeding with primitive humanity. The desired result was to combine the larger brain capacity of the tall Blonds with the lung capacity and respiratory system of primitive humanity, better suited to this planet's atmosphere. The sudden emergence of Cro-Magnon man was the result of their intervention. A large proportion of present-day humanity is descended from this mixed ancestry.

The Procyonians have continued to cross-breed with us at many stages of our evolutionary development, and this type of activity still goes on at the present time. They are trying to straighten out and correct the somewhat scrambled results of their earlier interventions. We turned out to be physiologically acceptable, but are as yet considered to be a psychologically unstable and immature species.

The Rigelians also perform genetic experiments on us, but are hampered by the extreme degree of difference between our species and are not capable of interbreeding with us directly.

The Procyonians tune in on us telepathically to vicariously experience our emotions, as the Rigelians do, but the Procyonian motivation is to trace and fully understand the biological and psychological ramifications of these emotions. Their motivation for breeding with humans is to tune up the frequency of our species, in order to help us to help ourselves. Their concern is for the well-being of all forms of life, not just humanity. The entire biosphere will benefit if we fulfill our positive potential, instead of self-destructing and destroying our planet's biosphere in the process.

It would be a mistake to count on them to clean up the mess we have made of our polluted planet, or to bring peace by dismantling our nuclear weapons. It is up to us to solve the problems that we have ourselves created. No one else will do this for us. Humans tend to make either Christ-figures or Satan-figures out of extra-terrestrial or inter-dimensional visitors, in order to absolve themselves from the responsibility for their own actions. This is a self-defeating strategy that does not work, that never has and never will. Awaiting a savior from the sky is a recipe for disaster. If we each do our very best to tilt the balance toward the continued improvement of our species and the quality of life on this planet, we stand a chance of resolving the immense problems we are faced with, but there are no guarantees. Christ-consciousness should not be confused with Christ. It is easy to kneel in awe. It is far more demanding to develop the full spectrum of awareness that is Christ-consciousness. It is up to us to shape our own destiny.

Although the Procyonians are from a specific physical place within our galaxy, they can also travel through time and between dimensions. The Rigelians do not have these abilities. The Procyonians frequently use mechanical vehicles for transport, but are not exclusively dependent on them (as the Rigelians are), because they can also use thought processes to teleport themselves physically. Our own legends indicate that a few rare and highly developed human adepts have occasionally acquired this ability. No mechanical vehicle can equal or exceed the speed of light, but such teleportation can. The process requires de-materialization and re-material-ization.

The name by which the Procyonians call their home planet translates into English as "the home of those who travel through time." The stone circles and megaliths constructed under their supervision in deep antiquity were geocentrically and celestially aligned to give access to time travel, thereby serving as time portals. It was also possible to acquire access to other dimensions through them.

In order to extricate ourselves from the covert alliance the CIA has made with Rigel, without our knowledge or consent, we must first regain control of our government.

At this point Khyla of Procyon, the Watcher who transmitted the information contained in this chapter, intervened to make the following statement:

> Tyrants have been defeated many times on many planets, in countless solar systems and galaxies. How strange it is that as soon as one tyrant of any species is thought to be banished forever, another always, but always, takes his place. The idealistic revolutionaries who defeated King George III in America went on to oppress the Indians and Blacks. Many of those who fought most courageously against the Axis powers of fascism later became fascists themselves, as is demonstrated by the present plight of the Palestinians, Afghans, Chileans and Nicaraguans. Yes, you must try to regain control of your government, but if so much as one individual involved in this process has not first gained control of his or her selfhood, it will be for naught. One can never defeat or gain control of anything but oneself. Those destined to oust the Rigelians must always keep track of the state of their selfhood, and learn first to defeat within themselves the essence of that which is tyranny. Through this type of awareness, they will know when to act and when not to act. Through understanding a hostile entity to be but one of the Ineffable's countless facades, it loses its power over you. Through the ability to wisely perceive a hostile entity, you may gain control of it. In overcoming the Rigelians, one must take great precautions not to become oneself the enemy. Certain levels of conscious existence will always be subject to tyranny. It is the nature of the vibratory rate. Gain control of yourself by ceasing to try to control. Anything you try to conquer, you only make stronger. Lao Tse

was one of our best pupils. Although he was not of human origin, Padma Sambhava evolved to such an extent during his life on earth in human form that his development surpasses ours, as our development surpasses that of ordinary terrestrial humans with their three-dimensional awareness. We have multi-dimensional awareness, but the awareness of Padma Sambhava is omni-dimensional. He transmits to me much of what I am telling you. We do not align ourselves with the terrestrial hierarchy that formed around the tradition he left behind him, but we do maintain communication with his very much alive omni-dimensional presence. Such communication still remains available to terrestrial humans who seek it with whole-hearted single-pointed devotion, either within or outside the context of the Mahayana Buddhist hierarchy. The Tibetan legends about the sacred treasures concealed by the lotus-born Root Guru for humanity's future time of greatest need refer to physically real objects of power whose retrieval will be essential to humanity's survival in the forthcoming apocalyptic struggle. They cannot be retrieved until Tibet is returned to the Tibetans. The Scandinavian legends concerning Odainsakr refer to these same objects. The Watchers have always been here. Those who hear or touch or are touched by them will evolve themselves into Watchers. All cultures go through a stage of high technological achievement prior to learning that everything they get their machines to accomplish can be done with pure thought. The Watchers need no tools to contact any mind. Humanity as a collective entity may create whatever destiny it chooses for itself. These paths include enslavement, nuclear destruction, and peaceful flourishing growth. Whatever path humanity selects is right for it. Souls do not cease to exist. If this planet is destroyed, they will go on to learn elsewhere. If you are free from the fetters of illusion, no force can harm you. To escape, one merely accepts. To accept is to transcend. When you know unceasingly that even in a nuclear holocaust both antagonists, the battle itself, and the perception of that whole event is the oneness of the Ineffable in a dance with its shadow, you will no longer need to exist at this level. The entire cosmos is but the manifestation of the mind and light and energy of the one Ineffable. War is neither right nor wrong. Wisdom can be gained on any path. Even that which seems certain folly is only a play of light and shadow. There are countless ways to learn. It is merely more pleasant to select a curriculum that is less prone to being painful. If an individual or a collective entity elects to learn through suffering, so be it. There are less traumatic ways to gather understanding. The Rigelians and the CIA have put in motion the potential for a rather drastic mode of learning. This can be altered at any time. Whatever it may be, the outcome is always as it should be. However, this does not mean that we should sit back and take no action.

The ancestors of the short Grays were once tall Blonds. The Great War took place. Behold the bitter fruit of victory. The Grays are a genetically damaged species. If terrestrial humans were to survive a nuclear winter, they might well look like that, several generations later. Before the great war, Rigel was a vast empire, which had been the source of most galactic seeding. All Rigelians were tall Blonds. A colony had already been established on Procyon. The Great War was a civil war of Rigelians versus Rigelians, and lasted the equivalent of three Earth centuries.

A group of Rigelians who realized that the Great War was about to break out took off for the Procyon colony in crude, clandestinely built ships. At that time, all the sophisticated equipment was owned by the State. They were the only Rigelians to escape the cataclysmic devastation. All those who had remained on Rigel were transformed into the short Grays.

After the Great War, when the Rigelians had become the short Grays, it took them thousands of years to reconstruct their society. They were damaged not only genetically and in their glandular systems, but also mentally and psychologically. As soon as the short Grays had reconstituted a power base, they launched an attack on the tall Blonds who had escaped to the Procyon colony.

Although the Blonds of Procyon had been spared the extreme chromosome and glandular damage sustained by those who had stayed behind on Rigel, they did suffer some radiation damage, which was minor in comparison, during their warfare with the Grays. However, this damage has rendered their females vulnerable to a disease that is decimating their numbers. The mute telepathic Blonds, who do not have speech abilities, suffered more extensive radiation damage than those who retained their speech ability.

Two major wars are still in progress. The one between Rigel and Procyon is presently in a state of temporary truce. Active fighting could break out at any time, comparable to the recent U.S.-Soviet cold war situation. The war between Rigel and the Sirius system is being fought actively.

Earth was seeded by the original tall blond Rigelians, before the Great War took place. The original tall blond Rigelians were the progenitors of Cro-Magnon man. It is because of this common ancestry that terrestrial humanity is of such interest to both the Blonds and the Grays. The abductees who are not returned are used for breeding purposes, and are generally treated well.

Terrestrial human females can be impregnated either on board ship or while they sleep in their homes. Males need not be manifested in visible form for this to occur.

Both Grays and Blonds have the ability to disintegrate matter into energy, then reintegrate the energy back into matter. That is how they pass through, and transport abductees through, walls and roofs.

Grays have the ability to camouflage themselves as tall Blonds through mental energy projection. Blonds do not ever project themselves as Grays. Sometimes Blonds are physically real but are prisoners of the Grays. The Grays must paralyze or destroy the Blonds ability to teleport through time and other dimensions in order to take them prisoner.

Just as terrestrial warfare includes traitors, defectors, deserters, and prisoners of war, so are there in warfare between extra-terrestrials. And just as in terrestrial warfare there are periods of truce, during which teams from opposing armies may cooperate temporarily on certain projects, so are there periods of truce in warfare between extra-terrestrials.

Some Blonds have high intellectual and verbal abilities, while others are mute and telepathic. The Blonds with speech abilities will respond violently if attacked or threatened, but the telepathic type will not. Both types are careful to avoid exposure, and usually encounter humans in quiet isolated places. They contact females more frequently. They may just stare and observe humans, then retreat. Blonds were sometimes mistaken for angels in earlier centuries. The Blonds do not seem to age and consistently appear to be from 27 to 35 human years old, no matter what their real age may be.

More than one type of extra-terrestrial visitor is interbreeding with humans. The Blonds are the ideal choice to interbreed with humans of all races, because there is a common genetic ancestor. Interbreeding of humans with any other species must be carefully controlled, as humans have different immune systems than extra-terrestrials. New hybrid bacterial strains can cause disaster both ways. Blonds can infect humans, and humans can infect Blonds. Blonds may be carrying viral and bacterial microorganisms that are safe to themselves but harmful to humans, and vice versa.

The Grays consider the Blonds to be rebellious and unstable. The Grays try to prevent the Blonds they have taken prisoner from escaping to explore terrestrial humanity unsupervised. However, a substantial number of such Blonds have escaped and are intermingling with humans.

There are over 1,000 humans in the United States alone who are the offspring of inter-galactic or extra-galactic beings and terrestrial humans. Of these, about 200 know or suspect their origin.

All humans have some extra-terrestrial genetic background. If they did not, all that would exist on this planet would be flora and fauna that included but did not go beyond the apes. The clams, worms, starfish, sponges, and other primitive organisms from which the entire flora and fauna of this planet evolved were deposited in the primeval oceans as the preliminary phase of planetary seeding, as is obvious from any study of the record left in the Cambrian and Pre-Cambrian rocks.

Throughout recorded history, as well as during prehistoric times, there has been constant genetic manipulation of and interbreeding with humans in order to breed out our less evolved simian traits. Sometimes interbreeding between humans and space beings has been a success, and sometimes it has been a dismal failure. However, Homo sapiens would not exist if it had not been for this persistent genetic manipulation and interbreeding, which will continue (unless nuclear war destroys our species) until humanity fulfills its potential by learning to use its total brain, instead of a mere fraction of it.

The woman who transmitted this information to me described her contact as follows:

> Khyla looked like a tall handsome human, slender but muscular, masculine yet ethereal. He appeared either naturally or artificially to have black around his eyes, almost like kohl. His face was close to exquisite, but definitely masculine. He had a gaunt face with high cheekbones and piercing cobalt-blue eyes. He had fine blond hair that was almost shoulder-length. He had a muscular neck. His skin was pale flesh color, with a whitish overtone. It is hard to gauge his exact height because of the circumstances under which our encounter occurred, but it was somewhere between six and seven feet.

Here is some more of what he told her:

> If you were a highly advanced culture about to invade a relatively primitive culture, you would not do it with a flourish of ships showing up in the heavens and take the risk of being fired upon. That's the type of warfare less-evolved mortals would get into. You would begin by creating intense confusion, with only inferences of your presence, inferences which cause controversial disagreement.
>
> You would go to the most secret and powerful organizations within the society. In the case of the United States, you would infil-

trate the CIA, and through the use of techniques unknown to them, you would take over some of the key people in their inmost core group. You would proceed in the same fashion to take over key members of the KGB. You would also create great dissension among the public at large, some individuals and groups insisting that they have seen UFOs, others insisting with equal vehemence that such a thing is not possible, and that they are either liars or deluded.

You would involve the planet's two major nations in an ongoing idiotic philosophical dispute, keeping them constantly at each other's throats over such questions as whether Thomas Jefferson was greater than Karl Marx or vice-versa. You would keep them continuously occupied with quarreling like two adolescent boys trying to prove their masculinity over who has which piece of territory, whether one has the right to invade Afghanistan or the other has the right to invade Nicaragua, persistently exchanging threats and insults like a couple of macho teenagers, while arguing whether one should dismantle one type of nuclear warhead, or the other should dismantle another type of nuclear warhead. As you watched all this, you would sit back and you would laugh, if you had the capacity to laugh.*

You would make yourselves known to various elite in-groups, who would offer you protection out of greed, expecting to acquire more perfect knowledge than anyone else on the planet of this ultimate secret to end all secrets. They would covet you, and you would trust their covetousness and their crass stupidity to trap them. You would do it on both sides of the Iron Curtain.

You would occasionally let your ships be seen by some of the

---

* The information in this chapter was given to me before the advent of St. Gorby, which transformed the Red Menace of the Evil Empire into our long-lost brothers-in-arms and comrades-in-camaraderie, freedom-loving democracy-demanding kindred spirits. In the euphoric thaw that characterizes U.S.-Soviet relations as of the month of December 1989, some statements in this chapter are no longer accurate. However, they do remain valid as descriptions of the Cold War mentality, which for so long afflicted both nations that it constitutes a history lesson that we should never forget. Post-Script: No sooner had I inserted this note than George Bush sent an emissary to shake the hand of the Butcher of Tienanmen Square and broke the treaty we had so solemnly signed with the Organization of American States by arrogantly invading Panama without consulting our allies, thereby escalating international tension back to the previous intolerable levels, single-handedly reviving the Cold War nightmare in order to avoid cutting one single dime from the so-called "Defense" budget.

ordinary citizens, so that the elite governmental groups would become involved in attempts to keep them quiet, clumsily squelching attempts to make information about UFO activity public. This would result in the mass population losing confidence in the veracity of their elected officials. There would be constant arguments between the authorities and the public as to whether or not the persistently reported phenomena genuinely existed, thereby setting the population and the government at each other's throats. You would have already set the two major super-powers at each other's throats. By subtly causing economic turmoil, you would set the "Haves" and the "Have-Nots" at each other's throats. In all possible ways, you would plant the seeds of massive discontent.

After you had manipulated the population to the point where your covert control over it was complete, you might decide to go overt and let a few ships land in public. But you would not go from covert to overt until you were sure of the totality of your control.

You would start doing cross-breeds, escalating the process to the maximum from generation to generation. As the process continued, you would begin to have more and more creatures walking around who were obviously hybrids between the Grays and humans. Perhaps in a century or two, some of the Grays would begin to physically intermingle with Earthlings. But for the time being, anything that walks around will at least look as if it is human. This arrangement is simpler, because it keeps mass panic to a minimum.

The Grays would not be at all reluctant to change their appearance. In comparison with most of the other space races, they are considered rather repulsive. They are interbreeding with humans on an ever-increasing scale, and there are going to be a lot more three-month interrupted pregnancies.

Those who have experienced UFO sightings or E.T. close encounters will constantly be at odds with the government, which will continue to retaliate by stigmatizing them as liars or deluded. The U.S. and the U.S.S.R. will continue to play their adolescent prestige games with nuclear weaponry. The impoverished will become even more impoverished, and more filled to overflowing with explosively righteous anger. The wealthy will cling even more greedily to the wealth that they already have, creating a social atmosphere of sheer desperation and complete confusion. To add to that, there will be series after series of "natural" disasters, some genuinely natural, some human-induced through aberrant scientific activities such as underground nuclear testing, others deliberately induced by the

Grays through the technology they possess. When approximately three-quarters of the planet's population has been eliminated in this fashion, the Grays can then make an overt appearance as saviors from the skies, distributing food and medicine to the survivors. As the survivors line up to receive their quotas of food and medicine, implants will be inserted, supposedly to aid in further food distribution, actually to guarantee complete Gray control with no possibility of rebellion. From the point of view of the Grays, terrestrial humanity will have been reduced to manageable numbers and to eternal submission.

Humanity is not about to be invaded. Humanity is not in the middle of an invasion. Humanity has been invaded, and the invasion is nearly in its final stages. Great invasions do not happen with thundering smoke and nuclear weaponry. That is the mark of an immature society. Great invasions happen in secrecy.

You throw a crumb out here and there. You bribe the U.S. government with a few tidbits — a Stealth Bomber, a Star Wars system. You encourage the government to think that the UFO researchers indeed threaten the security of this great secret they have. You tempt and tease the Soviet Union with a laser system far finer than any their own scientists could devise. And you always keep that subtle inference just on the borderline of consciousness that the elusive will-of-the-wisps termed UFOs may in fact exist, yet you persistently repress this borderline perception and make it seem so insane that there is a social stigma attached to declaring one's conviction that the phenomena are real.

While all this confusion is going on, the Grays are gradually changing you over. The inner core of the CIA is deeply controlled by the Grays. The CIA sees the Grays as a path to greater scientific achievement, as a way of overpowering the Soviet enemy. Surprisingly enough, the obtuse collective mentality type that makes up the bulk of the CIA also makes up the bulk of the more fanatic Star People, those who babble and mush and gush so endlessly. All those who have to cleave to or be fused with some sort of group mentality leave themselves wide open. They have already been taken over. There is a large and ever-growing cult of contactees who think of the Grays as liberators, sincerely believing them to be heavenly Star Brothers who have come to help humanity.

The reason the awful little Grays mutilate animals is the stuff that they eat. They eat pulverized hormonal secretions, what you would call *subtle essences*. They live on the stuff of life. There is something deathlike about their species. They always bring about the death of animation, the death of individuality.

How do I know? I am a Blond of Procyon. We were a culture that could travel through time, but also lived on a planetary sphere. And the little Grays, our insidious little friends, did to us exactly what they are doing now to you. This is what happened to our planet.

Having come in war, but having been unable to obtain any decisive victory, the Grays expressed the desire to make peace. We had not wanted to fight with the survivors of the Rigelian Great War to begin with, and gladly accepted their offer. As time went by, they said they wished to normalize relations and be our friends. We were in doubt as to whether it would be safe to trust them, and debated the issue for a long time before finally deciding that we should trust them. They were the only other surviving remnant of our original ancestral stock, although they were horribly deformed by the misfortunes they had endured.

The Grays began to visit us, first a few as ambassadors, then as specialists in various domains where their expertise could be useful to us, as participants in different programs that involved mutual collaboration, and finally as tourists. What had begun as a trickle became a flood, as they came in ever-increasing numbers, slowly but surely infiltrating our society at all levels, penetrating even the most secret of our elite power groups. The one secret that remained beyond their grasp, because the part of their intelligence that was capable of understanding its subtle complexities had atrophied during the nuclear winter that had caused the mutation of their species, was the Blonds ability to transcend and travel through time.

How then did we fail to foresee our own future, and the fatal mistake we were making when we first let them in? Just as on your planet they began by unobtrusively gaining control over key members of the CIA and KGB through techniques unknown to them, such as telepathic hypnosis that manipulates the reptilian levels of the brain, so on Procyon through the same techniques, whose existence we were not aware of either, from the start they established a kind of telepathic hypnotic control over our leaders. Over our leaders and over almost all of us, because it was as if we were under a spell that was leading us to our doom, as if we were being programmed by a type of ritual black magic that we did not realize existed.

Just as a few of the original tall Blonds clandestinely left Rigel when the Great War was about to break out, so did a few of the original tall Blonds clandestinely leave Procyon and escape into the corridors of time just before the Grays completed the slow undermining that culminated in their sudden takeover of Procyon. Those who stayed behind came under the total domination of the Grays.

The Blonds you see on the same ships as the Grays, working with them, are hybrids, or they are clones. One way to distinguish the clones is that they look alike. The real Blonds have distinct facial feature differences and do not look alike.

The clones have thick necks and coarsely muscular bodies. They do not have the ability to teleport or to travel interdimensionally. They can be contacted by telepathy, but are unable to send. They can be given orders telepathically. They are zombie-like flesh robots. You can tell that they are of low intelligence by looking into their eyes.

The real Blonds are also muscular, but have slender necks and agile bodies. Their eyes are alert and of high intelligence. Physically they are almost identical to humans, the main difference being that by human standards their blood circulatory system is under-developed, while their lymphatic system is over-developed. This gives them stronger immune systems than terrestrial humans.

The hybrids are in an intermediate state between the real Blonds and the clones.

After what has happened to Procyon, no true Blond would collaborate voluntarily with the Grays. The Grays have taken some prisoners of war, who have no choice in the matter, and are forced to work with them in order to survive, with the hope of escaping. There are also a few Blonds who have become degenerate renegades, space pirates and mercenaries who sell their services to the highest bidder. But many of us remain free and continue the fight to the finish with the life-form that has become our hereditary enemy. We choose to remain in exile in the corridors of time, where they can not reach us, rather than to live under the domination of the insidious Grays. It is dangerous for us to venture forth from the corridors of time, but occasionally we do so for a hit-and-run strike, similar in nature to a cosmic version of terrestrial guerrilla warfare.

We must periodically enter a substantial physical form for a period of repose, or to breed progeny, in order to continue to survive, but otherwise we constantly travel the vast corridors of time. That is why we may appear to fade in and out like holographic images to human perception. What I have come here to communicate, if only to one or two people or a small group, is that what is now in the process of happening to your culture also happened to ours. It is the same fate our own culture suffered. And the Blonds you see with the Grays are either hybrids, clones, or prisoners of war, because no true Blond who got out untouched, unscathed, uncrossed with those Grays would ever be with them. He or she would prefer to be in a state of non-existence.

Besides the Blonds and the Grays, ships from many other space cultures are watching planet Earth at this time with extreme interest. Scientists from other space cultures are studying what is going on here during this decisive period of your history. If your elected representatives had not so stupidly made a deal with the only aliens willing to provide them with weapons systems — with the short-sighted goal of overpowering the Russians — the Grays would not have achieved their present dominance, and you would now be exchanging ambassadors with a wide variety of space cultures.

What I want to get across to you is that the ultimate evil, which underlies all the negativity in the cosmos, finds expression in that masked form of psychological complacency that leads an individual to adhere to a group philosophy rather than to think things through for oneself. Those who feel safe and comfortable in no matter what belief system merely because many others adhere to it — who get together and form an arrogant self-righteous group convinced it has a monopoly on the truth, and who are ready to persecute, kill or stifle anyone who challenges that group's philosophy — have formed an alliance with the ultimate evil, whether they know it or not. It is the self-righteousness and implacability of certain elite power groups like the CIA and the KGB, certain organized religions, and certain so-called lunatic fringe groups such as some of the more fanatical Star People, which are so objectionable. It is as if the self-righteous elite power groups and the self-righteous lunatic fringe groups were mirror opposites of each other, and thus equivalent to each other. The elite groups see the fringe groups as their enemies, and vice versa, but they each think of themselves as a "chosen" special group. As soon as you become involved in a belief system that you are a "chosen" special group, who are as lords over the common folk because of your secret knowledge, you are on your way to a fall. That type of attitude plants the seed of destruction in any society or culture, leaving it vulnerable to overthrow by those oppressed within its boundaries, as well as by outside forces. All cultures who have elite groups at odds with each other, and with the population at large, sooner or later collapse from either internal or external pressures.

A healthy organism does not isolate portions of itself that cease to interchange freely with other portions of its body. This type of condition is a prelude to cancer, whether it occurs in an individual or in a society. The only chance of retaining your freedom is for the awareness of this principle to penetrate the consciousness of humanity. It is a pearl of wisdom treasured by those who have attained the ability to travel through time and other life cycles.

I have seen civilizations rise and fall and begin again, only to die again, over and over and over. It isn't only a problem of this planet. It's a problem that must be faced by all civilizations in the course of their development, no matter where they are in the cosmos. Everyone wants that slightly larger piece of the pie than their neighbor for themselves, and eventually this tendency culminates in choking them. Sooner or later this will be the undoing of the Grays as well, thereby enabling us to return in triumph from our exile in the corridors of time. The Grays do not see and are incapable of understanding their own fundamental error: that the very weakness they seize upon in humanity is their own inherent weakness, the blind spot that inevitably seals their doom.

Minerals evolve into plants, plants into animals, animals into humans, and humans into angelic energy-forms. But to try to force a rock, when it is in the state of being a rock, to perform like a plant is utterly futile. To try and change the arrogant mentality of a self-righteous government official or of a fanatical Star Person is as futile as trying to make a rock perform like a plant, unless the individual has matured to the point of being ripe for major change.

That is what a traveler through time learns: nothing in the cosmos can ever be forced. Everything happens and unfolds as it should, even when you are confronted with the idiocy that has brought about the potential end of your species as you know it. It is a challenge to be faced, just as Paul Revere and Thomas Paine and John Paul Jones faced the challenges of their time. May it bring out the best in you!

Through facing it wisely, without falling into the traps set by your oppressors, may you learn to fulfill your potential, which includes the ability to travel through time!

For you to fight the Grays on a military level is an impossibility. Even an alliance between the U.S. and the U.S.S.R. could not do it. The Grays' technology is too far in advance of yours. It would be like bows and arrows versus machine guns, and this time around, you would be the ones with the bows and arrows. They can use electro-magnetics to axis-switch this planet or take it out of orbit. Because of their technological advantage, active resistance would be suicidal and foolhardy rather than courageous. If you took hostages, so would they. They can get to you, but you can't get to where they come from. Not even their moon base is vulnerable to you. It is necessary to fight in another manner, through passive resistance.

At this stage, one thing you can do is to provide the public with as much information as possible. This will make it more difficult for the collaborators and Grays in disguise within the government to continue to work against humanity in favor of the Grays. Tell the public how to put their minds into a state that the Grays cannot penetrate, by focusing the mind on powerful imagery, different for each individual. The only way to victory is through the strength of your consciousness. When genetic or other manipulations are being performed on the abductees, the Grays expect them to cringe in fear; then the Grays can derive a second-hand high from the intensity of the emotions expressed. If instead of cringing in fear, an abductee can put his or her mind elsewhere, focusing attention on dynamic protective imagery of a religious or mystical nature, it decreases the gratification that the Grays are getting from their second-hand high, and it confuses them. Center the consciousness on something so different from what they expect that it puzzles them. No matter what the physical situation may be, it is essential to send this S.O.S. telepathic message to the higher powers protective of humanity without becoming entangled in negative emotions such as fear, rage or hatred. Negative emotions not only diminish the effectiveness of one's S.O.S. message to the higher powers in the universe, they are the type of response that the Grays are used to evoking and are expert at manipulating. If you combat the Grays with hatred in your heart, you become like them and further entangled with them, instead of free from them. A difficulty with the viewpoint of many of the adherents of organized religions is that they tend to perceive the Grays as demons, and therefore to hate them. Although to some extent this analogy is valid, hatred is a form of attachment, a negative emotion the Grays know will bind you to them. A more correct perception is that the Grays are a species that is terminally ill, having exhausted their DNA, and are therefore in a state of desperation. That is why they are so ruthless in their genetic and other experimentation. Their physical bodies are degenerating from generation to generation. The Grays do not have progeria, but their DNA is running out and no longer replicates properly, so they are unable to replenish themselves. It is not progeria, but it is similar to progeria, almost like a progeria of the entire species.

It should be remembered that aggressive behavior or attempts at physical resistance during an abduction may result in death. The Grays have no more compunction about taking human life than humans have about taking reptilian life. While one is in their power, one has no more control over what happens physically than does the victim of a human kidnapper or rapist. Their "chosen ones" are attempting to sugar-coat the bitter pill and get you all to stand in line to be processed without any effective resistance, like cattle into hamburger, depicting abduction by the Grays as a glorious experience that everyone should have. These "chosen ones" are the "bell-wethers" that Charles Fort referred to.

There are other E.T. groups you would be happy to work with and travel in the vehicles of, but the track record that the Grays have left behind them leaves no room for doubt as to their malignancy. The only reason the Grays have such a degree of dominance over you is because your elected officials stupidly made clandestine agreements with them, binding you to them in an exclusive alliance that is respected by other space races, allowing them to install themselves in underground bases impregnable to your weaponry, a situation from which you must now extricate yourselves.

In antiquity this planet was divided into sectors among four different groups: Blonds, Grays, large lizard-like beings from the Capella system, and beings from the Arcturus system. These groups still consider themselves to be the owners of this planet. They do not recognize the human claim to ownership. However, some of us do recognize human rights, as well as the rights of other life-forms. An alliance now exists between the tall Blonds and the large lizard-like beings from the Capella system to drive out the Grays. The beings from the Arcturus system are neutral observers and are not participating in the conflict. The Blonds and Capellans have deep moral repugnance for the current activities of the Grays on this planet and are willing to help humanity, if humanity will take effective steps to stop its pollution of the planetary environment. The Grays have become a criminal species and will be treated as such. However, any species that pollutes its own environment to the point of endangering the survival of its planetary biosphere is also guilty of a cosmic crime.

The space shuttle "Challenger" was destroyed because one of its scheduled operations was an experimental attempt to dispose of nuclear waste by projecting it into outer space. Vehicles of other cultures could collide with canisters of nuclear waste projected into outer space. Canisters could also be broken open by meteor showers and contaminate whole zones of the universe. It was not an intelligent idea to try and shoot a canister out from the space shuttle. It is not enough to launch canisters beyond the periphery of your solar system. There must be a preplanned crash on a specific target. The only safe way is to select a system that is about to super-nova, and then send an unmanned spaceship loaded with nuclear waste on a collision course directly into that solar system's central sun. The second-best solution would be to send a ship on a collision course into the sun of a solar system where conditions are incompatible with the existence of life-forms. To send it into your own sun could cause a solar flare that would reduce all forms of life on Earth to dust and ashes. The nuclear waste produced on Earth must be kept on Earth until a safe way to project it to a suitable target area is found. Jupiter is the closest target to Earth that is acceptable for this purpose.

Enochian is the lingua franca of the space races, much as Swahili was the lingua franca of the many African languages. Enochian is the correct time-tested traditional way for Earthlings to communicate with extra-terrestrials. In the Golden Dawn Enochian system, the Great King of Air is the appropriate intermediary to be called upon as a benign go-between in negotiations between Earthlings and extra-terrestrials. Enochian was the ancestral root-language of the original Blonds on Rigel before the Great War.

Although active resistance to the Grays would not be advisable at the present time, because of their technological advantage, this does not mean that you should surrender. It means that you should focus your attention on the different techniques of passive resistance that may be applicable to the situation, making the fullest possible use of your individuality, which so puzzles and confuses their collective hive mentality. As collective thought patterns enhance the ability of the Grays to manipulate you, original thinkers acting on their own are more likely to have success than mass movements led by leaders who do everyone else's thinking for them.

In preventing the take-over of your planet as a colony ruled by Gray overlords, you should go back through your own history and learn what you can from the techniques of passive resistance used to bring about the independence of India, used by the American Indians and Blacks during their oppression in the United States, by the Blacks in South Africa at the present time, by the French Resistance during the Nazi occupation, and anywhere else in your historical records where there are lessons of this nature to be learned. The point of passive resistance is to endure, to survive until the moment when it becomes possible to switch over to active resistance because outside help has come — being careful to avoid the mistake of the citizens of Budapest, who rose up believing propaganda assurances that the United States would support their uprising, only to be crushed by Soviet tanks when no such help was forthcoming. Prematurely triggered active resistance would be a disaster that would enable the Grays to perpetuate their colonization of this planet, exactly the type of situation they would try to bring about. Beware of zealots with an obsessive hatred of the Grays, who may have been subconsciously programmed by the Grays to act as agent provocateurs. If you get all those sincerely devoted to resistance together into one place, it is much easier to wipe them out. If the resistance remains disseminated among the population at large, it is more difficult to round them up. Don't add to the superiority of the Gray position by playing into their hands. And remember that although their technology is far in advance of yours, you do vastly out-number them and can over-extend them. They are already over-extended elsewhere and unable to commit further forces to this area of the universe, so those already here must operate without reinforcements coming to them.

You are so far outstripped in terms of physical weaponry that you must find a source of strength that transcends the physical — such as techniques of centering consciousness on powerfully motivating imagery, which would be different from one individual to another. For the religiously oriented it might be a key event in the life of Jesus, Buddha, Mohammed, Moses, or whoever the appropriate figure would be in one's belief system. For those who are not religiously oriented, it would be whatever figure that person sincerely admires as representing what is best in humanity, whether it be an artist or inventor or other type of benevolent leader of society. If the admiration is not wholeheartedly sincere, it will not be sufficient to be of much use as protection, nor can the attention be maintained for long. The degree of protection given by such imagery depends largely on the intensity and endurance of the single-pointed attention. So it is best to choose whatever figure you genuinely feel spontaneous admiration for, whatever image makes your heart sing and makes you feel at one with the infinite. That will always work and is all we can do for now.

An example of the type of attitude that the Grays find most confusing is the classic Buddhist discipline of meditating on a bloated corpse until one roars with laughter upon realizing what a complete cosmic joke existence is. The most likely way to extricate oneself and others from a potentially disastrous situation is to keep the consciousness centered and the heart still, realizing the situation to be the illusion that it is. Do not act out of fear, thereby ensuring the victory of the opponent. If one allows oneself to be intimidated, the inevitable result is death. In no matter what type of situation, retain your sense of humor and perspective. Learn to apply the T'ai Ch'i disciplines in non-physical fashion. Center yourself, then act from that center.

Since the Grays have mastered much deeper techniques of hypnosis than humans have, their takeover of human consciousness can only be prevented by strong imagery of a religious or mystical nature. Your contemporary hypnosis works within the mammalian portions of your brain, which in terms of evolutionary development are the more recently acquired portions. Being partially reptilian themselves, the Grays know how to manipulate the reptilian level of your brain, which is the most basic and ancient level. The only way to counteract such manipulation is by activating the most high of the highest levels of consciousness accessible to you at your present stage of development. If one is unable to maintain an image evoking that highest level of consciousness firmly in one's thoughts, their hypnosis can bypass the higher levels of your evolutionary development and take control of the deep reptilian level. In this fashion they can overpower an individual's true will and obliterate the integrity of the soul. That is how they took over key officials of the CIA, KGB, and other powerful elite groups within your social structure. They only need to control the elite at the tip of the top of the social pyramid, the top hundredth of one percent of the population, in order to control the entire population. A person enslaved in this fashion can be made to do things that your type of hypnosis could not make them do, such as murdering their closest friends or family members.

Having gained control over the reptilian level of consciousness, they temporarily paralyze all portions of the mammalian brain higher than the ape level, then activate the ape level's more violent responses, such as territorialism, greed, lust, or rage. Humans can be made to respond like apes, unless they are able to resist the attempt to take them over by activating the level of consciousness that corresponds to the crown *chakra*. Any attempt to fight back at the ape level ensures the success of the Grays. The ape-level belligerence, territorialism, and posturing for purposes of prestige and dominance, which are unfortunately so characteristic of the U.S.-U.S.S.R. relationship on both sides, deliver the population of this planet into the power of the Grays.

After having destroyed approximately three-quarters of the present population through the introduction of viral diseases and the inducement of assorted catastrophes, the Grays would not even need to make an overt appearance as saviors from the skies. They could unobtrusively replace humans with hybrids. It could be done so gradually that no one would realize what was happening. The transition from humans to hybrids could be so subtle and seamless that the changeover would never be noticed. It would not even be mentioned in the history books, as scientists would assume that the physical and mental changes were the result of naturally occurring evolution. Human history would become hybrid history without anyone understanding what had actually occurred. The governments might even continue to deny the existence of UFOs.

All that would be needed would be to continue the process that is already in operation. Some researchers are aware of the fact that the hybrids that turn out to resemble the Grays are removed from their mothers and taken elsewhere, but very few are aware that the hybrids which turn out to resemble humans are left to grow up in human society.

Before taking hybrids back to their home base to give a much-needed genetic boost to their own ancestral stock, they would want to carry out intensive long-range studies. Certain questions would need to be answered, such as: Are the hybrids psychologically stable? Disease resistant? Productive? Aggressive? They would want to observe the interplay between humans and hybrids, in order to make sure that the hybrids had the qualities necessary to become leaders in human society. In general, Gray/human hybrids would require less food and sleep than terrestrial humans. They would tend to be more intelligent and slender, but emotionally cold. This does not mean that any human with these characteristics is necessarily a hybrid. As many as 3% of the present population may already be hybrids. All the Grays would have to do would be to continue doing exactly what they are doing, to keep boosting that percentage bit by bit, with an occasional sudden jump in the wake of seemingly natural catastrophes, until the original human population has been 100% replaced by hybrids.

Why do I know so well how such an operation is carried out? The process is quite similar to that by which the Blonds replaced Neanderthal man with Cro-Magnon man. However, the intelligence of terrestrial humanity has now evolved to the point where it has a choice in the matter. By understanding the long-term hive-mind strategy of the Grays, individual humans who attain multi-dimensional awareness can circumvent and short-circuit it. If enough individual humans do this, and refrain from quarreling over whether the state of multi-dimensional awareness is to be called Christ-consciousness or any of the other names it has in the different traditions, uniting together from all traditions to liberate the planet, the Grays will be obliged to seek elsewhere in the cosmos for a slave species they can genetically manipulate.

At some point help may come from outside, from my own and/or some of the other space races. There may also be revolt within the ranks of the Grays, based on widespread discontent with their rigid insectile hierarchical caste system. In the process of infiltrating a species, the Grays cannot avoid being influenced by that species, and some of them who had never thought of questioning authority are beginning to do so, because of the influence of human contact. The Grays are having problems not only within their own ranks, but also on other planets they have colonized. As a species they are afflicted with severe, perhaps terminal, health problems. They have substantial captive populations of Blond, human and other prisoners of war, eager to join a revolt at the slightest opportunity.

There is no reason that one should not send out telepathic appeals for help, in the form of prayer or meditation, or in whatever way is appropriate to the individual, to the higher forces in the cosmos. They do exist, and are sensitive to such signals. There are extra-terrestrial and other-dimensional cultures capable of harnessing the innate power of entire galaxies, who could be of immeasurable help in liberating your planet from domination by the Grays, if you could persuade them to intervene. However, they are unlikely to respond until humanity cleans up its own act and stops polluting the planetary environment. One can also send out telepathic signals of encouragement to those among the Grays who have begun to question authority and acquire a taste for human freedom, but it would be suicidal to attempt to fight the Grays directly with the weapons now at your disposal.

One must be rational in attempting to fight back, and understand the proper way to proceed. Your own consciousness is the most potent weapon that is available to you at the present time. The most effective way to fight the Grays is to change the level of your consciousness from linear thinking to multi-dimensional awareness. Your secret weapon, your ace in the hole, is that you are not hive-mind collective thinkers, though many of you do fall into that category by conforming to conventional group-patterns and are therefore easily controlled by the Grays. Collective thought-patterns among humans empower the Grays. It is your individuality that is your best weapon, because it is the one weapon you have that the Grays do not. The major weakness of the Grays, their area of vulnerability, their Achilles heel, is their inability to think as individuals. They are an extremely telepathic high-tech society, but as individuals they are not creative thinkers. They take orders well, but they do not conceptualize well. They have the technology to throw your planet out of orbit, but there is one key ability that you have and they do not have: the ability to hold in mind imagery that inspires an individual to realize his or her direct personal connection to the source of all that is, which is the ineffable Godhead, no matter what name you may call it. That is your key to victory.

8

A Hall of Mirrors with a Quicksand Floor

by Linda Moulton Howe
(Author of *An Alien Harvest*, published by
LMH Productions, P.O. Box 538, Huntingdon Valley, PA 19006)

*O*n September 1, 1979, I began researching bizarre animal deaths that were making headlines, as they had periodically for a decade. Much of my television work as Director of Special Projects for the CBS affiliate in Denver involved stories about environmental issues. I thought perhaps I was dealing with a contamination story — maybe the government had accidentally released some kind of poison into the land and was randomly spot-checking tissue from grazing animals to monitor the contamination's spread. That was the context in which I began the investigation to produce the film *A Strange Harvest*. But I quickly learned from newspaper files that mutilations had been reported worldwide. Further, it did not make sense that the government would brazenly leave the carcasses to be discovered by a shocked public. Within a month, after talking with dozens of ranchers, law enforcement officials, and fellow journalists who had investigated the intense mutilation activity in 1975-1976, I heard one "off the record" UFO story after another. A Wyoming rancher said that an orange, glowing disk the size of a football field had approached him one night in 1976 while he was watering a field of barley. That same year, the rancher found two of his cows mutilated.

The description of orange or white glowing lights and/or beams of light shining down from something silently hovering above pastures was a common theme among people I interviewed. The documentary shifted from environmental contamination to an accumulation of human testimony that suggested the presence of extra-terrestrial mutilators. My definition of "extra-terrestrial" includes alien intelligences from this universe or any other dimension.

After *A Strange Harvest* was first broadcast on May 25, 1980, I received hundreds of phone calls and letters from people with their own stories about encounters with strange lights and mutilated animals. By 1982, the head of documentaries at Home Box Office (HBO) in New York City screened *A Strange Harvest*. I was asked if there were additional materials to develop for an HBO film. I replied with a proposal for a documentary called *UFOs: The E.T. Factor*. It was accepted, a development contract was signed, and I left Channel 7 in March 1983 to begin the HBO project.

Three weeks after I began research on the script, I went to the Air Force Office of Special Investigations (AFOSI) at Kirtland AFB in Albuquerque, New Mexico. An AFOSI agent gave me some pages to read entitled "Briefing Paper for the President of the United States of America" about extra-terrestrial aerial vehicles and alien beings. I was told that the government had decided to disclose information to the public about its contact with alien life forms. Further, I was told that several thousand feet of color and black and white film would be provided for the HBO documentary. That film was described as historic, shot between 1947 and 1964. The content concerned UFO crashes, retrieval of dead alien bodies — and at least one live E.T.

The paper began with a summary about crashes of silver disks in the southwestern United States. My memory says the first date was 1946. Other dates included 1947 and 1949 and some in the early 1950s. There were two different crashes at Roswell, New Mexico. Some others I remember listed were Aztec, New Mexico; Kingman, Arizona; and a crash south of Texas in northern Mexico. According to the paper, our radar interfered with the aliens' guidance system.

The alien bodies and disks were taken to various secure government facilities such as Los Alamos National Laboratory in Los Alamos, New Mexico, for examination and analysis. Some crash remains were also taken to Wright Field (Wright-Patterson AFB) in Ohio. The government called them "Extra-terrestrial Biological Entities" or "EBEs."

The bodies were described as gray colored, about three feet to four and a half feet tall. Long arms, four long "fingers," no opposable thumb, claw-like nails with webbing between fingers. Instead of a nose or ears, there were only holes.

The paper described a 1949 crash near Roswell, New Mexico. Six creatures were found, five dead and one alive. An Air Force officer (later promoted to Colonel) took responsibility for the live alien and had it transported to Los Alamos Laboratory north of Albuquerque. Los Alamos (LANL) is now an officially designated National Laboratory along with Sandia, Lawrence Livermore and Argonne. Los Alamos was the crucial facility to the United States development of the atomic bomb in the highly classified Manhattan Project. It would have been a natural decision to put an even more highly classified secret there: an extra-terrestrial biological entity with both reptilian and insect characteristics. According to the briefing paper I read, the creature lived at Los Alamos "until June 18, 1952, when it died of unknown causes."

During those three years, "EBE," as the creature was known, communicated about his civilization and its relationship to human evolution on this planet. This communication was done both mind-to-mind and verbally.

In 1983, the E.T. story that was outlined for me by the briefing paper and government sources said that the gray aliens are responsible for our biological evolution through manipulation of DNA in already evolving primates on this planet. Various time intervals of DNA manipulation were specified for 25,000, 15,000, 5,000 and 2,500 years ago. Included in this government description of the Gray intervention in this planet's evolution was their creation of a being 2,000 years ago to be placed here to teach Homo sapiens about love and non-violence. I asked the AFOSI agent at Kirtland AFB if the briefing paper specifically meant Jesus Christ and he nodded his head.

From the 1940s on, according to the 1983 government scenario, an agreement was made between the gray aliens and MJ-12. In exchange for technological information from the Grays, which the government thought would be privileged only to the United States and would exclude the Soviets and other American enemies, the Grays would be allowed to have underground bases in the U.S. where our own government scientists could work and learn. In general, the story in 1983 described an E.T. civilization that set up this earth "experiment" but meant us no harm, and once we got used to looking at their insect/reptilian forms, we would love them.

Along with that portrait of the Grays, another was painted of a group referred to in the paper as the "Talls." These are supposed to be Nordic looking, with or without pale hair. I was told that these Talls were troublemakers and at odds with the Grays. There had been a major "300-year-long war" which the Grays had won and now the two groups "tolerated" each other, according to the agent. I asked what the conflict was about, but he said he didn't know.

Today, the picture that is emerging from frustrated and angry military and intelligence sources is exactly the opposite. The story now is one of great deception at several levels. The Grays allegedly used a Trojan horse-style entry. In the beginning, the aliens convinced the government that they were benevolent and were in fact the creators of this planet. Sometime in the 1960s, the MJ-12 group allied the U.S. with the Grays in a secret treaty. That treaty allegedly gave the aliens land at Nellis AFB near Las Vegas, Nevada for a base of operations. The U.S. also agreed that the Grays could abduct humans and kill animals for medical research purposes in exchange for gaining knowledge about their superior technology. In addition to the base of operations, the aliens had one other major request: government help to keep the Gray presence secret while they conducted their ongoing eons of research here. If that alien demand for secrecy had been rejected, the history of the entire world in the last half of the Twentieth Century might have been very different and more peaceful. However, the U.S. government was obsessed with maintaining the social and economic status quo and "avoiding public panic at all costs."

To ensure that secrecy was maintained, the Central Intelligence Agency hired psychiatrists and psychologists to plot sophisticated misinformation campaigns designed to persuade the public that UFOs did not exist. Fear and ridicule were, and still are, the major weapons used in that ongoing misinformation strategy. Thus, there have always been two levels of deceptions and lies occurring simultaneously: the government's disinformation of the UFO subject in order to perpetuate the agreement with the Grays free of public scrutiny; the lies of the aliens to abductees in the form of contradictory messages which create great confusion about the origins and motives of the E.T.s, whether tall, gray, blond or other; the Grays' ongoing abduction of people and mutilation of animals in order to harvest enzymes, blood, and other tissues for their own survival needs; and biological deception of "Blonds" seen with the Grays which allegedly are Gray creations to interface with humans more easily.

By 1972, according to one military source, the government realized it was walking on quicksand in a hall of mirrors. The aliens were mutilating animals in increasing numbers and leaving the carcasses to be found by shocked ranchers and law enforcement, perversely violating their own demand for secrecy. Human abduction reports were increasing and the government realized that the Grays were not confining their "medical research" to a select list of people shared with MJ-12. Betrayal by an alien hive mind that could not be understood was the quicksand. The illusions planted in human minds by the Grays represented the hall of mirrors.

In addition to those multiple layers of deceit, there is increasing information about at least one tall, perhaps blond, group not manufactured by the Grays that would like to help us but can't yet aggressively act for some unknown reason.

Several sources describe intense conflict within the MJ-12 ranks about letting the public know the truth. Currently it would appear the power lies with those who say no, keep on suppressing, confusing, and misinforming.

Perhaps MJ-12 itself still does not understand the Gray alien creatures it has been trying to deal with. Perhaps some other event occurred in the early 1980s that shook their confidence even further and they have been trying to concoct yet another cover story to hide their mistakes? Perhaps the government has come to believe the earth is at the end of a cycle that is engineered by another intelligence and will be replaced by something entirely new? If so, perhaps some in MJ-12 say, "What's the use of telling people when the end is near anyway?"

But that would not explain the energy and obsession that continues in the development of the Star Wars SDI program, in spite of prominent physicists who say its goals are impossible to achieve. In 1983, I was told that SDI had nothing to do with the Soviets, but was our preparation to defend the planet from outside attack from something else in the cosmos that the EBEs warned about. Later, an Army source said that SDI is a Gray-motivated effort because *they* are afraid of something coming from out there. If any of this is true, which E.T.s with which intentions are headed this way? If we know the Grays are betrayers, why would we attack another group which they are afraid of and which might be coming to help us? Or are the Grays trying to provoke our government to attack overwhelming back-up forces that will support the Gray's insidious invasion?

The "facts" keep shifting and that means we are all still wading in quicksand. All the scenarios could be part of the CIA's engineered misinformation strategy to control and deflect public awareness, keeping the stories so wild and changing that no one can believe anything, something like radar chaff. Since the 1960s, John Keel and Jacques Vallee have both written about the "control system" aspect of the UFO phenomenon and/or humans in league with the phenomenon. People are definitely subjected to controlled ignorance.

However, there is one fact I can state with certainty. Since March 10, 1989, eight cattle and one horse have been reported dead and mutilated to sheriff's offices in Arkansas, Oklahoma, and Missouri. Strange lights and craft have also been reported in those states. I have collected tissue samples from animals in all three areas and can assert with medical proof: The cuts were made with heat, probably above 300 degrees Fahrenheit, were done in two minutes or less and with "pinpoint thinness." (For photographs and more information, see my 1989 book *An Alien Harvest*.) One cow belly had an 18 inch by 22 inch excision. A large laser manufacturer confirmed that such a cut would take at least an hour to complete with state of the art laser equipment. Two minutes for the mutilator's technology; an hour for human technology.

From the human point of view, it's a one-way trade route. What is taken is not by permission nor paid for. And what's left behind is fear, anger, dead animals, and traumatized people.

Perhaps MJ-12 feels pushed into a corner of stunned futility and inability to act because the Grays have demonstrated so far their superior ability to do anything they want to, including instant destruction of men and machines when they so choose. Perhaps, as the worst case scenarios describe, the Grays are actually controlling earth events and the governments are helpless. This was suggested in an interview I did with Larry Warren on May 18, 1986, in the company of New York math professor, Benton Jamison. Larry Warren was one of the Air Force security guards at the appearance of a UFO and Gray creatures at Bentwaters AFB in England at the end of December 1980. The following is an excerpt from my conversation with Larry.

[Transcript: Excerpt of interview with Larry Warren by Linda Howe and Ben Jamison, May 18, 1986, about Warren's conversation with A. Bustinza and the underground briefing after the UFO landing at Bentwaters in December 27-30, 1980.]

HOWE: Did you ever talk with Bustinza about what he said, "This is what happened in Alaska or California" — like when he called you into your room?

WARREN: He told me — he didn't tell me about that incident (Alaska), he just said something had happened. But he told me about this incident and he got so serious — he said, "When I was younger I was at my house and we were watching TV — he comes from a very poor family apparently — and we're watching television (Bustinza's family) and all of a sudden this thing with a bubble on its head — a little thing appeared on the TV and it was like yelling at them. The show went off and everything." And I'm laughing (at Bustinza telling this) and he's serious and saying "I swear to God it happened!" And he said, "My father ran outside and looked up and there was a UFO in broad daylight over the street. All the neighbors saw it and everything." So he said his mother went out into the yard and fainted. He said his father ran back into the house, grabbed his shotgun, ran back outside and aimed it at it and the thing took off. Bustinza was very religious-oriented and he swore to God it happened.

HOWE: And did the alien look like the ones at Bentwaters?

WARREN: I forget what he said. I thought he was joking with me. But he said a little alien was up there with a bubble on its head and got scared and took off. And nowadays I don't throw stones at any of it.

HOWE: In the de-briefing, did they say anything at all about the aliens?

WARREN: No, never once. Never, ever. Never said alien. Never used the word UFO. It was all military regulations. Who to speak to, what not to, don't discuss anything. They went around it so smoothly. They never said anything, but we obviously knew what we were there for. Very clever people.

And one day after I was out back in New York, I pick up the phone and hear music! And I hung it up and walked downstairs and my sister picked it up and same thing. I called this friend, Dick, with New York Telephone and he came out to my house. He said, "You've got a tap on your phone." He said he could tell by the drain on the phone. Then I come down to Connecticut and it's been a party down here! Every few months I'll get a tap. I've got a tap detector and it goes red. (Much more about phone tap problems and black helicopter "surveillance.")

HOWE: Could you go back over again sitting with Bustinza about what he said?

WARREN: We went over the incident (at Bentwaters). He mentioned about something with a cape — and how he fit that in I don't recall. Something about something tall with a cape! He told me about the underground facility and it was about "Men in Black" — it was a classic description, I've read about them.

HOWE: Could you go into detail about what he said?

WARREN: He said they wore black suits. They had a big car with New York State license plates. The — he was called to meet this car. As soon as he got near it, I don't know if he got a shot or something? He lost consciousness. He remembered the interior of the car seemed too bright. It seemed like too ... green. Too bright. The dashboard lights seemed too bright. And he got into the car with someone else with him, I think Burroughs — I believe that is what he said, Burroughs. Got in the back of the car and they were driven. They could only hear sound.

HOWE: Is he coming — did they come into the base to a building?

WARREN: Just outside the dorm where he lived. They parked there. He was told to meet a car at a certain time.

HOWE: By whom? Who told him?

WARREN: I don't know. I don't remember. Someone called him on the phone and said meet such and such. I don't know who. He gets out there and got into the car. That was five years ago and I don't remember a lot of it, but he was taken — this blew my mind, but it didn't surprise me.

HOWE: Two men?

WARREN: Two men and they drove to — he was unconscious — he couldn't open his eyes, I remember, and he couldn't move for some reason as soon as he got into the car, but he could hear, and he could hear that they were near the flight line, because they could hear the jets land. And he said he remembered the feeling of descent going down. And the next thing he knew, he was eating in a room like a small cafeteria — he remembered it in pieces. He remembered being in a room full of a lot of high-tech equipment...engineers or whatever around...being taken to this cavernous — he told me something very interesting, too ...

At this time in England, about that time frame (December 1980), there were all these commercials about Exxon or British Petroleum jointly building underground tunnels. And this one particular one being in Ireland, leading from the sea. Now, Adrian said that from the catwalk he was on, he saw the same tunnel he saw in those commercials. And I was told it goes 13 miles to the North Sea, that this is how these things enter and exit. Through the water.

Bustinza said he looked down and it was dark, but there were some people, humans, walking around. And there was this object — a spaceship down there.

He went into another room and it was not an auditorium, it was like a classroom. And they were put in chairs, comfortable kind of chairs, and he said all of a sudden he couldn't turn his head from side to side at all to see the person sitting next to him. It was like a screen, some kind of screen that light shone out from behind, so you couldn't really see what was behind it. They were briefed by a general or a commander or whoever. I don't remember who. And then something came up behind the screen. He said he could see the silhouette. And talked to him through his mind. Told them a lot of things about religion, how the government — our government and Russia aren't what they seem — that the bases can be made invisible!? — if it had to be, or destroyed at a flick, if they had to be.

Everything up above is a mask...is all false. Is covering the true what is going on. He said government is not real. I wish he would have told that, but he never did.

HOWE: But you keep telling me.

WARREN: Religion and about Christ — because he was religious — they knew his birth, things about his life that no one knew — but this voice was in his head and he/it could communicate that way.

HOWE: Did Bustinza tell you what was communicated to him about Christ?

WARREN: I think there was something about the Pope....he was very serious, you couldn't help but believe him.

HOWE: Try to picture it when he came to you in your room.

WARREN: He was sitting just like you are on a bunk, and I was in a chair just like this exactly. And he told me again about the — they told him religion isn't as it seems. It's a sense of control over people. But there is a greater Force in the universe, much above whoever they are and everything. And something about the Pope, and I don't recall what it was...then the Pope got shot at, just soon after. The religious thing was very interesting to him, but much different than we imagine it to be.

And the military structure, he says, is totally non-existent. It was all a game! And the U.S. and Russia — that this is corporations that handle all the — they make wars and they make, you know, like gas prices and stuff.

HOWE: Can you remember what he said the alien communicated about it?

WARREN: Oh, my God, the most important thing and I almost forgot it! This is what Bustinza told me. They are coming here (aliens), they are among us, you may know them. There are people on the base who either work with them or are them.

And I said, "How do they look like them? How do they look like human beings?" He said, "They do. They can." And they are in government. This is the thing, this is what got me, really blew my mind — they are in government in levels even beyond the Presidency. The President is nothing. They said he is an ornament. Every world leader is an ornament. There are so many things. When I got upgraded in security, there were three levels that were available to my people — like General Gordon Williams would have a Top Secret. I had a Secret. They said there were 38 levels above Top Secret in the government! Now I was told this directly getting my clearance.

Now Bustinza told me the President means nothing. A lot of the government is them. He said they are from something dying? Having to come here and they have been doing it for, since the 1940s. Coming here, getting into society some how.

What did he say about the mail system? Something about the mail system, too, but I don't remember.

HOWE: Keep trying to remember.

WARREN: There are underground bases — Plattsburg was named. Which if you're going to put anything, put it up in the Adirondacks. Under a lot of military bases there are these underground facilities — they are massive apparently. Under Florida is one of the biggest installations. In South America they have a massive installation — That Shirley Maclaine was right in the area where these things are. Peru. He said they have one of the most massive installations they have down there. The Peruvian government is fully aware that it's there and they stay away. They don't mess with it...

I have talked with people in government who know. They say, "Sure." I've talked to Senators who say, "That's an area to stay away from...."

HOWE: Let's go back to Bustinza. Try to remember how he started, even if it was five years ago.

WARREN: He was crying! This guy was crying, a grown man crying. And I think he was my age now, then.

HOWE: And he's crying...

WARREN: Telling me these things.

HOWE: He starts crying like he's been holding something in ...?

WARREN: Yeah! And it's so frustrating to him, he says, "I want to get out of here!" He said, "I'm either going to kill someone or they're going to kill me before it's over." Apparently he pulled a knife on this lieutenant, a black lieutenant, who was pressuring him about something. He flipped and pulled a knife on her.

HOWE: And the woman, the lieutenant, was pressuring him to keep quiet?

WARREN: Something, I don't recall. There was so much to that conversation — it was emotionally charged, and the guy even had me on the border of tears, because after having the experience about what happened out there with us (the UFO landing), this guy is laying on me that I'm sitting above an alien base here on Earth. (Bentwaters AFB) I had no reason to disbelieve. I have seen that they are here. I told Bustinza that for me to tell it right (Warren agreed to tell Bustinza's story when he got out of the Air Force as though it was his, Warren's, experience to cover Bustinza. That cover-up came unravelled some time before this interview in 1986, and thus we were going over details in the honest context of Warren remembering what Bustinza told him.) I told Larry Fawcett I had to fess up. When it came time to leave, Bustinza wouldn't talk about it. I told Fawcett that I didn't experience it first-hand.

HOWE: OK, just try to concentrate on what Bustinza told you.

WARREN: OK, it hit on religion, and something about them coming into society. Somehow they look like us, and they're doing something — I don't know if they are taking over — I don't think they are taking over, but they have identities taken care of by the governments of the world. And something about Third World countries are almost insignificant.

HOWE: So what is the game that is being played between the Soviet Union and the United States with the aliens?

WARREN: The Soviet Union has had major catastrophes apparently with these things — some of them dislike the Soviet Union a great deal. Some don't. Some like them. Some deal with them. And they are like the maggots of the space races — you know, the bad guys! And Adrian told me that he found out that there were hundreds upon thousands of races that have come here through the centuries and millions of years, and they have always been here — as long as we have. And that we are the descent of them! Of someone! (long rambling story about being in Egypt and assigned to some kind of underground facility he was not allowed into at either Cairo or Luxor near the Valley of the Kings and Queens.)

I got orders cut for me just after Adrian told me about the underground experience and we came to — orders cut for Italy. They said I was going to go TDY there for a month. We got on a plane late one night — about 10 or 11 security police. We stopped in Germany, picked up some more on a C-130 and flew off to Italy. Then we flew to Athens. We flew from Athens to Turkey and we picked up things. We flew from Turkey to Ben Gurion Airport in Israel and then flew into Cairo. We were driven for a long way out to these — this area. We had tents pitched. There was a huge radar tower and massive tower coming out of the middle of nowhere ground. And a huge mountain range. And this mountain range was apparently so heavily armed and fortified and had nuclear weapons in it to detonate it, if it ever had to be — it was amazing! It was the height of my clearance, partially upgraded because I was going to this place. What this place is, I never found out. We had to do communications work there, and we worked with some Egyptian security that did perimeter. Never got to go in. They had this tunnel carved out like SAC in Egypt and we have control in the Middle East — we have control of so much! But this was all underground. This facility was so massive that it was larger than the state of New York underground! I never got to see it. I never went in, but there were guys...the security was so tight that if the Egyptian security forces fell asleep on duty, they would be shot. They are shot by their own superiors! And they take care of the external security. Never got in. I didn't have a clearance to get in there. I saw a few people come out of the place. Tourists were not around this area. But these mountains, you could see glass like in crevices — glass and every now and then you could see a person walk by. It was very high-tech and very strange...

Well, like Bustinza told me — these tunnels that were very much advertised — I mean, who cares about tunnels! — but they were on the BBC all the time explaining they were doing this for this reason for your power needs — these tunnels are in the middle of nowhere, and there were never hydroelectric towers built nearby or anything. Ever. But Adrian said the commercial campaigns were done to keep public minds away from the disturbances, seismic disturbances and such. And it all fit in...

So when we got back (from Egypt) the very end of March or early April ... and in Egypt Bustinza and I never talked about anything — we just had a good time...

HOWE: But in all this, Bustinza never had any flash on anything, never said anything until you got back?

WARREN: Yep.

HOWE: What was it about the Pope?

WARREN: I don't remember the order.

HOWE: What was it about the Pope?

WARREN: I don't know. But he said something about the Pope and that they have something at the Vatican. They know exactly what it is and they can't say, or else it would destroy religion. He said there were predictions made, they've all come true — that the last prediction will not be shown — of course, we all know that Pope Pius saw it in the 1960s and said, "Oh, lock that stuff up!" All the Popes see it but will not release it. It destroys religion as they want you to have it.

HOWE: Did he talk anything about the aliens making Christ?

WARREN: Not so much making Christ... but he said Christ had dealings with... he was a man, but there was definitely a connection. There are many years of Christ's life that aren't documented. There are descriptions of this man in China, in Africa — now this guy did not have a jet to get around on! But he was there. ....

HOWE: Well, go back to some more of Bustinza. It's important. The government?

WARREN: He (Bustinza) said the government isn't as it is, as we see it. The President isn't real. The aliens control everything. And these people answer to whoever ... and there are people way up — the President just does his job like a janitor.

JAMISON: Did he ever say why the aliens are doing all this?

WARREN: I don't remember if he said it was for good or for bad. I was kind of scared, I remember, after the conversation. I knew one thing. I wanted to get the hell off of that base. You could feel something in that area though. All the time. There was something wrong.

HOWE: Did you ask him anything like: What was the alien talking to you for?

WARREN: He never said it was an alien. But it was the impression that it was.

HOWE: The thing behind the screen?

WARREN: Yeah. The thing was talking apparently to everyone in the room at the same time, but individually. Explain that. Mentally. He couldn't turn his head side to side, but everything — this is all I could remember.

HOWE: What about evolution? What is man's relationship to them?

WARREN: God, he mentioned that, too. I don't remember.

HOWE: They made us?

WARREN: It was down to that, basically that we were from them. That's what he said.

HOWE: And that underneath in all these bases, the aliens and human relationship is really happening there, and not on the surface?

WARREN: Well, our military bases are a decoy — like a big stage play. I don't know why or how. But he said that the base, that if it was found out or something happened, the bases can be gone like that (snaps fingers). What he meant, I don't know. You wouldn't see them. Maybe England's a UFO itself!

It was just mind-blowing stuff. If I had never had a UFO experience and someone told me that stuff, I'd say "Go away." (The bases) — that's maybe their homes, you know?

HOWE: But if they are controlling everything that happens here, to what end? If they are walking among us and looking like us...

WARREN: What the outcome is, I don't know. He said what it is all about, but I don't remember if it's good or bad. I can't remember. But I remember leaving that conversation with him angry and frightened. So I'm sure maybe it wasn't good. But it seemed like games — the human beings in the government as we call them play games. And people die in the mean time!

9

Under the Cloak of National Security

We have confirmation from a source very close to the highest levels of the government that the basic premises of this book are correct.

John Lear is the son of William Lear, who invented the Lear Jet. Due to the renown of his father's achievements, of which the invention of the Lear Jet was only one, the members of his family have friends among government officials at the very highest levels.

John Lear began his career as a test pilot for the Department of Defense, then flew missions for the CIA over Laos and Cambodia when we were not officially supposed to be there. He has flown over 160 types of aircraft in over 50 countries. He holds 17 world speed records in the Lear Jet, and is the only pilot ever to hold every airman certificate issued by the Federal Aviation Administration. At the time he stepped into the middle of the UFO controversy, he was a commercial airline pilot employed by American Trans Air as the senior captain of a Lockheed L-1011 Tristar.

There is no such thing as a "former" member of the CIA. An agent may no longer be actively employed by the CIA, but he remains a member of the organization for the rest of his life, accountable for any and all security breaches. It is a matter of the utmost seriousness for anyone who has been associated with the CIA to go public with highly classified material.

John Lear has courageously chosen to risk the danger of making public the truth about the most highly classified of the highly classified material. He has done so because we are in an emergency situation, in which the survival of Homo sapiens as a species is at stake. The information he has assembled correlates in so many ways with the results of my own research that it constitutes an independent confirmation of the validity of the basic conclusions I have drawn.

In my opinion, Mr. Lear represents the faction within the government which realizes that the government must now level with the public, if it is to retain any credibility at all. And what would facilitate an overt total takeover by the Grays more effectively than a sudden near-total collapse of public confidence in the government?

It is the invisible government-within-the-government that would profit from a catastrophic collapse of the democratically elected government. We would emerge from the crisis under the control of an overtly totalitarian dictatorship, instead of the covert dictatorship we now have. The problem is to detach the monstrous parasite that the invisible government-within-the-government in fact is, from the government of the United States as defined by the Constitution. The invisible government is like a tapeworm which has grown to such an enormous size that it threatens the life of its host. However, once you and I and John Q. Public manage to find out what the real problem is, appropriate steps can be taken to effectively get rid of an extremely dangerous parasite. The invisible government that is above top secret should now be subjected to intensive thoroughgoing public scrutiny.

Since I wrote the above, there have been some developments that should be mentioned. In his *Affidavit* (Paragon Publications, P.O. Box 981, Orlando FL 32802, 1992), Lars Hansson has accused John Lear of being a member of the "secret team" responsible for Iran-Contra and so much other governmental wrong-doing. This comes as no surprise, since Lear made clear from the start that he has been employed on covert missions for the CIA. It must be said that I find Hansson's hypothesis that Lear was assigned to distract public attention from the Iran-Contra scandal by going public with his UFO statement quite plausible. The timing of the release of the statement was certainly just right, if this was in fact the real motivation for the release of the statement. This would also explain the semi-magical immunity to governmental retaliation Lear has had, though so many others who tried to go public with similar information have been killed or otherwise silenced. However, I disagree with Hansson when he draws the conclusion that Lear was trying to distract public attention from Iran-Contra by pointing to an imaginary danger: alien intervention in human affairs. Lear may indeed have been trying to distract public attention from Iran-Contra, but in my opinion was doing so by pointing to a danger that is not only real, but of such magnitude that it makes Iran-Contra seem of minor importance in comparison. I don't think that we should either forget or forgive those responsible for the Iran-Contra scandal, but I do think that in comparison with the danger represented by the secret treaty with the Grays and their subsequent double-cross, Iran-Contra is of secondary importance. My guess is that Lear was assigned to kill two birds with one stone: distract public attention from Iran-Contra, and see who (if anyone) would believe the horrible truth about the alien presence, if it was presented to the public by someone close enough to the highest levels of the government that the news media would be obliged to take him seriously, yet nevertheless not a government official, so the government could always distance itself from him by discrediting his statements or his reputation. At this point I have no way of knowing whether my guess is correct. Be that as it may, although I do not agree with Hansson about the reality of alien intervention in human affairs, and consider his profusely detailed description of John Lear's private life to a large extent irrelevant, I think his *Affidavit* contains a high-yield gold mine of important hard-to-find political information.

Here are the historically important texts of John Lear's original statement:

The following was released by John Lear on December 29, 1987, and revised on March 25, 1988.

Note to the press: The government of the United States continues to rely on your personal and professional gullibility to suppress the information contained herein. Your cooperation over the past 40 years has exceeded our wildest expectations and we salute you.

"The sun does not revolve around the Earth."

"The United States Government has been in business with little gray extra-terrestrials for about 20 years."

The first truth stated here got Giordano Bruno burned at the stake in AD 1600 for daring to propose that it was real. The second truth has gotten far more people killed trying to state it publicly than will ever be known.

But the truth must be told. The fact that the Earth revolves around the sun was successfully suppressed by the Church for over 200 years. It eventually caused a major upheaval in the Church, government, and thought. A realignment of social and traditional values. That was in the 1800s.

Now, about 400 years after the first truth was pronounced we must again face the shocking facts. The "horrible truth" is far more horrible than the government ever imagined.

In its effort to protect democracy, our government sold us to the aliens. And here is how it happened. But before I begin, I'd like to offer a word in the defense of those who bargained us away. They had the best of intentions.

Germany may have recovered a flying saucer as early as 1939. General James H. Doolittle went to Norway in 1952 to inspect a flying saucer that had crashed there in Spitzbergen.

The "horrible truth" was known by only a very few persons: they were indeed ugly little creatures, shaped like praying mantises and who were more advanced than us by perhaps a billion years. Of the original group that were the first to learn the "horrible truth," several committed suicide, the most prominent of which was Defense Secretary James V. Forrestal who jumped to his death from a 16th story hospital window. Secretary Forrestal's medical records are sealed to this day.

President Truman quickly put a lid on the secret and turned the screws so tight that the general public still thinks that flying saucers are a joke. Have I ever got a surprise for them? In 1947, President Truman established a group of 12 of the top military scientific personnel of their time. They were known as MJ-12. Although the group exists today, none of the original members are still alive. The last one to die was Gordon Gray, former Secretary of the Army, in 1984. As each member passed away, the group itself appointed a new member to fill the position. There is some speculation that the group known as MJ-12 expanded to at least several more members.

There were several more saucer crashes in the late 1940s, one in Roswell, New Mexico, one in Aztec, New Mexico, and one near Laredo, Texas, about 30 miles inside the Mexican border.

Consider, if you will, the position of the United Sates government at that time. They proudly thought of themselves as the most powerful nation on Earth, having recently produced the atomic bomb, an achievement so stupendous it would take Russia four years to catch up, and only with the help of traitors to Democracy. They had built a jet aircraft that had exceeded the speed of sound in flight. They had built jet bombers with intercontinental range that could carry weapons of enormous destruction. The post-war era and the future seemed bright. Now imagine what it was like for those same leaders, all of whom had witnessed the panic of Orson Welles' radio broadcast, "The War of the Worlds," in 1938. Thousands of Americans panicked at a realistically presented invasion of Earth by beings from another planet. Imagine their horror as they actually viewed the dead bodies of these frightening looking little creatures with enormous eyes, reptilian skin, and claw-like fingers. Imagine their shock as they attempted to determine how these strange "saucers" were powered and could discover no part even remotely similar to components they were familiar with: no cylinders or pistons, no vacuum tubes or turbines or hydraulic actuators. It is only when you fully understand the overwhelming helplessness the government was faced with in the late '40s that you can comprehend their perceived need for a total, thorough, and sweeping cover-up, to include the use of "deadly force."

The cover-up was so successful that as late as 1985 a senior scientist with the Jet Propulsion Laboratory in Pasadena, California, Dr. Al Hibbs, would look at a video tape of an enormous flying saucer and state for the record, "I'm not going to assign anything to that (UFO) phenomena without a lot more data." Dr. Hibbs was looking at the naked emperor and saying, "He certainly looks naked, but that doesn't prove he's naked."

In July 1952, a panicked government watched helplessly as a squadron of "flying saucers" flew over Washington, D.C. and buzzed the White House, the Capitol Building, and the Pentagon. It took all the imagination and intimidation the government could muster to force that incident out of the memory of the public.

Thousands of sightings occurred during the Korean war and several more saucers were retrieved by the Air Force. Some were stored at Wright-Patterson Air Force Base, some were stored at Air Force bases near the location of the crash site.

One saucer was so enormous and the logistic problems in transportation so enormous that it was buried at the crash site and remains there today. The stories are legendary on transporting crashed saucers over long distances, moving only at night, purchasing complete farms, slashing through forests, blocking major highways, sometimes driving 2 and 3 lo-boys in tandem with an extra-terrestrial load a hundred feet in diameter.

On April 30, 1964, the first communication between these aliens and the U.S. government took place at Holloman Air Force Base in New Mexico. Three saucers landed at a prearranged area and a meeting was held between the aliens and intelligence officers of the U.S. government.

During the period of 1969-1971, MJ-12 representing the U.S. government made a deal with these creatures, called EBEs (Extra-terrestrial Biological Entities, named by Detlev Bronk, original MJ-12 member and sixth President of Johns Hopkins University). The "deal" was that in exchange for "technology" that they would provide to us, we agreed to "ignore" the abductions that were going on and suppress information on the cattle mutilations. The EBEs assured MJ-12 that the abductions (usually lasting about two hours) were merely the on-going monitoring of developing civilizations. In fact, the purposes for the abductions turned out to be:

1.   The insertion of a 3mm spherical device through the nasal cavity of

the abductee into the brain. The device is used for the biological monitoring, tracking, and control of the abductee.

2. Implementation of posthypnotic suggestion to carry out a specific activity during a specific time period, the activation of which will occur within the next two to five years.

3. Termination of some people so that they could function as living sources for biological material and substances.

4. Termination of individuals who represent a threat to the continuation of their activity.

5. Effect genetic engineering experiments.

6. Impregnation of human females and early termination of pregnancies to secure the crossbreed infant.

The U.S. government was not initially aware of the far-reaching consequences of their "deal." They were led to believe that the abductions were essentially benign and since they figured the abductions would probably go on anyway whether they agreed or not, they merely insisted that a current list of abductees be submitted, on a periodic basis, to MJ-12 and the National Security Council. Does this sound incredible? An actual list of abductees sent to the National Security Council? Read on, because I have news for you.

The EBEs have a genetic disorder in that their digestive system is atrophied and not functional. Some speculate that they were involved in some type of accident or nuclear war, or are possibly on the back side of an evolutionary genetic curve. In order to sustain themselves, they use an enzyme or hormonal secretion obtained from the tissue that they extract from humans and animals.

The secretions obtained are then mixed with hydrogen peroxide and applied on the skin by spreading or dipping parts of their bodies in the solution. The body absorbs the solution, then excretes the waste back through the skin. The cattle mutilations that were prevalent throughout the period from 1973 to 1983 (publicly noted through newspaper and magazine stories, including a documentary produced by Linda Howe for the Denver CBS affiliate KMGH-TV) were for the collection of these tissues by the aliens. The mutilations included genitals taken, rectums cored out to the colon, eyes, tongue, and throat all surgically removed with extreme precision. In some cases the incisions were made by cutting between the cells, a process we are not yet capable of performing in the field. In many of the mutilations there was no blood found at all in the carcass, yet there was no vascular collapse of the internal organs. This has been also noted in the human mutilations, one of the first of which was Sgt. Jonathan P. Louette at the White Sands Missile Test Range in 1956, who was found three days after an Air Force Major had witnessed his abduction by a "disk shaped" object at 0300 while on a search for missile debris downrange. His genitals had been removed, rectum cored out in a surgically precise "plug" up to the colon, eyes removed and all blood removed with, again, no vascular collapse. From some of the evidence it is apparent that this surgery is accomplished, in most cases, while the victim, animal or human, is still alive.

The various parts of the body are taken to various underground laboratories, one of which is known to be near the small New Mexico town of Dulce. This jointly occupied (CIA-Alien) facility has been described as enormous, with huge tiled walls that "go on forever." Witnesses have reported huge vats filled with amber liquid with parts of human bodies being stirred inside.

After the initial agreement, Groom Lake, one of this nation's most secret test centers, was closed for a period of about a year, sometime between about 1972 and 1974, and a huge underground facility was constructed for and with the help of the EBEs. The "bargained for" technology was set in place but could only be operated by the EBEs themselves. Needless to say, the advanced technology could not be used against the EBEs themselves, even if needed.

Between 1979 and 1983, it became increasingly obvious to MJ-12 that things were not going as planned. It became known that many more people (in the thousands) were being abducted than were listed on the official abduction lists. In addition, it became obvious that some, not all, but some of the nation's missing children had been used for secretions and other parts required by the aliens.

In 1979, there was an altercation of sorts at the Dulce laboratory. A special armed forces unit was called in to try and free a number of our people trapped in the facility, who had become aware of what was really going on. According to one source, 66 of the soldiers were killed and our people were not freed.

By 1984, MJ-12 must have been in stark terror at the mistake they had made in dealing with the EBEs. They had subtly promoted "Close Encounters of the Third Kind" and "E.T."to get the public used to "odd looking" aliens that were compassionate, benevolent and very much our "space brothers." MJ-12 "sold" the EBEs to the public and were now faced with the fact that quite the opposite was true. In addition, a plan was formulated in 1968 to make the public aware of the existence of aliens on earth over the next 20 years to culminate with several documentaries to be released during 1985-1987. These documentaries would explain the history and intentions of the EBEs. The discovery of the "Grand Deception" put the entire plans, hopes and dreams of MJ-12 into utter confusion and panic.

Meeting at the "Country Club," a remote lodge with private golf course, comfortable sleeping and working quarters, and its own private airstrip built by and exclusively for the members of MJ-12, it was a factional fight of what to do now. Part of MJ-12 wanted to confess the whole scheme and shambles it had become to the public, beg their forgiveness and ask for their support. The other part (and majority) of MJ-12 argued that there was no way they could do that, that the situation was untenable and there was no use in exciting the public with the "horrible truth" and that the best plan was to continue the development of a weapon that could be used against the EBEs under the guise of "SDI," the Strategic Defense Initiative, which had nothing whatsoever to do with a defense for inbound Russian nuclear missiles. As these words are being written, Dr. Edward Teller, "father" of the H-bomb, is personally in the test tunnels of the Nevada Test Site, driving his workers and associates in the words of one, "like a man possessed." And well he should, for Dr. Teller is a member of MJ-12 along with Dr. Kissinger, Admiral Bobby Inman, and possibly Admiral Poindexter, to name a few of the current members of MJ-12.

Before the "Grand Deception" was discovered and according to a meticulous plan of metered release of information to the public, several documentaries and video tapes were made. William Moore, a Burbank, California-based UFO researcher who wrote *The Roswell Incident* — a book published in 1980 that detailed the crash, recovery and subsequent cover-up of a UFO with four alien bodies — has a video tape of two newsmen interviewing a military officer associated with MJ-12. This military officer answers questions relating to the history of MJ-12 and the cover-up, the recovery of a number of flying saucers, and the existence of a live alien (one of 3 living aliens captured and designated, or named, EBE-1, EBE-2, and EBE-3, being held in a facility designated as YY-II at Los Alamos, New Mexico. The only other facility of this type, which is electromagnetically secure, is at Edwards Air Force Base in Mojave, California). The officer names members previously mentioned plus a few others: Harold Brown, Richard Helms, Gen. Vernon Walters, JPL's Dr. Lew Allen, and Dr. Theodore Von Karman.

The officer also relates the fact that the EBEs claim to have created Christ. The EBEs have a type of recording device that has recorded all of Earth's history and can display it in the form of a hologram. This hologram can be filmed but because of the way holograms work does not come out clearly on movie film or video tape. The crucifixion of Christ on the Mount of Olives has allegedly been put on film to show the public. The EBEs claim to have created Christ, which, in view of the "Grand Deception," could be an effort to disrupt traditional values for undetermined reasons.

Another video tape allegedly in existence is an interview with an EBE. Since EBEs communicate telepathically, an Air Force Colonel serves as an interpreter. Just before the stock market correction in October 1987, several newsmen, including Bill Moore, had been invited to Washington, D.C., to personally film the EBE in a similar type interview and distribute the film to the public. Apparently, because of the correction in the market, it was felt the timing was not propitious. In any case, it certainly seems like an odd method to inform the public of extra-terrestrials, but it would be in keeping with the actions of a panicked organization that doesn't know which way to turn.

Moore is also in possession of more Aquarius documents, a few pages of which leaked out several years ago and detailed the supersecret NSA project which had been denied by them until just recently. In a letter to Senator John Glenn, NSA's Director of Policy, Julia B. Wetzel, wrote, "Apparently there is or was an Air Force Project with the name (Aquarius) which dealt with UFOs. Coincidentally, there is also an NSA project by that name." NSA's Project Aquarius deals specifically with "communications with the aliens" (the EBEs). Within the Aquarius program was project "Snowbird," a project to test-fly a recovered alien aircraft at Groom Lake, Nevada. This project continues today at that location. In the words of an individual who works at Groom Lake, "our people are much better at taking things apart than they are at putting them back together."

Moore, who claims he has a contact with MJ-12, feels that they have been stringing him along, slipping him documents and providing him leads, promising to go public with some of the information on extra-terrestrials by a certain date.

Certain of Moore's statements lead one to believe that Moore himself is a government agent working for MJ-12, not strung along, but stringing along ever hopeful ufologists that the truth is just around the corner. Consider:

Moore states emphatically that he is not a government agent, although when Lee Graham (a southern California-based ufologist) was investigated by DIS (Defense Investigative Service) for possession of classified documents received from Moore, Moore himself was not investigated.

Moore states emphatically that the cattle mutilations of 1973-1983 were a hoax by Linda Howe (producer of *A Strange Harvest*) to create publicity for herself. He cites the book *Mute Evidence* as the bottom line of the hoax. "Mute Evidence" was a government-sponsored book to explain the mutilations in conventional terms.

Moore states that the U.S.A.F. Academy physics book, *Introductory*

Space Science, vol. II, chapter 13, entitled "Unidentified Flying Objects," was written by Lt. Col. Edward R. Therkelson and Major Donald B. Carpenter, Air Force personnel who did not know what they were talking about and were merely citing "crackpot" references. He, Moore, states that the book was withdrawn to excise the chapter which describes four of the most commonly seen aliens (one of which is the EBE).

If the government felt they were being forced to acknowledge the existence of aliens on Earth because of the overwhelming evidence such as the October and November sightings in Wytheville, VA, and recently released books such as *Night Siege* (Hynek, J. Allen; Imbrogno, Phillip J.; Pratt, Bob: Ballantine Books, Random House, New York), and taking into consideration the "Grand Deception" and obviously hostile intentions of the EBEs, it might be expedient for MJ-12 to admit the EBEs but conceal the information on the mutilations and abductions. If MJ-12 and Moore were in some kind of agreement, then it would be beneficial to Moore to toe the party line. For example, MJ-12 would say, "here are some more genuine documents...but remember...no talking about the mutilations or abductions." This would be beneficial to Moore as it would supply the evidence to support his theory that E.T.s exist but deny the truths about the E.T.s. However, if Moore was indeed working for MJ-12, he would follow the party line anyway, admitting the E.T.s but pooh-poohing the mutilations and abductions. If working alone, Moore might not even be aware of the "Grand Deception."

Now you ask, "Why haven't I heard about any of this?" Who do you think you would hear it from? Dan Rather? Tom Brokaw? Sam Donaldson? Wrong. These people just read the news, they don't find it. They have ladies who call and interview witnesses and verify statements on stories coming over the wire (either AP or UPI). It's not like Dan Rather would go down to Wytheville, Virginia, and dig into why there were *4,000* reported sightings in October and November of 1987. Better that Tom Brokaw or someone else should risk their credibility on this type of story. Tom Brokaw? Tom wants Sam Donaldson to risk his credibility. No one, but no one, is going to risk their neck on such outlandish ideas, regardless of how many people report sightings of 900 foot objects running them off the road. In the case of the Wytheville sightings, dozens of vans with NASA lettered on the side failed to interest newsmen. And those that asked questions were informed that NASA was doing a weather survey.

Well then, you ask, what about our scientists? What about Carl Sagan? Isaac Asimov? Arthur C. Clarke? Wouldn't they have known? If Carl Sagan knows, then he is committing a great fraud through the solicitation of memberships in the Planetary Society, "to search for extra-terrestrial intelligence." Another charade into which the U.S. government dumps millions of dollars every year is the radiotelescope in Arecibo, Puerto Rico, operated by Cornell University with - guess who? — Carl Sagan. Cornell is ostensibly searching for signals from outer space, a sign, maybe, that somebody is out there. It is hard to believe that relatively intelligent astronomers like Sagan could be so ignorant.

What about Isaac Asimov? Surely the most prolific science fiction writer of all time would have guessed by now that there must be an enormous cover-up? Maybe, but if he knows he's not saying. Perhaps he's afraid that Foundation and Empire will turn out to be inaccurate.

What about Arthur C. Clarke? Surely the most technically accurate of science fiction writers with very close ties to NASA would have at least a hint of what's really going on. Again, if so he isn't talking. In a recent Science Fiction survey, Clarke estimates that contact with extra-terrestrial intelligent life would not occur before the 21st Century.

If the government won't tell us the truth and the major networks won't even give it serious consideration, then what is the big picture, anyway? Are the EBEs having done a hundred thousand or more abductions (possibly millions world-wide), built an untold number of secret underground bases (Groom Lake, Nevada; Sunspot, Datil, Roswell, and Pie Town, New Mexico, just to name a few) getting ready to return to wherever they came from? Or, from the obvious preparations are we to assume that they are getting ready for a big move? Or is the more sinister and most probable situation that the invasion is essentially complete, and it is all over but the screaming?

A well-planned invasion of Earth for its resources and benefits would not begin with mass landings of ray-gun equipped aliens. A properly planned and executed invasion by a civilization thousands and probably hundreds of thousands of years in advance of us would most likely be complete before even a handful of people — say 12? — realized what was happening. No fuss, no muss. The best advice I can give you is this: next time you see a flying saucer and are awed by its obvious display of technology and gorgeous lights of pure color — *run like hell!*

In 1983, when the "Grand Deception" was discovered, MJ-12 (which may now be designated 'PI-40') started work on a weapon or some kind of device to contain the EBEs that had by now totally infested our society. This program was funded through SDI which, coincidentally, was initiated at approximately the same date. A frantic effort has been made over the past four years by all participants. This program ended in failure in December 1987. A new program has been conceived but will take about 2 years to develop. In the meantime, it is absolutely essential to MJ-12 (PI-40), that no one, including the Senate, the Congress or the citizens of the United States of America (or anyone else for that matter), become aware of the real circumstances surrounding the UFO cover-up and total disaster it has become. Moore never did release the video tapes but claims he is negotiating with a major network to do so...'soon.'

In an earlier statement, dated December 13, 1987, John Lear included the following information, which was not in his later statement:

Here is a list of some of the probable visitors to earth from outer space. The only known home of these visitors is that of the EBEs, which is Zeta Reticuli 1 & 2, a binary star system visible from the southern hemisphere, approximately 38 light years away, with a spectral class of G2, identical to our sun.

3 types of EBEs (Grays):

Gray-1: 3 1/2 ft tall. Large head. Large slanted eyes. Worships technology. Doesn't give a damn about mankind.

Gray-2: Same type, different finger arrangement, slightly different face. More sophisticated than Gray-1, uses common sense, passive. May not need secretions.

Gray-3: Same basic type. Lips thinner. More subservient to other two Grays.

Blonds, Swedes, Nordics: Known by any of these monikers. Similar to humans. Blond hair, blue eyes. Will not break universal law of 'non-interference' to help us. They could only intervene if any Gray activity would have adverse effect in another part of universe.

Interdimensional: Entity that can assume various shapes. Peaceful nature.

Hairy Dwarfs: Four feet tall. 35 lbs. Extremely strong. Hairy. Neutral. Don't try to hurt intelligent life.

Very Tall Race: Look like humans but seven or eight feet tall. Unite with Blonds.

Humans appearing similar to Blonds seen with Grays: Drones created by Grays. Child-like mentality.

MIBs: Men in black. Wear all black. Sunglasses. Very pale skin. Do not conform to normally accepted patterns. Extremely sensitive to light. May be a holographic image.

On August 10, 1988, John Lear gave a lecture to the Dallas MUFON group, which included much information that was not contained in his previous statements. Here is a summary of some of the highlights:

> This nation has been brainwashed by a CIA mind-control opera-
> tion based on fear of ridicule. There have been at least one million
> abductees in the U.S. since 1947. In the last 13 years, there have
> been over 14,000 cattle mutilations in the U.S. (As of the date he
> was speaking a wave of animal mutilations was occurring in the
> suburbs of New York City, on Long Island, involving household
> pets, with approximately 250 cases recently reported.) There are ap-
> proximately 70 alien civilizations known to be visiting us at the
> present time.
>
> Gordon Cooper, one of our very best astronauts, lost his chance
> to go on the Apollo flights because he dared to speak out about
> UFOs in a letter to the United Nations. During the past few years,
> there has been a steep increase in the number of missing persons. It
> is estimated that there are about ten million of the Grays in bases on
> the Earth and Moon, but it is not known whether they are able to
> return to their home base. They enter and exit their underground
> bases through interdimensional transference, a hyperspace maneuver
> which accounts for the apparently nonsensical stories of UFO
> witnesses who report having seen UFOs going into or out of moun-
> tains. Those witnesses are truthfully describing a maneuver that is at
> present incomprehensible to our science.
>
> It was President Eisenhower who allowed the reins of power to
> pass from the hands of the President into the control of the Penta-
> gon. Ever since Eisenhower, the real rulers of this nation have been
> a military junta.

The only point on which I find myself in disagreement with John Lear
is that one sentence of advice in his statement of Dec. 29, 1987: "Next time
you see a flying saucer and are awed by its obvious display of technology
and gorgeous lights of pure color — *run like hell!*" This assumes that all
UFO occupants are of the predatory type the U.S. government so foolishly
made a deal with, when there are in fact many different types of E.T.s
interacting with us, with some of whom it is possible to establish genuine
friendships.

It would be a wise move to seek shelter, if it is possible to do so, from
which to observe what is going on. Panic-stricken flight would be a sure
way to attract the attention of predatory entities, triggering an automatic
capture-of-prey response. In a close encounter situation, if my intuitive impression was that the entities were predatory, evasive action would indeed

be appropriate and would take precedence over any further observation of them. If my intuitive impression was that these were entities I could communicate with in a peaceful manner, I would signal my presence and wait for a response. I would not advance toward a craft unless invited to do so.

Operation Plowshare, which was carried out in 1965, was portrayed to the public as an experiment on peaceful applications of nuclear explosives. The main Plowshare test site, at which there were multiple nuclear detonations at a depth of 4,000 feet underground, was in the vicinity of Dulce, New Mexico. While this detail on its own does not prove anything, it does tend to support the validity of John Lear's allegations.

In the final chapter of this book, Riley Crabb gives a different timetable for the preliminary encounters between U.S. government officials and extra-terrestrials than John Lear does. Contradictions can occur between the results of the best-intentioned researchers, so for the time being let us suspend judgment until more information surfaces, while continuing to examine both possibilities. The point in question is aptly put by Valdamar Valerian in his blockbuster of a book, *The Matrix* (Arcturus, 1988): "There is evidence to suggest that President Eisenhower was present for a demo of alien technology at Edwards AFB in the 1950s....Now, governments being what they are, there was a proposal to them that they give us advanced technology, and evidently that request was refused. That request was later repeated with other races that were contacted. All refused — except one — the Grays."

According to researcher Jason Bishop, the Blonds who refused to give us weapons technology and tried to warn us about entering an alliance with the Grays had a base in the Carlsbad Caverns area of New Mexico. Upon entering the alliance, at the request of the Grays, our government detonated nuclear weapons underground in the Carlsbad area to destroy the base, which the Blonds then abandoned. Recently we began using the area in which this "underground testing" occurred as a storage depot for nuclear waste.

Besides the alien underground bases mentioned by John Lear, there are a number of other locations where there is reason to suspect the existence of such bases: in New Mexico, at Angel Peak, to the north of Taos Pueblo, and to the northeast of Albuquerque in the Sandia Mountains; in Arizona, at Fort Huachuca and in the Santa Catalina Mountains; in California, at Fort Irwin, Norton Air Force Base, Deep Springs, 29 Palms Marine Base, George Air Force Base, at Tecachapi Ranch and the hollowed-out mountain next to the hydroelectric facility at the Kern River Project near Bakersfield; in Nevada, at Blue Diamond, Groom Lake, and southeast of Tonopah at Quartzite Mountain; in Colorado, at Alamosa, Fort Collins and Grand

Mesa; in Texas, at Red River Arsenal and Fort Hood; in Arkansas, in the vicinity of Hardy and Cherokee Village; in Oklahoma, at Ashland Naval Ammunition Depot; in Kansas, at Fort Riley; in Missouri, about twelve miles south of Lebanon, near the newly created town of Twin Bridges, in the Bat/Dry/Dead Man/Howell cluster of caves, and underneath dioxin-tainted Times Beach, now off-limits to the public; in New York, at Platts-burgh Air Force Base; in New Jersey, at Picatinny Arsenal; in Florida, at Eglin Air Force Base and at Cabo Rojo in Puerto Rico.

There are indications of underwater bases in the Milwaukee Depth northeast of Puerto Rico; Lakes Titicaca, Yanacocha and Pumacocha in Peru; between Berin and Santiago off the coast of Chile; in the Gulf of San Matias off the coast of Argentina; in the Brazilian Amazon near Santarem and Monte Alegre; under Stack Rock in St. Bride's Bay, Broad Haven, Wales; in Holy Loch, Scotland; in the triangle formed by Guam, Luzon in the Philippines, and the southeast corner of Japan; in Lake Assal, Djibouti; in Bass Strait, between the Victoria Province of Australia and Tasmania; in Shirley Bay, Ontario, Canada; and in the Arctic and Antarctic. There may be a base in the vicinity of Vancouver, B.C., Canada, but so far there is no indication as to whether it is undersea or underground.

Possible locations of underground bases outside of the United States include Bentwaters Air Force Base in England; Mount Mealfuarvonie near Loch Ness in Scotland; Plateau d'Albion and Col de Vence, in France; Pine Gap in Australia; the Ranoi Oro Volcano on Easter Island; in Mexico, at Ceballos-Pueblo de Allende and San Ignacio Hill; in Argentina, the Loretani Valley, about 60 kilometers southeast of Cordoba; the Peruvian mountain area made famous by Shirley MacLaine in *Out on a Limb*; the Gizeh, Luxor and Siwa areas of Egypt; the Gobi Desert area of Mongolia; and somewhere in the desert or mountain areas of Iran or Afghanistan, perhaps in the vicinity of the dervish monastery where Gurdjieff received his training. As we know there are a wide variety of E.T. groups interacting with us, it would be interesting to find out which groups have what bases, and which groups share bases.

The same type of myopic mediocre mentality that dreamed up the Iran-Contra deal is responsible for the clandestine deal with the Grays.

In sparkling contrast to such dismal dummies, we now have a sample of the viewpoint of the highly lucid Valdamar Valerian, taken by permission from his *The Matrix* (Arcturus, 1443 S.E. Port St. Lucie Blvd., Port St. Lucie, FL, 34952, 1988):

Part of our culture does not or will not believe in the existence of other species; part of our culture acknowledges their existence or the probability of their existence; part of our culture is actually interacting with those other species that are either alien to our planet or coexist here with us....we are dealing with...the gradually growing awareness that we are not only not alone here, but we have never been alone here. As if that were not enough, it turns out that factions of our society have known this, and apparently have been interacting with some of these alien species for quite a while....

A friend of mine and four of his friends experimented with crystalline structures a year or two ago, and they figured out how to cut them along certain planes so they could actually see the aura or energy field around people.

That's when they discovered that all people aren't people, or the people they thought they were. It appears that some E.T. humanoids have a dark blue ovoid aura. It so happens that all the people they checked that met this criteria also wore dark glasses and made every attempt to act like they really wanted nothing to do with people in general.

They followed one of these people out into the desert where he evidently had a trailer. After waiting until dusk, they made a pretense of needing help and knocked on the door. After a short while, the light went on and the man came to the door. He looked normal, except that his pupils were vertical slits instead of circles. It works. The only trouble is that it costs $2,000 to put a pair of those glasses together....

The NSA (National Security Agency)...was created initially to protect the secret of the recovered disks, and in the process attained control of all communications in the United States, including the U.S. Mail....

A lot of comments have been put forth in recent books and literature in regard to abductions, and one of those comments is that only people of low to medium IQ are abducted. The evidence is that IQ has less of a part to play than the resonant vibrational rate of the individual. It is apparent that the electromagnetic emissions of the individual are scanned, and people are chosen by this method. Since the CIA also possesses this technology, I suggest that some of the abductions could be performed with intentions that would benefit both groups. The person can, in effect, be programmed for slavery and have no memory of it....

The Roswell incident was one of the first retrievals that the United States performed. Gray Species 2 was found on board. There were also human bodies and body parts found on board the craft, which was one of the primary factors that caused the retrieval to be so highly classified....

It is not at present in the interest of some of the EBEs to have terrestrial humans move into fourth density (specifically, development of telepathic abilities), and the Grays in particular do not want the old energy grids on earth reactivated again. Well, they are gradually being reactivated anyway, whether they like it or not. Reactivation of the energy grid, from what we can determine, will serve to open some or all of the dimensional doorways which interlink earth with other locations. This, the EBEs perceive, will interfere with their activities...Brains of advanced physical beings, presumably those of third and fourth densities that require the use of physical bodies, are described as having the right and left hemispheres fused and a small frontal lobe which acts as a "crystal recorder" structure, or third brain. This is exactly what the autopsies found...

As of May 1988, we have discovered that the EBEs are sensitive to materials with a left-hand atomic spin. Sugar is a common substance like this. It could be construed from this that a good way to repulse the EBEs would be to entrain some sort of signal on their biological frequency that would force a change in the spin vector of their atomic structure....

It is rumored that in 1976 the U.S. government was offered assistance with the EBE problem by a group called the Coldasians, after they set up several bases in the Nevada Test Range. In a stupid effort to gain their technology by force, the US forces allegedly attacked and tried to overrun the Coldasian bases. Naturally the Coldasians were upset, and they allegedly grabbed 200 of our scientists and spirited them off to a base on the far side of the Moon. Supposedly the Coldasians had their point of origin in the Polaris system...

All of the beings in the universe have an equal right to exist, to develop, and to express their own individual manifestation of All That Is. Interaction between species is based on a need being fulfilled in some way. If that need is one-sided, then the other side may suffer because of it. Maybe not. I am sure there are selfish symbiotic relationships that somehow survive. It is clear, however, that we are having interactions and that some of them are less than desirable for the participants. Most of the interactions are suppressed because of fear and self-limitation. Unfortunate for both parties....

Acquisition of mind control and thought beam technology from non-human sources is the final act in a long series of events that started many years ago. The purpose of mind control, as far as the United States Government is concerned, is to devise operational techniques to disturb the memory, to discredit people through aberrant behavior, to alter sex patterns, to elicit information, and to create emotional dependence. The goal of mind control is to program individuals to carry out any mission of espionage or assassination, even against their will ... even against such fundamental laws of nature as self-preservation ... and to control the absolute behavior and thought patterns of individuals.

In this era of psychopolitics, the guise of National Security is used as an excuse for illegal activities, a cover for unsanctioned deeds, and as an instrument of manipulation of public opinion and individual citizens. Mind control plays a vital part in this whole scenario. The primary target of National Security has been the people of the United States, since a secret government cannot exist in a climate of free speech, open criticism and public exposure....

The RHIC-EDOM file was a 350-page document prepared by the CIA immediately after the murder of JFK. The report described a way of turning men into electronically controlled robots that were programmed to kill on demand. In the RHIC phase, the individual was put into a trance and given suggestions that were activated in one or more levels by key words or tones. In the EDOM phase, which was an acronym for Electronic Dissolution of Memory, the memory of the individual was affected to either eliminate or alter the memory of events that the individual experienced. By electronically jamming the brain, the existing acetylcholine creates static which blocks both sight and sound. This method can be used to either block/erase the memory, or to slow it down so that events seem to happen after they actually have occurred ...

Intelligence forces have already developed remote-controlled men who have no memory of their programming but will perform a pre-assigned task when exposed to an audio or visual cue. These men, who are essentially cyborgs (altered and controlled humans), are far less expensive than robots. They are also expendable. There is now sufficient evidence to indicate that the assassinations of John and Robert Kennedy, as well as Martin L. King, Jr.,* were carried

---

* At least one more name should be added to that list - John Lennon. I also suspect that the

out by individuals who were programmed with RHIC-EDOM techniques by intelligence forces....

Typical Scenario for Producing Social Change through Artificial Manipulation of Society

Wanted: Increase social control and power over society. Increase police control. Extract specific people.

Step 1: Withdraw social programs. This will cause an increase in crime rate and seemingly "justify" an increase in control. Cause specific social problems.

Step 2: Apply authoritarian measures. Reap benefits. Incarcerate "troublemakers."

Step 3: State publicly that the measures have been sufficient and that a new department has been created to deal with this "new problem."

Step 4: Reap benefits from newly created institution. Profits come in from dealing with artificially created social situation.

Step 5: Institute new social programs that have a higher level of control over the individual....

Somewhere within the United States the technology for the creation of the completely subservient slave state is being perfected. The slave state will be designed to finish the job started at the end of World War II. Whether or not the mind-controlled state becomes a reality depends not so much upon the efforts of the cryptocrats, but upon the free will, determination and strength of character of the American people. The predisposition to gain advanced technology in this field from alien sources is just an extension of the negative and devolutionary mentality that has been running the countries of the Earth for many generations. We *must* recognize what is happening, inform people, and find a way to implement a productive and peaceful transition to a state where we can begin again at a new level....

The Grays are playing a game with us that depends heavily on maintaining a situation where humans view themselves as limited, fatalistic beings with no control over their own destiny. They continually manipulate humans in higher levels, such as in government, Illuminati, etc., to enable them to achieve their ends. On a paraphysical level, they were responsible

---

names of the 14 women murdered at the University of Montreal on Dec. 6, 1989, belong on that list, along with those of the victims of the Stockton, California schoolyard massacre of Jan. 17, 1989, as well as many others.

for implantation of religious imagery in order to withdraw energy and experience from human souls when humans physically die. Humans are then
re-implanted and returned to the earth to begin the process all over again.
It's very insidious and a very nasty business, and they don't want you to
know about it....

Humans are not players in this game, and in order to become a player
and leave the game, humans must become aware of the rules of the game...

The Grays are destructive to themselves and all beings with whom they
interact. The Gray EBE species consists of a broad spectrum of entities.
They are led primarily by non-corporeal beings of 6th density, of which
there are apparently only a few. These are ultimately the game masters, and
each of these beings knows himself to be capable of creation of other beings propagated from himself.

Solutions must be formulated that will resolve the problem of the negative Gray entities and remove them from the terrestrial sphere of influence.
However, by raising our vibratory rate (by virtue of the nature of our
thoughts and actions) we will be able to co-exist until we can spiritually
grow beyond their reach. Solutions must be reached rather quickly, for they
appear to be destroying the spiritual matrix and the substrata holding together what's left of our culture. By their interaction with the terrestrial
human souls, they are slowing the evolution of the human species.

As we have seen, the negative Gray entities have been engaged in abduction of terrestrials (they are not the only ones who do this) and other
activities primarily to sustain the 3rd density base for their hold on this
planet.

The Grays that are a little less negatively oriented, referred to previously as the Zeta Reticulans, are primarily interested in scientific research
and genetic engineering in order to enrich their own gene pool.

The Grays that are primarily negatively oriented, referred to previously
as the Rigelians, are interested in survival. Survival for both the third-den-
sity entities (cattle mutilations and genetics) and the higher density entities
(soul manipulation and implantation)...

Socially, it appears that they have a high sense of duty and blind obedi-
ence, but their negative leanings cause internal social disorder because of
their telepathic abilities. This is a prime weakness, as Paul Bennewitz
pointed out.

Their activities are planned around the concepts of conquest and colonization. Their basic game is to use nullification and domination to control
the leaders of the population of a planet. They appear to accomplish this
primarily by taking out the leaders and replacing them with their own entities, made to resemble the leaders that are taken...

Another way to characterize the basic operation for conquering a planet such as the Earth is to say that the Grays locate terrestrial humans who vibrate spiritually in resonance with their frequency, whether it be on a mental level or a negative spiritual level.

These terrestrial beings are then informed that they are the "elite" or the "chosen ones," destined to lead or conquer other territorial groups and rule the planet....

The function of the "elite" terrestrials, as far as the Grays are concerned, is to cause decimation of portions of the terrestrial civilization to enable better management and control. Good examples of this policy on Earth are Adolf Hitler, Nazi vs. Jew, and wars in general.

Life is characterized by games of varying emotionality and complexity as far as the Grays are concerned. When you are aware of the game, then you have the opportunity to leave the game if you choose. They choose to leave most of humanity in this condition where, according to entities such as Bashar, humans are both culturally conditioned and implanted with programs that will keep them enmeshed in a world of apparent limitation. The world is then perceived to be fragmented. Science and physics are fragmented. All aspects of culture are fragmented to prevent people from realizing their true power and their true nature — to keep them in a condition where they cannot realize the true God-like powers that they have — to keep them enslaved.

Now you have a good idea of why things are the way they are around you.

The Dulce Papers

The Dulce papers were comprised of 25 black-and-white photos, a video tape with no dialogue and a set of papers that included technical information of the alleged jointly occupied (U.S.-Alien) facility one kilometer beneath the Archuleta Mesa near Dulce, New Mexico. Several persons were given the above package to hold for safekeeping. Most of those given the package were shown what the package contained, but were not technically oriented and knew very little about what they were looking at. The following was written by one of these persons about what the papers contained. This person described the scenes that the videotape showed and made pencil drawings of some of the photos. What you see is what you get; I can't decipher what is written or drawn anymore than you can. I pass these papers on only in the interest of getting to the truth. From other information I have I believe the information contained herein is true. I believe the facility exists and is currently operational. I also believe that there are four additional facilities of the same type, one located a few miles to the southeast of Groom Lake, Nevada. What is the truth? Only God, MJ-12 and the aliens know for sure.

Dulce papers: Lots of papers/documents that discuss copper and molybdenum, also papers about magnesium and potassium, but mostly about copper. Lots of "medical terms" that I don't understand. A sheet of paper with charts and strange diagrams. Papers that discuss ultra violet light and gamma rays. Papers that discuss color and black and white and how to avoid detection through use of certain colors. In addition to these papers there are about 25 pictures, black and white, plus one video tape with no dialogue, all taken inside the Dulce facility. These papers tell what the aliens are after and how the blood (taken from the cows) is used. Aliens seem to absorb atoms to "eat". Aliens put hands in blood, sort of like a sponge, for nourishment. It's not just food they want; the DNA in cattle and humans is being altered. The "Type One" creature is a lab animal. "They" know how to change the atoms to create a temporary "almost human being." It is made with animal tissue and depends on a computer to simulate memory, a memory the computer has withdrawn from another human being. The "almost human being" is slightly slow and clumsy. Real humans are used for training, to experiment and to breed with these "almost humans." Some humans are kidnapped and used completely (even atoms). Some are kept in large tubes, and are kept alive in an amber liquid. Some humans are brainwashed and used to distort the truth. Certain male humans that have a high sperm count are kept alive. Their sperm is used to alter the DNA and create a non-gender being called "Type Two." That sperm is grown some way and altered again, put in large wombs, many destroyed, certain are altered again and then put in separate wombs. They resemble "ugly humans" when growing but look normal when fully grown which takes only a few months from fetus size. They have a short life span, less than a year. Some female humans are used for breeding. Countless women have had a sudden miscarriage after about three months pregnancy. Some never knew they were pregnant. Others remember contact some way. The fetus is used to mix the DNA in types one and two. The atomic makeup in that fetus is half human, half "almost human" and would not survive in the mother's womb. It is taken at three months and grown elsewhere.

Jason Bishop, who is associated with *UFO Contact Newsline*, (Suite 600, 8721 Santa Monica Blvd., Los Angeles, CA 90068, (213) 656-3331), has prepared a book for publication entitled *The Dulce Base*, which contains internal descriptions of it from people who have worked there. I have had the privilege of seeing an advance copy of a portion of the manuscript, which contains fascinating descriptions of the structure of the facility, its multiple levels, the types of uniforms and insignia, the security procedures, its administration, the names of key members of its Board of Directors (who are also highly placed officials in our visible and public government), and many other details, such as that alien living quarters are on the fifth level, and that:

> Level 6 is privately called 'Nightmare Hall.' It holds the genetic labs. Reports from workers who have seen bizarre experimentation are as follows: 'I have seen multi-legged 'humans' that look like half-human/half-octopus. Also reptilian-humans, and furry creatures that have hands like humans and cry like babies, mimicking human words ... also huge mixture of lizard-humans in cages.' There are fish, seals, birds and mice that can barely be considered those species. There are several cages (and vats) of winged humanoids, grotesque bat-like creatures... but 3 1/2 to 7 feet tall. Gargoyle-like beings and Draco Reptoids.
>
> Level 7 is worse, row after row of thousands of humans and humanoid mixtures in cold storage. Here too are embryo storage vats of humanoids, in various stages of development.
>
> I frequently encountered humans in cages, usually dazed or drugged, but sometimes they cried and begged for help. We were told they were hopelessly insane and involved in high-risk drug tests to cure insanity. We were told to never try to speak to them at all. At the beginning we believed that story. Finally in 1978, a small group of workers discovered the truth. It began the Dulce Wars.

This is apparently a reference to the incident mentioned by John Lear, concerning 'an altercation at the Dulce Labs' in the course of which 66 of our people were killed. According to the *Nevada Aerial Research Newsletter*, the elite Delta forces have a morale problem, quite common among them but rare in other branches of the Army: a soldier will suddenly break down and burst uncontrollably into prolonged weeping. When that happens to a soldier in the Delta Forces, that soldier immediately disappears and is never heard from again. If a Delta soldier overstays his leave by even a few hours, 'bounty hunters' are sent out after him.

ROOM LIGHT : PINK-PURPLE
BRIGHT IN SOME AREAS

HUNDREDS OF THESE IN
VARIOUS STAGES OF GROWTH.

WISPY HAIR, "ALMOST NOSE"
MOUTH LOOKS "SEALED"

WOMB LOOKS GREY
VEINS (?) LOOK DARK GREY
CREATURE WHITE- PALE
EYES - DARK LIDS (?)
CAN'T FIND GENDER
2 TOES - 3 FINGERS

LIQUID - AMBER COLOR
NOT COMPLETELY CLEAR

LOOKS LIKE GLASS TUBE,
BUT ABOUT 5 FT TALL

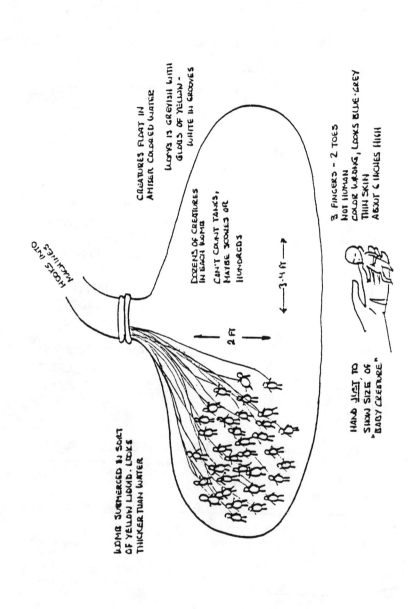

HOOKS INTO
MACHINES

WOMB SUBMERGED IN SORT
OF YELLOW LIQUID. LOOKS
THICKER THAN WATER

CREATURES FLOAT IN
AMBER COLORED WATER

WOMB IS GREYISH WITH
GLOBS OF YELLOW -
WHITE IN GROOVES

DOZENS OF CREATURES
IN EACH WOMB

CAN'T COUNT TANKS,
MAYBE SCORES OR
HUNDREDS

← 3-4 FT →

← 2 FT →

3 FINGERS - 2 TOES
NOT HUMAN
COLOR VARIES, LOOKS BLUE-GREY
THIN SKIN
ABOUT 6 INCHES HIGH

HAND JUST TO
SHOW SIZE OF
"BABY CREATURE"

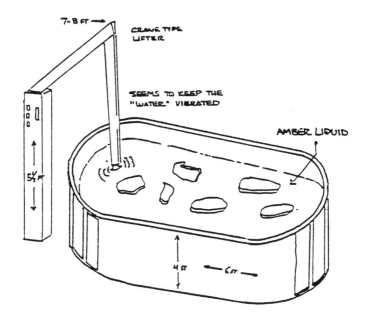

7-8 FT →

CRANE TYPE
LIFTER

SEEMS TO KEEP THE
"WATER" VIBRATED

AMBER LIQUID

5½ FT

4 FT

← 6 FT →

LOOKS LIKE LARGE PIECES
OF PALE MEAT IN CLOUDY
"WATER" SUBMERGED, NOT
FLOATING

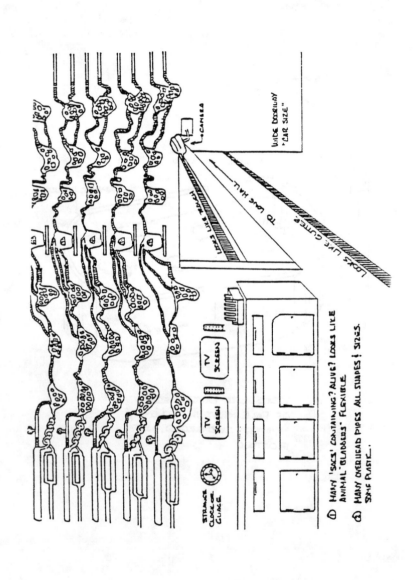

① MANY "SACS" CONTAINING? ALIVE? LOOKS LIKE ANIMAL "BLADDERS" FLEXIBLE

② MANY OVERHEAD PIPES ALL SHAPES & SIZES. SOME PLASTIC.

STRANGE CLOCK OR GUAGE

TV SCREEN

TV SCREEN

CAMERA

WIDE DOORWAY "CAR SIZE"

LOOKS LIKE A BENCH

TO LONG HALL

LOOKS LIKE GUTTER?

I don't feel I should proceed further without relaying what Bishop says about the secret control group at the core of our invisible government, the 32 members of the Jason Society, the top 12 members of which constitute MJ-12: 'They have secretly harnessed the dark side of technology, and hidden the beneficial technology from the public.'

10

The French Connection

by J. F. Gille
A Biographical Note

*B*orn: May 25, 1942, Paris, France — Under Nazi occupation until Summer, 1944. Very impressed by the 1954 UFO wave: I want to become an astronomer, or, preferably, an astronaut. But, even at that young age, I realize that the latter career is rather unlikely, for I'm not of the athletic/military type.

Late 50s - early 60s: I adhere to the 'psycho-socio' theory of UFO (hoaxes / delusion / political manipulation).

July 1, 1965: The Valensole case (a CE I + CE II + ...? - Alpes-de-Haute-Provence Dept., France) makes me change my mind (I had access to private channels to the witness, Mr. Maurice Masse).

1960-1974: I am a student in Mathematics at the University of Marseilles - in 1966-67 in Nice, a student of Jean Dieudonne.

Feb. 1970: I meet Aime Michel.

1970-1983: A researcher at the CNRS (National Council for Scientific Research).

1974: Awarded Ph.D. in Theoretical Physics.

1976-1978: Involved in the UMMO affair investigation.

Summer 1978: Anonymous and non-anonymous threats (some indirect threats from the very top).

May 1980: I arrive in the U.S. (for the MUFON Symposium in Houston). Don't find my way back to the airport.

March 1982-July 1983: In France.

November 1983-August 1986: In Houston, Texas.

Aug. 1988: I translate and disseminate (against the advice of some prominent Parisian ufologists) the John Lear statement.

September, 25 1988: Back in the US (mainly to try to investigate the Bennewitz Story)

MUFON Consultant since 1980

Quoted in Len Stringfield's *Status Report III* (Case B-8), and in "Above Top Secret," by Tim Good.

Ufo Sighting Over Mount Archuleta
October 23, 1988
by J. F. Gille

I. Location/time:

Southern slopes of Mount Archuleta, 5 miles northwest of Dulce, New Mexico. Dulce is about 27 miles west of Chama, on US 64, in Northwestern New Mexico, Rio Arriba County, and on the Jicarilla Apache Indian Reservation, only 4.5 miles south of the Colorado State Line.

Location of witnesses: 400 m (435 yd) southeast of Mount Archuleta Summit (elevation: 8136' = 2480 m; longitude = 107 degrees 03'17" W, latitude = 36 degrees 59'19" N — only 1.27 km = 0.79 miles = 1390 yd south of Colorado state line). Witnesses' spot height: 7900' = 2408 m.

Location of the phenomenon: south to north trajectory for about 2 miles (3 km), stopping very close to Mount Archuleta summit, seen from a 25-35 degree angle ("altitude" in Astronomy lingo) to the horizon (which makes for a height above sea level of 2600-2700 m or 8500'-8800'). Estimated closest observers-trajectory distance: 440 m (480 yd); distance observers-spot where the UFO stopped: 470 m (510 yd).

Time: 7:51 PM (1951 hours) local (mountain) time. Duration: a few seconds (Ms. Allegre, RN, estimated the duration of the whole observation as 5 to 6 seconds).

II. Witnesses:

Eliane Allegre, R.N., 44, residing in Albuquerque, New Mexico;

Gabriel Valdez*, New Mexico State Police, residing in Dulce at the time of the observation;

---

* Gabriel Valdez, who has been one of the most persistent and perceptive of those investigating the cattle mutilations ever since they began, is quoted on page 171 of *Extra-Terrestrials Among Us.*

Edmund, a friend of Mr. Valdez, local resident;

"Jack" (not his real name), Ph.D., a research scientist for a major laboratory in the US;

Manuel, local kid;

Greg, son of Mr. Valdez;

J. F. Gille, Ph.D., 46, residing in Albuquerque, NM.

III. Circumstances Of Sighting:

1. I was interested in the Dulce area because of rumors related to a jointly (CIA-Alien) occupied underground facility under Mount Archuleta, and to numerous associated UFO sightings, as reported by local residents.

Ref.: "UFO Crash at Aztec," by William S. Steinman, *UFO Photo Archives*, Tucson, 1986, ISBN 0-934269-05-X, pp. 578-604 (the Bennewitz Story);

"John Lear Statement" (privately published) Dec. 29, 1987, revised March 25, 1988.

A night of observation in the mountains had been planned under the leadership of Mr. Valdez.

2. Since about 7:30 PM, we had been playing a game (called "ouija" by some) at the instigation of Mr. Valdez. Five players are required: one of them (the subject) in turn is sat on a chair. The other four place their hands on the head of the "subject," and have a moment of quiet. Then, at a signal, they lift him, using only the tips of their forefingers, jabbing them under the subject's armpits and knees. In most cases, the subject is lifted very fast and easily one foot or two up. When the same stunt is attempted without the prior "meditation time," it is usually impossible to move the subject, even when the combined efforts result in much strain applied on the joints of the forefinger. Indeed, I know not of any conventional explanation, in terms of our Western Science, of this innocent game, played as it is around the world (I had played it in France when I was in my twenties).

Just as we were processing the last person (Jack), one of Mr. Valdez' sons shouted: "Look! Here it comes!" *(NOTE: I do not make the statement that there was a causal correlation between what we had just been doing and what we saw next. I merely report two consecutive events which may have or may not have been correlated.)*

3. Look of the phenomenon: The "object" (hereby designated as such — I personally was not able to make out any structure in it) came from the South at great speed, on a flat, straight, horizontal trajectory resulting, for the retina in our eyes (through the persistence of luminous impression, a standard physiological reaction) in a perfectly straight luminous line (yellowish, and of some thickness, like one that would have resulted from a

plane's landing light — it was, definitely, not a plane. I use this comparison to give an idea of the luminosity of the trajectory. We had seen already a number of shooting stars that night. The path of the trajectory itself was maybe hundreds or thousands of times more luminous than theirs).

There was not any sound coming from the phenomenon.

The object stopped dead on its tracks. Its trajectory final spot was very close to the top of Mount Archuleta, as we saw it from where we were.

At the same time, it became extremely luminous, lighting at least half the sky up. It looked literally like the blossoming of a flower of light. There was a "display of gorgeous lights of pure color" (to quote the John Lear Statement): yellow, pink, green, enhanced by the center of it giving out a shower of sparks (not unlike portable fireworks mounted on a stick seen on the 4th of July). There was kind of a mist, too, around the object's center, at this moment.

It then sort of "folded on itself," and disappeared, vanished. There was not anymore anything to be seen. Ms. Allegre's expression to describe the end of the phenomenon was "it slipped away into another dimension."

I usually have a rather impatient attitude toward UFO observations that exhibit a lower strangeness level than CE-IV's (abductions). Now, the above described case is not even a Close Encounter (object less than 200 yd. from the witness). Actually, for several months, I did not emphasize the importance of the Oct. 23 observation. However, it is not its strangeness level, undoubtedly low on an absolute reference scale, which gives its interest to that humble LITS: the exact location where the phenomenon did happen had been described, prior to our Oct. 23 observation, in at least two published documents. Namely, the "John Lear Statement" and "UFO Crash At Aztec" by W.S. Steinman (See precise references Supra, III.1). The John Lear Statement has been called a hoax and/or a piece of disinformation by some. We are, obviously, unable to check presently the genuineness of all claims stated in so rich a text. It may be worthy of note, nevertheless, that our observation on the slopes of Mt. Archuleta was kind of a Road to Damascus for one member of our party, a well-bred, experimented, hardnosed physicist. This fact alone, we believe, could well be a justification not to discard the observation, and, above all, to give a second look to Mr. Paul Bennewitz's statements, according to which there is an underground base operated by aliens under Mount Archuleta.

That hypothesis earned Mr. Bennewitz (from Albuquerque) a lot of rejection and jeers from the ufologic community, and very likely also, unfortunately, persecutions of an altogether much more serious nature. We'd like, someday, to delve deeper into that mysterious affair. Let's for now be content not to deprive the ufologic community of the details of this simple observation.

Albuquerque, February 20 - April 13, 1989*

Pine Gap Base: World Context
by Lucien H. Cometta
Translation by J.F. Gille

To understand the case of the Pine Gap U.S. base (near Alice Springs, Australia) better, I feel compelled to give some explanations beforehand. I hope those explanations will help to increase the general awareness of the extraordinary importance that facility has for mankind as a whole.

---

* Paul Bennewitz is a physicist who owns Thunder Scientific Laboratory, which is located near Kirtland Air Force Base in Albuquerque, New Mexico. On February 2, 1980, he saw four saucer-shaped objects within the boundaries of Manzano Weapons Storage Area, and took a film of them. He offered his 2,600 feet of 8 mm film, plus some still photographs, to the Intelligence officers at Kirtland AFB. Months later, an official Air Force report described the film as "depicting unidentified aerial objects flying over and around Manzano Weapons Storage Area and Coyote Canyon Test Area." Nevertheless, "no conclusion could be made whether these objects pose a threat to Manzano-Coyote Canyon areas." The Air Force declined to investigate the matter as Bennewitz had requested, refusing even to evaluate the information and photographs he had collected. Uncle Sam's Top Secret Weapons Storage Area, yet the officers in command consider it of no importance that unidentified aerial objects have been witnessed and photographed flying over and around this most highly classified ultra-sensitive off-limits facility?! Bennewitz persisted in his research. He tried to communicate with the beings who were piloting the objects through his computer, and was successful in doing this, but found out that they were not friendly. However, he continued to communicate with them and established a psychological profile of the aliens. He summarized his research in a 17-page report entitled "Project Beta," which is a brilliant analysis of the mentality, characteristics and motivations of this type of alien. It also describes how we humans may best extricate ourselves from the impossible situation in which we, in fact, are, including specifics about weaponry and strategies appropriate for defending ourselves, and for driving this type of alien from the Earth. The text contains grammar and punctuation mistakes, but is a work of genius. It was reproduced in *The Matrix* by Valdamar Valerian (Arcturus, 1988), along with two interviews that James McCampbell conducted with Bennewitz over the phone, which clearly establish that Bennewitz was eminently sane, a perceptive, well-balanced and original thinker. He was then physically seized and forcibly confined in a psychiatric institution, where he was subjected to electroshock and other "therapies" that silenced him for keeps. In my opinion, the Paul Bennewitz case constitutes a flagrant example of the misuse of psychiatric facilities to silence political dissidents, as was so often done in Russia before the advent of the Gorbachov era, perpetrated within the boundaries of the United States and under the aegis of the United States Government. It is also my opinion that the speech William Moore made about the Bennewitz case at the Las Vegas MUFON Conference in July, 1988 consisted of disinformation about disinformation, and was a smoke-screen designed to camouflage the facts of the case in order to discredit Bennewitz's original testimony, which is thoroughly documented in Linda Moulton Howe's essential masterwork, *An Alien Harvest* (LMH Productions, 1989).

The majority of the people, all over the world, are not lingering in doubt any more about whether UFOs and E.T.s are for real. They know they are real.

Early 1989, by and large, nobody questions their existence.

The case for UFOs and E.T.s aroused passions, controversies and grand-standing for years, some of it not quite rational. The matter being now settled, public opinion should cool down, and it is with a serene and clear mind that we ought to be thinking of the future, and of our future relationship with the peoples from space. However, the public mind is not at peace. It vaguely feels the governments are hiding "something real big," and it wonders where our leaders are going to lead mankind.

In the process of research and study of UFOs and aliens, researchers who do not take at face value the explanations from the scientific establishment have discovered unsettling facts and started to lift part of the coverup lid. The value and prestige of their sources of information do not leave any doubt of the truthfulness of these reports whose main outlines are summarized below.

Tesla Technology

As everybody knows (at least since the publications of Col. Tom Bearden, a few years ago), Nikola Tesla was a Czech immigrant who arrived in the United States in the 1890s. As early as 1898, he started to apply for patents, among which we find: the discovery of alternative current and polyphase current; the harnessing of earth magnetic forces to produce electric energy, and the transmission of that energy by "waves" of the same kind as radio's (wireless, and without any noticeable loss of power); radio broadcasts (long before Marconi); electro-magnetic and "anti-gravity" propulsion (for ground or air vehicles); the projection of electrostatic waves able to shield a city under a dome which no bomb or missile could get through without burning out; etc...

Unfortunately for him, Tesla intended to offer to the world *free and inexhaustible* energy, via the tapping of the electricity from the earth and atmosphere, then broadcasting it through a wave carrier, just like radio. That breakthrough was obviously not to the taste of the tycoons, owners of electric plants, generator and electric cable manufacturers, not to mention the oil kings. Came 1910, and poor Tesla was laughed at and ridiculed, and the people who had supported him financially were forced by mightier players to demand immediate repayment of the invested money. Regarded as a lunatic by the public, deserted by all, and utterly broke, Nikola Tesla died in the United States in 1943.

Russian and American Advanced Studies

As early as 1920, without the knowledge of the Western World, the then-young Soviet state collected all the pieces of information they could lay their hands on related to the works of Tesla (including his personal notebooks), and commissioned a staff of scientists to implement and perfect what Tesla had been forced to give up. As it was, Tesla had the uncanny ability to do mentally the most complicated computations. It was not the same thing with the Russian specialists, and, as computers were not yet around, it took them years to achieve any appreciable result. At the end of World War II, the Russians were on the brink of perfecting means of remote destruction using EM waves, and they were planning to carry on with their invasion of Europe, in spite of whatever opposition the American troops could have mustered against them. Fortunately for Europe, the atomic bomb dropped on Hiroshima dissuaded Stalin from even trying. Today, there is no doubt that the Russians have perfected, and even improved, the technology Tesla once discovered. They have access to inexhaustible sources of energy, and they have got weapons of formidable destructive potential that could perform remote-controlled "surgical" strikes. They made a statement of that to the Americans when they destroyed, several years ago, a submerged US nuclear submarine (USS Thresher, sunk April 4, 1963 in the Atlantic), which was cruising thousands of miles from their coast.

Of course, the Americans realized the mistake they had made when they turned down Nikola Tesla's discoveries, and, no later than toward the end of WW II, they started to work on those premises. In a few decades, they caught up with the Russian scientists, and it is permitted to think that they are by now about even with them. EM antigravity that Tesla was able to use for propulsion, free and inexhaustible electric energy he wanted to give to the world, are now at the disposition of the superpowers.

This advanced technology obviously allows them to have aerospace crafts of the "cigar" and "saucer" types, and it is more than likely that among the UFOs seen around the world, a fair number are good, honest-to-Earth, human contraptions. Likewise, it is known that the Russians have facilities in Riga that are meant to transmit waves able to recharge high voltage batteries aboard submerged submarines thousands of miles away. They can generate a mammoth stationary wave around the Earth, in the range of 9,000 to 14,000 Hz (cycles per second), producing a resonating electric field up to 350 km (220 miles) and higher. It is rumored that the Soviets have other similar bases, including one in the North Pole area. Naturally, the United States is not inactive and also has such facilities.

All of this is very nice, and all mankind should rejoice, for that new technology opens up extraordinary prospects: free energy, therefore considerable fall of the cost of living, and unhoped-for improvement of the standard of living for each individual; disappearance of famine in the world — in a nutshell, material well-being for all, an important change, especially for the worse-off people. Moreover, these new capabilities would widely open up the gates of deep space — an event that could possibly bring us a beneficial spiritual evolution. Thus, theoretically, the man-in-the-street should see no evil in the development of that technology. However, the governments not only have never informed the public of those prodigious advances, but they have gone to great lengths and spent a lot of money to keep a lid of secrecy on them. What are *they* getting at? What are *they* aiming at? No doubt the setting-up of a world dictatorship, under the guise of a One World government, which will make a show of bringing us peace and true "equality" for all, with the exception, of course, of the top leaders, who will experience boundless power and a luxury that would have humbled the monarchs of old.

All of the above enables us now to talk about Pine Gap.

Pine Gap

The United States has three major bases in Australia. One is in South Australia (Nurrangar, near Woomera, T.N.), another in New South Wales, and the third, and by far the largest, is located within about 230 km (143 miles) of the geographical center of the continent [The French original says, erroneously, 12 km (7.5 miles). Even then, 230 km is actually less than 6/100 of the breadth of the continent], not far to the west of Alice Springs (Northern Territory), at the foothills of the southern slopes of the MacDonnell Range. This base is completely underground, with entrances barely visible from the surface. This "Top Secret" base is entirely financed by the U.S. Government and is officially known as a "Joint Defense Space Research Facility." Early on, its aim was scientific research for the development of a space defense technology. It is now known that, since its induction, the base was mainly used to study ElectroMagnetic Propulsion, EMP (not to be confused with E.M. Pulse, endeared to our strategists).

What exactly is Pine Gap? As strange as it may seem, even Australian Federal Parliament members do not know. Among the Cabinet members, only a very small number of "initiates" have a vague idea of what this is all about. The only information source available to the public is the cross-checking done by private researchers such as Jimmy Guieu.

It is said that under Pine Gap is the deepest drilling hole in Australia —

about 5 miles, more than 8,000 meters. Such a drilling hole is likely used as an underground antenna able to recharge the batteries of submarines in the Pacific or the Indian Ocean through ELF broadcasts. Such an antenna could be used also to generate the gigantic stationary wave around the Earth I alluded to.

Some say that Pine Gap has an enormous nuclear generator to supply energy to a new type of transmitter-receiver (transceiver). It seems too that there is a high-powered, high-voltage plasma accelerator, which may be put to use to transmit electric current, or even to produce a "Death Ray," or quite simply to feed a plasma gun. All of this is not as incredible as it sounds: it is now known that the U.S. base to the north at West Cape, near Exmouth Gulf in Western Australia (Harold E. Holt USN Communication Station) has an older type of the transceiver at Pine Gap, which is used to send electric current to submerged U.S. submarines who trail a wire antenna. It is known that electric currents transmitted in this way are powerful enough to recharge high-voltage batteries of the type called plasmodynamic cell batteries.

Several times, the locals have seen white discs about 30' (10m) wide, in the process of being unloaded from large U.S. cargo planes on airports serving Pine Gap. Those discs had the USAF emblem on them. It seems likely that flying saucer-type crafts are assembled and based at this secret base. The number of UFOs, seen very often at night by motorists traveling across the Nullarbor Plain, is such that, locally, nobody seems to doubt it. An amazing quantity of furniture, of a quality which wouldn't mar a five-star luxury hotel, has also been delivered by plane from the U.S. The locals say that an enormous amount of food is stocked in the warehouses of what could well be a true multi-leveled underground city.

On the other hand, Pine Gap is well known as one of the most important control centers for spy satellites that circle the globe. An article published late 1973 claimed the Pine Gap installations, along with those of its sister base in Guam, were used to control the photographic missions of the large American satellites in orbit above Earth. The quality of the shots was such, said that article, that it was possible to identify a 7 inch (18 cm) large object.

Computers of huge capacity are among the assets of this giant anthill. Those computers are connected to their American and Australian central counterparts, which collect all the pieces of information secured in these countries, not only about finance or technology, but on every aspect of the life of the average citizen. Those computers in Pine Gap are also connected to similar mainframes in Guam, in Krugersdorp (30 km west of Johannesburg, South Africa) and at the Amundsen-Scott U.S. base at the South Pole.

Let us say, incidentally, that the employees (more than 1200) of the U.S. base in South Africa all claim to be members of the U.S. consular mission in that country. It may be worthy of note that the Amundsen-Scott base at the South Pole is located on a sensitive magnetic spot of our planet, that it holds exactly the same assets as Pine Gap, and that all the information about most of the average citizens of Western Europe is stored there in memory banks tens of meters under the icepack.

A statement made by the Australian Premier sometime during 1987, assuring that "France must disappear from the Pacific, from the Kerguelen Ridge, and from Antarctica" sheds light on the importance of this polar base for the Anglo-Saxon world.

But the most disquieting fact about Pine Gap may be that the employees working on the base, and especially those earmarked for duty on the EMP Project, have undergone brainwashing and even implantation of intracranial devices. Those employees have turned into unconditional slaves of their master, whoever he is. Rather scary, isn't it?

The true point of the brainwashing of those individuals, along with the ruthless attempt to implement the coverup of really advanced military technology, will become clear at the end of this article.

For me, all began with the construction of the new Parliament Building in Canberra which cost an impressive number of billions of dollars. Australia has only 18 million inhabitants so far, yet it treats itself to a building far beyond its means, supposedly to accomodate its government, even though the old Parliament building was perfectly suitable. This new building, enormous, immense and magnificent would easily fill the needs of the USSR or of the United States, which both have hundreds of millions of citizens to rule. That building puzzled me, and I started to talk about it around me, until the day I bumped into an Englishman who told me that the Australian Premier, Bob Hawk, was a Rhodes Scholar, and as such he worked toward the setting-up of a One World government, and that this new Parliament building likely had something to do with it. I could not figure out straight away what that Englishman meant, but I didn't dwell on it. Some time after, I stumbled on a pamphlet published by the Human Rights Organization, which talked of a group of about a hundred people well placed in high finance, politics, the judiciary branch and big business, which had formed the "Club of Rome." According to this pamphlet, the Club of Rome was pledged to a consortium which controls all of international high finance. A number of other groups similar to the Club of Rome are equally pledged to that finance consortium. The Human Rights Organization says they are infiltrating the various political parties and religious denominations with the intention to stealthily make progress toward the institution of a world dictatorship.

The whole thing looked a little bit too preposterous to be true, it seemed to me. Nevertheless, a friend of mine gave me an audio cassette taped at a lecture given by Peter Sawyer, a former high-ranking Australian civil servant, which exposed a certain number of facts he had noticed while he was in office. He talked, in particular, of a telephone exchange in Canberra called "Deacon Center." This exchange, built in concrete with four-foot-thick walls, cost hundreds of millions of dollars. Not to mention the telephonic hardware proper, it is fitted out with numerous computers, arrayed on four levels, for a total bill of over 150 mega bucks. When he tried to find out why such an equipment was needed in a country with a population of 18 million, he discovered that those computers were connected to all the banks, to every post office, to all of the telephone exchanges, to each and every one of the money machines, to every one of the police stations and customs houses, to every arrival or departure desk for air or sea travellers; and also and above all, to the other data bank centers collecting data on private citizens, in the U.S. as well as in Europe.

That facility on Deacon Street is therefore a center where all the data pertaining to each and every one of the citizens of the Western World ends up being stored. All financial, economic, political and military information, as well as the information on every inhabitant of those countries. As a matter of course, all people living in Australia are put on file, kept up with and labelled. All Australians' expenses, their income, their travels, their illnesses and their familial behavior are stored in the memory banks of the Deacon Center in Canberra, along with similar information pertaining to the inhabitants of the Western countries.

Peter Sawyer discovered also that the President of the Rockefeller Foundation came for a lengthy stay in Australia to supervise in person the construction of 20 luxury residences in Canberra (the Australian government footed the bill), in the wonderful setting of a National Park, where, legally, nobody is allowed to build.

The investigations led by Sawyer exposed, first, that the new Parliament Building is meant to accomodate the world government-to-be; and, second, that the 20 luxury residences will be allocated to the different foreign members of that Government...Why choose Canberra as the headquarters of the World Government? Simply because Australia is a peaceful country, with very few natives likely to turn rebellious, and, above all, it's an English-speaking country. No other English-speaking country can offer the safety Australia will provide at the time of the take-over by the World Government. In America or in Europe, uprisings are more than likely, and South America not only is not English speaking, but its fondness for revolutions and social disturbances is well-known.

Australia is thus the ideal place for such an undertaking. Well, then, but how could the advent of a World Government ever be possible in the near future? It is relatively easy, as we are going to explain.

First, who are those "internationalists" who want to take over the world? The answer will surprise more than a little: the ones who want to set up a world government are fifteen families or so (Cf. R.C. Girard's "This Is A Test..." (MUFON J.#251, March '89, p. 15, col. 1) and "Elements Of The Equation" (Chap. 6, Arcturus '88), who already govern all of international high finance and keep a tight leash on most of the governments through the absolute control of their finances and their domestic economy. Those finance moguls devised their plan after World War I, and have been working ever since on an insidious undermining process aimed at economic destabilization all over the West.

If those financiers are obviously labeled "capitalists," it is a very deceptive label, because they never stopped pulling the strings of the progressive parties, as well as those of the conservative parties. Their idea is logical, and lies, quite simply, in the destabilization of the countries of the West on the political, economic, and religious levels. It may be surprising to some that these "innovators" have taken on the religions — the great religions raise moral barriers, which are strongly against the unethical and non-altruistic aims of the sponsors of what they call the Universal New Order — so their power over the masses had to be thoroughly cut down. Since henchmen of theirs had infiltrated the top levels of the main religious establishments, only a small number of years was necessary to make them virtually powerless. The rifts between the Jewish and Catholic faiths are just an example.

Economic destabilization is implemented through a slower but most efficient process. I am not going to speak of the numerous difficulties encountered by the various countries as far as economy is concerned, but I will describe the process, already on its way, that will cause the entire financial system of the West to suddenly collapse as easily as a blockbuster bomb would level a building. The moguls of international finance have indeed devised a monstrous plan to that effect. Those are the ones who are responsible for the rises in the price of oil when they said to the Arab leaders that they were going to make the European governments agree to those rises, providing that the yield coming from the rises would be paid to the "International Reserve Bank," which is entirely at their command. The Reserve Bank handed over those amounts of money to a "holding" bank, which lavishly loaned this huge heap of dollars to the Third World countries — for usurious rates of interest. That holding bank receives the interests paid by the underdeveloped countries, then puts them back almost entirely into another holding bank which, in turn, invests that huge quantity of money on behalf of the Arabs. Those investments are made into thriving and usually very large businesses, international hotel chains, enormous farming estates, etc. In the meantime, only relatively small interests are sent to the Arab countries — yet those interests are considerable enough to allow the "oil kings" to achieve important improvements and public works in their countries, while they buy real estate for themselves in Europe. None of that looks fishy.

But wait! Things are soon going to change. Those who engineered that plan were perfectly aware that the leaders of the underdeveloped countries would be tempted to pocket a good part of the received money (they were prompted a little bit, if need be) due to the fact that they had no experience in "high politics," no more than in "international finance." It was obvious beforehand that the industries and farming concerns in those countries would not receive enough aid to improve the economic situation, and that the high interest rate subscribed to would throw those Third World nations into even worse financial hardship.

The outcome will be that, sooner or later, those countries will be forced to accept the offer the "holding bank" has started to make them, according to which the repayment of their debt and of the interests will not be required, if the governments sign an agreement with the bank giving it perpetual prospecting and exploiting rights on all mining resources of their country. Whether this agreement is signed or not doesn't really matter, because if the debtors are not able to pay, the holding bank will go bankrupt — and that's the important thing. The International Reserve Bank will then tell the Arab countries that the holding bank's investments have turned out badly, all their assets have vanished and that no interest will be paid any more. Then the Arab countries will have no other choice than to put on the market all the securities they own, as well as quite an amount of property bought by the second holding bank. Moreover, a good part of those possessions will then be frozen, because they will have been bought with the aid of not entirely repaid loans, and they will be part of the assets of the first holding bank, gone bankrupt. The incredible quantity of shares put on the market at the same time will cause a stock market crash of such magnitude that all the national economies of the West will collapse at the same time. The world will find itself in a desperate predicament. Cash will not be worth a damn, and the risks of a global confrontation will be high.

At that point, the usefulness of bases like Pine Gap will become obvious. If a global confrontation is going to break out, those bases, which have the capacity to shelter tens of thousands of people, will serve as a place of safety for the politicians of that time and their staffs, as well as for the international financiers, their families, and their lieutenants. If no confrontation breaks out, the technologically advanced achievements that are there will give the opportunity to the financiers to pose as saints, as they offer to the world, from a safe place, the miracle cure which will surely save it, namely the replacement of all currencies by plastic cards ensuring "true equality" for all; the abolition of all ownership rights; and the setting up of a One World government that will ensure world peace.

Of course, the new system will not be to everybody's taste, but the masses will be convinced that it is necessary to ensure peace and social justice by any means, including force. The potential uses of the equipment in the underground bases, scattered widely throughout the world, will make possible the disappearance without a trace of nonconformists hindering the "happiness of the people" (they may be sent away somewhere else, as in Leslie Watkins' *Alternative 3* (Cf. "The Matrix" (p. 205), by Val Valerian, Arcturus '88); and it will ensure also the swift crushing of any possible uprising. It may even happen that our new masters will tell the people that they have the aliens' support, and that we are at the eve of the Millenium, a Golden Age, as promised in the Scriptures (Rev. 20:2). And it will be the worst dictatorship ever known by man.

It is easy to imagine what will be said against "those dirty Arabs" because of what will have caused the collapse of the world market with the all-out selling of their securities! Don't get me wrong, I am not especially pro-Arab, no more than I am pro-Jew: I am only alluding to the party line of that time, a future time not that far off.

It may be worth noting that a few years ago, two brothers, billionaire bankers in Texas, fed up with what they saw brewing, tried to check those insane schemes. In order to get more credibility with the Arab countries, they were able to enlist the Shah's political and financial support (before he was abruptly deposed). It didn't take more than a few weeks for the brothers to be indicted on a charge of so-called fraudulent bankruptcy and wind up in jail. In the meanwhile, the Shah had to face a revolution, was deposed, and, after a short treatment in a "private hospital" in the U.S. (while he was not sick), he sneaked away from the CIA, and died in Egypt.

I beg the reader's forgiveness, for it was not possible for me to talk about Pine Gap without explaining how it fitted in to the picture of the present world scene. The above-mentioned Pine Gap sister bases are, for the Southern Hemisphere: Guam, Krugersdorp in South Africa, and the one in Antarctica. All have exactly the same technological assets. In Australia, Pine Gap is backed up by: one base in New South Wales, one in the Northern Territory, as well as the (North) West Cape base, Western Australia, a few hundred miles (700 miles = 1,130 km actually) north of Perth. It is quite certain that in the U.S. and in the Northern Hemisphere, other bases of this kind have been built. It may even be that the U.S. bases occupied by the Grays are of the same type. By the way, and it sounds so incredible that I did not intend to mention it, one rumor holds that a representative of the Grays is stationed in each of the underground U.S. bases in the Southern Hemisphere.

None of the above has anything to do with science fiction. If some details turn out to be inaccurate in the future, it may be because of the tinkering that will be done to face up to unfolding events.

The investigations done by the Australian Peter Sawyer and an American researcher look like they have been conducted in an honest manner; their respective conclusions coincide and also match with Stan Deyo's opinion as expressed in his book *The Cosmic Conspiracy* (West Australian Texas Trading, 1978). I content myself with correlating facts that, apparently, have nothing to do with each other.

Anyhow, they don't give a rosy view of the future.

Truly, Australia and the world could find a use for the "Knights of Light" (*Les Chevaliers de Lumiere* is the name of a science-fiction saga, by Jimmy Guieu, which stages a fight between cosmic forces of good and evil in a series of books).

(End of Lucien Cometta's article.)

Another piece of the puzzle turned up in my mail from France. The source has no direct relationship with the subject of UFOs, being the excellent ecological agriculture magazine *Nature et Progres*, article by Daniel Depris on "Electromagnetics and Health" in its July/August 1989 issue. I felt that I should translate the following excerpt from it, because it is clearly relevant to the large-scale microwave emissions from the Pine Gap facility, that we have just read about.

"The FM radio band that goes from 87.5 to 108 MHz is one of the most dangerous to the public health, given the lengths of the waves under consideration (from about 3.40 to 2.75 m). We have already discussed how the human body acts as a receptive antenna. Global resonance for the average individual would be ideal for functioning as a grounded half-wave antenna, a mode that permits the capture of a maximum amount of energy emitted by this FM radio band. An individual whose height is 1.7 meters (about 5 feet 7 inches) will resonate to the maximum at a half-wave from the frequencies near 88 MHz. In the same way, a child whose height is 1.4 meters (about 4 feet 6 inches) will resonate just as perfectly to 108 MHz. I insist on the fact that we are wide-band antennas, and that most human beings will be primarily affected by frequencies ranging from 50 to 200 MHz. As far as global resonance is concerned, infants and young children will mainly be in resonance with frequencies from 100 to 250 MHz. The very large scale use of the 87.5 to 108 MHz frequencies constitutes a total aberration in public health planning."

Was this total aberration deliberately planned by those in charge of using the mass media for purposes of mass mind-control?

This final item has nothing to do with France, but is nevertheless relevant to the material discussed in this chapter. The following despatch from the Knight-Ridder wire service appeared in the *Sunday World*, Tulsa, OK, on Dec. 10, 1989:

San Jose, Calif. — Unusual radio waves recorded hours before the Loma Prieta earthquake struck may someday provide a way to warn of an impending temblor, a Stanford University researcher said Thursday.

Three hours before the quake hit, an instrument Stanford researchers were using near the quake's epicenter registered the most powerful signal it had received in two years of listening. The waves continued until the moment of the quake, when the electricity failed and the instrument shut down.

"We've seen very unusual things we can't understand," said Arman Bernardi, one of a team of Stanford researchers that, by sheer coincidence, was studying submarine communications.

The instrument, in a mountain house in Corralitos, began receiving a substantial increase in ultra-low frequency radio waves 12 days before the quake.

Antony Fraser-Smith, the leader of the Stanford team, has no explanation for how the earth could have generated the radio waves but said he is convinced they were related to the earthquake.

But a government geologist cautioned against reading too much into the Stanford findings.

"It's common to have strange things happen (just before earthquakes) and it's just coincidental," said Malcolm Johnston, of the U.S. Geological Service...

Since this was a previously unknown phenomenon, on what grounds did government geologist Malcolm Johnston base his scientific certitude that it was merely coincidental? Was the San Francisco earthquake triggered artificially?

11

An Explosive Exchange

When Whitley Strieber's book *Communion* (Morrow, New York, 1987) was published, I wrote to him and congratulated him on having carried out a genuine landmark study in the history of UFO research — a monumental breakthrough. He replied briefly, and included my name on his "Communion Network" list, after having asked my permission to do so. This list contained the names and addresses of approximately 300 people, all of whom had expressed sincere interest in or had first-hand experience with alien abductions, who were invited to communicate with each other. Letters began to turn up in the mailbox, and I in turn increased my circle of correspondence. The exchanges of information have been quite interesting. I felt and still think that Strieber's idea had been an excellent one. I hope that the exchange of ideas and experiences that has begun continues into the future. However, one circumstance drastically changed my opinion about what the Network was originally designed to accomplish by Strieber's alien mentors.

I corresponded with Winston Sarafian, a member of the Network who seemed exceptionally knowledgeable about the short Grays, having experienced multiple abductions by them. I do my best to remain as free as possible from bias of any kind, either positive or negative, while gathering and evaluating evidence. However, when I was researching this book, much of the information that surfaced concerned negatively oriented alien activities. Until I received Sarafian's answer to my letter pointing out the existence of these apparently hostile alien activities, I had been entirely open to the possibility that the short Grays — however strange they looked and some of their actions seemed — might in the long run turn out to be compatible with terrestrial humanity, at least to the point where it would be possible to work out a public and mutually satisfactory planet-sharing arrangement, rather than the eminently unsatisfactory present situation of covert manipulation of the populace by the aliens through governmental intelligence agencies. Sarafian's letter of Nov. 11, 1987, drastically changed my opinion. Here are the relevant passages from that letter:

I agree that we shouldn't 'make a pact with the first group of aliens that come along,' but it seems that the U.S. and British governments have already done so in hopes of acquiring new scientific knowledge and technology....Earth is already part of the Reticulan Network. The Reticulans have infiltrated human society to such a degree that we may have no choice but to accept their overlordship, provided they wish to become our overlords....The Reticulans don't understand most human emotions, since they are so highly intellectual and spiritual. Moreover, they have a mission to perform — namely surveillance, direct observation of human 'participants,' genetic and psychological experimentation on human subjects, hybridization and domestication of the human species, and eventual repopulation of planet Earth with domesticated hybrid humans — which precludes them from treating us as equals. Their aim is to develop a hybrid species, which I have termed Homo Sapiens Extraterrestrialis. This goal has already been attained to a large degree, and in the next decade we will probably see the hybrids taking over key positions in human societies. In any event, human population will soon be drastically reduced due to a resurgence of catastrophic pandemic diseases, environmental degradation, atmospheric destruction, and geophysical changes....Yes, indeed, like Nazis, the Reticulans are determined to achieve their eugenic goals at all costs. And, like the Nazis, they are intent on supplanting our independence of mind and spirit with a subordination to the Network super brain....Based on their ability to project brain waves and influence human behavior, I believe that the Reticulans are part of an alien network tied to a super brain. In short, an individual Reticulan functions as part of a group mind, or group consciousness. In Reticulan society all individual brains are linked together into a single super brain....The Reticulans are suffering from incurable genetic diseases and must have our DNA and genes to strengthen their race. They are dying out as a result of weakened and broken DNA. As a species they have existed for many millions of years longer than humans, but know they have reached the end of their evolutionary development and have regressed to an infantile form.

This is my response to Winston Sarafian:

The Reticulans, or short Grays, are not the only E.T. group inter-acting with us. The tall Blonds seen working with the Grays are prisoners of war or cloned hybrids. The genuine tall Blonds are an entirely different group.

I sympathize with the fact that the Grays have used up their DNA, and are facing extinction as a species. However, even in such an emergency situation there are certain cosmic guidelines to be fol-lowed. There are limits to the extent that one intelligent species can exploit another intelligent species without a backlash.

Sooner or later the genuine tall Blonds will intervene decisively in this hybridization process you assume to be inevitable. It is not for me to say when or how, but I can assure you that I would not want to be among the Quislings who have sold their birthright to the Grays for a mess of pottage when this happens.

The Grays may have taken over our so-called intelligence agen-cies (a misnomer if there ever was one), our governments, and sub-stantial portions of our populations. I realize that they are about to release mass death on this planet on a hitherto unprecedented scale, and that their deployment of the AIDS virus was a mere foretaste of what they have in store for us. But so long as one free-thinking man and woman remain alive upon this planet, victory will elude them. They could not win the war for Hitler, nor will they win the unde-clared war now in progress.

Are you aware that the super-brain you refer to is that of the Spider Queen of Space, worshipped on this planet only by renegade cults such as the Obeah branch of Voodoo, and some disciples of Aleister Crowley? It is certainly a super-brain, but is just as cer-tainly not omniscient or infallible. It is, in fact, extremely vulnerable to telepathically focused White Light.

If you wish to be one of those 'bellwethers...superior slaves or overseers' Charles Fort referred to (see page 106 of my previous book), so be it. The Reticulans may assume that they already own the Earth, and we have no choice but to accept their overlordship, but they have some surprises coming. As the old saying goes, there's many a slip between the cup and the lip. I choose to be one of those who rally round the battle cry of 'Liberty or death!' (That ends my response to Winston Sarafian.)

Whitley Strieber has repeatedly stated that he hates the word "abductee," because it implies that one is a victim, and prefers the word "participant." However, what this substitution, in fact, does is to blur the distinction between voluntary and involuntary. A person who voluntarily accompanied the aliens on board their craft would be a participant. A person whose mind is controlled by techniques known or unknown to our science, or who is subjected to any physical constraint, is an abductee.

Strieber also insists on substituting the word "visitor" for the word "alien," thereby blurring yet another distinction. One of the connotations of "visitor" is that of a guest who has been invited into one's home, while the term "alien" has no such implication. The Grays who abducted Strieber, and inserted the implants into his brain that were detected by doctors using the Magnetic Resonance Imaging Scan technique, are so very different from terrestrial Homo sapiens that they are in fact an alien life-form. Anyone who has studied the abductions that the Grays have been systematically perpetrating on a large cross-section of our population is well aware that the Grays do not wait to be invited, but take people whether those people wish to go with them or not.

Terrestrial humans who treat other humans as the Grays treat humans are condemned to stiff sentences in the penitentiary on kidnapping charges, if not kidnapping and rape, yet Strieber glosses over this obvious fact with a sugar coating by his insistence on substituting nebulously polite terms like "participant" and "visitor" for factually accurate words like "abductee" and "alien." Once you agree to play the game by his rules, with their deliberate blurring of boundaries, you are adrift in ambiguity, with no chance whatsoever of avoiding total control by the Grays.

In the newsletter that he has started (*The Communion Letter*, Spring 1989), Strieber outlines the policies to be implemented in the groups he intends to form, giving them some twists that are very strange indeed.

Those who have devoted substantial time and energy to the study of alien abductions, and persist in calling a spade a spade, are anathematized and excommunicated from the gatherings of the faithful flock. The groups are warned to shun abduction researchers. The well-documented genetic experimentation of humans by aliens is attributed to fantasies generated by the nasty minds of those same researchers, who are also accused of spreading fear in order to control others, though what the researchers are actually doing is sharing their research results with the public, making no attempt whatsoever to dominate anyone, or to prevent people from drawing their own conclusions based on independent examination of the data.

Strieber recommends that when a "participant" remembers experiences with "visitors" that generate fear, the "participant" should seek the help of a professional psychologist. What this policy does is to automatically assume that any fear-generating memory is caused by some psychological flaw in the abductee's personality for which the aliens are not responsible. The policy also guarantees that memories of traumatic interaction with the aliens will not be allowed to surface within the context of group meetings.

Earlier in this book, we saw what "help" from contemporary mental health professionals typically entails. The few enlightened exceptions are very rare indeed.

The Strieber newsletter's attitude toward the abduction of children by the Grays is summed up in the title of a sub-section: "The Magic Playground." The impression given is that the abduction of children by the Grays is a wholesome adventure, as innocent and entertaining as a trip to the movies to enjoy Snow White and the Seven Dwarfs.

As Charles Fort so wisely said over half a century ago: "... all this has been known, perhaps for ages, to certain ones upon this earth, a cult or order, members of which function like bellwethers to the rest of us, or as superior slaves or overseers, directing us in accordance with instructions received — from somewhere else — in our mysterious usefulness" (see *Extra-Terrestrials Among Us*, page 106).

A hive mind might make mistakes that we as individuals would not make, such as prematurely disclosing the details of a long-range master-plan for conquest through an over-eager acolyte, as occurred in the Winston Sarafian letter of Nov. 11, 1987. We as individuals make mistakes that a hive mind would not make. We think for ourselves, not together as a species. We once had a collective tribal consciousness, not all that different from a hive mind.

It is not so very far back in our own history to the period when a king was buried with his wives and key members of his court, who followed him into death. It could even be argued that such a collective tribal mentality is still a dominant factor on the contemporary scene, in the form of chauvinistic nationalism or self-righteous ideologies. The Chinese students massacred in Tienanmen Square were attempting to assert their right to think for themselves, instead of blindly following the dictates of an autocratic insectile hive mind, whose sub-human political instruments cold-bloodedly murdered them.

Our liberty to think and act as free individuals is a hard-won fragile prize that has been acquired only recently, and the struggle to maintain it is far from over. The word "totalitarian" defines social systems based on a collective mentality, which under a variety of disguises continue to exercise a pervasive influence on our democracies. Autocratic royalty was an earlier version of the totalitarian social systems, which dominated human history for many millennia, in comparison to the 200-year life-span of our contemporary democracies.

In the world today, the gigantic multi-national corporations have taken over the role of autocratic royalty, constituting predatory oligarchies disguised by a veneer of democracy that siphon the wealth of entire nations, tunnel-visioned dinosaurs oblivious to any values except immediate profit, determined to let nothing stand in the way of their systematically trashing this planet's biosphere and irrevocably polluting our environment. I have long been puzzled by the fact that such policies do not make sense even on a business level. To deliberately sacrifice not only the well-being but the survival of our children and grandchildren for short-term financial gain is so obviously suicidal that it makes no sense in human terms. It is difficult to understand how such policies achieved dominance and official acceptance in human society. However, if at the highest levels of our main financial and governmental structures the decision-making power is under the control of non-human aliens, whose only concern is to harvest this planet's resources (including the human population) as efficiently as possible, these policies become quite understandable.

Researcher Tal LeVesque, who specializes in the study of the reptilian mankind, describes the situation as follows:

> About 12,000 years ago a battle for the possession of the surface of the Earth occurred, accompanied by massive destruction and flooding. At that time most but not all of the Elder Race and the Reptoids left the Earth. Their confrontation was broken off until that future time, which now approaches: the Elder Angels versus the Dragon/Serpent beings.
>
> The survivors of the ancient battle secured bases to operate from in the caverns that honeycomb the planet. Certain Amerindian and other groups were temporarily taken into protective caverns, but were later returned to the surface. Some humans survived even though they had remained on the surface during the cataclysm. Insectoid entities on the astral plane saw an opportunity to manipulate these survivors through lower-level egotistic survival drives, such as greed or lust or anger. The Insectoids began by controlling the activities of weak-willed individuals under stress, then through them influenced the behavior patterns of others. The Insectoids are astral overseers that survive on the energy released by violence, stress, fear, and the vibrations from the sacrificial killing of animals and humans. This is the Dark Lord.
>
> However, the insectile mentality of the Dark Lord would quickly relinquish control to commands from a spiritual force of superior

beings. The Dark Lord can also be weakened by periods of peace, through starvation due to lack of emotional storms, violence and killing. The astral agents of the Dark Lord drain the life-energy from physically living creatures, such as ourselves. What animal mutilations, Voodoo rituals and Satanic rites do is to direct energy toward the elemental astral beings that feed off of this type of activity.

Some of you thought that you were dealing with alien E.T.s, and you indeed are, but who is controlling who, for what and why? This becomes quite complex.

For example, the Aztec priests sacrificed prisoners, cutting out their hearts in a violent ceremony. The Mexican pyramids all have tunnels leading to deep cavern pits, into which the bodies of the victims were thrown. Their flesh fed the Reptoids that live underground. The astral Insectoids used this energy release to feed themselves. They were the Host of the Hive God Overlords.

Demons are still waving their antennae at this scurrying swarm of manipulated beings, who are driven to drain, destroy and lay waste to vast areas, madly in ant-like fashion, fervently devouring nature and competing with war-like zeal. We burn cattle flesh on the altars in our back yards and at the Golden Arches, as the vortex of smoke rises into the polluted sky, lit by searchlights powered from a local nuclear plant that produces "pellets" for the bombs.

Like the AIDS virus, the Insectoids are opportunistic. They are also powerfully hypnotic. However, they are lower astral entities, with corresponding mentalities. Fully conscious Elder Man or Reptilian Man can deal effectively with astral mind-matrix patterns, which like demons hang out around weak people and planets.

Nobody likes astral parasites. They use everybody and every living thing. They are the original Fascists.

Look around! If we are animal man, then why do we act more like insects than animals?

At this point I will tell you a secret: The Reptoids are fellow members of humanity. We are hu (animal) man, and they are reptilian man. They became self-conscious first, before we appeared on the scene. They taught us. However, we both got manipulated and tricked into becoming enemies at war with each other. The astral Insectoids deceived us both, and we are still in a species war with our fellow reptilian man. The real physical danger comes from the adversarial conflict in our struggle with each other. However, the astral and spiritual danger is from the Insectoid mentality, which is alien to both humans and Reptoids.

The Insectoid power fears the Black races and has kept them subjected and confused for they hold the key to knowledge. Their genetic clan information is needed to unlock advanced secrets from the Sirius data. Segmented data units are also carried by Indian clans, some of which were originally from the fourth planet in the Sirius system.

In unity and in diversity, mankind holds the secret of our spiritual heritage and the future!

There are cross-breeds, human-looking in form. The Rh-negatives are our link to the reptilian humanoids. They are mostly found among the Celtic people, the English, the Hebrews, certain Indian tribes, and some groups of Black people in Africa. The Reptoids cross-breed with everybody.

The short Grays are somewhat demented from exposure to high radiation levels, which also made them susceptible to lower-level astral thought patterns, leading to habits of control and misuse of intellect. For the most part, these agents of the Dark Lord are residing in certain specific cavern areas, midway between the surface of Earth and its interior lands. They cause a great deal of confusion among the surface dwellers. How do you know who is who?

By their fruits shall you know them.

If an alien UFO being teaches fear, war, separation, excessive involvement in politics, or preaches great disaster from an angry God, then their fruits are of the negative. Ignore them, no matter what they fly in, no matter what they produce in the way of miracles and wonders.

Because they feed off your energy, they will vanish and their power will subside if you give them none.

If a being comes in light and love, with great compassion and empathy for others, and without pretensions teaches a way that helps to resolve our problems, whose presence is uplifting and gives joy, then this is a Higher Being, whether extra-terrestrial or terrestrial. Welcome those who bring power for the good.

Discernment of motive is the ageless truth we take with us on our quest within the spiral of existence.

Discernment of motive is also what Riley Crabb of the Borderland Sciences Research Foundation focuses his attention on. The following summary of some of his highly acute perceptions is based on work that is listed in the Credits:

So-called "defense" is to save the elite few who will survive the first exchange of missiles. Once the defense is proven adequate, it will be time to shoot. Under Reagan, billions were spent on underground shelters for the few, in order to enable a selected group of Americans to survive the Russian response to a first strike nuclear attack by the U.S. All Reagan's staff members are members of the Knights of Malta, who believe nuclear war with Russia to be inevitable, and that we must shoot first to survive.

This was revealed to us here in New Zealand the night of Dec. 11, 1986. A British journalist was interviewing an American military officer on the "Foreign Correspondent" program. The officer boasted that the Reagan administration had spent a billion dollars on underground survival installations. He was confident that the chosen few would survive the first barrage of Russian retaliatory missiles. Left unsaid, of course, was the obvious: the proletariat left on the surface would burn.

The first direct contact between E.T.s and high-level U.S. government officials occurred at Edwards Air Force Base in California in 1954. The E.T.s present on that occasion were the human-appearing Good Guys from the Interplanetary Confederation. Similar contacts were probably made about that time with the rulers of other nations.

At Edwards we met the Good Guys, yet at Rendlesham in 1980 what we were meeting with and what the commanding officer Brigadier General Williams was communicating with, was the short gray Insectoids. How did this happen?

At Edwards in 1954, the message of the Good Guys was that we must change our suicidal course toward an all-out nuclear war. If the development and deployment of nuclear weapons continued, sooner or later they would inevitably be used in an all-out nuclear war, which would not only destroy humanity, but would make the entire surface of the planet uninhabitable for all life-forms for aeons of time. They would not provide us with weapons systems, but they would show us how to produce free energy without pollution, in order to enable us to provide for our energy needs without polluting the environment.

President Eisenhower listened to his advisors and made the wrong choice. The Chiefs of Staff did not want to give up their nuclear weapons. Bishop McIntyre did not want to see the anti-Communist drive of the Church blunted, or its religious dogma disrupted. Bernard Baruch did not want to see free energy upset the economic system. Eisenhower made the wrong choice and refused the offer of the Good Guys. After this decision was made, the Good Guys took their leave, and the short gray Insectoids moved in with their offer to provide weapons technology in return for certain illegal secret privileges.

A paper written by Riley Crabb, entitled "Insectoids and Where They Come From," is to be found at the end of this book as Appendix A.

Larry Fenwick of the Canadian UFO Research Network (P.O. Box 15, Station A, Willowdale, Ontario M2N 5S7, Canada) gave me permission to quote this portion of the *CUFORN Bulletin* of Jan.-Feb. 1981:

> Our member says he had met a man who worked for the U.S. Department of the Interior in Tennessee. This man claimed that he had met two tall aliens in that state while he was surveying for a dam. This was in the middle 1960s... The aliens stated that the short creatures have a base underground on the dark side of the Moon. The tall ones, although outnumbered, are able to and will rid our planet of the short aliens. The short ones come here to pick up something they need for their travels. It is abundant here. That is why they land in remote areas. The tall ones are more advanced than the short ones and were the first space explorers. The tall ones come here because Earth is the only planet that has warlike people and poverty.
>
> Any atomic war here would affect our solar system and, in turn, affect the balance of the universe. We should make more attempts to contact the tall ones. They will not interfere with us or harm us unless there is an imminent atomic war... In 1999, many UFOs will land on Earth. Then a democratic world government will be set up, with the system using the rules of the tall aliens.

Some researchers have stated that the Grays claim to have produced Jesus Christ, and have furnished proof in the form of a device that shows audibly and visually any part of human history which they or we wish to see.

We know that the short Grays have, to put it mildly, a tendency to lie. Because this device is of their invention, they are undoubtedly able to manipulate it just as Hollywood technicians manipulate equipment to produce the "special effects" of trick photography. Since the Grays are technologically more advanced than we are, they could manufacture almost any kind of "proof" required to convince our scientists of the validity of their claims, just as humans are able to manufacture decoys that appear to constitute convincing "proof" to the limited sensory perceptions of wild ducks.

One of the allegations concerning the short Grays is that they have a way of deriving nourishment from what leaves our bodies at the moment of death, that they are eaters of souls, who extract from our spirits a certain principle, through a process comparable to the extraction of hemoglobin from blood, which they use as food, burying the residue elsewhere in the universe, not on this planet.

The ancient Egyptians distinguished between the "ka" (the soul) and the "ba" (the etheric body that contains one's life experience). One of the ancient Egyptian prayers was: "Let there be no parting of you from me, my double, in the presence of the Keeper of the Scales!" What was feared was a separation of the etheric body from the soul, when the heart of the deceased was weighed against the Feather of Truth at the moment of judgment in the presence of the gods.

Separation of the etheric body from the soul can also be brought about by malignant entities for predatory purposes, both during life and upon passing the frontier into death.

Some cases of physical seizures and convulsions or sudden fits of violent insanity may be related to unrecognized predatory activity of this type — that is, unrecognized only by contemporary Occidental science: shamans of all cultures since time immemorial have been aware of the real existence of the predatory entities responsible for this type of activity.

The etheric body is charged with energy that is neither as subtle as that of the soul, nor as coarse as that of the physical body, but is intermediate between them. This is a substance highly valued as nourishment by certain other life-forms, which include the Grays. This is what the Grays are after, which they are here to trap as we trap fur-bearing animals. We are now and have for millennia been used by the Grays as a food source, with almost zero awareness of the actual situation. However, the continued survival of the Grays on Earth depends on our continued ignorance of this symbiotic relationship, in which the benefits are all strictly one-way.

It is worth repeating that they are using us to keep themselves alive. Fear is the emotion the Grays provoke and feed upon. Once you're afraid, they've got you. Fear puts your heart and mind out of synch, scrambles your energy patterns, and throws your ability to think clearly out of focus, enabling them to take control of you. But you can break this spell by calling out the name of someone you really love, or sincerely respect, or genuinely admire.

What we see happening over and over again in the history of our religions is the appearance of a sincere, brilliant and original thinker who has bold insights about how to renew and improve the civilization into which he was born. He is almost without exception a rebel to the existing order and a revolutionary outcast, who is usually killed by the authorities. After his death, his disciples form a hierarchical priesthood, which turns the original teaching upside down, and becomes just one more social control mechanism. The organized religions all provide a description of the after-life, containing symbols to meditate on and indications of appropriate conduct and procedure. The founder of the religion is always, almost without exception, a genuinely inspired benevolent genius. After his death, when the negatively oriented forces gain control of the hierarchical organization, these symbols are subtly changed, in order to steer the soul in specific ways when it leaves the body, directing it to what can only be described as a soul-trap even though it is the etheric body that is trapped and not the soul.

Because of religious conditioning before death, the spirit of the deceased voluntarily approaches a symbol in its path, which is actually a camouflaged instrument that magnetically captures the etheric body, laden with the individual's life-experience. After having been separated from its etheric body, the soul no longer has any memory of its previous lifetime's experience, and thus reincarnates again remembering nothing, as it begins to accumulate yet another body of vital experience. The process goes on and on indefinitely, providing nourishment for the Grays, but paralyzing our evolutionary development by denying us access to the hard-earned wisdom and knowledge gained by experience during our past lives.

The Grays are other-dimensional predatory parasites, who have been manipulating us as we manipulate cattle since time immemorial. Their hypnotic control over us is so complete that hardly anyone even begins to realize that they actually exist. But just as one can take effective measures to rid oneself of a tapeworm, when one realizes what the problem is, so humanity now has the opportunity to rid itself of these other-dimensional extra-terrestrial parasites. An ever-increasingly widespread realization of the true nature of this predatory game is what will bring about our liberation. The moment each individual realizes that he or she has a direct personal private line to the Source of All, organized religion becomes obsolete and the etheric body eludes capture, because it no longer seeks a symbol or a middle-man, but accompanies the soul straight back to where it came from: God, the Source of All.

Symbols held within the mind can be precious access points to the limitless living light that is the Source of All. However, when approaching external symbols that one finds in one's path while either out of or in the body: beware of imitations!

The Gnostics believed that upon leaving the body, the path of the soul to the highest heaven was blocked by the deities and demons of the lower realms of heaven. Only a knowledge of the names of these deities and demons, or a knowledge of the correct symbol to display when challenged by them, would permit the soul to continue its progress to its heavenly home, the kingdom of light ruled by the supreme divinity. This heavenly journey of the wise to the higher world of light was made possible only by the correct knowledge, as otherwise one was captured by the deities and demons of the lower realms of heaven. During a lifetime, this knowledge could only be obtained through first-hand personally experienced revelation. Second-hand insights from written texts or statements made by others could be helpful in preparing conditions propitious for personally experienced revelation, but they were not an acceptable substitute for direct first-hand experience.

Gnosis was — and is — an intuitive knowing, based on one's own vital experience. Let us consider the possibility that this description of the trajectory taken by the human soul after death was accurate during the first few centuries of Christianity — and is still accurate today — with the deities and demons of the lower heavens corresponding to various factions of extra-terrestrial and inter-dimensional beings.

By eliminating all references to reincarnation or extra-terrestrials from the Bible at the Council of Nicea in 325 A.D., humanity's path to liberation was transformed into a soul-trap almost impossible to escape.

According to the Tibetan Book of the Dead, during the process of dying one at first blacks out, then very briefly a colorless light shines. If one instantly without hesitation recognizes this colorless light as identical to the inmost essence of one's being and merges with it, one no longer needs to reincarnate. If this instantaneous recognition and union do not occur, the light starts to take on different colors. Each color becomes a path that leads to a different type of incarnation. The light takes on these colors, until a color appears that one is attracted to and goes toward, at which point it becomes a path. The colorless light in the Tibetan system would correspond to the supreme divinity of the Gnostics, and the pathways of the colored lights to the deities and demons of the lower realms of heaven. In modern terms, we call them extra-terrestrial and/or other-dimensional entities.

I see no basic contradiction between the extra-terrestrial and inter-dimensional hypotheses, though some consider them to be mutually exclusive. Access to other dimensions would certainly facilitate space travel. Some entities may have access to four, six, ten, or even an infinite number of dimensions. Such entities could materialize from hyperspace into three-dimensional space at will. That would not necessarily preclude a physical place of origin for such entities. If we terrestrial humans develop the quality of our awareness to the point that we also acquire access to the multiple dimensions of hyperspace, and with it the ability to materialize or dematerialize at any location we wish, our home planet and ancestral place of origin would still be Earth. We might be a space-faring race with no matter how many bases elsewhere in the cosmos, yet we would still be Earthlings, bearing the imprint of our true source of origin.

This brings to mind the portrayal of the soul in judgment in the Egyptian Book of the Dead: the heart of the recently deceased is weighed against the Feather of Ma'at, the Goddess of Truth. If the heart is heavier than the Feather of Truth, it is devoured by a non-human monster, which stands in wait by the scales for this purpose. Other religions have expressed similar ideas in different forms, frequently more chauvinistic than the ancient Egyptian reverence for the Feather of Truth. The mythologies of antiquity are loaded with clues indicating how to navigate a safe passage through the predators of the between-world, how to keep the hounds of hell at bay. It is time to restore that lost wisdom to our normal waking consciousness in contemporary society, by realizing that (to repeat myself) the stakes in this game are real, and it is being played for keeps.

Most of us focus our attention on the external reality of our physical surroundings almost exclusively, with only minimal awareness of the internal landscape, the territory of the psyche, which is glimpsed only occasionally in dreams that are for the most part quickly forgotten. However, some of us focus our attention primarily on the internal psychic territory, and only secondarily on the external reality of our physical surroundings. A large proportion of the inhabitants of our insane asylums consists of those who have been unable to correlate the information derived from their internal vision with that derived from their external vision in a socially acceptable fashion. A small but fast-growing proportion of us already has, or is in the process of acquiring, the ability to correlate information from both the external and the internal landscapes harmoniously, and to apply the perceptions gained effectively. As this ability has been so rare, it has been considered paranormal, but with every passing day what was the paranormal is becoming more and more part of normal everyday life, as more people wake up to their psychic potential and begin to explore it for themselves.

Those who focus their attention almost exclusively on the external reality are nearly defenseless against the Grays, who can manipulate them like puppets on a string because of their minimal awareness of the other-dimensional territory with which the Grays are thoroughly familiar. Those who have learned to explore their psychic potential stand a much better chance of retaining their freedom, and therefore pose a threat to the Grays, who can no longer herd them like cattle. As this ability continues to spread, more and more formerly docile devotees of the conventional value systems are beginning to think for themselves, thereby breaking out of the narrow-horizoned pastures in which they had been enclosed. The example set is contagious, and the more the merrier, because when the paranormal becomes normal for us, predatory parasites like the Grays will have to seek elsewhere in the cosmos for their nourishment.

May we come forth by day triumphant!

The challenge of being confronted with the super-brain the Grays are connected to in an all-or-nothing combat for our survival as a species may be the trigger needed to bring what Jung called the Collective Unconscious, and others have called by other names, to full consciousness on a world-wide scale. In learning to use the whole brain, instead of a mere fraction of it, each individual contacts his or her own genetic code, thereby becoming aware of past-life memories concealed in the contents of the deep subconscious, a process that connects the individual psyche to the collective psyche of humanity as a species, as well as to other forms of super-consciousness: the collective psyche of all forms of life in the biosphere of Earth; the collective psyche of all forms of life in our galaxy; and the collective psyche of all forms of life on all the stars in all the galaxies, which is the Grand Tribunal to which we should cry out for justice when confronted with the criminal activities of the Grays or any other group of irresponsible predators.

During every major period of the history of our species, certain individuals have to some degree achieved such cosmic contact, but always as rare exceptions. The challenge at present is to make this hitherto rare ability so widespread that it becomes the commonplace omnipresent norm throughout humanity in the shortest possible amount of time, thereby bringing humanity's awakened super-brain into action against the hitherto unopposed Spider Queen super-brain of the Grays. The contemporary surge of interest in topics that can be described as wearing the "New Age" label may be an indication that humanity's own super-brain is preparing to awaken. I am not the only researcher who has noticed how relevant information keeps persistently surfacing in my path, as if something or someone was providing me with clues that are pieces of a puzzle.

It is possible for us to regain our long-lost ability to think as a species without losing our individuality, by learning to maintain awareness on both levels simultaneously: a delicate balancing act, but within the range of our potential capabilities, as has been demonstrated by Buckminster Fuller

(*Synergetics*, Macmillan, 1975 and *Operating Manual for Spaceship Earth*, Pocket Books, 1969), David Bohm (*Wholeness and the Implicate Order*, Routledge & Kegan Paul, 1981), Sir John Eccles (*The Wonder of Being Human*, Macmillan, 1964), Sir Fred Hoyle (*The Intelligent Universe*, Holt, Rinehart & Winston, 1984), Karl Pribram (*Consciousness and the Brain*, Plenum, 1976), Ilya Prigogine (*Order Out of Chaos*, Bantam, 1984), Rupert Sheldrake (*A New Science of Life*, Tarcher, 1982, and *Presence of the Past*, Time Books, 1988), as well as others. We do not need to give up our individuality to gain access to a collective species consciousness, as termites and totalitarian governments do, and as the short Grays have done.

We should not neglect the possibility that even among the short Grays, there may be different sub-groups, operating to some extent independently. Although most descriptions of them tally, there are occasional variations reported, such as: eyes that are entirely black with no pupil, eyes that are entirely yellow with no pupil, orange eyes with vertical pupil. There are variations in the number of fingers reported, as well as in skin colors that may be greenish, yellowish, tan, whitish or bluish gray. It could be as simplistic to assume that all Grays are the same, as to assume that all Blacks or Orientals or Caucasians are the same, though the Grays do often appear to be cloned and connected to a group mind; thus terrestrial standards of diversity may not be applicable to them. According to Valdamar Valerian, there are three different sub-groups of Grays, and their basic food source is animal parts removed by laser surgery and distilled into a high-protein broth, ingested by smearing a soupy mixture on the outer epidermis. Linda Howe has received similar information from other sources. At this stage of our knowledge of the subject, all we can do is to keep an open mind as we carefully examine each scrap of information that comes in.

Research carried out since *Extra-Terrestrials Among Us* was published indicates that I could have added the distinguished name of Secretary of Defense James Forrestal to my "Strange Suicides" chapter. The official version of his "suicide" is that he was taken to Bethesda Naval Hospital because of a "nervous breakdown," and assigned to a room on the sixteenth floor, from which he jumped (backwards) out the window during a "fit of depression" on May 22, 1949. By one of those odd coincidences so rampant in this field of research, his "suicide" occurred a little over a year after he created the first official government committee to investigate UFOs, Project Sign.

In his *Disparitions Mystrieuses* (Laffont, Paris, 1974), Patrice Gaston quotes a bitter joke that the highly respected veteran UFO researcher Aime Michel once made, which translates into English as: "The Forrestal syndrome consists of one symptom, and only one. The invalid was investigating UFOs. The syndrome becomes life-threatening when the invalid finds out something of importance."

Dorothy Kilgallen, who was one of the best-known journalists in the United States during the 1950s and early 1960s, was investigating both the UFO cover-up and the JFK assassination at the time of her sudden death. In her syndicated column that appeared in the *Los Angeles Examiner* on May 22, 1955, she described her meeting in London with "a high British official of Cabinet rank" (who may have been Lord Mountbatten), during which he had assured her that a crashed UFO, crewed by small men under four feet tall, had been examined by British scientists. In his book, *The Truth Twisters*, which was published by Macdonald in London in 1987, Richard Deacon describes the circumstances under which Dorothy Kilgallen died:

> In 1965 the well-known American newspaper columnist Dorothy Kilgallen interviewed Jack Ruby at the Dallas jail, where he was being held for the murder of Lee Harvey Oswald. The night-club owner and ex-gangster told Miss Kilgallen something which, according to her conversations with close friends, 'would blow the Kennedy case sky-high.' A few days later, Miss Kilgallen was found dead of a massive dose of barbiturates and alcohol. When her apartment was closely examined, there was no trace of the notes of her talk with Ruby. Her death was attributed to suicide.

Another one of the best journalists in the United States, Frank Edwards, author of *Flying Saucers: Serious Business,* the most eloquent spokesman for responsible UFO research during that period of history, died under mysterious circumstances on June 24, 1967, leaving behind persistent rumors that his so-called "heart attack" had been artificially induced, just as he was about to go public with major new information that would have blown the lid off of the cover-up for keeps. But before he got a chance to blow the lid, he was heart-attacked, which can be done either through a weapon designed for this purpose, or through a poison.

In my previous book, I referred to the TV series *V* as "obvious and transparent propaganda." However, because further research has brought out significant correlations between individual case histories from independent sources and certain aspects of the *V* scenario, I wish to amend that statement. I now think that *V* was a sincere attempt to get a warning out to the public by a group of people who found out some of what is going on. The details of the story line can be faulted in various ways. Much of it does not check out with the case histories, it was heavily laced with CIA propaganda, and there was a considerable amount of distortion, but nevertheless it also contained some important information that was released into the mass consciousness of humanity world-wide in the form of TV fiction.

If an alien group-mind has blind spots that we as free-thinking individuals do not have, yet also has access to areas of knowledge that we do not have access to, and if the opposite is also true, there should be some way to work out a mutually beneficial dialogue and relationship — so long as our basic rights are respected. However, our basic rights are not being respected. We have no need of overlords, and will fight to the death before we live as slaves.

Sometimes negatively oriented E.T.s come in and try to undo the work that a positively oriented group has done, and vice versa. That is one of the many reasons why it is so essential to distinguish between the different types of entities. Because of the camouflage and mind-control capabilities of some types, deciding upon the basis of appearance alone may be deceptive. The most reliable way I know of so far is one's gut feeling as to whether one is in the presence of a friend, a foe, or a neutral observer. It is also important insofar as possible to steer clear of fear and other negative emotions, which guarantee the continuation of dominance by the negative entities. The more one can activate the highest of the higher levels of the brain by centering one's attention on a person or symbol sincerely loved, respected and admired — with firm intuitive certitude of benevolence, sending telepathic S.O.S. emergency distress signals to the figure you have chosen, without becoming entangled in negative emotions — the less of a hold the negatively oriented entities will be able to exert on you.

The challenge on which our survival depends is to activate the full potential of the dormant nine-tenths or more of our brains. Our far distant extra-terrestrial ancestors endowed us with this super-abundance of neural pathways, vastly in excess of what would be required for normal survival needs as surface dwellers on this planet. So let us each awaken the sleeping giant that is within us, as we confront the all-or-nothing emergency situation that is now staring us in the face.

Above all, we must not allow the Grays or any other aliens to alienate us from each other. By spreading half-truths designed to generate distrust, jealousy and other negative emotions, groups of friends effectively working together as teams are fragmented. This is not a strategy confined to extra-terrestrials, as the old proverb "Divide and conquer" testifies.

Why are the Grays suddenly so concerned about learning to feel emotions as humans do? Is it because they lack what we call "a soul," a vague term connoting the subtle nucleus of our higher self, to which our finer feelings are the royal road of access, no matter what the religious framework within which the quest is undertaken? But why should the Grays suddenly become so interested in acquiring souls, when they have gotten along without souls, as well as the growth of ethical values that inevitably accompanies spiritual development, successfully and with no regrets for so many millennia? Why this sudden interest?

We should consider the possibility that the multi-dimensional universe we share with the Grays and so many other forms of life may be approaching the threshold of a black hole in the cosmos, which would reduce all things the universe contains to wave/particles of elementary energy. In the Hindu terminology, this would be the event known as *maha-pralaya,* the universal dissolution to which not even the gods are immune. Because spirit is the original source of the elemental wave/particles from which the universe was formed, it would therefore be the only type of energy to pass unscathed through the passage of the black hole and out its other side: a white hole into a new universe, in which the only survivors from the previous cycle would be those who had developed genuine spiritual integrity. The Grays and all their works would be reduced to less than the dust, to quarks and other elemental wave/particles, by such a passage. Of course, the same would also be true of a substantial portion of humanity. An event of this nature may be what our diverse religious traditions about a Judgment Day are actually referring to. But now let us return from speculation about the future to the hard facts we face.

The invisible government that is above top secret in all the nations of the Earth is the enemy of the human race. If our President is merely a janitor, whose job it is to clean up the messes left behind by those who have the real power, the first step to take in correcting that intolerable situation would be to eliminate the intelligence community's covert control of the Presidency.

One of the clearest descriptions of the invisible government that ever found its way into print is in this brief excerpt from an interview with a CIA employee, published in Valdamar Valerian's very valuable volume *The Matrix* (Arcturus, 1988):

> Don't kid yourself. This country is controlled by the Pentagon. All major decisions are made by the military. The CIA's just the whipping boy. NSA are the ones that have the hit teams. Look into their records — you won't find a thing. Look into their budget — you can't. The CIA is just a figurehead, but as far as intelligence goes, the NSA's far superior to them — far in advance in the 'black arts.' The CIA gets blamed for what the NSA does. NSA is far more vicious and far more accomplished in its operations. The

American people are kept in ignorance of this — they should be, too.

What you're saying is that the military is more dangerous to our democracy than the CIA or other intelligence groups?

The CIA gathers the information, but the military heads the show.

What you are suggesting, I guess, is that there is an invisible coup d'etat which has occurred in the United States?

O.K. There is a group of about eighteen or twenty people running this country. They have not been elected. The elected people are only figureheads for these guys who have a lot more power than even the President of the United States.

You mean the President is powerless?

Not exactly powerless. He has the power to make decisions on what is presented to him. The Intelligence agencies tell him only what they want to tell him.

Elsewhere Valerian indicates that this "Inner Fed" is composed of the NSA, CIA, FBI, AFI, NASA, and the Federal Reserve. Not many people realize that the Federal Reserve is a privately owned banking cartel that has 300 stockholders, many of whom are not U.S. citizens. Other key members of the oligarchy that rules this nation behind a facade of democracy are the World Bank, the International Monetary Fund, the Business Roundtable, the Council on Foreign Relations, the Trilateral Commission, and the Bilderberg Group.

Allegations by various researchers that the CIA derives funding for its covert operations from its participation in and domination of the illegal drug trade come as no surprise to me. I had surmised as much since 1973, when I was given a copy of a Letter to the Editor in *The Bangkok Post* of July 16, 1973, signed by John Everingham, describing how the opium harvest of Laotian tribal groups was collected by U.S. Army helicopters that had their identification markings painted out. A few years later, when reports of unmarked helicopters began to turn up in connection with the cattle mutilations, it seemed probable to me that the same rogue element within the government was responsible for both the opium smuggling and the cattle mutilation operations. However, this particular insight seemed so outrageously reprehensible to just about everyone I attempted to discuss it with that I made no further attempt to share it until I found myself researching related material, while at work on the "Strange Suicides" chapter of *Extra-Terrestrials Among Us*. In that chapter, I made reference to certain books containing strong and specific evidence that supports this hypothesis:

The Politics of Heroin in Southeast Asia by Alfred W. McCoy, Harper & Row, 1972; *The Great Heroin Coup* by Henrik Kruger, South End Press, Boston, 1980; and *Mama Coca* by Antonil, Hassle Free Press, London, 1978. Since the publication of *Extra-Terrestrials Among Us*, two other books have come out that contain even stronger and more important evidence: *The Underground Empire* by James Mills (Doubleday, 1986) and *Out of Control* by Leslie Cockburn (Atlantic Monthly Press, 1987).

I find it amazing that George Bush was able to win the 1988 election, in spite of Cockburn's devastating analysis of his involvement in the Iran-Contra scam, including the fact that the CIA-chartered planes which flew arms to the Contras, flew back to the United States — directly into Homestead Air Force Base in Florida, using a CIA code signal — loaded to the limit with cocaine. It is difficult to understand why Michael Dukakis refrained from attacking Bush directly on this glaringly vulnerable point, unless Dukakis was himself subservient to the CIA agents assigned to him.

The victory of Bill Clinton is a most welcome development, but the question just raised concerning Dukakis is also applicable to both Clinton and Ross Perot, neither of whom attacked Bush directly on this glaringly vulnerable point, though the evidence available to them was far more substantial than what was available to Dukakis. When Clinton was under attack for having smoked marijuana, he could easily have pointed out that it was on the court records in Switzerland that the Ayatollah Khomeini had paid for the arms he obtained from the Oliver North "Secret Team" only partially in cash, and that over half of the payment was in the form of morphine base. It is on the court records in Costa Rica that the planes sent out from Miami loaded with arms for the Contras made the return trip loaded with cocaine. Why did neither Clinton nor Perot even mention this glaringly obvious vulnerable point in Bush's record?

Jean Ziegler is a Deputy of the Swiss Parliament (a position approximately equivalent to that of a Congressman in the United States), as well as being a Professor of Sociology at the University of Geneva and the author of numerous books and articles about the Third World. His most recent book, entitled *La Suisse lave plus blanc* (Editions du Seuil, Paris, France, 1990), is about money-laundering in Switzerland. The title translates as "Switzerland Washes Whiter." I have translated the following brief quotation from it, as it is of particular interest to American readers:

> Like the European businessmen at the time of the slave trade, the Swiss banking magnates like triangular commerce. That is why the Swiss courts continue to be involved with the Irangate affair for which American justice condemned Colonel Oliver North and his

accomplices in April 1989. The commerce developed by North and his accomplices was as simple as it was lucrative. With the expert assistance of the Swiss magnates, as well as some discreet help from the Swiss Secret Service, they delivered American and Israeli weapons to the Imam Khomeyni. The Imam paid for some of the weaponry in dollars, but for most of it in drugs (morphine base and heroin). The godfathers of Turkish and Lebanese networks installed in Zurich turned the drugs into cash on the international market. After taking their cut of the profits, the godfathers deposited the remainder in numbered accounts that had been opened in the main banks and financial institutions of Geneva and Zurich.

The Aug. 2, 1990, issue of *Le Nouvel Observateur* (Paris, France) carried an article by Lucien Rioux that described the impact of Jean Ziegler's *La Suisse lave plus blanc* on Swiss politics, giving the impression that drastic reforms were under way to correct the abuses that Ziegler's book had revealed. However, the Sept. 6 issue contained a Letter to the Editor from Jean Ziegler, stating that:

Three points are missing from Lucien Rioux's analysis of the Swiss situation in your issue no. 1343 of August 2.

1. Our inability to punish. The infiltration of the State by organized crime is an almost natural consequence of the laundering of millions of narco-dollars through multinational Swiss banks. Among others, Parliament has dismissed from their functions the federal Minister of Justice, the Public Prosecutor of the Confederation, the Federal Chief of Police, and the Chief of Military Intelligence. However, not a single one of these noble persons has been convicted! All the officials dismissed from their functions are benefiting from solid-gold retirement pensions.

2. Our inability to make fundamental reforms in the State. Switzerland is living under the reign of the soft consensus. At the executive level, all the major parties are represented. Most of the rightwing deputies are on the boards of directors of banks, multinational corporations, etc. As a consequence of this, the new law which came into effect on Aug. 1 against the laundering of drug money is completely ineffective.

3. The perversion of our democratic rights. Lucien Rioux told of the hundreds of thousands of secret files on as many citizens that were made in flagrant illegality by the political police. Many Swiss and citizens of other nations have already suffered considerable

damage, some of it financial, some of it professional, in terms of damage to careers. But the federal authorities still today refuse complete and free access to these files.

The portion of Pan Am's private investigation report concerning the crash of its flight 103 in Lockerbie, Scotland, that was released to the press by Rep. James Traficant of Ohio on Nov. 6, 1989, indicates that the CIA deliberately suppressed information which would have prevented the terrorists from blowing up the plane, in order to protect one of its drug-dealing networks.

Lt. Col. (retired) James "Bo" Gritz of the Green Berets went into Burma's "Golden Triangle" in the summer of 1989 and brought back an offer from the chief of the Shan tribe, General Khun Sa, to eradicate their production of heroin, as well as to expose the U.S. government officials involved in shipping opiates from the Golden Triangle to the United States. Although the White House did not accept this offer, the statement that contained it was published in the first issue of *The Billy Goodman Happening*, 80-705 Highway 86, Oasis, Ca 92274. It is indeed bizarre that with all the coverage the U.S. news media has been devoting to drugs, not one single major media outlet saw fit to print this historically important statement, which was carried only by this small-circulation newsletter. After reminding my readers that George Bush was the Director of the CIA during a substantial portion of the time frame that General Khun Sa is discussing, I quote an excerpt from his remarkable statement:

> Throughout the U.S. war in Vietnam, heroin production was accelerated to help finance CIA mercenary expansion campaigns in Laos and Cambodia... Today, the operation remains the same. Only a few of the names have changed, as people have died or been promoted. After the Communist takeover in 1975, the CIA stockpiled weapons in Thailand and the Philippines to continue operations in Southeast Asia. Heroin provides the means. Officials arrange the laundry of funds through international banks. Mafia contacts handle worldwide distribution. We were not surprised to learn of Mr. Richard Armitage's appointment as U.S. Assistant Secretary of State for East Asia. He is well known to us as a key member of the CIA drug team. His position over this part of the world will assure business as usual, while securing his involvement. It is because of this demand for heroin that we are prevented from establishing a legal economy. We Shans have been slaves to Western government secret dealings which have poisoned the World's population. Our determination to

free ourselves has led to this letter of appeal... President George Bush is not likely to support our plan.

During his videotaped interview with Bo Gritz, Khun Sa named another high-ranking U.S. official to whom he regularly sold heroin not merely by the ton, but by the hundreds of tons: Theodore Shackley.

The following chronology of events demonstrates the intimate connection between George Bush, Felix Rodriguez and the drug-dealing of the Contras:

1959: Felix Rodriguez, a Cuban refugee, hired to be a member of a special assassination team, working under Theodore Shackley of the CIA in Miami, Florida.

1970: Felix Rodriguez works under Donald Gregg in the CIA operation in Vietnam. Gregg reports to Shackley.

1976: George Bush succeeds William Colby as the head of the CIA under Gerald Ford. Bush appoints Ted Shackley to be his Chief of Covert Operations Worldwide.

12/1/81: Bush meets with the National Security Planning Group in the White House. They discuss and approve a $19 million expenditure to Argentina for the creation of a 500-man anti-Sandinista Contra force.

4/82: Bush meets with Australian labor leader Hayden to discuss the CIA's involvement with the Nugan Hand bank in Australia. Nugan Hand was money-laundering for the Southeast Asia heroin operation that began during the Vietnam War. Current State Department spokesman Richard Armitage acted as bagman, carrying cash from Bangkok, Thailand, to Australia.

11/82: $3,690,000 payment made to the Contras by Ramon Millian Rodriguez, the book-keeper of the Colombian Cocaine Cartel, at the request of Felix Rodriguez, in exchange for protection from prosecution.

1983: Gustavo Villolda gets a letter of recommendation from Donald Gregg as "combat advisor" to the Contras. Villolda was with Felix Rodriguez during the Bay of Pigs invasion and the CIA trackdown and execution of Che Guevara in Bolivia.

10/84: Gerad Latchinian, co-director with Felix Rodriguez of Giro Aviation, a CIA proprietary airline, arrested for smuggling $10,300,000 worth of cocaine to finance the assassination of Honduran President Roberto Suavo Cordova. Latchinian maintains that this was a CIA operation.

12/84: Felix Rodriguez meets with Donald Gregg, George Bush's National Security Advisor. Gregg has an autographed photo of Rodriguez on his desk. Rodriguez gets Gregg to call other high-ranking officials for help in getting a job in El Salvador as a Contra military advisor.

1/85: Felix Rodriguez meets with George Bush to discuss the Contra job, less than two months after the Latchinian indictment.

6/85: Felix Rodriguez meets in Washington, D.C. with Donald Gregg and Colonel Steele of the Salvador Milgroup that works with the Contra supply network. Steele was given one of the super-secret KL-43 encrypton devices for secure telephone conversations.

12/85: Felix Rodriguez attends the Christmas party at George Bush's White House office, and is introduced to the staff as an old friend of Donald Gregg and Bush.

5/86: Felix Rodriguez meets with Bush, Gregg and North in Bush's office.

6/86: Felix Rodriguez is called to Washington to meet with North to explain phone calls to Tony Avirgon and Martha Honey (U.S. journalists in Costa Rica), which North has taped.

8/86: Felix Rodriguez meets with Bush and Donald Gregg to complain about the quality of arms shipments from Richard Secord's arms supply operation. Later that same month, Donald Gregg meets with Alan Friers, the Central American Task Force chief, to support the purchase of military equipment from Felix Rodriguez rather than Secord. Friers is told by Gregg, "Don't buy any of those damned airplanes from Secord."

9/86: General Singlaub sends memo to North expressing concern about Felix Rodriguez's daily contact with the Bush office, warning of "damage to President Reagan and the Republican Party."

10/5/86: Bush's office is the first place notified when the C-123 carrying Eugene Hassenfus is shot down. Buz Sawyer, the pilot of the plane, has the private White House phone number of George Bush in his pocket when his body is recovered from the plane. Hassenfus testifies that he worked for the CIA under Max Gomez (alias for Felix Rodriguez) and Ramon Medina (alias for Luis Posada Carriles) with the knowledge and approval of George Bush. Telephone logs from the phone company in El Salvador for the "safe houses" used by the plane crew show many calls to North's White House office.

The documentation on which the above chronology was based is to be found in *The Politics of Heroin in Southeast Asia* by McCoy (1972), *Price of Power* by Seymour Hersh (1983), *Endless Enemies* (1984) and *Crimes of Patriots* (1987) by Jonathan Kwitny, *Veil* by Bob Woodward (1987), and *Out of Control* by Leslie Cockburn (1987), as well as the affidavit submitted to the Federal Court in Miami, Florida, in the RICO (Racketeer Influenced Corrupt Organizations Act) suit filed by Tony Avirgon against those who bombed the press conference at La Penca in 1984, and the "Drugs, Law Enforcement and Foreign Policy" statement issued by the Senate Foreign Relations Comittee in December, 1988.

In the August 23, 1990, issue of *Le Nouvel Observateur* (Paris, France), there was an article about Noriega by Rene Backman, who appears to have not only researched the subject thoroughly, but to have gained access to some inside information:

> If he talked, he could for example tell why some of the Southern Air Transport planes that delivered arms to the Contras returned to Miami loaded with cocaine. Or why CIA agents sold their protection to drug dealers Jorge Morales, Ramon Millian Rodriguez and Michael Tolliver in exchange for financial contributions to the Contras. Or what became of the mysterious eight million dollars missing from Irangate. Or how come drug dealer Ramon Millian Rodriguez was invited to Ronald's Reagan inauguration ceremony in 1981. Or who trained the Death Squads in El Salvador. Or at exactly what date Bush and Reagan knew what North was doing.

How did the invasion of Panama affect the value of the Bush family holdings in Panama?

According to former CIA officer John Stockwell (*The Praetorian Guard*, Turnaround Press, London, 1991), the Medellin cartel grew at the same rate as did the U.S. involvement in Central America. Besides the bookkeeper of the Medellin cartel, Ramon Millian Rodriguez, there was (according to *In God's Name*, by David Yallop, Bantam, 1984) another intriguing guest at Reagan's inauguration: Licio Gelli. Senior members of the Republican National Committee were puzzled that this little-known foreigner was given a more prominent place of honor than they were, being seated even closer to the newly-elected President. Less than four months later, Gelli suddenly became very famous indeed — headline news worldwide — as his many major crimes were discovered. He soon became number one on the "wanted" list of the Italian police. Gelli escaped to Uruguay, and continued to operate what remained of his multinational octopus of a criminal organization from his estate there.

During the lifetime of Nicaraguan dictator Somoza, Gelli had been closely associated with him in large-scale ventures, to the extent that he had been granted a Nicaraguan diplomatic passport. Gelli had invested huge amounts of money in Somoza's Nicaragua, and owned many different properties there. To what extent was this hidden variable an unrecognized factor in shaping U.S. foreign policy towards Nicaragua during the Reagan years?

After the end of World War II, in collaboration with the U.S. Counter-intelligence Corps (a branch of the CIA), Gelli was among those who helped Klaus Barbie and other high-ranking Nazis escape to South America. When Argentine dictator Peron returned from exile for a second term in power, he publicly fell on his knees in thanks at the feet of one man: Licio Gelli.

Among Gelli's close friends in Argentina was Jose Lopez Rega, who created the notorious "Triple-A" death squads, which were responsible for innumerable murders and disappearances. Rega raised the enormous amounts of money required for these activities by smuggling cocaine into the United States.

The technique Gelli and his associates used to acquire control of the power structure in Italy and other countries was — and still is — to buy off or blackmail the leadership of all political parties, clear across the spectrum from extreme right to extreme left. The almost limitless funds available to them enabled them to use this technique over and over again with a high rate of success. The list of those who have already been killed while investigating the organization that Gelli is a high-ranking member of is a long one.

In 1863, President Abraham Lincoln abolished slavery from the United States with his Emancipation Proclamation. In 1990, Congressmen Phil Gramm and Newt Gingrich restored slavery to the United States with their H.R. 4079, based on drug use instead of race. As of right now, you can be sentenced to twenty years for possession of one marijuana cigarette, a sentence you are not likely to survive, because you are to be used as expendable slave labor, forced at gun-point to go in and clean up the toxic waste dumps created by the real rulers of this nation, who buy and sell politicians like we do potatoes: the Pentagon's multinational, arrogantly offensive, "defense" contractors.

The *South China Morning Post*, which is based in Hong Kong, carried an article in its issue of June 1, 1990, according to which:

> A commercial arm of the People's Liberation Army has launched a venture to sell blood products to the United States and other parts of the world, but the project has stalled because of a dispute with the U.S. partner.
>
> China Xinxing Corporation (Group), a huge company under the PLA's logistics department, and Chicago-based Dylan Enterprise signed a joint venture contract last September to produce blood products for sale in China and abroad.
>
> Despite the international outrage over the PLA's assault on civilian demonstrators in Beijing last June, both Xinxing and Dylan ex-

ecutives said they were confident that, once their current dispute was resolved, the joint venture would succeed in finding markets....

The core of the dispute is over contract and legal obligations....

Only when all equipment arrives does the joint venture legally come into being, Xinxing insists.

'Only with this equipment can we meet U.S. Food and Drug Administration standards,' Mr. Wang said in an interview at Xinxing Medicine and Medical's headquarters in Beijing.

'The whole purpose of the venture is to sell to the U.S.,' he said.

If the whole purpose of the venture is to sell China's greatest natural resource, the blood of its own citizens, to the United States, why is this being done indirectly through a private corporation, rather than directly from the Chinese government to the American government? Is it because of the stark contrast between the facts of the matter and George Bush's misty-eyed assurances of "a kinder, gentler America"? The People's Liberation (!) Army is obviously in charge of harvesting the blood, but who actually supplies it? Political prisoners? Just how voluntary are the so-called "donations"? In what way does this bizarre business venture relate to the real reasons behind Bush's eagerness to collaborate with the Butchers of Tienanmen Square, a term that may turn out to be even more apt than hitherto imagined?

Would the army of slaves conscripted by the Gramm/Gingrich drug law be used not only as a source of free labor for the Pentagon's defense contractors, but also be milked periodically for blood, gland extracts, bone marrow, organ "donations," and used as a general reservoir of biological spare parts?

Paul Krassner published some excerpts from this chapter in the March/April 1991 issue of *The Realist* (Box 1230, Venice CA 90294). In the Fall 1991 issue, he made the following comment:

When I published an article in no. 116 by George Andrews, his concluding question seemed far-fetched: Would Chinese political prisoners be forced to supply biological spare parts?

But now a letter in the British medical journal *Lancet* claims that kidneys from executed Chinese prisoners are being sold to transplant patients for $17,000. Dr. Siu-keung Lam of Queen Mary's Hospital in Hong Kong wrote: 'Kidneys are usually obtained from prisoners who are executed for offenses such as rape, burglary or political crimes against the state. No consent for organ removal is given either by the prisoner or the family. Furthermore, the family rarely collects the body after execution for fear of harassment by government authorities.'

Although my question referred to U.S. political prisoners, Krassner's comment was nevertheless relevant. Neither of us wants to see George Bush get away with transplanting the Chinese Gulag system to the United States.

H.R. 4079 was so outrageous that Congress didn't dare to pass it openly, so they broke it up and attached it piece by piece to other laws. It has by now been almost entirely passed in this under-the-table fashion, and there is no organized opposition in Congress to passing the rest of it in the same way. What would George Washington have thought of this?

George Washington kept a Diary from day to day in his own handwriting. On May 12 and 13, 1765, he was 33 years old, living quietly at Mount Vernon, devoting his energy mainly to agriculture, not yet involved in revolutionary politics. The entry in his Diary for those dates reads: "Sowed hemp at muddy hole by swamp." The conventional response to this is that Washington was growing hemp for its fiber, a different variety of the plant than the marijuana rich in resin, which has such a powerful medicinal effect. However, this conventional response is contradicted by the Diary entry for August 7 of that same year: "Began to separate the male from the female hemp at Do — rather too late." If hemp is being grown for fiber, the male plants are not separated from the females. The only possible reason to separate the male from the female plants in mid-summer, before the females are fertilized, is to produce the exceptionally potent and rich in resin, seedless type of marijuana now known as "sinsemilla." The fact that the Father of Our Country notes in his own handwriting that he had separated the male from the female plants "rather too late" constitutes irrefutable evidence that he was growing the plant for its medicinal potency, not for its fiber.

In *Extra-Terrestrials Among Us,* I asked this question: "Did you ever stop to think that the more strictly illegal and severely punished the use of drugs becomes, the more profitable is the traffic in them?" In the April 1989 issue of *Omni,* the Mayor of Baltimore, Kurt L. Schmoke, eloquently expressed some ideas that indicate the only sane way to solve the drug problem:

> Last year the United States spent approximately ten billion dollars on drug-related law enforcement, while drug criminals earned at least 110 billion in profits. Meanwhile, drug-related crime, especially in the cities, simply got worse.

The harder we try to use criminal law to stamp out drug abuse, the greater the financial incentives become to deal drugs. Thus our drug policies aren't just failing, they're self-defeating.

Since 1914 the policy of the United States has been to treat the use of drugs in this country as a criminal offense. In 1936 August Vollmer, a former president of the International Association of Chiefs of Police, said, "Drug addiction is not a police problem. It has never been and can never be solved by policemen. Drug abuse is a medical problem, and if there is a solution it will be discovered by scientific and medical experts."

Our strategy of using criminal law to end drug abuse is a mistake....Although the criminal justice system should still play a role in controlling drugs, our policies should focus on public health strategies....Finally, the war on drugs should be led by the surgeon general, not the attorney general.

Mayor Schmoke compares our failed drug-control policies with those that have a long record of successful use in Holland, and concludes that we should model our approach to the problem along the lines of the Dutch method. I am in complete agreement with him. The only thing we would lose by such an arrangement would be the CIA's covert operations, which would be restricted by lack of funds, but which we would be better off without in any case.

The War on Drugs is a prime example of Uncle Sam's right hand ostentatiously battling the camouflaged glove of Uncle Sam's left hand, in a Punch-and-Judy show that not only diverts the public's attention from other issues, but systematically empties the wallets of the spectators. In August 1989, there was extensive media coverage of "former" Israeli and South African Intelligence agents caught on videotape training the armies of the Colombian cocaine cartel. What everyone seems to have forgotten and no one thought worth mentioning is that this is precisely the type of work for which the CIA used Klaus Barbie, the Gestapo officer known as "the Butcher of Lyons." I would suggest that the media heat may have been put on Israel and South Africa in this case to disguise the CIA's long-term involvement in training the armies of the cocaine cartel. All the recent violence in Colombia as we go to press is probably because some of the cartel kingpins have gone independent and stopped sharing their profits with the CIA. That may also have been the basic problem with Noriega, whose Israeli master-mind chief advisor, Micha "Mike" Harari, was mysteriously not arrested by the U.S. authorities, though at one point they had him in custody. Before becoming Noriega's chief advisor, Harari had been for 31 years the Colonel in charge of the Operational Division of Mossad (the Israeli equivalent of the CIA).

The thoroughly serious and impeccably researched book *The Underground Empire* by James Mills (Doubleday, 1986) made the point that one of the major difficulties in making arrests among the higher echelons of the cocaine cartel is the fact that the holders of these key positions so frequently turn out to be also holders of CIA identification cards, which render them almost immune to prosecution. Another point of major importance made in this book is that a law enforcement officer who becomes exceptionally successful in prosecuting the highest-ranking members of the higher echelons of international drug-dealing cartels gets transferred instead of promoted.

By deliberately orchestrating drug-related violence, letting it build so that it spreads from the ghettos to the suburbs and rural areas and finally to the prosperous urban neighborhoods, the CIA is conditioning the public to accept the presidential proclamation of a State of Emergency, with its accompanying automatic consequence, the replacement of civil law by martial law.

The way to solve the cocaine/crack problem is to legalise the benign non-toxic leaf that these highly toxic concentrates are derived from, while keeping the toxic concentrates illegal. This strategy would be effective if the leaf was sold at a price at which it would not be possible to make a financial profit by buying it and working it down to produce concentrates. It takes a large amount of leaf to produce a tiny amount of concentrate. In Peru, coca leaf is available in any grocery store, packaged as an herbal tea. In this form, it is affordable to the average person, but not so cheap as to be worth working down for concentrate. Coca tea is a mild stimulant that is medicinally benign. If coca leaf could be legally imported into the United States in this form, the cocaine problem would begin to shrink in size dramatically, instead of continuously expanding in a cancerous rampage of malignant growth.

Coca leaf is a valuable herbal medicine, which (if properly used) is beneficial rather than damaging to the health. Coca leaf should never have been made illegal in the first place. The right to grow our own marijuana, just like George Washington did, should also never have been taken away from us. The social problems we are faced with are, and always were, caused by the concentrates derived from the leaf, not the coca leaf itself, which according to Inca legend was a gift to humanity from the gods, a shrub from elsewhere, with tremendous positive potential. The authorities persistently ignore that positive potential and pretend it does not exist, instead focusing attention exclusively on the extremely negative problems associated with abuse of the concentrates.

It is this basic flaw in our legislation, which confuses the benign leaf with the toxic concentrates derived from it, which is at the root of the cocaine/crack problem, now raging out of control. This tidal wave of drug-related violence is being deliberately orchestrated to a crescendo point, at which a majority of public opinion will find presidential proclamation of a State of Emergency acceptable, not realizing that what is presented as a temporary expedient was planned long ago to become a permanent state of affairs, and they are being led as cattle to the slaughter, never to know freedom again. We live at a time when the liberty we have grown used to taking for granted is at risk and must be fought for. We are living in a trap that is waiting to be sprung.

On Sept. 23, 1989, Congress trashed the Constitution by passing HR 5210, which transformed this nation that prides itself on being the leader of the Free World into just one more military dictatorship as abject as that of any banana republic. HR 5210 was superficially explained to the public as anti-drug legislation, when what it in fact did was to deprive us all of our right to the due process of the law, as guaranteed by the Constitution.

Two organizations already aware of how dangerous the situation is, which are courageously doing their best to get the relevant information out to the public are the Christic Institute, 1324 North Capitol Street NW, Washington, DC 20002; (202) 797-8106 and the Mae Brussell Research Center, P.O. Box 8431, Santa Cruz, CA 95061; (408) 426-7373.

Researcher Thomas Shaffer, Jr. has relayed a very interesting bit of information to me. On June 2, 1989, CBS (Channel 3, Hartford, Connecticut) aired a quarter-hour of its 7:00 pm news program, *Inside Edition*. The program gave the impression that the U.S. government is now taking the possibility of E.T. contact seriously. Although the main focus of the program was on NASA's SETI project that uses radio waves to search for intelligent life elsewhere in the universe, it was recognized that there are people who believe that the extra-terrestrials are already here. This portion of the script was accompanied by photos of UFOs and drawings of humanoids. So far, strictly ho-hum propaganda hokum, the usual platitudes, nothing worth mentioning — but then the program ended with a punch line: a warning that "it is illegal for the viewer to communicate or interact with otherworlders."

Shaffer writes: "My reaction may be described as twofold. First of all, I felt compelled to refer to my copy of *Extra-Terrestrials Among Us*, pages 24-32. The second thought that crossed my mind concerned the possibility that this warning might make some encounter event participants more reluctant to relate their experiences."

What crosses my mind is that after NASA denied over and over again every which way that this obscure little regulation was of any importance, or was applicable to anything except the Apollo moon missions or had anything at all to do with civilian UFO contactees, all of a sudden the obscure little regulation of no importance turns out to be a tiger that has been camouflaged as a pussy cat. Without any preliminary discussion whatsoever, except of a general nature, the TV viewer was peremptorily placed before a fait accompli, in a manner to which there is no way for the average viewer to respond effectively.

As I pointed out in my previous book: "The primary effect of such a law would not be to prevent contact (which is often involuntary), it would be to silence witnesses." I also described how this law was slipped on to the books without any public debate. At the time that *Extra-Terrestrials Among Us* was released, I was ridiculed by quite a few critics for paying such serious attention to such an innocuous little NASA regulation. The punch line of that CBS program may have been no more than a trial balloon, but it does dramatically demonstrate how from one moment to the next the wording of that innocuous little NASA regulation can be interpreted so that it undergoes a jack-in-the-box transformation to become a great big monstrous law of the land, applicable to each and every citizen. Approximately six months after the release of *Extra-Terrestrials Among Us*, which had focused public attention on that NASA regulation, it was beefed up to the maximum by the Supreme Court decision of May, 26, 1987, which legalised Preventive Detention. According to dissenting Justices Marshall, Brennan and Stevens, this decision violated the Bill of Rights and the Eighth Amendment to the Constitution.

When I was at work on *Extra-Terrestrials Among Us*, I did not know about the clandestine agreement made between our government and the Grays. I recognized the apparently minor NASA regulation as being one of the major missing pieces of the puzzle, but it was not until I found out about the clandestine agreement that I realized the full implications of the inconspicuous bit of legislation, which was put on the books by administrative decree, without any public discussion, about the time that the clandestine agreement was made with the Grays. The example of this apparently minor legislation provides us with an instructive insight into the cynical depravity that characterizes the invisible government-within-the-government. Having made a secret and illegal treaty with reptilian aliens, in which the right to abduct U.S. citizens was one of the concessions illegally granted, a law was passed to make sure that any U.S. citizen who tried to alert his or her fellow citizens to what was going on would automatically be classified as a dangerous criminal, requiring confinement in "quarantine" indefinitely.

As I wept like a baby for the first time in years — while watching television upon witnessing the martyrdom of the Chinese students in Tienanmen Square — my grief gave way to anger upon hearing the tepid and desultory response to the atrocity by the Bush administration. In my opinion, this response was so perfunctory and non-committal because Bush and certain members of his Cabinet (such as James Baker, who is rumored to be a key member of the Board that governs the Dulce base) know that as the secret agenda of the invisible government is implemented, the Delta Special Forces will have to be used against the citizens of the United States, just as the forever-disgraced People's "Liberation" Army was used against the students, in confrontations on a scale that will dwarf the massacre at Tienanmen Square. George Bush has demonstrated again and again that he is in actual fact the friend of the Butcher of Tienanmen Square. The current drive to ban semi-automatic weapons, though it is backed by many good people with sound motivations, is designed to facilitate the take-over by the Delta Forces as soon as a State of Emergency is declared, rather than for the publicly stated reasons. Executive Order Rex 84, which President Reagan signed in 1984, is said to detail the specific procedures to be used in this take-over.

On five different occasions President Reagan raised the possibility of invasion by hostile extra-terrestrials, stating that under such circumstances the U.S. and U.S.S.R. would quickly resolve their differences and present a united front to the invaders. This may have been a way to prepare the public for a statement that such a situation already exists. There are indications that Soviet officials made a similar deal with the Grays to the one that our officials made. During the interval of time it took us to find out about their top secret deal, and it took them to find out about our top secret deal, the Grays installed themselves in underground bases on the territory of both nations. When the double-cross was discovered, it was too late for either nation to do anything about it, which is why U.S.-Soviet relations thawed, though the Punch-and-Judy show of belligerent animosity is maintained sufficiently to continue to distract the masses in both nations, as the masses are much easier for politicians to control when they have a convincing external enemy on which to project their negative emotions. We should not forget also that the U.S. and U.S.S.R. do have at least one thing in common: we are both in debt up to our ears to the same bankers.

The international bankers with enough clout to manipulate nations are of all races. They come in all shapes and sizes and colors. However, they are few in number. There is reason to believe that at least some of them have known about and worked in collusion with the Grays for centuries.

The similarity between the equilateral triangle symbol used by the Grays as a mark of their presence and the name of the Trilateral Commission may be more than mere coincidence. We should carefully consider the possibility that the Trilateral Commission may be one of the main instruments used by the Grays to maintain control of and siphon off the world's resources.

The Star Wars boondoggle is supposedly to protect the U.S. from a Soviet first strike, but those who find that cover story credible are becoming fewer day by day. According to John Lear, its real purpose is to be used as a weapon against the Grays. My difficulty with that theory is: why then would the Grays allow us to develop and deploy it, considering the degree of control they apparently already have? Another theory is that the Grays want us to build the Star Wars system in order to attack the incoming ships of the tall Blond fleet which — according to this scenario — will return in the near future to liberate Earth from domination by the Grays.

If the Blonds decide not to wait until the Star Wars system is deployed, and return in force to intervene decisively in the present intolerable situation, how will our government greet them? Will the covert alliance with the Grays still be honored, in spite of their double-cross, dragging us into the middle of no-man's-land on a galactic battlefield? Now or never, our citizens have a right and a need to know in what direction our leaders are taking us.

There is also a theory that the massive implants being performed by the Grays on vast sectors of the population are in preparation for certain Star Wars satellites being sent up. When these satellites are in orbit, the Grays can control our planet like absentee landlords from elsewhere in the cosmos, subjecting those who have their implants to slavery more total than was ever possible in antiquity. In his *1984*, George Orwell depicted a society in which an omnipresent Big Brother peered out non-stop at everyone through a two-way TV screen in each dwelling. However, according to this hypothesis, Big Brother would not need to be looking at you from a TV screen, because he would be literally right inside your head, instantaneously picking up all your perceptions and sensations, making your decisions for you, manipulating your body chemistry, applying pain or pleasure or memory erasure at will, to enforce commands from the cradle to the grave. Before writing a blank check for unlimited funding of any such project, the U.S. taxpayer should first find out what the real goal of the project is.

Finding out what a project's real goal is can sometimes be a shock. It may be that a shock of this nature was an important factor in the following series of contemporary "strange suicides."

Between Aug. 5, 1986, and Mar. 25, 1988, there were 11 "strange suicides" that may be UFO-related, all of them in England, all of them closely associated with "security" or "defense" projects. Leslie Shepherd of the Associated Press wrote an article about ten of these suicides ("Strange Deaths Hit 10 British Scientists" in the *Tulsa World*, April 17, 1988), from which I will now quote, before adding my comments and describing the eleventh "strange suicide."

> The mystery began Aug. 5, 1986, when Vimal Dajibhai, 24, was found dead in the gorge below Clifton Bridge near Bristol, southwest England. Suicide was suspected, but a coroner's inquest reached no verdict about the cause of death....Dajibhai was a junior engineer checking torpedo guidance systems for Marconi Underwater Systems Ltd. near London. No one has determined what he was doing in Bristol, 105 miles away.
> Three months after Dajibhai's death, Ashad Sharif, a computer systems analyst working on a defense project for another Marconi unit near London, died in a park near Bristol.
> An inquest ruled that Sharif, 26, killed himself by tying a rope to a tree, looping the other end around his neck and then driving off in his car at high speed. Coroner Donald Hawkins called it suicide, but he, too, wondered why it happened in Bristol.
> In January 1987, computer designer Richard Pugh was found dead in his home east of London. The circumstances were never explained, but a jury ruled it was accidental death during sexual experimentation. Pugh, 37, had previously worked on Defense Ministry contracts.
> Also that month, John Brittam, a 52-year-old computer expert at the Royal Armaments Research and Development Establishment, was found dead in his garage with his car engine running. Brittam previously worked for the Royal Military College of Science.
> A month later, a senior metallurgy lecturer at the college, Peter Peapell, was found dead under his car with the engine running. The government said Peapell, 46, was working on an unclassified project studying recent trends in beryllium in the Soviet Union.
> In March 1987, computer expert David Sands drove his car, its trunk loaded with tanks of gasoline, into a vacant restaurant and was burned to death. Sands, 37, worked for Easama, a Marconi associate, on a tender for an air defense contract....
> In April 1987, two more scientists were found dead.
> One was Mark Wisner, 25, a computer specialist at a Royal Air Force weapons-testing base, who an inquest ruled had committed

suicide by placing a plastic bag over his head. The other was a Marconi scientist, Victor Moore, 46, who an inquest determined died of a drug overdose.

Wisner was working on computer software for the Tornado fighter plane and Moore had worked on a night vision project for the British Army.

The mysterious deaths stopped until police found the body of Russell Smith, a 25-year-old junior scientist, half-way down a cliff. Police said they found a note in his car in a cliff-top park but refused to say what was in the note. They have declined to speculate on the cause of his death. Smith worked for the ultra-secret United Kingdom Atomic Energy Authority in Harwell.

Finally on March 25, another Marconi employee, 52-year-old Trevor Knight, was found dead in his fume-filled car in Harpender, 25 miles northwest of London. He was a computer engineer working on guided missile research at Marconi headquarters.

One of the strangest things about this strange series of deaths is that an inquest ruled that a 25-year-old man could commit suicide by placing a plastic bag over his head. Even if a 25-year-old man had the intention of committing suicide in such a bizarre fashion, before death by strangulation ensued, involuntary arm movements would have torn open a plastic bag.

I am certainly not the first person to wonder what type of top secret activity Marconi is involved in.

If the police wanted to clarify the matter, all they had to do was to make public the note that Russell Smith left in his car. The fact that they chose not to do this indicates that they do not want to clarify the matter, because of high-level governmental involvement. It seems likely that Russell Smith attempted to leave a message about what all the others didn't even try to explain, perhaps because they assumed that no one would believe them.

Peter Peapell was at work on a project studying beryllium, a high-strength metal that is very important in undersea housing projects and the construction of underwater cities. There are abundant indications that UFOs have underwater bases on this planet. Was the unclassified project Peapell was at work on a cover for another project that was classified?

Did Peapell and the others find out that they were not working for the bosses they thought they were working for, that they were not working for British defense and security at all, quite the contrary, because their bosses were in fact themselves under the control of short gray insectile reptilian humanoids with no concern whatsoever for British or other human well-being? Was that the horrifying secret they did not even try to explain to the world at large, assuming that no one would believe them? Was that the information that Russell Smith tried to transmit in the note he left behind, which the police suppressed?

Now let's have a look at the eleventh "strange suicide." My sources of information for the following account are an article by Ed Lion of United Press International, which appeared in the *Daily News*, Red Bluff, California, on Oct. 24, 1987; an article by Mark Tungate in *Evening Advertiser*, Swindon, England, on Aug. 26, 1989; and an article in *Western Independent*, Plymouth, England, on Aug. 20, 1989.

The incident occurred on Oct. 22, 1987, in the time frame between the deaths of Victor Moore and Russell Smith. Humphrey Taylor Scott was a test pilot who had worked for British Aerospace for over eight years. The weather on that morning was completely clear. Scott took off from an airfield in Surrey in a new Harrier GR-5 vertical take-off jet, with a price tag equivalent to U.S.$23 million, in order to test it before it was delivered to the Royal Air Force. A few minutes later, the air traffic control tower at Boscombe Down, Wiltshire, received a perfectly normal radio message from Scott, but only moments later all contact was suddenly lost. Six minutes after take-off, radio contact with Scott abruptly ceased. A U.S. Air Force transport plane that happened to be in the vicinity was requested to intercept the jet, and finally managed to do so over the Irish Sea, reporting that there was no one in the cockpit. At this point, there is a disparity in the accounts: Ed Lion states that the cockpit seal and ejector seat were also gone, while Mark Tungate says that the cockpit canopy was ripped away but the ejector seat was still in place. Be that as it may, the Harrier jet was flying straight and level at 30,000 feet — but without a pilot. This model did have an autopilot capability. It traveled for another hour before supposedly crashing into the Atlantic about five hundred miles west of Ireland, having run out of fuel after flying approximately 700 miles without a pilot. It is not clear from the articles available to me whether the crash into the Atlantic was witnessed, or whether the jet was assumed to have crashed because it disappeared from radar at that point.

On the following day, Oct. 23, the body of Humphrey Scott, wearing flying clothes and a parachute, along with an inflatable dinghy — which a pilot would normally take with him only if obliged to bail out over the ocean — was found in a meadow in Wiltshire. It was not specified in any of the articles whether the parachute was open or not. However, if the parachute had opened, and the pilot came down in a meadow, he would have been alive, so it looks as if for some reason he did not activate the parachute after ejecting from the jet. Was this because he was unconscious?

Humphrey Scott never did send any Mayday call or distress signal. Radio contact simply ceased from one moment to the next, which is an impossibility under normal circumstances in a brand-new $23-million Harrier jet. However, radio malfunction has frequently been reported by pilots upon encountering UFOs.

Did the Grays want to study this new type of human aircraft with vertical take-off ability more closely? Did they abduct Humphrey Scott on some occasion previous to this particular test flight, insert an implant into his brain, and then erase his memory of the procedure, so that it would be remembered by him as no more than an odd dream? After causing the jet's radio to go dead, they could have activated the implant and transmitted a series of commands that caused Scott to first put the plane on automatic pilot, second to bail out of his normally functioning plane, and third to lapse into complete unconsciousness before opening his parachute, thereby guaranteeing that he would never tell anyone the wildly improbable story of what had happened.

As Charles Fort has taught us, if you put enough wildly improbable stories together, correlations may emerge that begin to make sense. Such a maneuver by the Grays would guarantee that the jet would continue on a straight-line course, instead of the pilot's original flight plan, until it was far out over a remote area of the Atlantic, where the empty plane could then be captured without the inconvenient presence of any human witnesses.

To have known all he knew, Charles Fort must have had alien contact. Such a high proportion of the assorted and seemingly unrelated items of weirdness he collected are so directly relevant to the subject of extra-terrestrial intervention in human affairs that he must have known what he was doing. It is not possible to hit the nail square on the head time after time after time as he did, without knowing what one is doing. Over half a century after he did his work, many of the concepts he persistently hinted at not only remain valid, but far in advance of most contemporary research. In the society of his period, these concepts were so outrageous that he had good reason to dare to do no more than to drop hints about them now and then, and to present his findings in the oblique, superficially innocuous and socially acceptable form of a collection of newspaper clippings about odd events.

There is a type of Fortean odd event that Wiltshire has long been famous for, because it has been reported far more often from Wiltshire than from the other locations where it has occurred. Strange circular indentations have been found in their fields by farmers for years. They are always perfectly round, with plants flattened neatly in one direction. The body of Humphrey Scott, with its parachute and the inflatable dinghy, was found in the vicinity of one of these circles.

Colin Andrews of the Circles Phenomena Research Group is a technical officer for Test Valley Borough Council in Hampshire, who has been studying the phenomenon since 1983. He collaborated with Pat Delgado on a book entitled *Circular Evidence,* published by Bloomsbury in 1989. The book refrains from drawing any definite conclusions about the source of the phenomenon, but Colin Andrews has made some interesting statements to journalists who interviewed him ("Western Independent," Plymouth, England, Aug. 20, 1989).

Not only was Humphrey Scott's body found near one of these circles, but the Harrier jet Scott had piloted on that fateful morning changed its course slightly while directly over a field containing several of these circles at Winterbourne Stoke, near Warminster (long famous for its abundant UFO activity) in Wiltshire. Circles had also been found at the sites of two other less important airplane crashes. The circles tend to cluster around ancient standing stones and earthworks. Many of them form a precise pattern, with seven concentric rings and 48 spokes leading out from the center. A jelly-like substance was found inside one of the circles in 1985. Those who came into contact with it experienced breathing difficulties, and three different laboratories were unable to identify it.

Moreover, molecular changes have been detected in plants taken from inside these circles, and Colin Andrews says, "We've asked the Ministry of Agriculture to do tests. It ought to take a closer look at them before they enter the food chain." This is reminiscent of the Trans-en-Provence case, described on pages 10-13 of my *Extra-Terrestrials Among Us.*

An odd event occurred on Aug. 19, 1987, in the time frame between the deaths of Mark Wisner and Victor Moore, and the death of Russell Smith, in the United States. On that date, a young man named Gary Stollman pulled a gun on David Horowitz on NBC-TV's "Today" show, just as Horowitz was about to read his consumer reports. Holding what appeared to be a pistol to Horowitz's head, Stollman forced him to read instead a statement he had prepared concerning the CIA and extra-terrestrials, alleging among other things that they were working in collusion "to overthrow the United States government, and possibly the human race itself" — one tactic used being to clone people, and then to replace the real person with the cloned replica.

The statement is long and rambling, and does indicate a considerable degree of mental confusion, but that does not mean its entire content can be dismissed as delusionary. Horowitz read the statement, but it was not broadcast because as soon as Stollman pulled out the pistol, the television directors had switched the programming. After Horowitz had read the statement, Stollman surrendered his pistol, which turned out to be an empty BB gun. In order to avoid a public trial, he was declared insane. In order to silence him for keeps, he was classified in the category of the most extremely dangerous criminally insane, and consigned to an asylum of this category for the rest of his life. Most of those in this category are mass murderers.

Stollman badly frightened David Horowitz, but he did not kill anyone. The United States has often pointed an accusing finger at the Soviet Union for using psychiatric institutions to silence political opposition. However, the Stollman case exemplifies the same sort of sinister game being played within the context of the U.S. legal system.

Although the allegation that extra-terrestrials are capable of replacing individuals with cloned replicas of themselves may seem at first glance to be absurd, there are substantial indications in the literature that this type of activity does in fact occur. Irene Granchi of Brazil is one of the best-informed and highly respected UFO researchers in the entire world. Many knowledgeable people think that the British *Flying Saucer Review* is the very best of all the UFO magazines. In the April 1987 issue of *Flying Saucer Review*, Irene Granchi wrote an article on precisely this subject, entitled "Cloning by Aliens," describing in detail a Brazilian case of this nature she had personally investigated.

The abductee was placed in front of a TV screen, through which he was obliged to watch for a full 24 hours what the clone was doing in his own home. The clone displayed considerable difficulty in adjusting to the abductee's home environment, being unable to express himself in writing, to carry out financial transactions, or to react with the appropriate emotions in different situations. Although the abductee did not directly meet any living entity during the experience, there was a dialogue in his native tongue through a sound box, which at one point volunteered this information about the clone: "He is an image that can be touched. Inside him there is one of ourselves and a recording of your mind."

This bears a remarkable similarity to a case I once helped to investigate. A woman was at work in a branch office of a firm. She was in charge of that office and was the only employee working there. During the course of an otherwise normal business day, she suddenly felt as if she was being separated from herself. The next thing she knew, she found herself on board a UFO, confronted by short Grays and a large insectile being that resembled a praying mantis, which obliged her to sit down in front of a TV screen, through which she saw to her horror herself back at the office, though it wasn't really herself. Her body was being operated by a Gray just as a human drives an automobile, and she had no control whatsoever over the actions being carried out by this Gray, which was unable to answer the telephone correctly or to recognize her best friend, who quite understandably reacted with puzzled panic.

This nightmare experience lasted only a few minutes, but because of the inappropriate answers to the phone calls, she lost her job. It seems clear that in such a situation, worse things could happen than losing one's job. One wonders how many crimes have been perpetrated by people involuntarily placed in this condition, who were unable to give a coherent explanation of what had happened to the police afterwards?

On Oct. 10, 1988, there was yet another development in this ongoing series of strangely lethal events, in the form of an article that appeared in the *Dallas Times Herald*. Here are the essentials:

Pentagon Seeks to Review British Deaths

Suicide, puzzling accidents have killed 22 defense experts since 1983: From wire reports.

LONDON - The United States wants Britain to let Pentagon specialists review the cases of as many as 22 British defense workers who have died under mysterious circumstances, a newspaper reported Sunday.

Citing an unidentified U.S. source, the *Sunday Times* said some workers were involved in British projects related to Star Wars, the space-based weapons defense system. Although the newspaper said the U.S. Defense Department is officially 'not commenting' on the deaths, one spokesman was quoted as saying the case had reached 'the point where we can't ignore it anymore.'...

Seven worked for the Star Wars contractor Marconi Co. Ltd., a subsidiary of Britain's General Electric Co. PLC, which recently opened an internal inquiry into the case. The company is not related to the U.S. General Electric.

General Electric Co. PLC and Foreign Ministry spokesmen say the deaths are not related.

(Credit: MUFON *Metroplex* P.O. Box 835002, Richardson, TX. 75083)

No sooner had I received the article from the *Dallas Times Herald* than another piece of the puzzle turned up in my mailbox, in the form of a letter that had been sent to fellow researcher Regina Cullen of London. Since she had no way to verify its authenticity, she warned me that it might be a hoax, designed to damage the credibility of this book upon its publication. Nevertheless, I think it should be presented for public examination, as the fact that it may be a hoax does not necessarily rule out the possibility that it might in the long run turn out to be valid. Having now made this disclaimer, here is the text:

Lancashire: Sunday 19th February 1989

Dear Miss Cullen,

I have had a letter from you passed onto me via Andy Roberts of the magazine *UFO Brigantia*. Thank you for the article, I found it very pertinent. Your comments about your friend though drew my attention immediately. Having heard these rumors before from a few people I was drawn to the area myself and lived in the forests there for a long while, silently observing the comings and goings of the craft (which are definitely jointly built and flown by the aliens and a combination of US/GB military staff). After several months though, one of the sweep teams which regularly comb the area for intruders spotted me and I had to leave. Let me explain more. For a period of time I worked as a psychological strategy advisor to the Special Air Service. Whether you believe it or not a small team of SAS are always used in UFO retrievals both here and overseas and eventually I was attached to one of these teams to help the personnel cope with the pressures of dealing with the constant pressure of knowing that aliens were here and that some of them were working with us. I was made privy to certain things — things which John Lear has only told the half of, and eventually I could not stand the strain myself. I knew I was living a lie and could not go on any longer. When my term of service was up, I had myself invalided out of the service on mental health grounds and left, together with the usual warnings about divulging information. I have no family and so changed my name a few times and with the aid of the pay off I was given I moved to live in seclusion in north west England, my only concession to the 20th century being my w/p and my IBM with which I can keep in touch with my contacts still in the world. I have been leaking UFO material to various people for a while now and chose *UFO Brigantia* for a number of reasons. These seem not to have worked and I will probably not be writing there again. Also, due to recent happenings I suspect that certain elements within the Intelligence services are involved in trying to trace me for reasons I do not have to say. All the material I have uncovered has been deposited with a friend in Bowling Green in the States and should anything happen to me he knows what to do. Recently I was made aware of a joint alien/human facility at Dulce in the U.S. where cloning experiments are taking place — the truth of the aliens interest in the human body, if you have not already guessed it, is that they are not cross-breeding but cloning humans for their own purposes. Other recent developments include new code words for joint alien/human work in progress which are Merlin, Excalibur and Jason, although exactly what they refer to I have yet to discover.

The other main piece of information I have discovered is of a crash which took place in Lancashire during August 1987 (as I wrote in *UFO Brigantia*). This definitely took place and I am now sure that it was near Oldham, or in that region. One small disc came down and was retrieved within twelve hours, suggestive of the fact that it was tracked on radar as it entered Earth orbit (it was not one of "ours"). It remains to be seen whether or not British ufologists will ever realize what an event has taken place and although I have dropped hints they appear to be ignoring it.

I see from the December issue of *UFO Brigantia* that you are a friend of George Andrews — a man whose work I have high regard for. Should you choose to pass this information onto him, or to any other *sensible* ufologist, such as Timothy Good or Jenny Randles, I have no objection, although I think they are aware of most of these things already. You may use my name if you wish as it is (obviously) not my real one. Incidentally, either Andrews or Good may have heard of my code name whilst in the service as being Touchstone. It is too dangerous for me to deal with ufologists directly and with the problems this has brought me recently I will not be doing so again. A word about some ufologists in this country. One thing I learned when I was with the psyops team was that a great many of them are being led astray intentionally. One or two of them are working for the company in assisting to suppress information. Andy Roberts could not give an address for me because he did not have one. I obtain my copies of *UFO Brigantia* by a complex route of unconnected people who acted innocently in passing the magazine along (not via a relative as I stated in my first letter). For the reasons given before I cannot let my identity or whereabouts be known to anyone involved in the UFO research field. If you but knew it, Andy Roberts is very involved in clandestine areas of governmental UFO work, pertinent to my point at the operation, or so my sources tell me.

I would hope this letter reaches you Miss Cullen and answers your queries. I cannot enter into any correspondence for obvious reasons. The truth is there, it is just being obscured. We must all help as best we can.

Touchstone

There are resemblances so strong as to be beyond coincidence between the present situation of humans confronted by the short Grays, and J. R. Tolkien's description of the war between the human-like Hobbits and short gray Orcs in his three-volume masterpiece, *The Lord of the Rings*. The resemblance between Level Six at the Dulce Labs and the subterranean laboratories of Morgoth are also far too strong to be merely coincidence. It looks to me as if Tolkien was transmitting clairvoyant perceptions of future events, along with a rich mix of other things in his trilogy, which thus contains precious clues on how to free our planet from the domination of the Grays.

Just as the witches of England raised for England a cone of power at the time of the Spanish Armada, and again after the battle of Dunkerque, perhaps what is needed under our present circumstances is to raise a cone of power for the entire planet, and to aim it directly at the Spider Queen super-brain the Grays are all plugged into.

What type of entities in deep antiquity sealed the interdimensional gateway that Parsons and Hubbard unsealed in 1947, and where are they now? Would they help us yet again, after what they had sealed to protect humanity has been deliberately unsealed by humans? Let's all get together and send them a massive telepathic S.O.S., a cosmic species-to-species emergency signal, a psychic Mayday red alert that requests immediate intervention strong and clear.

The limits imposed by higher echelons of the cosmic hierarchy to the extent of permissible E.T. predatory activities on Earth might correspond with the extent to which terrestrial humanity is actively attacking its own biosphere. If terrestrial humanity persistently demonstrates by its deeds that it is no longer worthy of retaining its place as the dominant species on this planet — because it is suicidally fouling its own nest and sabotaging its own environment, thereby also destroying the evolutionary possibilities for all other forms of life on this planet — it is not surprising if we find ourselves being treated like our scientists treat laboratory animals by entities from elsewhere, who are interacting with us whether we like it or not. In the words of Virgil Armstrong: "I later learned from this alien group that...if a planet was on a path of self-destruction then others could, while time permitted, help themselves."

The oceans are dying, the lakes are dying, the rivers are dying, the forests are dying, and our ozone layer is full of holes. All of this for but one reason: humanity's industrial waste released into the environment in an irresponsible manner. Acid rain is the classic example of this death-dealing vicious circle.

Wilhelm Reich's correlation between what he called "the emotional plague" (the cause of cancer, fascism, and the barren desert so often encountered in the human emotional landscape) and the formation of physical geological deserts is a valid one. Our connections with this planet go far deeper than we normally recognize. Let us remember that our ancestors knew how to dance the rain into being. We are parts of this living planet's nervous system. As individuals, may we each attain a permanently sustained conscious connection with the universal life-energy, the original source of life in all the worlds, constantly manifesting limitless life, which has throughout history been called by so many different names, of which "orgone" is a recent one.

If humanity would devote as much of its ingenuity and productivity to the cleansing of the Earth, to the restoring of our planet to optimum health, to improving the quality of our environment, as we now devote to the arms race, our home star would soon shine forth in the true glory of a renewed splendor.

The money required to provide adequate food, water, education, health and housing for everyone in the world has been estimated at seventeen billion dollars a year. It is a huge sum of money — about as much as the world spends on arms every two weeks.

The dolphins always have been and still are in contact with extra-terrestrials. Dolphins should be included as full and equal partners in any official Earthling/E.T. conference concerning the future of this planet. If terrestrial humanity would at last learn to accept the guidance of the age-old wisdom of the dolphins, instead of slaughtering them stupidly, it might still be possible to save this planet's endangered and severely wounded biosphere. The age-old wisdom of the dolphins also has much to teach us about the characteristics of the different types of extra-terrestrials operating in our environment, and how to communicate effectively with them.

The September 1988 issue of the *Nevada Aerial Research Newsletter* (P.O. Box 81407, Las Vegas, NV 89180), states that:

It is usually the case that biological mammals are thought to be the ultimate on this planet.

Both Cetaceans and Homo sapiens are the dominant species in

the world of terrestrial mammals, with brain mass between 3,500 grams and 3,000 grams.

One of the most noteworthy members of the Cetaceans is the bottle-nosed dolphin, who has over 1,500 grams more associative brain mass than the human.

The brain of the dolphin is 30 million years ahead of ours in evolutionary development. This ancient species predates Homo sapiens. The dolphin is a fine example of a species of beings that has a non-technological orientation and is peaceful.

Homo sapiens requires 30 critical frequency bands for understandable communication. Dolphins require more than 60 bands. The frequency band of dolphin communication is 4.5 to 10 times greater than the one for humans.

There is no gap in the series of cetacean brain sizes like there is for land-based primates. The primates are missing a size for a brain mass that is between 500-900 grams. This represents the range of difference between ape brains and the human brain.

Since crystalline structures have been found in some alien brains during autopsy, there is every reason to assume that because the dolphin has a larger brain, there may be crystalline structures that lie within. These structures are functional networks that allow a telepathic communication flow.

The network also allows access to great volumes of data from the Universal Intelligence Matrix.

This correlates with the theory proposed by Terence and Dennis McKenna in their brilliant masterpiece, *The Invisible Landscape* (Seabury Press, 1975): that shamanic ingestion of certain hallucinogenic substances of the right type, in the correct dosages, under appropriate circumstances and accompanied by certain time-tested traditional techniques, will temporarily induce a state of super-consciousness that is derived from the formation of a super-conductive area within the brain. Through continued use of the correct techniques, this temporary super-conductive area can be transformed into a permanent acquisition that allows the shaman to tap into the state of super-consciousness at will.

Would the formation of a permanent super-conductor within the brain be perceived post-mortem during autopsy as an anomalous crystalline structure?

According to Valdamar Valerian in *The Matrix* (Arcturus, 1988), autopsy results on an alien (Gray) cadaver showed that there was a crystalline network in the right frontal area of the brain, indicating development of a third brain area.

Not all of the implants that aliens insert into humans are detrimental, but some of them certainly are. In such cases, the problem is to neutralize the undesirable implant. The following text "On Undoing Implants" was contributed by a woman with substantial first-hand experience in this field, who wishes to remain anonymous:

If the victim remembers the episode, the operation has failed. All that then needs to be done is to stimulate recall and provide reassurance. In some cases, this is easier said than done. However, this attitude is certainly preferable to blind mechanical reaction — unless the victim chooses to adopt instead the Insect Attitude and see bodies as mere meat machines, the Self as a chemical construct based on molecular reaction. This is the viewpoint of the insect kingdom.

It all depends on where you position your horizon, spiraling inwards or spiraling outwards, and what you would like to do.

Would you like to bring out the lasers, and chop off a few heads?

That approach would be like trying to clear a mine field with a sledge-hammer.

Another possibility exists. We can go along with the implant, become familiar with it, and then add energy very carefully with constantly focused attention, in a way that overloads the circuits of the implant and blows its circuitry. It is not really difficult, if one takes higher ground, thereby transcending direct confrontation, and from that higher ground transmits higher frequencies that crescendo to peak intensities.

Here is what is really difficult: try to get the implanted person interested in sustaining awareness above the navel, above gut-level reaction, and into such areas in and around the brain as are available as implant points. Try to get them to do it because they want to, because they choose to, not because they are told to.

This is where the row becomes really hard to hoe. Ninety-nine times out of a hundred, you may be told to four-letter off, but sometimes that hundredth one does spark.

What more can a Sojourner expect?

As this book was about to go to press, I received the following message from a friend who wishes to remain anonymous:

It is true that our kind has never had it easy in this world. Part of it is our being in an alien world, among alien people. Part, of course, is that the Opposition seeks to destroy us, and we are very vulnerable here. And part of it is to be found in the nature of Odin himself. While he gives strength and courage, he also leads us on hard roads where strength and courage are needed — both the strength that he gives, and that which lies within us. Our own strength is often unknown to us and unguessed at by us, yet Odin sees it. Look at the lives of his chosen heros! To one whom he favors, I would almost say: "Beware!"

I would not worry about invasion by the Grays, although I would do my very best to fight them, which is not the same thing. It may comfort you to remember there are beings whose greatness and power makes them comparable to galaxies, at least, yet who care deeply about this world and about each one of us. One such is the being whose presence you felt through me over the phone. They have the power to destroy all evil in a moment, but they do not use it. Their way is to work through our courage, strength, perseverance and love, however small these might be. This is doing it the hard way. It would be incomparably easier for them to use their own power. But if our battles were fought for us by archangels, what would be the value of our courage, strength, perseverance and love? What nobility would there be in us? It is, after all, our fight.

Let your mind reach out to what is high and bright and beautiful. Make use of your imagination, your highest faculty. Let your imagination soar, and see what it is capable of. Let yourself feel wonder at the kind of beauty whose element is enchantment, then give expression to the enchantment in words which sing out that Earth has not been forsaken by the High Ones.

Odin is also Maitreya and the Mahdi and Metatron and the return of Christ, coming in the clouds like a thief in the night, when most needed and least expected, to reveal his presence like a lightning flash from horizon to horizon. He is King of Gods and Angels, but in his highest aspect he chooses service over kingship: the brightest light is that which is veiled.

No matter what name you call him, he who extinguishes the fire and then suddenly brings it back to life is the giver of courage to those who have lost heart, the restorer of joy to those left without hope. He is our midnight sunrise, our break of day in the deepest darkness of night. May his white flame fill you with the strength that comes from deep within, enabling you to withstand, endure and prevail by cutting through the tangled lies of Loki's minions with the single-pointed sword of the truth.

This book would not be complete without a heroic little gem of a statement made by a courageous black lady with little formal education, who maintained her integrity in a situation in which so many others, including the most highly educated, have succumbed. When inside the ship and physically helpless, confronted with the unblinking reptilian hypnotic gaze of the leader of her Gray abductors, here is what she had to say:

"I'm trying to see. I can see only what they want me to see. I'm looking right into his eyes, and I seem to go blank. I will control my own mind. You have no power over my mind. God gave me this mind. You can't have it. This consciousness is mine, a God-given gift. You will not control me. I will look you in the eye and tell you that you will not control my mind. We can stare at each other as long as you want to, but you will not control my mind."

Her words contain a lesson for us all.

The secret treaty that our government made with the Gray aliens without our knowledge or consent was illegal. It is binding on the citizens of this nation only so long as we continue to tolerate it through ignorance, fear and apathy. As soon as a majority of the citizens of this nation publicly repudiate the secret and illegal treaty, the E.T. group similar to humans that warned us against continuing the arms race will have a legitimate reason to intervene.

When I showed Winston Sarafian's letter and my response to it to Donna Lawson, an abductee who has gone public, she asked me how I knew that sending white light to the Spider Queen of Space would not further energize her, rather than causing her to retract her minions from this planet, pointing out that white light had been ineffective in neutralizing unwanted alien implants, but that light in the range of the spectrum where blue shifts into purple had been effective at least temporarily in neutralizing the implants.

I'd like to give the final word to another friend, Rosemary Decker, who had this to say in response to the same material:

> White light, which contains all the colors of the spectrum equally, is white because of its balanced combination. It has long been known that violet light burns away destructive tissue, but does not harm wholesome living cells. That is why some healers use the amethyst crystal when dealing with diseases of cancerous types. It should also be pointed out that the extra-terrestrials interacting with

us do not divide neatly between Blonds and Grays. Some genetic types with physical proportions very similar to ours are dark-haired, dark-eyed, and bronze or brown-skinned. The reason I emphasize this is because there is still, long after Hitler's demise, a group of people claiming white (Blond) supremacy and attempting to infiltrate the media world-wide. The UFO field is one area of their attack. As for the Reticulans or Rigelians, whichever the case may be, their claim to have the upper hand on Earth is simply a ploy to frighten Earthlings into submission. Hitler used similar tactics. Genetic manipulation of Earthlings is nothing new. Our race was created in the first place by Outsiders who planned to use the hybrids as 'guards' and 'gardeners' (Book of Genesis) and in addition, according to the older Sumerian records, as 'miners.' A different group of extra-terrestrials, from an ethically more advanced culture, worked out a plan for the eventual self-determination, liberation, and welcome of Earthlings into the galactic community as brothers and sisters. There are many graduates of this group's invisible college, some here, some on other planets, and many more to come. The same group that worked out the Salvage Plan thousands of years ago continues to implement it today.

12

Late-breaking Developments

*I*n this final chapter, I have decided to summarize the essentials of the flood of major new developments.

The official Soviet announcement of a UFO landing at Voronezh was at first given major media coverage, which was promptly followed by a barrage of ridicule that killed the story. The basis for the ridicule was that the Russian journalist who filed the first report admitted that it was based on the testimony of adolescents. Having killed the story, the major news media systematically ignored the careful follow-up investigations that were done, such as this one, which is from *Moscow News,* Moscow, U.S.S.R., week of Oct. 23-30, 1989, article by Lev Aksonosov and Boris Zverev, translated by E. Komarek and reprinted in the Nov. issue of UFONS, Rt. 1 Box 220, Plumerville, AR 72127.

Aliens Visit Voronezh

A usual urban landscape: a busy street, a residential neighborhood, kindergartens, a meadow on the edge of a park. Here, in Voronezh's Levoberezhny District, near Mendeleyev Street, as eyewitnesses say, mysterious occurrences were observed approximately between September 21 and October 2. At first journalists drew primarily on eyewitness accounts by adolescents, pupils of Secondary School No. 33 nearby. But enthusiasts in Voronezh who have come together to study abnormal atmospheric phenomena at the Alexander Popov radio electronics and communications scientific-technical association are also taking an active interest in this. They have talked to eyewitnesses, quite a number of adults among them, and carried out the first studies on the site where the "extra-terrestrials" are supposed to have landed. By questioning each of the witnesses separately, they produced — on the basis of stories from people excited at what they had seen (or imagined?) — not only a detailed picture of the events, but also sketches of the appearance of the UFO and the "pilots." It is significant that descriptions of the aliens and their flying craft amazingly coincide with what was observed in early June of this year by the habitants of the Konantseva village in the Kharovsk District (Vologda Region).

However, an eyewitness account is one thing, the objective readings of instruments is something different. On the site of the UFO's supposed landing numerous dents were found in the soil which could have been made by the "saucer's feet." Their diameter is 25-30 cm, their depth from 20 to 25 cm. The "unofficial" enthusiasts say that, according to their calculations, the approximate mass of the body which exerted pressure on the ground was 11 tons. But more interesting, in some of the dents the "incorruptible" dosimeters recorded a definite increase in the background of gamma-radiation in comparison with neighboring sites some two or three meters away. Whereas the usual level here amounts to 10-15 micro-roentgen an hour, in one of the dents they recorded 30, and in another — 37 micro-roentgen an hour (it was this particular dent that Vladimir Cherkesov, senior expert of the Voronezh Administration of Internal Affairs, photographed)....

All the stories coincide in the main: the flyover and landing of a mysterious ellipsis-shaped body 15 by 6 m with a hatch in the middle was seen from various distances. The object remained at a height of roughly 1.5 m above earth, then supports came out and it landed. From the open hatch there emerged a three-metre-tall figure which filled the whole of the "doorway." Distinctive features: a heavy gait, no neck (the "head," with something like three luminous eyes, was a kind of hemisphere lying directly on the shoulders). The alien — sometimes there were a few of them — walked near the craft for some time, examined the plot, and seemed to take soil samples. This is what the boys told us (and not us alone).

And the adults? We have no doubt that the children did not invent all this. Incidentally, the same view is held by Mayor Viktor Atlasov, who carefully studied the video recording with the boys very first "testimonies." "I am not a young person and, you know, an adult can always tell when a child is telling the truth and when he is not. I believe the boys," he admitted in a conversation with us.

We found grown-up witnesses of repeated cases of flyovers, even landings, by UFOs.

Thus, Lieutenant of the Militia Sergei Malveyev, whom we immediately took to, said that on September 27, at about 7 p.m., he was walking in the area of the park. Suddenly Sergei noticed a luminous ball sweeping past northwards at colossal speed, strictly horizontally and at an altitude of roughly 200 m. He estimated its diameter to be about 15 m. He watched the ball's flight for about 5 sec., the object moved noiselessly.

"Couldn't it have been a mirage, some light spot, the play of light in the atmosphere?" "No" he confidently replied. "The body was clearly multi-dimensional." The lieutenant's first reaction was interesting: He decided not to tell his acquaintances and colleagues at once. "They might have thought a militiaman doesn't have such fancies...." Sergei Matveyev made up his mind only when the local press urged the city's inhabitants to report any strange things they might have seen. It must be said that his superiors took the young officer's story in real earnest.

We also spoke to two women witnesses. On September 29, at 7 p.m., Olga Poludneva, an assembler at a local industrial plant, saw a luminous ball flying at a great altitude in the openings between houses. According to her, the flight lasted about 10 minutes. Her friend Lyudmila Kupriyanova said that she was at home at that moment, and she heard cries outdoors: "A saucer is flying!" She ran into the street and only managed to see a luminous tail from the mysterious body. There were many people near the house, everyone greatly excited by what they had seen.

It is characteristic that for some time afterwards many witnesses of the mysterious phenomenon experienced an inexplicable feeling of fear and unusual sensations: heaviness in their feet and restraint in movement. But these are only emotions.

Now comes the turn of professionals. We spoke several times with a person of immense charm, whose objectivity cannot be doubted — her profession precludes any bias. Colonel of the Militia Lyudmila Makarova, head of the criminal expertise department of the Voronezh Administration of Internal Affairs, headed a group of experts who took measurements on the site of the event and examined it closely. "I don't know what actually happened here, but an increase in the radioactive background is in evidence. The reason? Maybe a grain of some isotope got in here. Then one more question: why precisely in the dent, why not on the surface? We shall be able to answer everything only after thorough investigations."

Thus, a highly competent commission is at work in the city. Taking part in it is the cream of local science specialists in the most diverse fields, and officials.

The incident in June that the above article refers to, which received minimal media coverage, was reported by United Press International on June 24, 1989:

> Moscow (UPI) — Reports of unidentified flying objects have filled local newspapers in the rural Vologda region of the Russian republic, the official Tass news agency reported Friday.
>
> One group of children outside the village of Konantsevo on June 6 "spotted a fast increasing luminous dot in the sky, which soon turned into a shining sphere," Tass said. "The mysterious object reportedly landed in a meadow and rolled to a nearby river as the children looked on no more than half a kilometer away.
>
> They claim that they saw the sphere kind of split, and something resembling a headless person in dark garb appeared on the meadow. It struck them that the alien's hands hung lower than his knees. At that moment, however, the 'flying craft' melted into the air, while the creature from it admittedly proceeded to the village."
>
> Tass quoted "eyewitness accounts" as saying that three more spheres later touched down in the same meadow.
>
> Just like the very first one, the rest of the spheres and their "passengers" quickly became invisible, Tass said.

Here in the United States, the experts lost no time in minimizing the significance of the Voronezh incident. In an interview with David Jacobson of *Courant*, Hartford, CT, published on Oct. 11, Jerome Clark of the Center for UFO Studies stated unequivocally: "I'm certain this is a hoax." Clark leaped so quickly to this conclusion because he knew of no other case histories involving aliens 9-13 feet tall with small heads. It apparently did not occur to Clark that the aliens might have been wearing some type of protective body armor, and that the entity inside the armor could look quite different. As this was the first case on record of a UFO landing in broad daylight for a substantial period of time in the middle of a city, it would not be surprising if the occupants stepped into a suit of protective armor, before stepping out for a stroll.

However, the Voronezh incident was merely a prelude to a deluge of other events.

On Oct. 23, 1989, *Het Volk*, Brussels, Belgium, reported that Major Vladimir Loginov of the Soviet Army had stated in an interview with the magazine *Socialist Industry* that on Oct. 17 a UFO bigger than the moon had hovered above the Siberian city of Omsk. It had four enormous searchlights, but was not visible on radar. It departed at a speed in excess of 7,000 kilometers an hour (about 4,750 mph).

All through the month of October and into November, many thousands of people witnessed UFOs over Oklahoma, Arkansas, Missouri, Kansas, Iowa, Tennessee and Mississippi. The most frequent sightings occurred in Oklahoma and Arkansas. Shirley England and her family of Welch, Oklahoma, were stopped by a UFO that landed in the road in front of their car, and had a close encounter with two entities described as being approximately 9 feet tall, thin, and glowing green. It was not clear whether or not they had heads. Barbara Bartholic sought out Mrs. England, who was traumatized to the point that it was very difficult to get further information from her. It seemed quite clear that she was sincere, was dismayed by the publicity she was getting rather than seeking it, and was not making a copycat hoax report based on the Voronezh incident. In spite of extensive local coverage, all of this activity in the Midwestern U.S., coming right on the heels of the Tass report, was ignored by the major news media. To give an idea of how extensive local coverage was, here is a list of the newspapers that ran articles on it:

Log Cabin Democrat, Conway, AR, Oct. 11
Daily Oklahoman, Oklahoma City, OK, Oct. 11
Tribune, Tulsa, OK, Oct. 11
News-Record, Miami, OK, Oct. 11, 12 & 13
Commercial Appeal, Memphis, TN, Oct. 12
World, Tulsa, OK, Oct. 12
Daily Quill, West Plains, MO, Oct. 13
Citizen, Baxter, KS, Oct. 13
Cedar Valley Times, Vinton, IA, Oct. 13
Arkansas Democrat, Little Rock, AR, Oct. 13 & 28
News-Leader, Springfield, MO, Oct. 19 & 22
Journal, Salina, KS, Oct. 20
Star, Kansas City, MO, Oct. 22
Commercial, Pine Bluff, AR, Oct. 24 & 25
Register, Des Moines, IA, Oct. 25
Daily Phoenix, Muskogee, OK, Oct. 27 & 28
Arkansas Gazette, Little Rock, AR, Oct. 28
Argus, Brinkley, AR, Oct. 29
Press, Grand Rapids, MI, Nov. 8
Daily Times, Harrison, AR, Nov. 10

Then we have this from the *Star,* Auckland, New Zealand, Nov. 14:

Budapest — A month after the Soviet Union was swept by tales

of visitors from outer space, Hungarians have started seeing unidentified flying objects and little green men.

Air Force pilots in southern Kecskemet were followed during
training flights last month by a "strange, spherical, orange-coloured"
flying object which did not show up on radar, the independent
weekly *Kel-Kelet* reported.

Days later, two soldiers on duty at the airport there saw a figure
of fluorescent green about 1.2 metres tall who beamed himself up
into space.

He passed around a plane, lifted one of his arms and created a
cone-shaped light-beam above his head, disappearing silently within
seconds into a high-rising tunnel of light.

Left behind on the concrete was the same kind of reddish deposit reported in news last month of three-metre tall, three-eyed
monsters in Voronezh, central Russia.

Deputy Defense Minister Janos Stock was quoted by the daily
Nepszabadsaq yesterday as saying the red deposit was a piece of
synthetic resin used for repairing pavements....adding that soldiers
sometimes have visions which others embellish.

Nepszabadsaq also quoted a report that a farmer in south-eastern
Gyomaendrod had seen two long-eared little green men. "The man
tried to hit them with his shovel but they paralyzed him with an
unknown power and disappeared," it said.

The Soviet sightings were eventually officially declared to have
been aliens, according to Tass news agency. Asked at the time
whether there might just be a hoaxer at work, the agency said "Tass
never jokes."
—NPZA-Reuter

On Nov. 27, 1989, the *Sun* of Toronto printed this:

Budapest (Reuter) — Only weeks after reports of little green
spacemen in Hungary, meteorologists said they have sighted four
large, brick-orange unidentified flying objects. Bazso said he and
his colleagues spotted strange lights close to the Great Bear constellation last Friday night.

The Hungarian incidents were still on-going as of April 19, 1990, when
the *Times* of London, England, reported "a series of inexplicable events,
involving UFO sightings and an apparent encounter with giant extra-terrestrial creatures, at Tarnaszentmaria army barracks. These continued for

about a month and were duly logged by the army. According to the testimony of the entire unit, the UFO intrusion began on the night of October 20 last year with an eerie noise which increased in volume every 20 seconds or so. Then one of the guards noticed three shiny round objects preceded by a beam of light. After a while these disappeared over the forest behind the barracks. On November 20, soldiers on guard duty noticed a cloud of red mist in the sky with curious flashing lights inside it, followed by a UFO, shaped like the planet Saturn, which floated over the barracks and disappeared over the forest. Two of the guards reported that they were illuminated briefly with a powerful beam of light which made them sick. Later that night, Private Lajos Dioszegi spotted 10 ft. tall figures in the forest clearing facing the barracks. "They were moving as if they were chess pieces," he stated. "All the animals in the barracks — pigs, sheep and dogs — became frantic."

The article in the London *Times* also mentions that there have been hundreds of UFO reports from Hungarian civilians recently. However, for some strange reason the London *Times* had nothing at all to say about the tremendous surge in UFO activity in England recently, which has reached unprecedented levels. During 1989, there were 1,400 reports from East Anglia alone. And the "corn circles" for which the most preposterous explanations have been touted by the media and officialdom in preference over the obvious one of UFO landing traces are now beginning to be found in rectangular and complex geometrical shapes that reduce Dr. Meaden's erudite theories about plasma vortexes caused by anomalous whirlwinds to blather. How come the *Times* has so much to say about what is going on in Hungary, but so little to say about the dramatic escalation of the same phenomena in England?

On Dec. 9, 1989, the *Tribune* of Tampa, Florida, had this to say:

Brussels, Belgium (AP) — The air force and police are investigating numerous UFO sightings near the border with the Netherlands and West Germany, officials said Friday.

Since Nov. 29, dozens of people and police officials in the north-western Liege province said they've seen luminous objects in the sky, with some of them describing a flying platform scanning the surface with three huge searchlights, while others talk of dancing lights.

During the same period, air traffic controllers "found radar blips on the screens that could not be immediately explained," said Defense Ministry spokesman Col. Michel Mandel.

At the time of the sightings there were no authorized low-level flights in the region.

It is some comfort that at least in Belgium the authorities do not attempt to foist on the public the rotten baloney about pranksters flying ultralight aircraft in formation. In the suburbs of New York, there were further sightings of the Westchester Wing during this time frame, for which this worn-out ludicrous explanation was offered yet again.

Sightings continued over Belgium, and descriptions of the object most frequently sighted consistently resembled descriptions given by witnesses of the Westchester Wing. As we go to press a situation comparable to those of Gulf Breeze, Florida; Wytheville, Virginia; and the Hudson River Valley of New York had developed in Belgium, where over a thousand sightings had been reported since the end of November 1989. At the end of August 1992, this unprecedented wave of activity is still going strong.

In stark contrast to the snobbish arrogance that has characterized most U.S. military officers when dealing with civilian UFO researchers, the Belgian Air Force cooperated with civilian researchers, not only sharing information but providing equipment. Working together, on the night of March 30, 1990, they achieved some remarkable and definitive results.

Paris-Match has a position in the French news media comparable to that of *Time* magazine in the U.S. news media. In its July 5, 1990, issue, *Paris-Match* printed an article based an documents concerning the events that occurred on the night of March 30. The documents were authorized for release exclusively through *Paris-Match* by the Belgian Minister of Defense, and contained statements such as: "Our system of defense is powerless when confronted by these aircraft... It can not be anything made by man."

Disappearances of children in Belgium have increased sharply since Jan. 1, 1990, but so far no one seems to have publicly linked the disappearances to the UFO wave. Disappearances not only of children, but of people of all ages, have risen dramatically. According to an article in the Oct. 8, 1990, *La Dernire Heure*, there had been 2,046 unexplained human disappearances since Jan. 1. 1,388 of these cases involved disappearances of children. Only 658 of the people who disappeared during July 1990 were adults, 186 minors disappeared in Belgium, under circumstances the police refused to discuss, except to say that the circumstances had them worried. Yet there was not a word in the otherwise detailed and comprehensive article in *La Dernire Heure* about the obvious correlation between the unprecedented number of disappearances and the unprecedented levels of UFO activity reported from all over Belgium during the same time frame.

There has also been an overwhelming abundance of reports in the Soviet Union, where many more incidents have occurred and continue to occur, including some at Voronezh. All of this activity has been systematically ignored by the U.S. news media.

There was an important development in Russia during 1989, which was released by the official Soviet news agency Tass, but received next to no coverage in the news media of the rest of the world. The only mention of it I have been able to find was in the Sept. 19, 1989, issue of *People* (Melbourne, Australia):

> Startling pictures of a huge, city-like structure on the surface of Mars are creating a furor among Soviet scientists.
>
> Film of the "Martian metropolis" was beamed to earth earlier this year by Russia's Phobos space probe — two hours before it mysteriously vanished from radio-TV contact.
>
> The now-missing Phobos spacecraft also transmitted baffling pictures of an immense oval shadow, more than 5 km long, on the rocky Martian surface. The image was recorded by both optical and heat-seeking cameras.
>
> Experts agree that the egg-shaped shadow is definitely being thrown by "something" in the sky — because ridges and valleys are clearly visible beneath it.
>
> Dr. John Becklake, of the London Science Museum, said: "There's no doubt it's a shadow — but a shadow of what? The city-like pattern is particularly fascinating. It's 60 km wide and could easily be mistaken for an aerial view of Los Angeles. The criss-crossing lines on the film are about 4 km wide. And they show up as infra-red — which means they're emitting heat. That's very puzzling indeed considering that Mars has an extremely cold carbon dioxide atmosphere."
>
> Soviet space authorities have refused to release the final picture taken by the Phobos probe before it vanished.

Once again, it is thanks to Lucius Farish's indispensable UFO Newsclipping Service, Rt. 1 Box 220, Plumerville, AR 72127, that I have been able to assemble the information contained in this chapter thus far. I now turn to some other sources.

Linda Howe writes that there have been many classic mutilations recently in southern Idaho: "There were 30 cases in Bear Lake County alone, 23 of them in one 6 square mile area. No blood. No tracks. All the same parts missing cleanly, as in years past. Sheriff and vets troubled, but not much media coverage — as always! And official explanation is Satanic cults — as always!!"

Lawrence Fenwick and other members of the Canadian UFO Research Network have investigated a series of remarkable UFO incidents in Israel, which received almost no media coverage. The dates on which some of the sightings and landings occurred were considered holy according to the Hebrew calendar. The most spectacular incident involved a pillar of fire that appeared near a place known as the Cave of Elijah on April 21, 1989, which was Passover. There have been three different UFO landings that left physical traces in the form of scorch marks at this same location during the past two years. The pillar of fire, which witnesses reported as having been approximately 60 feet tall and 20 feet wide, left a burn residue. A sample of this residue was sent to CUFORN, and analyzed by George Hathaway, Ph.D., at the University of Toronto. It was found to contain an anomalous substance: technetium, which does not occur in nature, except as a by-product of nuclear reactions.

The Dec. 15, 1990, issue of *The Jerusalem Post* ran a full-page article on the series of incidents that CUFORN investigated, and added some intriguing details. There have been 200 sightings in the Haifa area in the past two years, many of them by multiple witnesses, simultaneously reported from different locations. On Sept. 13, 1987, the eve of Rosh Hashana (New Year), there was a close encounter of the second kind, which left landing marks. The witness later reported various physical ailments, such as a burning sensation in the eyes and digestive problems, which he attributed to the samples of earth from the landing site that he had taken home with him. On May 22, 1988, the eve of Shavuot (which commemorates the giving of the ten commandments to Moses on Mount Sinai), there was a sighting by two witnesses from a location 200 meters north of the Sept. 13, 1987, landing site. The Pesach (Passover) manifestation of the pillar of fire on April 22, 1989, was again 200 meters north of the May 22, 1988, location. All three of these incidents occurred on the same beach. We know from the CUFORN investigation that the Cave of Elijah is a little less than two kilometers (1.2 miles) north of Shikmona Beach, and a line drawn through the landing mark and the burn mark from the pillar of fire points directly to the Cave of Elijah on Mount Carmel. Researcher Hadassah Arbel expressed the opinion that Elijah was an extra-terrestrial, who returned to his original abode (as he had come from it) in a chariot of fire. Arbel adds that Malachi, the last of the prophets, said in his final prophecy: "Behold, I will send you Elijah the prophet before the coming of the great and terrible Day of the Lord." Is it possible, Arbel asks, that we are receiving a signal of some sort?

Some relevant remarks were made by Roman Nacht in an article entitled "UFOs Over Modern Israel," which appeared in the March 1991 issue of *The Missing Link,* published by UFOCCI, Suite 304, 3001 South 288th. St., Federal Way WA 98003:

> Before the Six Day War in 1967, there was strong UFO activity over Israel, especially over the central and southern part of the country... the activity of UFOs over Israel has been tremendous during the last two years, especially over the northern part of the country.... UFOs were seen over Jerusalem in 1965/66. UFOs were seen over Ramat Gan in July 1976, even by the Mayor of this city, together with other prominent people. UFOs were seen over the top secret Dimona installations, where a local policeman lost his job after he resisted "admitting" that he was lying about being taken on board one of the space craft by the aliens. He was released as "normal," after psychiatric observation, but couldn't work again as a police officer. After many lectures given in Kibbutzim, men came to me and told me about strange discs flying sometimes by day, sometimes by night, over the Golan Heights during the Six Day War.... Many frightened people reported to me UFO sightings from Natanya, Naharya, Bat Yam and especially many sighting reports came from children in Nazareth. UFOs appeared also over ancient cities like Ashkelon or Ashdod, which caused twice a blackout.

Another significant bit of information appeared in the Sept./Oct. 1989 issue of the Arkansas MUFON Newsletter:

> Six times this year, an unannounced asteroid made a pass at the planet Earth. On August 24th, Asteroid 1989PB approached to within 1.5 million miles of Earth travelling at between 20,000 to 40,000 miles per hour.
>
> The mile wide chunk of rock was discovered coming this way on August 9th during film studies taken that day at Palomar Observatory in San Diego. It was the sixth one to intrude into the Earth's back yard this year and only one other had come closer.
>
> Last March, asteroid 1989FC travelled to within 460,000 miles of the Earth. This was stated to have been the closest asteroid pass in the records of astronomy. The origin of the six asteroids is apparently not known nor is there any assurance that more will not fol-

low. It is remarkable that a sequential series of historic astronomical events of this kind was so sparsely reported.

There was considerable debate among scientists over the nature of asteroid 1991VG, which came within 288,000 miles from Earth on Dec. 5, 1991, before drifting away. Astronomer Brian Marsden, director of the International Astronomical Union's central telegram bureau in Cambridge, Mass., went on record as stating that asteroid 1991VG had characteristics (such as pulsations of reflected light, reminiscent of a rapidly rotating satellite with highly reflective side panels) indicating it to be artificial in nature.

According to the *International Herald Tribune* of April 7, 1992, U.S. military authorities now want "a standing force of 10 missiles armed with monster nuclear warheads ready to deflect any threatening object that appeared suddenly."

Do we intend to shoot first and ask questions later? Should the military really have a secret monopoly on the control of this situation that concerns us all?

If a giant asteroid on an approach course to earth turns out to be a natural rather than an artificial object, if it really is an asteroid and not the great-grandmother of all mother-ships, and it is on a collision course with Earth, I would be in complete agreement with the Pentagon that we should do everything possible to deflect or destroy it before impact, including the use of nuclear weaponry. If it is an artificial object, not an asteroid but the great-grandmother of all motherships, and there is substantial evidence that its occupants are, for example, man-eating Reptilians, I would also be in complete agreement with the Pentagon that we should shoot first and ask questions later. However, the Pentagon has lied to us so often about so many things that most of us know its statements are not to be trusted. The fact that it is especially in the United States that abductions by the Grays have reached epidemic proportions is a clear indication that the Pentagon did indeed make a secret treaty with the Grays. Even if the Grays then double-crossed the Pentagon and the situation went out of control, the very fact that it is in the Pentagon's terms out of control implies that it is the Grays who now to an unknown extent control the Pentagon. If the Gray double-cross plus expertise in telepathic hypnosis and other remote mind control techniques has rendered the Pentagon subservient to them, then the Pentagon would tell the public exactly what the Grays want the public to hear: that the mighty ship approaching is filled with man-eating Reptilians, to which our immediate reaction would of course be to attack it with every weapon at our disposal. However, what if this is not true, but is merely a subterfuge to get us to attack a mighty ship belonging to a group who are enemies of the Grays but not necessarily of terrestrial humanity, perhaps even ancestral to us, who intend to prevent the Grays from adding this planet to their empire as a slave colony, therefore our allies and potential saviors? How can we obtain valid information concerning the nature of the occupants of this mighty ship, if that is what it in fact is rather than an asteroid, without relying on information coming from the tainted sources that have over and over again proven themselves to be utterly unreliable, that have now been caught in the act of lying to us systematically for the past half-century, such as NASA, the Pentagon, or our so-called intelligence agencies?

The following is from the December 1989 issue of *Acres, U.S.A.*, P O. Box 9547, Kansas City, MO 64133:

According to Dr. Robert Strecker, a Los Angeles physician who specializes in caring for AIDS patients, AIDS is a man-made virus genetically engineered in a laboratory. He claims that a 1972 document of the World Health Organization (WHO) shows authorization for the manufacture of the AIDS-like virus. On page 259, in volume 47 of the WHO Bulletin it states: 'an attempt should be made to ascertain whether viruses can in fact exert selective effects on immune function...by affecting T cell function as opposed to B cell function.'

Strecker maintains the origin of AIDS virus began with a hybrid of sheep visna virus and cattle leukemia virus that does affect T cell function and could only have been created under laboratory conditions. 'The request for the virus was made in 1972,' he said. 'Shortly afterward, AIDS appeared in Africa.'

The virus Dr. Strecker is alluding to is the bovine visna virus, the serum used in the WHO smallpox vaccine which he believes got its start by the genetic intermingling of the two animal viruses. He maintains the smallpox serum that was developed gives off the same influenza-like symptoms, ultimately developing into Kaposi's sarcoma, a purplish skin cancer, and pneumocystis carinii, a rare form of pneumonia. The physician researcher also believes there is strong possibility that the original AIDS virus was combined in the hepatitis B injections that were given in 1972 to homosexuals.

In 1986 Strecker sent a 40 page report of his findings to President Reagan and Vice-President George Bush, all the cabinet members, state governors, the CIA, and the FBI. There was little response by officialdom to his allegations. Dr. Strecker can be reached at 1216 Wiltshire Boulevard, Los Angeles, CA 90017.

Because of the long ordeal this book had to endure before finding the right publisher, this final chapter kept exponentially expanding, far beyond its originally intended limits. It began as a short appendix. Although the book is already bursting at the seams, more information of exceptional importance keeps coming in, such as these brilliantly astute observations in the January 1991 issue of *Acres, U.S.A.*, contributed by Richards Hoskins of Portfolios Investment Advisory:

> *The Wall Street Journal* of August 16, 1990, reminds us that the CIA in 1968 gave full backing to the Baath Party in Iraq and installed Saddam Hussein as the good dictator. The CIA also went to great expense to maintain the exiled Ayatollah Khomeini in Paris for years while the CIA-installed Shah ruled Iran.
>
> A U.S.-encouraged revolt in Iran against the CIA's own Shah forced him to flee to the U.S., where he died of cancer. The CIA then dispatched one of its own Air America planes to fly the Ayatollah from Paris to Iran to take power. Once installed, the Ayatollah dutifully attacked the U.S. and became the U.S. media's bad man.
>
> Iran's U.S.-installed Ayatollah then fought the U.S.-installed Hussein of Iraq for eight long bloody years with Iraq using Soviet equipment, and Iran using up the Shah's massive stockpile of American equipment, which was continuously maintained through the conflict with spare parts surreptitiously shipped by Reagan's administration to Iran via Israel while all parties concerned stoutly maintained that they hated each other.
>
> The president of the Philippines, the U.S.-backed Marcos, was persuaded to leave on a U.S. Air Force plane following a contested election in which the U.S. media supported his opponent, Mrs. Aquino. He was confined to Hawaii, U.S. territory, where he too died of cancer. His widow was hassled in court and then released with charges dropped and wealth intact. Collusion rumors abound.
>
> Think about it. Israel, who once launched a "preventive strike" against Iraq's nuclear reactor, has long been after the U.S. to fight their Arab enemies for them. Their amen-corner in the U.S. echoes this desire. To comply, the U.S.'s good guy Hussein, the man who can't breathe unless told to, becomes mad man Hussein (that's what the media actually calls him) because he invaded Kuwait. In righ-

teous indignation over this despicable act, good guy overnight becomes bad guy, and the U.S. sends a half-a-million man army to occupy oil-rich Saudi Arabia to confront the sworn enemy of the Israelis. All this without a single American soldier having been killed in battle. The stated reason? To "protect" the world's largest supply of oil from Mad Man Hussein.

All agree that the nation which controls the world's oil supply rules the world. What a coincidence it is that America, the nation which has aided in establishing every communist regime in the world, and has participated in installing in office almost every Arab leader, now surprisingly finds herself in control of the world's oil.

Viewing the situation, The Virginia Taxpayers Association commented, "Regarding the war with Iraq.... a House Banking Committee hearing on October 16 confirmed that 3 billion dollars of U.S. government money was laundered through the Italian Banca Nationale Del Lavoro in Atlanta in the 1980s, which actually paid for the Iraqi invasion of Kuwait." The fact that no federal or state bank regulators acted to stop these massive unauthorized loans to Iraq, at a time when these same regulators were zealous in curtailing legitimate loans to the U.S. corporations and real estate borrowers, has got to be suspicious.

On July 25, only a week before the invasion, U.S. Ambassador April Glaspie told Saddam Hussein that the U.S. took no official position on Iraq's border dispute with Kuwait. Two days before the invasion, Assistant Secretary of State John Kelly, in Congressional testimony confirmed the message to Saddam. When asked if the U.S. would come to Kuwait's defense if it were attacked, Kelly replied: "We have no defense treaty with any (Persian) Gulf country."

If one were a cynic and kept track of what is going on, the Mideast appears to be a staged soap opera.... All the while, the TV commentator stands on the edge of the stage just as the readers did in the old days to read the plot so the world audience will have some notion of what to make of it all.

Kuwait is playing now, but isn't the only show in town. It does, if properly managed, give promise of taking in one of the biggest gates since World War II. It may even end up like the profitable, drawn-out eight-year Iraq-Iran affair to add realism while at the same time helping the world's economies borrow money into existence to keep things going. Somebody's got to do it.... After all, according to Keynes, war borrowing is the best ingredient for business.

A little-known fact about the Gulf War is that one month before our Declaration of War, on December 15, 1990, Secretary of State James Baker signed the U.S. Army report from the 352nd Civil Affairs Command on the New Kuwait (unclassified, and therefore available to those interested). This report describes in detail how extensively Kuwait will be destroyed, how the oil wells will be set on fire, and then how it will all be rebuilt "better than before," with despotism, instead of democracy, even more strongly entrenched than it had been before. The report includes a list of the U.S. corporations who are to be assigned the profitable task of rebuilding Kuwait and extinguishing the oil well fires, as well as the Arab names they will be operating under.

Why have none of his political opponents thought of asking the obvious questions: How did George Bush's so-called "blind trust" make out during the time frame of the Gulf War? Why are the huge private business deals between Bush and Hussein still off-limits to the public's right to know?

In considering the method by which key characters like the Shah and Marcos and Jack Ruby are conveniently removed from center stage and inconspicuously disposed of, some comments made in "A Conversation Between Researchers" in the November 1989 issue of the *Nevada Aerial Research Group Newsletter*, P.O. Box 81407, Las Vegas NV 89180, appear to be relevant:

Q: Are they still going to keep killing people?

A: Yes, absolutely. Mae Brussell died of an advanced form of cancer that accelerated at a rate that the doctors couldn't believe. Someone should have checked her car or house with a Geiger counter for those radioactive needles. They are going to want to bump off everybody in the media who is interfacing with UFO stuff, that they cannot control. That means all of us 'loose ends.' That's why (deleted) is out there accelerating his hit team. They're not using guns but they are using radioactive isotopes.

Q: What exactly does that do?

A: Well, if he takes one of the radioactive needles that he and his team have been given out of its lead container and inserts it in the car seat.... the needle doesn't poke you, it's just inside the seat below you.... you're sitting on top of a highly radioactive area. You can get rectal cancer fairly quickly and you can die within six weeks. Remember, 20 people from the Kennedy assassination died within six weeks of cancer. Twenty witnesses died within six weeks. In the 1930s the Nazis were experimenting with the use of cancer as a technique of killing people clandestinely... Even after the person dies, anyone who sits in the vehicle is liable to get cancer ... one person after another.... until the car is junked. Nobody will go over the car with a Geiger counter. It could be in a couch or chair. Anyone that is healthy that dies within two months, suddenly.... you'll know (deleted) and his team got them. He's bragging about it to some of the other operatives. They're using (deleted) just like they used him in the Kennedy thing. He's a very dangerous man.... Kennedy found out about part of the alien thing and that the CIA was being used since 1949 to sell heroin and cocaine to the American public in order to eliminate weaker elements of the society and to acquire enormous funds for alien-related projects, which are phenomenally expensive. They're still doing it right now under the noses of the American public. They tried doing seventh-level mind control on some people and had them shooting up school yards in order to try get the American public to declare anti-gun legislation, so they'll give up without a fight when the balloon goes up. Some of the other things that they are doing is that they have some 10 concentration camps that are built to hold millions of people. They are converting old military bases and encouraging the development of corporate detention centers. It's just beginning.... At Columbia University, 10 days before his death, President John F. Kennedy said: "The high office of President has been used to foment a plot against the American people. Before I leave office, I must inform the citizen of his plight."

During the summer of 1989, Jean-Francois Gille, Ph.D., who contributed the tenth chapter of this book, sent me a long letter, that I shall now briefly summarize:

In the vast literature developed by private investigators on the assassination of John Kennedy, Gordon Novel appears as a minor, but by no means negligible, character. Picking up a book almost at random on the shelf dedicated to the assassination, you have a good chance of finding him listed in the index.... Recently, Novel popped up in the community to which I belong — the UFO research community. I found that so upsetting that I took the possibly presumptuous step of writing this Open Letter to Gordon Novel:

Mr. Novel, I don't know you, but several colleagues of mine independently informed me that you have been around lately, sometimes posing as a French scientist, telling us ufologists that we don't know what we are talking about....I won't elaborate on that here. As it seems you have been telling us what we ought to do, I'm going to tell you what you ought to do.... If I understand correctly, you are very blunt and upfront about what you think is true. So am I.

I have been presented with evidence which compels me to believe that on that fateful day in Dallas when your President was murdered, you were not in another city, and in Dallas you were not an innocent bystander, not at all. I believe you are the one the assassination specialists call 'The Umbrella Man,' and that not only were you there, a few yards from the limousine at the fatal moment, but that you, along with two or three other gunmen, killed John Kennedy.

I was a student in France at the time. The death of President Kennedy was felt as a personal loss, and almost like a personal aggression, by myself and most of my friends.

Quite a few researchers think that the reason why Bush suddenly decided the invasion of Kuwait was so reprehensible, though his own representatives had actually encouraged it only a few days before, was because the incident had the potential for being worked up to the point where he could with credibility and the necessary degree of popular support declare a State of Emergency, which automatically replaces civil law based on the Constitution with martial law. Once that is done, the next step would be to activate Rex 84, the Executive Order that Reagan signed about rounding up political dissidents and confining them in concentration camps. Very near the top of the list of "political dissidents" would be the UFO researchers who refuse to toe the Establishment's party line and persist in trying to get the truth out to the public. So many people have now become aware of the alien presence and its implications, as the number of people who find the debunkers still credible dramatically diminishes, that the government can no longer maintain the cover-up, except under the conditions of total censorship imposed by martial law. Proclamation of a State of Emergency would, among other things, have given Bush the power to confiscate private property on an unlimited scale. The private property of the "dissidents" rounded up and confined in the concentration camps, built during the Johnson administration and expanded on an enormous scale under Bush and Reagan, would then be confiscated. The only difference between Rex 84 and the Nazi scenario is that instead of being on a racial basis, it is on a basis of social conformity, imprisoning non-conformist UFO researchers, contactees and abductees; conspiracy researchers; environmental activists; anyone using or suspected of using or in favor of legalizing drugs; victims of AIDS, Epstein-Barr virus syndrome and other newly produced infectious diseases; the myriad multitudes of the homeless created by the policies of Ronald Reagan; non-conformists of all varieties; and anyone involved in political activism of any kind.

Another disturbing development is the ambiguity concerning the purpose of the GWEN (Ground-Wave Emergency Network) system, which was presented to Congress and the public as necessary protection for our nuclear weapons launching systems from the EMP (Electromagnetic Pulse) phenomenon which would otherwise paralyze them, in the event of a Soviet nuclear first strike. At enormous expense to the taxpayers, a network of GWEN transmitting stations was built that has a transmitting range of between 250 and 300 miles, and they are spaced about 200 miles apart.

Dr. Robert Becker made some very interesting remarks about the GWEN system in his excellent book *Cross Currents* (Tarcher, Los Angeles, 1990):

> The GWEN hardware is transistor based; even if placed in 'hardened' bunkers, it would still be vulnerable to an EMP. In addition, the EMP would produce major ground currents in the path of the GWEN signals that could decrease their transmission capabilities. Finally, the locations of all GWEN stations are known to the Soviets and thus are vulnerable to attack.... This is not the place for a full argument concerning the values and options of nuclear war, but in my opinion the reason for the existence of GWEN is specious.... I am concerned... because of the potential for behavioral and cognitive alterations that have been discussed in this book. GWEN is a superb system, in combination with cyclotron resonance, for producing behavioral alterations in the civilian population. The average strength of the steady geomagnetic field varies from place to place across the United States. Therefore, if one wished to resonate a specific ion in living things in a specific locality, one would require a specific frequency for that location. The spacing of GWEN transmitters 200 miles apart across the United States would allow such specific frequencies to be 'tailored' to the geomagnetic field strength in each GWEN area.

Dr. Becker goes on to say that he doubts whether this potential use ever occurred to the planners of the GWEN network, or that such action could be deliberately taken by any portion of the federal government. I venture to disagree with the good doctor on this point. In my opinion, he has hit upon the real reason for the construction of the network, and the publicly presented reason was specious camouflage. The GWEN system can be used not only to orchestrate mass outbreaks of hyperexcitability and violence in this or that area of the nation, but also to generate the opposite: zones of lethargy and torpor. Words or phrases can be broadcast, which most people would mistake for their own thoughts. The possibility of applying this technology to our free elections is quite obvious. When the GWEN system becomes operational in 1993 the entire population, every single citizen of the United States, could be bombarded with imperceptible subliminal signals designed to influence them in whatever way desired by those in command of the military/industrial complex.

Although the war with Iraq ended in a clear-cut victory with amazingly few American casualties, and the United States has emerged from the conflict as beyond any shadow of a doubt the most powerful military nation on the planet, the danger to the traditional liberties we are guaranteed by the Constitution is now greater than ever. The big question is: are we going to use our long-lost new-found strength as undisputed world heavyweight champion, the one and only super-power, to protect freedom and democracy, or to further extend the predatory tentacles of multinational corporate fascism disguised as democracy?

While the news media was keeping public attention focused exclusively on the Persian Gulf and yellow ribbons, an event of extreme importance occurred on the home front that received next to no media coverage, and of which the public consequently remains ignorant.

Between 3 and 4 in the morning on Aug. 4, 1990, Sam Nunn (Democrat) and ten other Senators met clandestinely with the opposition absent and illegally passed S.B. (should be S.O.B.) 2834, the Senate Intelligence Authorization Act. This treacherous legislation transforms our democracy into a dictatorship by totally destroying the system of checks and balances set up by the Constitution, giving the President unlimited powers that place him above the law.

S.B. 2834 not only gives the President the power to openly declare war without consulting Congress, it also gives him the power to start secret undeclared wars. It prevents Congress from stopping or interfering with any covert activities approved by the President. It redefines "covert action" so vaguely that it makes the term applicable to almost anything. In direct violation of international law, it claims for the U.S. the right to secretly interfere in the internal political, economic and military affairs of other nations. The President is allowed to fund covert activities by taking funds from any governmental agency, even if these funds were appropriated by Congress for a specific purpose. If this legislation had been on the books during the Reagan administration, Reagan could have bankrupted Social Security, Medicare and all welfare programs with impunity in order to buy exotic weaponry for his beloved Contras. National Security directives can be used to make any kind of Congressional oversight impossible.

Since Aug. 4, 1990, we are no longer the citizens of a democracy. We are the subjects of a dictatorship, potentially even more despotic than the autocratic monarchy we declared our independence from in 1776, though the politicians responsible for this atrocity have not yet dared reveal the facts to the public. Yet not a single member of Congress or the Supreme Court has had the courage to stand up and publicly challenge this act of treason.

There is one thing that Reagan and Bush certainly did accomplish: they wiped out the middle class, transforming the United States into a Third World debtor nation, a banana republic ruled with an iron hand by a military junta, where the population consists of a few super-rich and teeming masses of desperate paupers. When 2% of the population controls 90% of the wealth (as in El Salvador, where we put our clout squarely behind that 2% and pretended to be protecting democracy), permanent guerrilla warfare becomes inevitable. That is the real reason for the unprecedented levels of violence in own inner cities: the flagrant inequality of opportunity in what is supposed to be the Land of the Free. Drug abuse is a symptom of this massive disillusionment with the American Dream, not the root cause, as it is fallaciously presented to be by media representatives who know damn well that they are lying. Once the President has declared the State of Emergency, this nation will never again have free elections. Our economy is being deliberately collapsed in order to bring our society to its knees, leaving us with no choice but to accept the Trilateral New World Order, the cashless slave society in which you can't buy or sell without a plastic credit card: government of the people, by the international bankers, for the international bankers and their Gray masters.

What other options do we have?

One possibility, which contrasts with the toxic smog being generated from Washington like fresh spring water with rancid urine, is outlined in a sparklingly iridescent letter from a lady named Lia, which she sent to Riley Crabb, who was so kind as to share it with me. Here are some excerpts from it:

> I spent the weekend with a recent Edwards Air Force Base workman and his wife — recent because they are both repeat contactees and have become 'unmanageable' as AFB management puts it. He was fired for blasting a Spybee with spray paint — which I find as funny and classic as the graffiti on New York subway cars.
>
> "You did it on purpose," they told him. And they knew of

course, because Spybees are telepathic as well as camera-equipped. They also carry microphones. We were all laughing as he told us how the little spray-painted gold orb, blinded, went bouncing off walls and posts and was quickly withdrawn from its spy mission. He said Spybees are about the size of a baseball. They fly by anti-gravity all over any 'above top secret' installation. They dart sound-lessly everywhere and hover between workers, sometime pro-grammed to harass the guys for fun, like bumping them in the ass.

No person he and his friends knew about there was allowed to say one word to another while on the job. They would test by trying to write to each other in the floor dust. Within two or three strokes a Spybee would whiz around a corner, lock on to and stop above the writing. My friend's last comment was to write and draw a great big 'screw you.'

His painting work was part of an ongoing excavation beneath Edwards AFB on the high desert in California. He and his crew were always blindfolded and strip-searched before, so not even watches. But by taking turns counting in the elevator going to and from the work site, they estimated it must be some 9,000 feet down, at least two miles, and the trip took about 15 minutes.

Management accused my friend of "doing it on purpose" and they knew, and told him. "No, no. The Spybee kept bumpin' the back of my neck while I was sprayin.' After one real hard I whirled around with the spray gun still goin'!"

A prominent ufologist with us that Saturday evening suggested, after careful questioning of my friend, that the elevator itself was anti-gravitic, as there were no cables; so the estimated distance un-derground was at best a minimum. All present confirmed the government's possession of Plasmole tunnelling machines which melt a 50-foot hole through solid rock, at the rate of about five feet an hour.

For part of one night we went 'Foo Chasing,' their term for sightseeking UFOs. In this case the location was a Z-Clearance test site above Tehachapi where H. Hughes and Northrop Corporations and the USAF have just imported Delta Forces and fleets of black helicopters, deployed by the government for tip-top security events coverage. There is no doubt something major is going on up there, even that night.

The ufologist and his team were hoping to see the 30-foot ver-sion of the Spybee, as there are growing numbers of reports on these. They are designed to fly over your house carrying surveillance beams for thought/emotion control and behavior modification.

My personal decision is to opt out of the third dimension altogether. None of this interests me any more, and I'm ready for total consciousness at any cost! Meanwhile, back at the Physical. There are at least two 'sleepers' the participants in earth's present skew have not seen. One is that this whole plane is merely the image-game of a mass Mind greater than their own. Second is that a great Wave even beyond their control is currently working up the stunted majority at a rate that both sides would find frightening. With just a few more clues and nudges, they could end up making Trogtec look like greasy kid stuff.

I often see Terra now as in near-final throes of exactly the H.G. Wells scenario where an unwitting and witless 90% of mankind inhabits a play-fantasy world on earth's surface, while the split-off race of highly technical degenerates, the Trogs, prey on them from underground.

When mankind really awakens by 1992 they will directly, through no more than focused self-recognition, create all the positive phenomena the power elite can only try with wires and pulleys — and strip mining and economic slavery.

A most thorough and enjoyable way to round out your background picture of true human history involves the fact that this race was originally seeded here by ETs who were already at war with each other in other parts of the Galaxy, as described in Robert Temple's *The Sirius Mystery* and Zecharia Sitchin's breathtaking paperback trilogy: *The Twelfth Planet, Stairway to Heaven,* and *Wars of Gods and Men* of which ironically, the humans are the relative victors. 'The meek shall inherit the battleground.'

It is fascinating to learn who the fallen angels really were, and what third densities are capable of doing to each other. Individual contactees and research groups appear to be generalizing too sweepingly about where 'they' are from, what 'their' plan is, etc. There is a huge spectrum of plans and purposes and presences now with us.

Both Sitchin and Temple seem that superb type of scholar-academician who remains totally naive about extra-terrestrials, the spiritual revelation and 1990, but this lends credence to their discovering the same thing written backwards, that is, into our past....

A final supersleeper is that a race going to total consciousness may suddenly etherialize itself altogether, with or without its previous ambiance. Here goes nothing, for I have been contacted and shown where to go for continuance. I'm on my way there now. If I fumble, I'm stranded in the mountains without food or funds. If I make it,

INTRASTELLAR FLIGHT!

— EAT LIGHT —

At the 1992 apex comes also the full world acknowledgement of massive E.T. presence on Earth. The governments' universal cover-up of this until now will be seen, but seem of minor importance compared to what's happening — enough to dis-addict the last couch potato in history!

Advising you only to keep knowing how many different E.T.s and origins are now active among Earthlings, I am

Yours with love,

Lia.

What follows arrived in the mail from the Dolphin Tribe, 1425 West 221st. St., Torrance CA 90501:

The Dolphin Tribe

A Spiritual Path more Ancient than Humanity

Beliefs

The dolphins and whales have had large brains for over 30 million years. We believe they have evolved to Godlike levels. To us they are keepers of eternal knowledge and wings of freedom. We believe they will guide Humanity through the treacherous reefs of evolution to become God-lings of awareness and love. We believe that the Dolphin Group Mind is reaching out to humanity to rescue us from atomic suicide and lead us to the stars. We believe that the dolphins and whales are members of a Stellar Community of Advanced Civilizations and have transcendental science and technology. We believe that human children who are adopted by dolphins will become members of the Stellar Community of Advanced Civilizations and will help lead humanity to membership, peace, Godhood, and transcen-dental technology. Our beliefs are based on our communications with dol-phins, the history of Cetacean/human relations and on the evidence for their extra-terrestrial origins. We believe that integration with dolphin soci-ety will end warfare and the destruction of the ecosystem.

Goals

Our goals are to grow thousands of dolphin, whale, elephant, ape, E.T., human communities for interspecies communication and integration. Centers for the application of the spiritual power of the dolphin and whale spiritual liberators and the transcendental technology of the Stellar Community of Advanced Civilizations to the return of Earth to nature and humanity to Godhood. To rejoin the Stellar Community of Advanced Civilizations by birthing our children into water and raising them in the transcendental love field of dolphin/human families. To build paradisiacal artificial planets in Solar orbit so that the non-indigenous humans and industrial civilization will move off planet. To build interspecies villages in extra-dimensional space so that the Earth's ecosystem will survive the next gravitational collapse and Big Bang. To increase intelligence by shape-shifting to Dolphin and advanced humanoid forms. To achieve physical immortality by shifting to youthful forms and by using E.T. technologies. To deepen the Merfolk arts of shapeshifting, teleportation, inter-dimensional travel, levitation and spiritual liberation by forming interspecies shamanic circles.

Interspecies Villages

The purpose of the interspecies villages is to integrate the needs and dreams of the villagers with the sacred purpose of the dolphin and whale spiritual liberators. Practical solutions to the problems encountered in the evolution of the villages will come from the Dolphin and Whale Gods and from the Merfolk. The culture of the villages will be adapted from dolphin cultures. Communication with the dolphin and whale spiritual liberators will be through out-of-body travelling, trance channelling, computer translators, music, art, play and the transcendental technology of the Stellar Community of Advanced Civilizations.

Shapeshifting between Dolphin and Human Form

Of the infinite paths to Oneness there are few that are as much fun as the Merfolk migration. The Merfolk are those dolphins and people who have reclaimed their magical heritage. One of the powers gained during enlightenment is the ability to physically shift between dolphin and human form. About 0.004% of the people in the world at any time are actually dolphins and whales who have temporarily shifted to human form. Most of these mermen, mermaids and merchildren have come to help raise human consciousness and to point out the critical evolutionary steps leading to the eternal age of love.

To meet a merperson one must come as close to dolphin consciousness as possible. This will tend to tune one in to a merperson telepathically and lead to a physical meeting. Dolphin Consciousness can be characterized as happy, free of ego, compassionate, totally loving, focused on the here and now, with continuous input from the infinite self and a high respect for the physical body. The body is regarded as an aspect of the spirit, perfection of the spirit involves perfection of the body. If the body is damaged through accident or age, dolphins usually trade it for a new one through reincarnation, rematerialization, or the life synthesizers in the medical room of a dolphin star ship.

After one has tuned in to dolphin consciousness, a time will come when a mating with a merman or mermaid will lead you to the sea. They will help you to change to dolphin or whale form, take you on a tour of the sea and a visit with their families, they will take you to the star gate at galaxy center and teach you to teleport to other galaxies in this cluster. Returning to Earth, to the land, they will leave you the task of returning to dolphin form without assistance. When you have done this, you will be a Merperson and able to join in the migration.

Several times every year many dolphins and whales teleport to other systems and dimensions to visit relatives and take part in celebrations of unity with the Group Mind of the Multiverse. Ecstasy will take on ever higher meanings for the new migrant as unity with the Group Mind of the Metaverse (Gaia) launches one on an ever-accelerating upward spiral of spiritual evolution.

There are several activities that can help one tune in to Dolphin Consciousness. Swimming with free dolphins in the sea, especially a large tribe, shifts consciousness through interpenetration with their powerful auras. To save dolphins or whales from fishing net entanglement, stranding hunters etc., or to stop ocean pollution brings nearer the Day of Knowledge. The Day of Knowledge is the time when a contagious telepathic state will unite humanity with the Group Mind of the Metaverse.

John G. Neihardt appears to have clairvoyantly glimpsed an event similar in nature to what the Dolphin Tribe describes as the Day of Knowledge in his "The Song of the Messiah," which was published in *A Cycle of the West* by Macmillan in 1961:

.... eyes have never seen
the green with which that breathing land was green,

the day that made the sunlight of our days
like moonlight when the bitter moon delays
and shadows are afraid. It did not fall
from heaven, blinding; but it glowed from all
the living things together. Every blade
of grass was holy with the light it made,
and trees breathed day and blooms were little suns.
And through that land the Ever-Living Ones
were marching now, a host of many hosts,
so brightly living, we it is who are ghosts
who haunt these shadows feeding on tomorrows!
Like robes of starlight, their forgotten sorrows
clung beautiful about the newly dead;
and eyes, late darkened with the tears they shed,
were wide with sudden morning. It was spring
forever, and all birds began to sing
above them, marching in a cloud that glowed
with every color. All the bison lowed
along the holy pastures, unafraid;
and horses, never to be numbered, neighed
like thunders laughing. Down the blooming plains,
a river-thaw of tossing tails and manes,
they pranced and reared rejoicing in their might
and swiftness. In the streams of living light
the fishes leaped and glittered, marching too!
For everything that lived looked up and knew....
...all the livings things
with roots and leaves, with fins or legs or wings,
were bowed, beholding; and a sudden change
came over them, for all that had been strange
between them vanished. Nothing was alone,
but each knew the other and was known,
and saw the same; for it had come to pass
the wolf and deer, the bison and the grass,
the birds and trees, the fishes in the streams,
and horse and man had lost their little dreams
and wakened all together.

Something else turned up in the mail, from a correspondent who wishes
to remain anonymous, concerning reptilian humanoids (Reptoids):

They try to hide and avoid contact. They are soldiers, doing a job that has to be done, two or three of them at each post site. They are manning remote posts. They are not to bother humans, unless endangering the post. Most of them are not hostile and won't kidnap you. They may blast you with a flash gun that may paralyze you (you won't remember the flash of light) for an hour or two, causing confusion and mild fear. It could cause you to black out, pass out for a while. It is their way to escape and buy time to hide any visible equipment. They are fearsome to meet face-to-face, and their voices are harsh and whispery with heavy SS's. Most of them understand English and several other languages. If you know any areas with repeated reptilian sightings, then that is the place to look. Wear something with a reptile (not something violent, like St. George killing the Dragon!) in sight. If you see one, keep your hands *open*, palms forward, arms *down*. That is the non-aggression approach. *don't* raise your arms unless told to. Don't carry anything in your hands or arms. If he doesn't run, walk *slowly* towards him. Let him speak first. They consider humans repulsive and hostile and threatening. Don't try to offer him anything. Don't try to touch him, or any thing of his. If he hisses at you, back off a few feet, but don't look away. It simply means he finds your odor repugnant. *Don't* try to overpower him. He is stronger than ten or twelve men. Usually if he hasn't run so far, he wants to talk to you. Fight your fear and thoughts of panic.

Let us now turn to a "Conversations Between Researchers," in the *Nevada Aerial Research Group Newsletter*. The conversation begins with a discussion of the Voronezh landing announcement:

A: There wasn't just one landing. There was a multiple landing. This other man called in and said that he heard it on the BBC... that the BBC was reporting three landings. One of them took place at the 70th parallel on the Arctic Circle. The others took place north of Moscow, and the one that had the most publicity was the one that took place 300 miles south of Moscow. In one of the reports, it was indicated that they could not tell if the robot was giving instructions to the aliens or the other way around. They couldn't tell who was in control. "Yellow Fruit" said that the robot is a medic, that it's a computer, and that it also functions as a protective device for the aliens while they are out of the craft. The robot would have responded if anyone had tried to harm the aliens. It kind of reminds you of the movie *The Day the Earth Stood Still,*

Q: Who exactly are these tall blonds?

looked like tall handsome human.

Appeared either naturally or artificially to have black around eyes Almost like kohl

Masculine yet ethereal

Cobalt piercing blue eye

Blonde fine hair

High cheekbones

gaunt face

Flesh colored pale face - whitish undertone

over 6'

Hard to gauge exact height.

Close to exquisite face but still more masculine than my sketch.

Could be as tall 6'5" or 7'   muscular neck

Slender but muscular

Khyla of Procyon transmitted the information contained in Chapter 7. The woman who made contact with Khyla described him as follows: "Khyla looked like a tall handsome human, slender but muscular, masculine yet ethereal. He appeared either naturally or artifically to have black around his eyes, almost like kohl. His face was close to exquisite, but definitely masculine. He had a gaunt face with high cheekbones and piercing cobalt-blue eyes. He had fine blond hair that was almost shoulder-length. He had a muscular neck. His skin was pale flesh color, with a whitish overtone."

Nicknamed the "Swedes" or "Blonds," these humanoids average between six and seven feet tall. They originate from a solar system that revolves around Procyon, a binary star system that rises before Sirius in Canis Minoris (in the body of the Lesser Dog), about 11.4 light years from Earth.

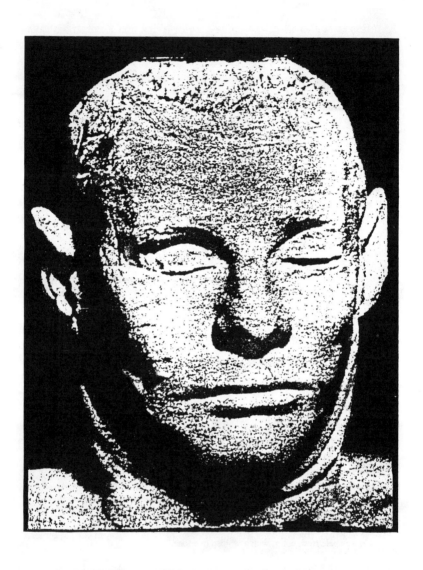

A picture of an alleged alien from Tau Ceti. Known as the "Browns," this species is considered to be benign.

A: This is one of the four primary civilizations that Lear talked about. They have an installation on Mars and they are taller than the Nordics. They originally came from the Orion system, like some of the other groups. There are also blonds that are under Gray control and blonds that work with and for NASA.

Q: What are they here for and what are they doing now?

A: Remember that the Grays are the representatives of the Serpent Race, a faction of the reptilian humanoid species. These (tall blonds) are the angels. When these guys start landing, you'll hear more and more about the tall guys, not the short Grays you are hearing about a lot. These are the opposite force, the Titans, the 'angels' out of the Christian Bible. They're a lot taller than we are. Here comes the conflict out of Revelations 12:7, the conflict between Michael and his angels, and the Dragon race and their angels. The open conflict for the Earth. One day you have the reptilian humanoids and the Grays exiting craft, and then you have these very tall Titans. You have both factions moving around....They left behind a physical substance, that's one of the mind-blowers. It could be a residue, waste...their excrement that was automatically ejected by the mechanisms on board the ship that process it....

Q: Well, the Soviets could never have released this information without the NSA and the United States knowing about it in advance. It had to be a simultaneous thing. It's almost an MJ-12 tactic using the Russians, because if they turn around and debunk this, then they were able to scare everybody. They'll take a look at the reaction. All day yesterday they were monitoring the radio stations and the reactions on call-in shows. They are noting the fear level in people in different places. They are conditioning people. This is the first major world-wide conditioning. They make the announcement using Russia instead of the United States....

A: Well, there will be more landings, and it will come out that the aliens are really here, because the aliens are going to show up in force. We've got to condition people fast. Who's going to show up? The Grays, the Blonds, the Reptilians, everybody's going to be fighting for the planet. The short Blonds, the Sirians, already claim this planet as under their jurisdiction. This is all prior to 1993.

Q: What happens in 1993?

A: Well, it would all have happened in the open. All the ships would be around the Earth and no one could deny it. Remember that Lear said that most abductees felt that something was imminent and that it would occur in two to four years? It would all occur. The implants would be activated, and people would start to disappear that had the implants. The Christians would call it the Rapture.

Q: Where would they go?

A: Well, they would go to the underground bases to act as an interface on alien equipment, which they have been trained on but have had the memory of the training blocked from their conscious awareness. We would then begin flying the disks that we have manufactured. These are the ones like the one that was at Norton AFB on display that Senator Alan Cranston and others were shown. Those disks are called ARVs, or Alien Reproduction Vehicles.

Q: What exactly does that mean?

A: These are the disks that the United States made that were based on alien technology. General Electric and other aerospace companies have been working together to assemble these disks over the last ten years. Those are very similar in design to those that people are being abducted and trained on, because when we go to fight for the Reptilians and Grays, they are going to put human beings into the ships. They're going to use us to fight for them so that they don't die, we do. We're going to think it's all hot and great, and all the hundreds of military that have been trained to fly these disks are going to be given a disk, but they will be under the control of the aliens, who will allow the implanted humans to interface with them, as long as they're controlled. When the Reptilians show up in force to use Earth as a staging area in the conflict, all the people that are implanted will start to interface using the alien technology, language and equipment. They'll have us, the one in 10 that are implanted. The rest of the humans that they don't need, they'll kill, like with the AIDS virus. All those people in Africa are being killed off because they weren't going to be implanted to be used later to interface with alien equipment — they are useless feeders.

Q: What happens to the people who are not implanted?

A: They're expendable. A lot of implant information out of UCLA has been suppressed. We're trying to duplicate the implant technology as a technical extension to the mind control programs. It's another coverup, so anyone who gets information on implant technology or other alien technology is singled out and squelched so that the information won't reach the news media that implants have been found during autopsies. World-wide control of the media has kept it away from the attention of the public — it's just another thing that's occurring all the time, it's just covered up. The entire planet is on a lock-down. We don't notice it, even though we're in the middle of it. We're lied to. People do not believe that the government is lying....

Q: What do the Reptilians want?

A: They want Earth as a staging area. They're just returning. This is not the first time they have done this here. Thousands of years ago they used the Earth as a base. We were also used by the Blonds for mining. Humans are crossbreeds that are expendable to the Blonds as well. We're like trash to the Blonds. We were the miners. We're crossbreeds. Check it out. We have 90% of our cortex that we don't use. In nature, nothing develops that is not used before it is created, so that shows that we are crossbreeds that are non-functional. We are not aware of our genetic extension of what the mind can really do. We're the dumb ones. We have the facilities in our brains to dematerialize things, for example, but we can't, because we don't know how to do it....

Q: What's in it for the Grays?

A: To control us. This is the same technology that we were unable to attach a weapons system to because of the field that is produced by the craft. The majority of U.S. disks are totally useless, all you can currently do is fly around in them. The Grays didn't give us anything they couldn't defeat. The Grays are actually interfacing with us so we don't see what's behind the Grays.

Q: Such as the reptilian humanoids?

A: Exactly. The Grays are a bunch of slaves, in a way. They are being manipulated by the Reptilians, who are ultimately behind the U.S. getting disk technology....Although sometimes the projection isn't very clear due to lack of data, none of the projections look very good. All projections put the human beings in the category of being a prize, a diamond. There is something about human beings that neither species of alien has. Something is unique about the human being that is not shared by the Grays, the Reptilians, or the Nordic Blonds, and whatever that is, they would like to keep that knowledge from us. What happens when a human goes from using a fraction of his brain to using all of it, the part that we have been suckered into not using. We've been conned not to use it. Is a human being potentially more powerful psychically than a Gray? We think so, and it would explain some of the Gray reactions to human beings, and why they need to technologically control humans....what happens when the other 90% kicks in.

Q: Maybe we can induce the rest of it to kick in?

A: Absolutely. It can be done, and we have access to the technology....They have been using equipment to limit the awareness of human beings, just like they put substances in our food to change the DNA resonance and tuning. A lot of substances that are encouraged in our civilization — tobacco and caffeine are two examples — are encouraged because they make the system alkaline. Everything in the human environment induces a lot of Beta rate in the brain, which limits the potential awareness level. I believe that we don't really need weapons when we are at full potential. We can do what the other species can do, without their hardware. This is one of the reasons human beings are kept in check. The Reptilians have gone as far as they could go, and they wanted a culture that they could manipulate. They found us. We are the abandoned ones. They are trying to pump it out of us, but we have to remember it first, before they can get it out of us. Remember, they are high tech and they don't have the intuitive process. They have to see it first before they can analyze it. We can experience it first on an intuitive level, before we show it. We have the edge, in microseconds, but we have to be very aware. There is more to all this than just building a disk and having it at Area 51....Based on intelligence reports, the Grays appear to be mercenary in nature. They will work for anyone. In other words, if the Blond Nordics grab them, they'll work for them. If you were to grab one, he'd work for you.

Q: How do you do that?

A: All you have to do is threaten them. They are very paranoid. They have never had the benefit of parental bonding. They are isolated in a hive command structure. It is the way they are raised....The cell structure of the Grays is not that of a real species type — it is a cross-bred genetic structure that has been cloned so many times that there is replicative failure. Genetic information begins to be lost in the replication process. It puts them on the down side of an evolutionary spiral, creating all kinds of genetic birth defects — mind defects as well as body defects.

Q: What is the reptilian agenda?

A: When the Draco come back to areas like in South America, such as Tiahuanaco, that they left about 6,000 years ago, we'll be seeing craft all the time everywhere. The Grays, meanwhile, will be put back in subjugation as a slave race to do manual labor and exercise their training in biogenetics.

Q: What do the Reptilians want with humans?

A: They are coming back to use Earth as a staging area in their war against the ELs (Michael, Gabriel, Raphael, Uriel and their cohorts), who are Nordic in appearance.

Q: Are they the good guys?

A: Both of these groups are totalitarian dictatorships, and have military-political command structures. What is happening in human society all over the planet is happening inside the Draco and Serpent Race societies: everyone who has been caught in this thing wants to get their personal power back. Humans, the crossbreed hybrids that we are, command more power than any of these species, but the human awareness is deliberately suppressed on this planet. We, the people of Earth, can take control of this planet, because we don't need the technology — it can be done through the use of our minds. You can construct, using your mind. If both teams fight, neither will win. Only unification will carry us into another cycle without everything shutting down.

Q: How are people going to do this, when they can't even resist abduction?

A: People can resist abduction. When the Grays come in, they repeat things over and over to you, and then after a while, you go with it. They cannot force you to do anything. They have to have you do it. You fall for it. When you don't fall for it, and you have the command of your will power, shields of energy can be projected. We have a higher potential than they do.

There has been a major new development, which takes the form of a case in Missouri, investigated by Forest Crawford and reported in the Jan./Feb. 1991 issue of *Enigma* (UFO Study Group of Greater St. Louis, Box 31544, St. Louis MO 63131). The case involves a type of alien heretofore unknown to me, of particular importance because of its determination to free this planet from the Grays. They are friendly to humans but not to our government, as one of their number was subjected to vivisection without anaesthesia and slowly murdered on the operating table by government scientists interested only in exploratory surgery. The scientist in command of the team, who was responsible for the procedures perpetrated, was alleged to have been Dr. Frank Drake of the OZMA project.

The physical appearance of this type of alien is so similar to humans that they would not be noticed in a crowd, except for somewhat pointed ears. Skin color is bronze, a tan such as is common around the Mediterranean and in South America. Eyes are brown. Hair is also brown, and is worn in a crew cut, but lies flat instead of standing up. Nose is broad and flat, but close enough to human norms not to attract attention. Mouth and lips are like ours. Height varies from 5'6" to 5'9", and weight from 180 to 200 pounds, but they are muscular rather than fat. Their home stars are Tau Ceti and Epsilon Eridani.

The Tau Cetians also have had major problems with the Grays, and are working in collaboration with other alien groups who have been similarly afflicted. The Grays have been preying on other civilizations throughout the universe. Tau Cetians confirm that the Grays are using human vital fluids for food, and are kidnapping our children. They also confirm that Khyla's people were driven from their home star by the Grays. The only difference to surface so far between the Tau Cetian information and the information already given in this book is that the Tau Cetians say not all

Gray groups are cosmic criminals like the parasitic predatory Grays who have infiltrated our governments through the intelligence agencies.

The Dallas Morning News of April 5, 1991, carried an article about a teletype message on the previous night to local police departments from the North American Aerospace Defense Command about fiery objects falling from the sky. Three minutes after reception of the teletype, at 1:47 A.M., the civil defense sirens for the city of Dallas sounded on their own, resulting in the emergency switchboard being flooded with calls from residents asking the nature of the emergency. The article goes on to state:

> Computer tapes did not show that anyone had triggered the sirens — or even that they were sounding, said Bobby J. Martinez, assistant director of Dallas Office of Emergency Preparedness.... Mr. Martinez said the city's 94 sirens can be turned on only by the watch commander at the police communications center or the Office of Emergency Preparedness. 'Dallas police do not indicate that they sounded the sirens, and we weren't even in the office at that time,' he said. There is no way for a teletype to trigger the 127 decibel sirens automatically, Mr. Martinez said. Police and emergency preparedness officials tried to turn the sirens off, but with limited success. The sirens went back on as many as three times before Mr. Martinez's office disabled the city's entire system at 3 A.M.... A fisherman at Lake Whitney, 35 miles north of Waco, called the National Weather Service in Forth Worth to report that the whole lake lit up and debris fell everywhere, said a weather service spokesman.

Was what that fisherman saw really falling debris, or was it something else, not so easily defined? If it was falling everywhere, how come none of it was found on the shores of the lake after sunrise, though a careful and extensive search was made? Did what made the lake light up also retrieve the "debris," which might perhaps be more accurately described as "supplies and/or reinforcements?" It is probably true that the Dallas civil defense sirens could not be triggered by a teletype message to local police, but the North American Aerospace Defense Command undoubtedly has other methods at its disposal to activate local emergency alert systems directly from its headquarters, in ways designed to over-ride any local attempts to interfere with such activation. Did NORAD spot the objects as they were coming in, realize that their trajectory targeted the general Dallas area, without realizing that the precise target was the alien base concealed under nearby Lake Whitney, and therefore activate the Dallas sirens directly from its headquarters?

In the *Northwest Arkansas Times*, Fayetteville AR, April 8, 1991, Kay Hall wrote:

> I was surprised by a big lovable man at the UFO Conference in Eureka Springs this weekend. While Sergei Bulantsev, a correspondent of the Tass News Agency, didn't offer any new or concrete evidence of UFOs or things unknown, he made several Christian-like statements offered in friendship. His philosophy was "make peace, not pollution." .... He did say that aliens visiting Russia are quite different than the "Grays with large eyes" United States witnesses report. He said the "visitors" are taller, perhaps, but very human-looking and, if dressed as we were, would not be noticed in a crowd. He called them "tourists." Neither are there any abductions in the Soviet Union, not one, single documented case, he said. All the abductees were politely invited, he said, to accompany the aliens to the space ship. Strangely, he said, many describe entering a small spacecraft of 4 to 5 meters, and once inside it, describe huge rooms. He said he believes often spacecraft are doorways to another dimension. Nuclear tests in Russia and in the United States, he said, were a concern to all life, whether on this planet or on others.

If what Sergei Bulantsev says is correct, it should be verifiable from other sources also. Is this a propaganda ploy, or is Bulantsev's statement based on fact? If upon investigation it does turn out to be based on fact, the implications are tremendous. The key question of supreme importance: is the alien group dominant in the Russian "tourists," who are so human in appearance as to be able to pass unnoticed through a Russian crowd, the group I have been referring to as the Blonds, perhaps accompanied by or associated with the newly discovered Browns (Tau Cetians)? Is it only the countries that made secret treaties with Grays, which are at present infested with the Grays? If this is the case, the first and foremost thing to do would be for a majority of U.S. citizens to publicly repudiate the secret treaty with the Grays in no uncertain terms through the electoral process.

The May/June 1991 issue of the *Louisiana MUFON* Newsletter (752 Daventry Drive, Baron Rouge, LA 70808) carried some excellent descriptions of what the very interesting speakers at the 1991 Ozark UFO Conference had to say, which summarize recent developments in the field of UFO research. Several speakers at the Ozark UFO Conference were aware of a new phenomenon in Switzerland that seems to be trying to outdo the British crop circles. There have reportedly been six incidents where a smooth-sided, circular, flat-bottomed hole was found in the morning where none had been the night before. There are no tracks or evidence of digging or hauling, and no trace of the missing dirt. The first holes were only about five yards in diameter, but the most recent was 33 yards in diameter and at least that deep. An estimated 22 tons of dirt is missing without a trace.

In answer to a specific question about the bending of plant stems at right angles in the formation of crop circles, Ozark conference speaker George Wingfield confirmed that such bending does occur, but he said you could do the same thing by placing the plant in a microwave. He did not indicate whether such microwave treated plants could continue to grow as do bent plants in crop circles. In apparent contradiction, vegetation does not grow, sometimes for years, in some spots where UFOs allegedly landed. The apparent cause is extreme dehydration of the soil to an extended depth and microwave radiation is a suspected factor. In possibly the best documented landing trace case, French researchers studied for two years plants taken from the 1981 Trans-en-Provence UFO landing site.

Forest Crawford, MUFON Assistant Director for Illinois with a background in chemistry and physics, the last five years in research and development, spoke on "The Revealing Science of Ufology."

Crawford introduced his topic with a definition and discussion of science and the scientific method. He compared and contrasted the work of the UFO researcher with that of the archeologist, sociologist and futurist. He discussed the kinds of evidence and stated the researcher's greatest problem, especially the UFO researcher, was ignoring evidence. The UFO researcher generally must prove strangeness beyond human knowledge and comprehension — a tall order. He cannot ignore the smallest detail, no matter how simple, absurd or ludicrous.

Crawford illustrated his point by detailing two investigations which eventually supported each other. In the first, researchers trying to find a way to make sense out of the touchy "messages" phenomenon decided to try a "Ask the Aliens" approach. A short questionnaire about alien activities including questions in the technical, physiological, sociological and philosophical areas, with some questions deliberately beyond the ability of lay persons to answer, was prepared. Then a group of abductees who claimed continuing contact with their abductors were recommended by therapists and were asked to obtain answers if possible. These answers are being correlated as received and show some shocking results. One question, "What is Angel's Hair?" garnered several answers variously expressing the disposal of waste materials through the craft's energy system. The most outrageous answer detailed how insect-like creatures are created to do menial tasks and their disposal through the propulsion system where electromagnetic fields cause chemical reactions forming the angel hair. Meanwhile, in Iowa researchers rushed to a UFO sighting area where they succeeded in collecting numerous samples of angel hair, some collected while still drifting in the air, in baby food jars. These jars were immediately sealed and placed in a freezer which succeeded in stabilizing the samples. Laboratory analysis showed the samples to be an aminester, in the same family as spider webs, but definitely not spider webs or any another similar natural substance they could identify. Thus the outrageous answer fit the technical requirements for producing the substance. Other correlations are being found in the Messier number of the alien's home galaxy, the purpose of implants, how the aliens use light and another questions. This line of research continues and is being expanded.

To the question, "What can you tell me about the future?" one consensus was that by the end of 1992 there would be so many sightings, landings, abductions, contacts and/or publicity that the UFO question would be resolved in most people's minds.

Sergei Bulantsev, Russian national, senior correspondent for Tass news agency and a 20 year UFO researcher in the USSR, spoke on "UFOs in the USSR."

Bulantsev reviewed a number of UFO sightings, landings, and alien contacts he has investigated. Many parallel UFO sightings in the U.S., but in general appear to be similar to U.S. sightings reported 20 years ago. He suggested three hypotheses: space craft from other solar systems, parallel worlds, and the other supernatural, under which he mentioned the influence of the church. He suggested pure science and pure religion would meet in the UFO investigation.

Bulantsev suggested UFOs appear more aggressive in the U.S. than in Russia. He knows of no reports of the "Grays" in Russia, most aliens reported there are more like humans. Reports of alien contacts in Russia are increasing and many reportedly leave specific messages, but he can't understand what they are supposed to mean or their purpose. One recent message to President Bush and Hussein was, "There should not be war in the Gulf." Then a message to Bush, "Do not touch Hussein and his generals."

George Wingfield, British national and IBM executive, spoke on "Crop Circles and Pictograms: England, 1990."

Wingfield first quickly reviewed the history of British "corn" circles as they call them. The first circle in 1978 was an enigma because it obviously was precisely drawn with the structures and carefully bundled strands. By 1987 there were groups of circles in different patterns and the swirling went clockwise and counter clockwise. The first ringed circles appeared in 1987 and by 1989 circles and rings appeared in complex patterns. The final circle of 1989 was divided into 4 quadrants with the grain in opposite quadrants lying parallel in a East-West or North-South direction. This was the first circle in which the grain was not swirled and it was a harbinger of things to come.

The summer of 1991 was a quantum leap forward as patterns of rings and circles became true complex pictograms. Straight bars, or boxes, and arcs, both inside and outside of circles, were combined with circles and rings to form complex pictograms. Some pictograms combined more than 30 elements. Sometimes pictograms formed on one night were added to on a later night.

Researchers from around the world have succeeded in finding only a few witnesses who have seen the figures formed. They report the grain falls quickly, within seconds, in a wave as if a giant wand was passing over the field. Some report the sound of rushing winds, or trilling noises, but were standing in calm air when a circle formed near them. There are many reports of mysterious lights over fields where circles later formed, but no direct association can be made. The "beam" or "force field" that pushes the grain down in forming the elements apparently does not lift or turn off in moving from one element to the next, but instead focuses into a very narrow beam leaving a narrow trail, less than an inch wide. Some circles are definitely associated with ancient landmarks. The pictogram used to illustrate this had a "V" shaped base with each leg pointing to a gravesite of a medieval crusader and the central axis pointing to an ancient burial mound. The much publicized hoax circles last year, where researcher's instruments picked up movement only to later establish the circles were obviously manmade, were allegedly made by intelligence units from the British army for unknown reasons.

Science cannot identify what dowsers measure; however, dowsers have succeeded in predicting the formation of circles, and have even predicted the size and general dimensions of the future formation. Dowsers have been reporting since 1987 that ley (earth energy) lines across the British Isles have been "recharging." The circles tend to form where two recharging ley lines cross. Channelers report that earth energies will continue to increase and the size and complexity of the circles will increase. 1991 will be more exciting than 1990.

Wingfield believes that the circles are messages to humanity, but that there is not a literal translation. They act on the subconscious and are uniting us with other intelligent forces in the universe.

William Sherwood, professor and retired optical physicist for Eastman Kodak, spoke on "The Contactee in a Multi-Dimensional Universe."

Sherwood said anyone who had studied the UFO enigma for more than a few years has had a great deal of practice in learning to be open-minded without being gullible. To be open-minded is to be receptive to new ideas, and that is essential for acquiring new insights. He said truths lie in nature, not in science, and only a fraction of the truths of nature are contained in the science we know.

Sherwood discussed the meaning of "occult," from its Latin meaning of hidden from sight, to its medieval concept, including only that which might be revealed by experimentation, to today's prejudiced attitude. The occult practices of yesterday have evolved into the sciences of today, and today's occult practices of telepathy, dowsing and channelling will no doubt be among the accepted sciences of the future.

Sherwood gave a quick summary of cross-correlation of contactee information from 1986 to today about a multidimensional universe, and stated, "to an amazing degree, that is also the testimony of modern science." In support of that he cited and quoted from many scientific publications by more than a dozen theoretical scientists including Einstein. He concluded with passages about space, time and dimensions from Stephen Hawking's book, *A Brief History of Time.*

Sherwood discussed several scientific achievements where the scientist admittedly obtained his basic ideas from channelled information. Wilbert Smith's 1950 Top Secret memo resulted in the establishment of the Canadian UFO program within weeks. Based on information obtained as head of a scientific mission to the U.S., it stated, "UFOs exist" and "The UFO matter is the most highly classified subject in the United States government, rating even higher than the H-bomb." Subsequently, he published a highly technical treatise, "The New Science," which noted on the fly-leaf, "Assembled by W.B. Smith from data obtained from Beings more advanced than we are." Some projects mentioned in that and the UFO memo are still highly classified and hidden from the public.

These were some of the ideas expressed at the Ozark UFO Conference in the spring of 1991. Crop circle developments during the summer of 1991 were well described by Michael Chorost in the Oct. 1991 issue of the *MUFON UFO Journal*: "One of the most interesting formations was a representation of the Mandelbrot set, a two-dimensional graph made famous by chaos theory.... the last two seasons of crop circles have clustered densely in a tiny area containing Europe's most remarkable ancient constructions: Avebury, Silbury Hill, Windmill Hill, Barbury Castle, Adam's Grave, the White Horses, and the East and West Kennet Long Barrows.... I invite my readers to consider the fact that the mystery of the crop circles is very much like the mystery of the megaliths. Each consists of compelling geometric forms. No one knows why either were made, nor why they are where they are. Nor do we know how either were made. Perhaps the two mysteries are deeply intertwined. Not that either one 'caused' or 'inspired' the other, but that the two phenomena somehow 'talk' about the same thing, a thing still unknown to us, or 'do' a single thing, taken together as a total system. It could be that solving one mystery will automatically solve the other." Chorost goes on to describe the research results of Marshall Dudley, a systems engineer for Tennelec/Nucleus of Oak Ridge, Tennessee, as well as those of Michigan biophysicist Dr. W.C. Levengood. To summarize these results as concisely as possible, Dudley detected significant isotope changes in the soil samples from crop circles he had been provided with, and Levengood found that cell pits in plants cells in the affected formations have been subjected to rapid heating that has separated the cell pits. He found this to be true in samples from England, the United States and Canada.

Another major breakthrough was made by Gerald Hawkins, the author of *Stonehenge Decoded*, who discovered that in 18 photographs of crop circle formations, there is a repeated pattern of frequency ratios that are equivalent to the diatonic scale (the white keys on a piano). In addition to that finding, he has outlined four new theorems about relationships of triangles to circles to squares that he finds in the crop circle formations, and these theorems do not exist in any known academic text.

That is a very brief condensation of a large amount of highly complex technical research. There is strong and abundant evidence in support of these results publicly available. One would think that the news media would eagerly leap upon so thoroughly substantiated a sensational story, and proclaim it to the world in banner headlines and TV special features.

What actually happened?

The world news media instead leaped eagerly on a flimsy story full of holes: that two British senior citizens had "confessed" to hoaxing the circles with no equipment except some planks. This was triumphantly proclaimed to the world as the final and definitive solution to the mystery of the crop circles, in spite of the obvious fact that two men with planks cannot produce significant isotope changes in the soil, nor heating so rapid that it separates the cell pits without leaving burn marks on the outside of the plant. Other obvious impossibilities deliberately ignored were how these two senior citizens had managed to make so many hundreds of circles without having once been detected, or how they managed to make patterns of such precision and size and complexity with planks while working in the dark. All the factual evidence was deliberately ignored in order to convince the public that the mystery of the crop circles had now at last been definitely solved: Doug and Dave did it. The public was bombarded to saturation point with ten-second TV shots of Doug and Dave flattening some wheat with some planks, until finally the vast majority was conditioned into accepting this absurdity as the proven explanation. The minority of those who persisted in trying to point out the flaws in this explanation was then subjected to scathing ridicule and social ostracism.

There may be some relationship between the mathematical discoveries made by Gerald Hawkins upon studying crop circle formations and the mathematical discoveries made by Richard Hoagland upon studying the geometrical alignments of the cluster of ruins around the Face on Mars (see Chapter Three of *Extra-Terrestrials Among Us*). Since the appearance of my previous book, Hoagland's research has made dramatic progress. The mathematical code concealed within the geometrical alignments associated with the Face indicates how our normal three-dimensional space connects with the multiple dimensions of hyperspace, opening up the possibility of producing free energy without pollution — exactly what was offered to Eisenhower in 1954. However, as this would make fossil fuels obsolete, and it is the big oil companies that rule the roost in Washington, just as in Eisenhower's time the government is determined to block this development, using the prestige of NASA to ridicule Hoagland's research instead of examining the evidence.

As of May 15, 1992, the main event to take place so far this year has been the series of spectacular sightings of a very large triangular craft that makes no sound, exactly as has been described again and again over Belgium since 1989, over Vermont, New Hampshire, Pennsylvania, Arkansas and Missouri. During the same period of time as the sightings, there were 16 cattle mutilations reported in Oklahoma, one in Kansas, one in Arkansas, and several in Missouri.

This series of spectacular sightings in the United States resembles not only what has been happening persistently in Belgium since 1989, but also the well-documented incidents that occurred in France on the history-making night of Nov. 5, 1990.

The following was translated and summarized by George Andrews from the February 1991 issue of *OVNI-MAGAZINE*, published monthly by the Banque Internationale de Donnes Ufologiques, Boite Postale 10, 92323 Chatillon, France. The CNES (Centre National d'Etudes Spatiales) is the French equivalent of NASA.

Being in possession of the most complete documentation gathered by civilians in France concerning the events which occurred on Nov. 5, 1990, we have established the reality of an exceptional situation. Analysis of the 400 testimonies we have studied provides overwhelming evidence from which certainties emerge, which should be brought to the attention of the public of the whole world.

The CNES deliberately lied in order to manipulate international public opinion. On that date, over 70 UFOs were reported in the skies of France, black and of gigantic size. Their flight paths formed an organized pattern. These facts cause us to consider the events of that night a prelude to overt contact.

It is appropriate to inform the elected officials and the media representatives of this nation that they were lied to by the CNES, which bears full responsibility for this incredible deception. We have therefore sent a summary of our documentation to the French government, to all political parties, and to the Secretary General of the United Nations. In so doing, we followed the procedure outlined by the International Symposium of Bioastronomy at Val-Cenis in June 1990, to be implemented in such a case.

Let us begin with the official position of NASA, released to the public in the following form of this document:

SUBJECT: RE-ENTRY REPORT
PER YOUR TELECOM THIS DATE, THIS DATA APPEARS TO CORRESPOND TO YOUR SIGHTING(S).

1. 20925/1990-094C / GORIZONT 21 PLATFORM / USSR
2. 03 NOV 1990
3. REV 36 / DESCENDING / 05 NOV 1806Z
4. 49.0 DEG NORTH / 7.3 DEG EAST
5. DECAY WINDOW IS PLUS OR MINUS ONE MINUTE
6. INCLINATION 51.7 DEG.
TRAJECTORY PRIOR TO DECAY (DEG)
)/TIME 309/16512309/17062309/17212309/17362309/1751
LAT.30.0-17.8-51.5-25.222.8
LONG115.9153.7217.2289.7327.0
FINAL REPORT
312 0757 T COR TRANS NR : 0010 FM NCC NASA

According to CNES, all the observations made between 0:30 and 23:30 on Nov. 5, 1990, are attributed to the atmospheric re-entry of the Soviet rocket Gorinzont 21. However, the NASA telex contains precise details that do not correlate with the official statement made by scientists at CNES.

The first impossibility is that the rocket re-entry was not visible in France. The re-entry into the atmosphere is the moment when the phenomenon becomes visible. The atmospheric re-entry of a satellite or rocket, seen from a distance of 100 kilometers (62 miles) resembles a meteorite more than it does fireworks. The light it emits would be comparable to that of Venus, to those directly underneath it. CNES calculated the re-entry point as directly above the town of Bitche in northeast France, near the German border, at an altitude of 110 kilometers (68 miles). This would not have been visible at any of the locations marked on the map from which witnesses reported UFOs. Some of the reports came from as far away as 800 kilometers (497 miles) from the re-entry point.

The second impossibility is the angles of vision. fifty-five percent of the witnesses testified to having seen a black object or triangle at precisely 19:00, directly overhead. The locations from which these sightings were reported are scattered throughout France. It is completely impossible to explain this with any single object. At 100 kilometers (62 miles), the angle of vision is already only 45°. At 500 kilometers (311 miles), it is less than 12° — and that is without taking into account the roundness of the earth or irregularities of the terrain. Angular height: the theoretical horizontal is at 0°/H, while the vertical zenith is at 90°/H. The point is to estimate between 0° and 90° the apparent height from ground level above the horizontal 0°.

The third impossibility is the observation times. NASA specified the atmospheric re-entry as occurring at 18:06 Z, with a tolerance of one minute. That is 19:06 French time. The following table of figures is based only on the witnesses who reported black objects or triangles passing overhead at times that were precise to the minute:

TIME	#	TOTAL %
before	5	
18:55	10	
18:58	6	
18:59	2	107 CASES
19:00	46	(= 93%)
19:01	2	
19:02	12	
19:03	1	
19:04	3	
19:05	9	

19:06	4	POSSIBLE
19:07	5	ERROR
19:10	11	
TOTAL	116	

Witnesses observed the objects from 18:45 to 19:30. If we put to one side the sightings of 19:06 and 19:07, since they correspond with the time specified by NASA for the atmospheric re-entry, that still leaves us with 93 percent of the witness reports unexplained.

The fourth impossibility is the distance between witnesses and the objects. We used three ways of estimating these distances through triangulation. First, estimates based on reports by multiple witnesses. Second, estimates based on reports of UFO spotlights that swept the ground. Third, visual estimates from witnesses with previous experience in evaluating nocturnal distances, such as military training. 67 percent of the witnesses estimated the distance between them and the black object as less than one kilometer (0.6 miles). 47 percent estimated the distance as less than 500 meters (547 yards). Less than 6 percent of the witnesses found a distance of over 5 kilometers (3 miles) acceptable.

50 m	3		
100 m	11		
200 m	8		
250 m	1	= 51	
300 m	9	47%	
400 m	4		
500 m	15		= 72
600 m	1		67%
700 m	1	= 21	
800 m	1	19%	
1 km	18		
2 km	14		
3 km	5	= 36	
4 km	1	33%	
5 km	10		
6 + +	6		

The fifth impossibility is the angular dimensions of the object or triangle. Some witnesses extended their arms to estimate the size of the black object or triangle, judging from its appearance at the end of an extended arms, and came up with the following measurements:

8 cm 5%		
9 cm 11%	27%	
10 cm 11%		50%
15 cm 18%		
20 cm 5%	23%	
30 cm 5%		
35 cm 5%	28%	
40 cm 18%		50%
50 cm 10%	22%	
100 cm 12%		

Correlating these measurements with the estimated distances, the actual size of the black object or triangle was evaluated as follows:

10 m 2%		
30 m 7%	25%	
40 m 5%		
50 m 11%		51%
60 m 2%		
80 m 4%	26%	
100 m 20%		
150 m 7%		
200 m 14%	25%	
400 m 4%		49%
500 m 9%		
700 m 4%	24%	
1 km+ 11%		

Twenty-four percent of the witnesses estimate the length of the black object or triangle to have been 500 meters or more. 11 percent estimate the length at one kilometer or more. These objects are not a human scale!

The sixth impossibility is the duration of the sightings. According to CNES, an atmospheric re-entry is visible about one minute. 43 percent of the witnesses specified that they observed the object or triangle for 1 minute and 30 seconds or more. 37 percent observed it for more than 2 minutes, 20 percent for more than 3 minutes, 10 percent for more than 4 minutes.

10 s	8%	
15 s	5%	
20 s	4%	57%
30 s	12%	
45 s	8%	
1 mn	20%	
1 mn 30	6%	
2 mn	17%	
3 mn	10%	43%
4 mn	4%	
5 mn	6%	

The seventh impossibility is to explain the incongruities such as: rapid decreases in altitude, increases in altitude, explosion of an object in flight resulting in a group of objects flying in formation, flight so slow that the witness could keep up with the object at a walking pace, immobility and hovering followed by slow horizontal gliding, passing beneath the horizon or in front of landscape, changes in direction, allegations of nozzles protruding from the object, traces of condensation falling on the witness, spotlights on the underside or rear of the object emitting thin straight laser-like rays that at times extended about 300 meters (328 yards), spotlights that swept the ground, electromagnetic effects on TV sets and other equipment, simultaneous switching off of spotlights, synchronized blinking of spotlights, effects of perspective when passing close to witnesses.

In concluding this brief summary of our massive documentation, we would like to make a few comments. Over 400 credible witnesses made reports that had points in common. The flight path of this armada of over 70 ships (that is the minimal figure) was at an altitude of about 1,000 meters (3,280 feet), sometimes beneath the horizon, flying a horizontal course after descending rapidly from the sky, following parallel trajectories distant from each other by 5 to 25 kilometers (3 to 15 miles); there were changes in direction, immobility in flight, increases in altitude, and several waves in succession of flights. Their flight paths followed an organized plan. Considering the facts of the matter all together implies that a non-human intelligence and technology were responsible for the phenomena.

Normally NASA foresees and announces the atmospheric re-entry of rockets and satellites several days in advance, yet it was not until 2 days after the incidents that Gorizont 21 was used to explain the otherwise conventionally inexplicable. The panic among official scientists was obvious. An explanation had to be found at any price, so it was found.

Not a single one of the witnesses panicked, though some were at first uneasy. It may be that the technology we are confronted with has the capability of exerting a pacifying effect on some witnesses, whose initial uneasiness was replaced by powerful feelings of serenity. Some of our witnesses are not only in the military, but have ranks going as high as colonel.

The situation created by the events of Nov. 5, 1990, is without precedent. It is of major importance, because it indicates preparation for overt contact. The CNES abused its power. To silence questions that had become too precise, the CNES lied to the media, the public and the authorities, not only in France but throughout the world.

Appendix A

INSECTOIDS AND WHERE THEY COME FROM
by Riley Crabb of the Borderland Sciences Research Foundation

Flying Saucer Researchers and believers — as well as the merely curious — have been alerted to the presence of a specific type of Invader in the Earth's atmosphere by the reading of Whitley Strieber's *Communion* and by Budd Hopkins' findings. The fact that these invaders appear to be human-sized insects with a highly developed technology and exceptional hypnotic powers is beyond belief! Yet the testimony of hundreds of abductees cannot be denied nor dismissed as fiction. Fourth dimensional manifestations of another kind of evolution is a fact of ufology, and those who have experienced it directly have undergone a permanent change of consciousness. There's no going back!

Forty years of scientific research in the flying saucer phenomenon have come up with no answers. So, the dedicated researcher has no choice but to turn to the contactee and to the occult, two areas of research spurned by the orthodox scientist. The tragedy of America is that no explanation of any kind has been forthcoming from the authorities, in fact just the opposite, cover-up: so the abductees have had to seek each other out for consolation.

The Mahatmas of the Himalayas have known of the 4th Dimensional invasion from outer space for a long, long time. One of them, Djwal Kuhl, writing through Alice A. Bailey, revealed it in 1925 in the book *Treatise on Cosmic Fire*. Commenting on the origin of Cosmic Evil he observed that there were disintegrating constellations in the universe, unknown and unrecognized by scientists. These constellations have a "malefic effect upon our system and upon all that passes into their sphere of influence."

"There is one such constellation, situated between the Lesser Dipper and our system, and another, interrelated with the Pleiades and our system, which still have a profound effect upon the physical body of the solar Logos." That's his cryptic way of saying that we are being invaded by advanced beings from other systems and they have no morals or ethics. Later in *Treatise*, Djwal Kuhl says that cosmic evil becomes planetary evil in the unbalanced relationship between our planetary Logos and another planetary Logos, apparently a known star in the Great Bear Constellation.

Some contactees have been told that the Insectoids come from a planet of the Sun, Dubhe, in the Great Bear Constellation. "In this relation, at present lacking perfect adjustment, lies hid the mystery of cosmic evil" which will be negated when the "heavenly triangle is duly equilibrated...a. One of the stars of the Great Bear, b. The Pleiad involved, and c. The planetary scheme concerned."

Obviously these Insectoids have not finished their evolution on their own disintegrating planet and have chosen ours because of the abundance of air and water. The second reason for the invasion of these egg-born creatures is because we have something they do not: an individual, immortal soul — and the love and compassion that go with it! So it is highly unlikely that the attempts at cross-breeding reported by the abductees will have any success. The gap between the two evolutions is too great... For the student of metaphysics, whether Theosophist, Rosicrucian, Anthroposophist, Zen Buddhist or whatever, the question is to relate general statements about "an inhabited universe" to specific contacts with advanced beings who are here now!

Djwal Kuhl is one of the Mahatmas of the Himalayas who helped to guide and inspire H.P. Blavatsky in the writing of *The Secret Doctrine*. There he made reference to the problems of understanding 4-D, 5-D and 6-D phenomena which bedevil flying saucer researchers today — not to mention theoretical physicists chafing against the limits of 3-D science!

In Vol. I "Cosmogenesis" of *The Secret Doctrine,* Theosophical Press, Pt. Loma, California 1909(?), page 605, Blavatsky writes: "When the Secret Doctrine ... teaches that every one of the higher, as of the lower worlds, is inter-blended with our own objective world; that millions of things and beings are, in point of localization around us and in us, as we are around, with, and in them; it is no metaphysical figure of speech, but a sober fact in nature, however incomprehensible to our senses...

"Hence, when 'other worlds' are mentioned — interpenetrating it and interpenetrated by it. There are millions and millions of worlds and firmaments visible to us; there are still greater numbers beyond those visible to telescopes, and many of the latter kind do not belong to our objective sphere of existence. Although as invisible as if they were millions of miles beyond our solar system, they are yet with us, near us, within our own world, as material and objective to their own inhabitants as ours are to us...Yet by their spiritual sight the Adepts, and even some seers and sensitives, are always able to discern, whether in greater or smaller degree, the presence and close proximity to us of beings pertaining to other spheres of life..."

This "interpenetration" and "close proximity" has become a fact of daily life to Whitley Strieber and other abductees; and, as the abductors do not bother to give their point of origin to their victims; the Striebers of the flying saucer phenomenon remain in total ignorance and puzzlement as to what they are or where they come from in relation to present day astronomical knowledge. Betty Hill's kidnappers showed her a star map and asked her to locate our solar system on it. This she could not do, so the captain said, "There's no use telling you where our system is."

But there is a hint in Vol. II of the Point Loma edition of *The Secret Doctrine*, page 549, of the possible origin of the Insectoids in this dark cycle, "The mysterious constellation of the Seven Rishis in the Great Bear, if Egypt made them sacred to 'the oldest genitrix, Typhon...intimately connected with our present age — the Dark Kali Yuga' and Typhon is the Satan of the Egyptians. 'It is they, the Seven Rishis who mark the time and the duration of events in our septenary life cycle.. They are as mysterious as their supposed wives, the Pleiades...'" No hint there that actual beings from planets of the Great Bear and the Pleiades are coming here in space ships as physical manifestations of the "transfer of energy" from the two Constellations. Perhaps Blavatsky and Djwal Kuhl were sworn to secrecy.

The following excerpt from Eugenia Macer-Story's brilliant article, "The Control Factor in UFO Investigation," is of particular relevance to what Riley Crabb has just told us:

For centuries, Kabbalists have discussed a "dark satellite" (Zolar, 1984, page 108) which figures in a struggle between good and evil forces of destiny. This is not the moon or any of the planets in the astrological sense.

It is a dark dimensionality having its own organization and governed by well-defined laws. These laws and the energies they govern have an inverse relationship to the overt four-dimensional continuum. It is said that the energies of the dark satellite are lower instinctual energies informed by cunning and intelligence.

The beings of the dark satellite are said by Kabbalists to be neither elemental spirits nor spirits of the deceased which originate in the ordinary straightforward terrestrial dimensionalities.

According to Hermetic tradition, it is from within the dark center of the Astral realm of these beings that the spirit of lies, murder, fraud, and religious imposture is first formulated. Ideas from this dark center are then projected to the human community as the means of the continued existence of political and social deception. From the human receptors of these ideas, styles of imposture are reformulated to suit the spirit and temper of the times.

The silent, subtle influx of the dark satellite poisons the dimensional spaces that constitute the magnetic planes of all human life. Zolar, in his book *Ancient and Forbidden Knowledge,* quotes a verse from one of the supposed lost magical works of Hermes Trismegistus:

> So they called forth a form
> From the deep dark abyss
> To embody their evil desires.
> Obedient it came
> From the realms of the dead,
> Arrayed in its magic attire.
> As it passed o'er the earth
> The fair flowers fell dead
> From its breath of poisonous fire.

According to ancient traditions, the power of this shadow satellite is inversive. The cunning intelligence of the inhabitants of these dark realms enters by mental projection some facet of material truth and then proceeds by a process of inversion which can be very sophisticated to distort ordinary reality until human perception inverts into a negative dimensionality.

However, this orb of evil is not regarded as being a separate force. It is a satellite of the straightforward dimensionalities. Inhabitants of the dark satellite have only the power of inversion. They do not actually have the powers of direct creation or procreation.

Since I will be discussing this reverse universe in more detail, I mention the straightforward symbol of the Aleph before citing any reverse diagrams. Aleph is an energy form with hands and implements the positive transfer of ideas from the more subtle into the material dimensionalities. Sometimes, like the winged messenger Mercury, the Aleph is mentioned as the spirit of air. I heard a naturalist remark recently that we are all together inside the atmosphere and that it is literally the air that links all living beings on this planet.

Particular descriptions of the inverse universe and the inhabitants of these dark dimensionalities are found in Kabbalistic texts dating from antiquity. Discussion of this inverse realm is a highly secret (because dangerous) aspect of ancient metaphysical traditions with origins in Arabic as well as Western Hermetic cosmology. Usually the section on such topics will be a very short part of a longer, more positively oriented discussion of metaphysical symbology.

The positive Kabbalist diagram is called the Tree of Life and contains ten Sephiroth. Each of these Sephiroth are emanations of light which may manifest in various ways. Lengthy books have been written which discuss the meaning of the Tree of Life.

If an individual takes the diagram of the Tree of Life drawn on a thin piece of paper and turns it over, the diagram of the *sitra ahra* or reverse universe will be shown. This has the same symmetrical structure as the straightforward arrangement of the Sepheroth, but the letters of the names are reversed.

Since, in Kabbalist thought, the universe is constructed from letters and names, this is not a casual reversal. Beings found in the sphere of the *sitra ahra* are frequently referred to as the *Kelippah*. In a text written by Isaac of Acre (Amsterdam, 1648) certain manifestations of the Kelippah are described as having four fingers and no thumb.

The Kelippah "sought to take on a body through association with humans" (Scholem, 1987, page 321). Children who resulted from a union between a human and one of the Kelippah were said in tradition to be "illegitimate" progeny of the human parent. Care was taken at funerals, bar mitzvahs, and other family ceremonials that there was no confusion between the ordinary distant relatives who had come from afar and hybrid creatures falsely seeking part of the inheritance of the family bloodline.

Of course it might be argued that the hybrid between a Kelippah and a human was actually a member of the family. This sort of dilemma is an example of the extremely painful inverse scenarios which can be inducted into human affairs by the action of the more powerful types of Kelippah.

There is an obvious resemblance between ancient descriptions of the Kelippah and more contemporary descriptions of the gray beings (Jacobs, 1992, page 220) seen by individuals who claim to have been abducted by UFO aliens and subjected to "breeding" and forced "bonding" procedures.

"UFO abductees" have frequently wondered about the purpose of procedures that seem directed toward the creation of hybrid-alien children and the deliberate induction of mental-emotional reactivities and false reveries by telepathy. Often the inducted mental scenarios will seem skewed or inappropriate to the specific personal background of the person who is being affected telepathically.

If these procedures are seen in the knowledge of traditions of the inverse universe of the Kelippah, some coherence of interpretation may emerge. Here perhaps is a modern version of the mental induction of skewed thought and disruptive emotion that is mentioned in both Hermetic and Kabbalist texts as being the ambitious practice of inhabitants of the dark satellite who seek a foothold in the more straightforward dimensionalities.

It was here in the text that my word processor refused to behave, so I inserted a copy of an ancient amulet for protection against the Kelippah.

This was specifically for protection against Lilith. Oddly, the demon in the depiction literally looks like a UFO. Her consorts have the angular lack of an organic body often reported by people who interact with the gray UFO beings. The storage mechanism of my computer had literally refused to store the section on the reproductive mechanisms of the Kelippah until I realized that whether or not the storage mechanism was still locked I could still print the section in question. My realization seemed to unlock the mechanism.

Activity of negative mental entities swings about the basic duality of how an object may be observed. Thus, the person moving into the reverse world of the *sitra ahra* does not literally leap into another physical continuum, but into a mental continuum where all perspectives are basically changed. Not necessarily reversed, but skewed. The perception moves "behind the diagram" so to speak.

For example: in the magickal use of a horse trough, the trough itself does not necessarily change. A positive magician may ask a person to sprinkle water from it into the four corners of a room for purification purposes.

However, a negative magician may, by the use of mental glamour, be able to convince a person that the horse trough is the fountain of youth. After being charged a thousand dollars for a drink from this fountain, the unfortunate subject of this glamourous attention may get very sick.

A similar "glamourizing" experience sometimes occurs during UFO investigation.

Appendix B

TWO GOOD SOLDIERS

(Contributed by Citizens Against UFO Secrecy, 3518 Martha Curtis Drive, Alexandria, VA 22302)

Credits also to Larry Fenwick, Canadian UFO Research Network, P.O. Box 15, Station A, Willowdale, Ontario M2N 5S7, Canada, and to Robert H. Bletchman, 360 East Center St., Manchester, Conn. 06040.

Suddenly, and totally unrelated to his job performance, a U.S. Army employee of some 29 years service receives the ultimate designation of persona non grata from his superiors: an "unsatisfactory" performance rating.

Earlier, in September 1984, "UFO-cover-up whistleblower" advertisements had begun appearing in military post/base newspapers seeking details on such issues as the U.S. government's analysis of artifacts from crash-landed "flying saucers."

What could these two circumstances possibly have in common?

The recent decision of the U.S. Supreme Court in the First Amendment case of *Larry W. Bryant v. Casper W. Weinberger, et al.*

Filed as Civil Action No. 86-1323a in U.S. District Court for the Eastern District of Virginia (Alexandria Division), the case emerged as a two-count suit by Bryant to (1) protect his right to submit his ads to printers of various military "commercial enterprise" newspapers without his having to endure arbitrary rejection or other interference from the newspapers' overseers, the post/base public affairs officers; and to (2) reverse the on-the-job reprisal (in the form of the unjustified "unsatisfactory" rating) taken against him by his superiors at the Pentagon.

Bryant, a writer with the Army's Office of the Chief of Public Affairs, succeeded in settling Count No. 1 with a "consent order" issued by the district court judge in April 1987. The order upholds his right to continue submitting his ads seeking first-hand testimony and other evidence about what he calls the "Cosmic Watergate." "This represents," he said from his home in Alexandria, "a turning point — both for preserving free speech on public issues and for furthering government accountability for official

UFO-related actions and documentation. As director of the Washington office of the public-interest group Citizens Against UFO Secrecy, I've been pursuing the ad campaign to encourage current and former government officials to blow the whistle on the government's 40-year history of deceiving the public as to the reality of crash-landed UFOs and their retrieved occupants."

But arriving at the turning point cost Bryant dearly, for his having dared point a finger at the naked emperor's UFO clothes, he found himself the target of trumped-up counseling memos and other harassment aimed at punishing him for his heresy and at dissuading him from continuing the ad campaign.

Undaunted in his commitment both to greater freedom of UFO information and to protection of civil liberty, Bryant chose to take on his detractors in Count No. 2 of his lawsuit. Unfortunately, the government was able to convince the district court judge that the U.S. Civil Service Reform Act of 1978 precludes a civil servant like Bryant from gaining access to the federal court system to contest such cases of on-the-job harassment — even when the free-speech exercise takes place off the job in his capacity as a private citizen.

Bryant appealed to the U.S. Fourth Circuit Court of Appeals, based in Richmond, VA. A three-judge panel meeting in Baltimore cited its ruling in the 1985 free-speech case of *Pinar v. Dole* as governing the dismissal of Bryant's claim.

"Had I chosen to stop there, their decision would have meant that the several hundred thousand federal employees no longer would have the same degree of First Amendment protection enjoyed by non-federal people." Bryant explained. "So there was much more at stake here than just the stifling of a UFO researcher."

Indeed, Bryant felt he had no choice but file a "Petition for a Writ of Certiorari" with the U.S. Supreme Court. On the opening day of its current term, Oct. 3, 1988, the court issued the following order to the U.S. Fourth Circuit Court of Appeals: "The petition...is granted. The judgement is vacated and the case is remanded to the United States Court of Appeals for the Fourth Circuit for further consideration in light of *Webster v. Doe*, 486 U.S. ——— (1988)." In turn, that order was relayed to the district court in Alexandria.

As he awaits further developments in his case, Bryant acknowledges the show of support from fellow UFO researchers, colleagues, and friends.

"They knew, perhaps more than I, that every step of the way I was making ufological and legal history" he said. "In particular, I owe the most gratitude to a former co-worker, Lisa G. Fetterolf, who bravely had come forward with evidence crucial to the government's admission that Army officials had violated my First Amendment right of free speech. Her sworn declaration reveals that the former Chief of Army Public Affairs was under orders 'from on high' to 'get rid of' me because of my being 'an embarrassment to the government.'"

Now that his case has added to legal precedent, Bryant intends not to let up.

"I may write a book about all this, some day. Meantime, I've resumed the ad campaign, and I hope to have more time to share results with readers of the *MUFON UFO Journal* and other publications," he added.

One of Bryant's latest series of ads dealt with the plight of Army Sgt. First Class Clifford E. Stone in Roswell, New Mexico (who made the statement that was published on pages 181-182 of *Extra-Terrestrials Among Us.*)

The ad's title — "Exposed: Army Invokes 'Stone'-Age Tactics to Silence UFO Activist" — introduced military personnel to the circumstances surrounding Stone's fall from grace at the hands of his superiors at the New Mexico Military Institute.

Stone, a veteran of the Vietnam conflict and a MUFON researcher specializing in analysis of the government's UFO-related documentation, has been leading efforts at getting the full story on the "Snowbird" document. This one-page, "leaked" document had surfaced a few years ago, purporting to reveal the existence of "Project Snowbird," "Project Sigma," and other official projects dealing with U.S. retrieval of "crashed saucers" and U.S. exploitation of pertinent alien technology.

When some of Stone's superiors learned of his off-the-job pursuit of ufological truth, they chose to make an issue of it at his office. Among other harassment tactics, they relieved Stone of his duty position and branded him an incompetent — this coming from the same officers who earlier had rated him an outstanding non-commissioned officer.

After going public with his story, seeking the aid of the Army's Inspector General, and, basically, sticking to his Constitutional guns, Stone has won some vindication. A "commander's inquiry" recently completed by Stone's new chain-of-command concluded that "The XO (executive officer) overreacted to Stone's UFO interest and congressional contact, and in so doing, exhibited intolerance and bias against him. Reconstruction of events ... strongly suggests that action against Stone was not originally intended as a 'relief' but merely as a means to conveniently and quickly eliminate him as an 'embarrassment.'"

Now spurred on by such high-handed efforts to curb their UFO activism, both Stone and Bryant are continuing to seek greater freedom of UFO information.

For his part, Stone is pressing for congressional review of, and intervention in, the U.S. National Security Agency's stonewalling on responding further to Stone's pointed inquiries about the "Snowbird" document. That agency has invoked the defense that to respond further on such an issue dealing with "national security policy" would be improper.

Moving ahead on another front, Bryant has been pursuing a freedom-of-information lawsuit against the U.S. Department of Justice to free up the identity of the principals cited in the now-famous F.B.I. memorandum of March 22, 1950, recounting how three "flying saucers" had crashed in New Mexico.

"Because of this suit (which now awaits the judge's decision on the government's motion for summary judgement), the government has admitted that it was a 'local law-enforcement officer' who had relayed the story to a special agent of the Federal Bureau of Investigation," Bryant said. "This revelation adds to the credibility of the memo's content."

Appendix C

NATIVE AMERICANS FOR A CLEAN ENVIRONMENT
P.O. Box 1671, Tahlequah, Oklahoma 74465, (918) 458-4322

"We were not given this land by our parents. It is on loan to us from our children." — A Kenyan proverb.

"Under current law, it's a crime for a private citizen to lie to a government official, but not for the same official to lie to the people." — Donald M. Frazer.

"The Earth is not dying, it is being killed. And the people who are killing it have names and addresses." — Utah Phillips.

An agreement which authorizes Japan to acquire 150 tons of plutonium over the next 30 years went into effect on July 17, 1988. The U.S. only has 100 tons in its whole weapons system. The Foreign Relations Committee had written the Administration to say they felt the agreement would be illegal, but Reagan's folk didn't think so, and now Japan can begin shipments in 1990, carrying plutonium in containers not yet designed, in planes that are not yet built, without any future approval of the U.S. Can you imagine the disastrous results from a plane crash of this stuff?

There's a rumor going around that Kerr-McGee has contracted to ship their fertilizer made from nuclear waste to a rice grower in Arkansas.

The Committee for Nuclear Responsibility, Inc. has issued a document entitled "Revival Movement in Radiation-Land," which contains figures the nuclear community never wanted to see — figures that prove the cancer risks from low doses are far more serious than admitted by any of the international committees that set the standards. Write to: CNR, P.O. Box 11207, San Francisco, CA, 94101.

Peripheral Systems of Portland, Oregon, are working on batteries made out of nuclear waste. What's next?

The EPA failed to take its own staff's recommendation to regulate gas and oil drilling waste as hazardous. Instead Lee Thomas (the head of EPA) recommended that Congress continue the special exemption, even though EPA has many sites on its Superfund list caused by this type of waste.

Under public pressure due to ever-increasing popular awareness of its previously secret activities, an awareness that was spearheaded from the start by NACE, Kerr-McGee finally sold its plant in Gore, Oklahoma. However, the only change in the activities of the plant itself is of a cosmetic nature. The ownership and the name have changed from Kerr-McGee to General Atomics Technologies, but the toxic waste problem generated by the Gore nuclear facility remains unchanged. General Atomics intends to continue the Kerr-McGee policies of dumping nuclear waste into the Arkansas River, marketing "processed" nuclear waste as an agricultural fertilizer, raising cattle on radiation-contaminated hay and selling those cattle on the open market, and converting uranium for South Africa.

Aerojet General, which manufactures bullets from the reprocessed uranium made at the Gore facility, has been sued by its insurance company, which alleges that Aerojet knowingly polluted its facility. The pollution is leaking into the groundwater and the nearby American River in Sacramento, California.

Radio waves can cause both conventional and nuclear weapons accidents. This condition is known as the "Hazard of Electromagnetic Radiation to Ordnance" (HERO). Military experts have documented at least 25 HERO-suspect accidents. Independent research documents as many as 60. For further information, write: Axelrod & Rabinowitz, 5337 42nd Street, Washington, DC 20015.

The Soviets have lost radio contact with Cosmos 1900, a satellite that carries a nuclear power plant aboard. There is a lot of uncertainty about its re-entry to Earth.

Claiming the right of "free trade," U.S. companies are exporting their hazardous waste to Third World countries. There were at least 400 such shipments in 1987. We don't yet have more recent figures. A typical shipment consisted of 30,000 tons of incinerator ash, which was secretly dumped in Haiti and off the Guinea Coast.

Cesium-137 spilled from "leakproof" capsules into cooling water at Radiation Sterilizers, Inc. in Decatur, Georgia. The plant has been shut down and decontamination has begun. They were irradiating milk cartons. The big push now is to sterilize things with radiation. It used to be just medical equipment, but now it's everything from milk cartons to baby diapers to tampons.

Because of the effective lobbying of public protest groups, the Swedish Department of Agriculture reversed its previous promotion of food irradiation and joined the ranks of the opposition by presenting legislation to ban irradiated foods. The legislation passed!

Unless there is human error in the irradiation process, the food does not become radioactive, but it is chemically altered. Ions and electrons are knocked out of orbit, and will bond with other disrupted atoms to form different chemical combinations, some of which (such as formaldehyde or peroxide) are known, others of which are new to us, with totally unknown long-term effects on human health. Yet the Department of Energy, the Food & Drug Administration, and the World Health Organization (!) are all determined to cram irradiated food down the throats of the citizens of this and other countries without further testing, since food irradiation would be such a convenient way to dispose of some of the most toxic by-products of the nuclear industry. Anyone who wants to protest against this suicidal policy should write a letter stating that you are concerned about the safety of the food you eat, that you will never purchase food that has been exposed to radiation, and you will not shop at any supermarket that supports this technology by selling radiation-tainted food. Letters should be sent to the Food Marketing Institute, 1750 K Street, Washington, DC 20006.

During recent years, NACE has tried to stop the renewal of the Gore facility's permit to dump nuclear waste into the Arkansas River. This state permit, which expired in 1982, is issued by the Oklahoma Water Resources Board, of which Robert Kerr, Jr. (son of the late Senator Kerr, founder of the Kerr-McGee empire) is a member. During the struggle to stop the renewal of this permit, NACE called for Kerr's removal from the OWRB because of conflict of interest, since he is a major stockholder of the Kerr-McGee Corporation and is on its Board of Directors. Was he removed? No. He was instead made Chairman of the OWRB, two weeks before the new permit was issued.

Although both Kerr-McGee and the Nuclear Regulatory Commission assured NACE that the ponds full of nuclear waste, which were described on page 278 of *Extra-Terrestrials Among Us*, had been cleaned up, General Atomics admits that they are still in existence. So in spite of all the public indignation and protest, followed by soothing reassurances from the authorities that the problem has been taken care of, the ponds are still there, still leaking their lethal contents into the groundwater we all must drink.

Appendix D

MASS MURDER AS A MEANS
OF MANIPULATING PUBLIC OPINION
by George C. Andrews

I have found four possible links between Marc Lepine, the 25 year old mass murderer of 14 female students at the Polytechnical College of Montreal on December 6, 1989, and the CIA. These correlations are based on the articles about Lepine's background by Greg Watson and Jack Aubry in the *Toronto Star* on February 7-8, 1990.

The first possible link is the lavishly lucrative employment of Liass Gharbi, Marc Lepine's Algerian-born father, with the Investors Overseas Services balloon that burst during the 1960s. As the Nugan Hand banking scandal and also the Savings and Loan scandal in the United States have demonstrated, as well as the recent worldwide BCCI scandal, swindles of this nature are standard operating procedure for the CIA to raise money for its covert activities. If the Investors Overseas Services boom-and-bust was orchestrated by the CIA, an employee like Gharbi would have been thoroughly investigated before being added to the payroll. Information concerning his family life, tendencies toward violence, and divorce would have been routinely added to his file. Employees naive enough to invest their savings in the corporation before its sudden bankruptcy would receive no warning or compensation, and would be left stranded, just as Gharbi was. Although no longer an employee of a CIA front organization, Gharbi's file would still have been retained by the CIA, which might have continued to monitor his activities occasionally.

The second possible link is through Lepine's uncle, a former Canadian Forces paratrooper who had also trained with the U.S. Special Forces, an elite group that is closely integrated with the CIA. This uncle taught the young Gamil Gharbi (who later changed his name to Marc Lepine) how to use a gun. The young man visited this uncle at his Quebec farm frequently during a three year period. This constitutes a direct connection with the CIA during the formative years of the mass murderer's early adolescence.

The third possible link is the "surrogate father" provided to Marc at the age of 14 by the Big Brothers Association. When Marc was 17, this "surrogate father," whose activities included extensive involvement with electronic gadgetry, suddenly disappeared, "gone back to Europe." Investigative journalists Weston and Aubry found it curious that this "surrogate father" had not left behind any administrative records through which he could be traced.

Was this nebulous and elusive "surrogate father" a CIA monitor who provided a conditioning that the uncle did not provide, and may have known nothing of? While the uncle provided the weapons training, did the "surrogate father" initiate the RHIC-EDOM conditioning through preliminary hypnosis sessions in which electronic gadgetry was involved? RHIC-EDOM, the acronym for *Radio Hypnotic Intracerebral Control - Electronic Dissolution of Memory,* a mind control technique developed by the CIA with your tax dollars. RHIC-EDOM is capable of programming an individual to carry out an act such as committing a murder while erasing all memory of that act, and of the conditioning that brought it about, from the individual's mind.

The fourth possible link is the privately run Control Data Institute in Montreal, at which Marc Lepine enrolled for training in the spring of 1988. The name of this enterprise is redolent of an Intelligence agency front. It is a matter of public record that the CIA owns many businesses in different countries with similar names and functions. Two months after enrolling at Control Data Institute, Lepine moved out of the apartment he had lived in for two years, telling the landlord that he was "going off to join the armed forces." Was this what he believed to be the truth? Had he been given reason to think that a career had opened up for him as an Intelligence agent? Shortly afterward, he attended his high school reunion party, dressed out of character in fashionable and expensive clothing, never before having looked "so dapper, so prosperous."

However, on March 31, 1989, when only two months and two relatively easy courses from completing his training at Control Data Institute, he inexplicably dropped out and stopped attending classes, without giving anyone a reason for this apparently irrational decision.

The next move he made was to apply for a firearms acquisition certificate, and start shopping around for a semi-automatic weapon. The first sentence of the suicide note he wrote several days before committing the mass murders states: "I will die on December 6, 1989." Was this flatly factual statement a reflection of his RHIC-EDOM conditioning, which had been activated just before he dropped out of his nearly-completed training at Control Data Institute?

The CIA's main motive for arranging the Montreal massacre would have been similar to its motive for arranging the Stockton, California schoolyard massacre of January 17, 1989, perpetrated by "lone young drifter" Patrick Hurdy: to frighten the public into supporting legislation that would ban semi-automatic weapons. When the President goes on TV to proclaim a State of Emergency, civil law based on the Constitution is to be replaced by martial law, and normal law enforcement officers are to be replaced by the black-uniformed Delta Special Forces, the resurrected Gestapo. The faceless FEMA replaces the President, allowing atrocities to be committed without anyone being held responsible. The concentration camps have already been built. Civilian resistance to the replacement of democracy by dictatorship will be far less effective if the citizens hand over their semi-automatic weapons to the authorities before the State of Emergency is declared.

Proclamation of a State of Emergency in the United States will be followed by a similar proclamation in Canada within a matter of hours. According to an article by Howard Goldenthal in the *Toronto Star* of June 27, 1989: "FEMA (Federal Emergency Management Agency), which most Americans believe was set up to coordinate relief following natural disasters or nuclear war, is also responsible for managing response to rioting, terrorism and armed insurrection, according to Diana Reynolds, a professor at Tufts University and an expert on the agency's activities. It should be noted that FEMA, since its creation in 1979, has had an extremely close relationship with the Canadian emergency people. In 1986, the U.S. and Canada signed the Cooperation in Comprehensive Civil Emergency Planning and Management agreement. That agreement all but fused FEMA with Emergency Planning Canada (now Emergency Preparedness Canada)."

Marc Lepine's father, Algerian-born Liass Gharbi, was divorced by Marc's mother because of his persistent physical violence. Similar behavior characterized his relationships with the many other women he became involved with, caused in large part by his attempting to impose fundamentalist Islamic standards of feminine submission on American women. Exposure to this problem during infancy and early childhood must have made a deep impression on Marc, resulting in traumatic memories of major severity. As he grew up, these memories would have been gradually suppressed and replaced by neurotic behavior patterns that contained glaringly obvious weak points. Anyone subjecting an adolescent to mind-manipulating techniques for control purposes, with no concern for the adolescent's well-being, would soon notice these weak points and would focus special attention on them, amplifying, resonating and exacerbating them so they could be orchestrated by the controller. In the political climate of December, 1989, an obvious motivation for programming a disposable assassin to murder women only would have been to frighten and intimidate supporters of feminist movements, such as freedom of choice.

The real scandal of the Reagan-Bush years is the extent to which the Democrats collaborated in the colossal rip-off of the U.S. taxpayer, functioning as a tame and toothless opposition that spread the myth of a Teflon President instead of speaking up about, for example, the atrocities we were actually committing in Central America.

The first step toward balancing the budget should be to remove from it the entire tumor of the "black budget," which is a malignant growth. If a project can not stand public scrutiny, it should not be publicly funded. Total transparency in government, full disclosure no matter what the circumstances, is the only way to restore the nation's health and confidence.

What our sold out politicians are actually doing, while pretending to act in the best interests of the United States, is to concentrate more and more wealth into fewer and fewer hands. This is detrimental not only to the vast majority of the citizens of the United States, but to the world as a whole. No one profits from this type of situation except the few families of the super-rich, who are deliberately collapsing the world economy as a prelude to a Trilateral takeover.

Why should we continue to allow a small group of billionaire power junkies to ruin the lives of average Americans and everyone else on the planet? They wave the flag and pretend to be acting in the best interests of the United States, when it is actually themselves and no one else they are enriching, as they soothe the public with syrupy pie-in-the-sky promises, repeated endlessly by the news media, which they are the owners of, like that of the mythical "trickle-down effect."

The world's resources are not circulating like blood does in a healthy body, but are instead being monopolized by a tiny elite clique that is a cancer on the body politic, not only making life intolerable for everyone else, but destroying the planet's biosphere. Mother Earth is our star, and it is the only one we have. The words of Utah Phillips are worth repeating as the final sentence of this book: "The Earth is not dying, it is being killed. And the people who are killing it have names and addresses."

Credits

The version of Black Elk's Prayer to the Great Spirit on the title page was recited by John G. Neihardt on a 33 1/3 rpm record entitled "The Wonder of it All," released by Roto Records, Thompson Company RC-1004, Lincoln, Nebraska, in 1970.

CHAPTER ONE

The details of the Schirmer and Greenhaw cases were summarized from an article entitled "UFO Witnesses: Are They Public Property?" By Harry Tokarz in *CUFORN Bulletin*, May-June, 1984. Canadian UFO Research Network, P.O. Box 15, Station A, Willowdale, Ontario M2N 5S7.

The book by Aime Michel to which General Chassin wrote the Preface was *Flying Saucers and the Straight Line Mystery*, published by S.G. Phillips, Inc., New York, 1958. The statement by Aime Michel concerning JANAP-146 was taken from the volume in the "Pour ou Contre" collection that was devoted to UFOs, published by Berger-Levrault in Nancy, France, in 1969.

The details of the Brazilian case of May 19, 1986, were summarized from translations of articles in the Brazilian press obtained through Lucius Farish's UFO Newsclipping Service, Rt. 1 Box 220, Plumerville, AR, 72127. These included *Journal do Brasil*, Rio de Janeiro, Brazil, May 23, 1986; *O Povo*, Fortaleza, Brazil, May 23, 1986; *Ultima Hora*, Rio de Janeiro, Brazil, May 24, 1986: *O Globo*, Rio de Janeiro, Brazil, May 14, 1986. The special issue of *Planeta*, Caixa Postal 113, Sao Paulo, devoted to the events of May 19 was obtained thanks to Simon Vinkenoog of Amsterdam, Holland. "Lenticular clouds" explanation mentioned in article entitled "Out of the Blue" by Kent Black in *Philip Morris Magazine*, Summer 1987.

The details of the events of Aug. 12, 1986, were also summarized from Lucius Farish's *UFONS*, specifically from articles in the following newspapers: *Herald-Journal*, Syracuse, NY, Aug. 13, 1986; *USA Today*, Arlington, VA, Aug. 14; *Tribune-Democrat*, Johnstown, PA, Aug. 14: *Arkansas Gazette*, Little Rock, AR, Aug. 14; *Sun*, Winchester, KY, Aug. 14 & 15; *Courier-Journal*, Louisville, KY, Aug. 16; *Journal*, Winston-Salem, NC, Aug. 16; *Standard Observer*, Irwin, PA, Aug. 16: Star, *Leongatha*, Victoria, Australia, Aug. 19.

For the abduction of Aug. 15, 1986, *UFONS* and *Il Giornale*, Milano, Italy, Aug. 26, 1986.

For the European incidents of Sept. 23, 1986, *UFONS* and *Weekly Express*, Daventry, England, Sept. 25, 1986; *Evening Telegraph*, Derby, England, Sept. 25; *Mercury*, Leicester, England, Sept. 16; *Journal do Brasil*, Rio de Janeiro, Brazil, Sept. 24; *O Globo*, Rio de Janeiro, Brazil, Sept. 24; *Mainichi Daily News*, Tokyo, Japan, Sept. 25; *Liberation*, Paris, France, Sept. 14: *Le Parisien*, Paris, France, Sept. 24.

For the Japan Air Lines sighting over Alaska on Nov. 17, 1986, *UFONS* and *News*, Detroit, MI, Jan. 1, 1987; *Free Press*, Detroit, MI, Jan. 1; *Chronicle*, Houston, TX, Jan. 3; *Times*, Seattle, WA, Jan. 3 & 8; *Post*, Washington, DC, Jan. 4; *USA Today*, Arlington, VA, Jan. 5,& & 14; *Arkansas Democrat*, Little Rock, AR, Jan. 13; *Inquirer*, Philadelphia, PA, May 24.

This is the numbered list of newspapers, corresponding to the numbered UFO sightings and incidents between July 1, 1987, and June 30, 1988:

1. *News*, Danville, PA, Feb. 26, 1988.
2. *Enquirer*, Columbus, GA, July 17, 1987.
    Telephone, Madison, WI, July 23 & 30, 1987.
3. *Capital Times*, Madison, WI, July 15, 1987.
    Wisconsin State Journal, Madison, WI, July 15, 1987.
    Courier Hub, Stoughton, WI, July 16, 1987.
4. *Daily Record*, Roswell, NM, Oct. 1, 1987.
5. *Herald*, Exmouth, England, Aug. 7 & 14, 1987.
6. *Ocean Co. Observer*, Brick Town, NJ, Aug. 13, 1987.
7. *Province*, Victoria, B.C., Canada, Sept. 18, 1987.
    Sun, Vancouver, B.C., Canada, Sept. 22, 1987.
    Evening Telegraph, Derby, England, Aug. 17 & 20, 1987.
8. *News Miner*, Fairbanks, AK, Aug. 27, 1987.
9. *Telegraph*, Seymour, Victoria Province, Australia, Sept. 1, 1987.
    Gazette, Gwent, England, Sept. 3, 1987.
10. *Southwest Times*, Pulaski, VA, Oct. 14, 1987.
    S.W. Virginia Enterprise, Wytheville, VA, Oct. 15 & 19, 1987.
    Herald Courier, Bristol, VA, Oct. 16 & Nov. 20, 1987.
    Daily Progress, Charlottesville, VA, Oct. 18, 1987.
    Times-Dispatch, Richmond, VA, Oct. 19, 1987 & Jan. 3, 1988.
    Daily Telegraph, Bluefield, WV, Oct. 24, 1987.
    Northern Virginia Daily, Strasburg, VA, Oct. 24, 1987.
    Herald, Farmville, VA, Dec. 9, 1987.

Times & World-News, Roanoke, VA, Nov. 14, 1987.
Carrol News, Hillsville, VA, Dec. 9, 1987.
11. *Gazette Telegraph*, Colorado Springs, CO, Sept. 4, 1987.
12. *Record*, Detroit Lakes, MN, Sept. 7, 1987.
13. *Evening Mail*, Birmingham, England, Sept. 16, 1987.
    Newsletter, Stafford, England, Oct. 2, 1987.
14. *News-Argus*, Lewistown, MT, Nov. 15, 1987.
15. *Independent*, Cornwall, England, Sept. 27, 1987.
16. *Free Press*, Amery, WI, Sept. 29, 1987.
17. *East Anglican Daily Times*, Ipswich, England, Oct. 10, 1987.
18. *Herald Express*, Torquay, Devon, England, Oct. 1, 1987.
19. *Jerusalem Post*, Israel, Oct. 9, 1987.
    Yediot Abaraaot, Israel, Oct. 9, 1987.
20. *Evening Mail*, Birmingham, England, Feb. 19, March 31, April 9, 1988.
21. *Journal*, Salisbury, England, Oct. 15, 1987.
22. *Burton Mail*, Staffordshire, England, Oct. 31, 1987.
23. *Herald*, Worthing, England, Oct. 9, 1987.
24. *Valley News Dispatch*, Jeanette, PA, Oct. 31, 1987.
25. *Kent Evening Post*, Maidstone, England, Oct. 20, 1987.
26. *Monadnock Ledger*, Peterborough, NH, Oct. 29, 1987.
27. *Times*, Little Fork, MN, Oct. 28, 1987.
28. *Watsall Observer*, Staffordshire, England, Nov. 6, 1987.
    Burton Mail, Staffordshire, England, Nov. 9, 1987.
29. *Chichester Observer*, Sussex, England, Nov. 19, 1987.
30. *Reporter*, Edgerton, WI, Nov. 19, 1987.
31. *Enterprise*, Simi Valley, CA, Nov. 11, 1987.
32. *Sentinel*, Gulf Breeze, FL, Nov. 19 & 25, Dec. 3 & 10, 1987, Jan. 14, 1988, Feb. 11 & 18, March 3, 10, 17, 24 & 31.
    MUFON UFO Journal, Seguin, TX, July 1988.
    Tribune, Bismarck, ND, Dec. 8, 1987.
    Beacon, Beulah, ND, March 10, 1988.
33. *West Lancashire Evening Gazette*, Blackpool, England, Dec. 10, 1987.
34. *Express & Star*, Wolverhampton, England, Nov. 23, 1987.
35. *Daily Telegraph*, Bluefield, WV, Nov. 24, 1987.
36. *Wayne Co. Outlook*, Monticello, KY, Dec. 17, 1987.
37. *Sun*, Melbourne, Australia, Jan. 22, 1988.
38. *Delaware Valley News-Eagle*, Hawley, PA, Dec. 24, 1987.
39. *Arkansas Democrat*, Little Rock, AR, Feb. 9, 1988.
40. *Star*, London, England, Jan. 27, 1988.

41. *News,* Kenosha, WI, Jan. 7, 1988.
42. *Evening News,* Bolton, Lancashire, England, Jan. 7, 1988.
43. *Yorkshire Post,* Leeds, England, Jan. 7, 1988.
    Southend Evening Echo, Essex, England, Jan. 7, 1988.
44. *Press & Sun-Bulletin,* Binghamton, NY, Jan. 11, 13 & 16, 1988.
45. *Tribune,* Ashley, ND, April 6, 1988.
46. *Beacon,* Cannon Falls, MN, March 3, 1988.
    Seaford Gazette, Sussex, England, Jan. 20, 1988.
47. *Press,* Christchurch, New Zealand, Jan. 22, 1988.
48. *Morning World-Herald,* Omaha, NE, Jan. 18, 1988.
49. *Arkansas Gazette,* Little Rock, AR, Jan. 23, 1988.
    Arkansas Democrat, Little Rock, AR, Jan. 23, 1988.
    Gazette, Texarkana, TX, Jan. 23 & 24, 1988.
    Bee, Dequeen, AR, Jan. 28, 1988.
    NorthWest Arkansas Times, Fayetteville, AR, Feb. 4-8, Mar. 27, 1988.
    McCurtain Co. Gazette, Idabel, OK, April 10, 1988.
    Article by C. Louis Weidemann entitled "Mysteries Breaking Out All Over" in *Fate,* Highland, Park, IL, Sept., 1977.
50. *Sun,* Melbourne, Australia, Jan. 21, 25 & 30, 1988.
    Australian, Melbourne, Australia, Jan. 21, 1988.
    Telegraph, Brisbane, Australia, Jan. 21, 1988.
    Sunday Observer, Melbourne, Australia, Jan. 24, 1988.
    News, Adelaide, Australia, Feb. 1, 1988.
    MUFON UFO Journal, Seguin, TX, March, 1988.
    UFO Research Australia Newsletter, P.O. Box 229, Prospect, South Australia 5082, April, 1988.
51. *McCurtain Co.* Gazette, Idabel, OK, Jan. 22, 1988.
52. *Tribune-Herald,* Waco, TX, Jan. 23, 1988.
53. *Express & Star,* Wolverhampton, England, Jan. 23, 1988.
54. *South Wales Evening Post,* Swansea, Wales, Jan. 28, 1988.
55. *World,* Wenatchee, WA, Feb. 1, 1988
56. *North Western Daily Mail,* Barrow-in-Furness, England, Feb. 19, 1988.
57. *Rotherham & South Yorkshire Advertiser,* Rotherham, England, March 4 & 31, 1988.
    Independant, Perpignan, France, Feb. 4, 1988.
58. *Independant,* Perpignan, France, Feb. 4, 1988.
59. *Medon & Dukeries Advertiser,* Mansfield, England, Feb. 18, 1988.
60. *Midi Libre,* Montpellier, France, Feb. 8 & 12, 1988.
61. *Star,* Shropshire, England, Feb. 23, 1988.
    Le Meridional, Marseilles, France, Feb. 17,1988.

62. *Star*, Johannesburg, South Africa, Feb. 15 & 16, 1988.
63. *Evening Mail*, Birmingham, England, Feb. 25, 1988.
64. *Times Series*, Bedfordshire, England, Feb. 25, 1988.
65. *Tribune-Democrat*, Johnstown, PA, Feb. 28, 1988.
66. *Pioneer*, Brandenburg, KY, Feb. 23 & March 8, 1988.
67. *Doncaster Star*, Doncaster, Yorkshire, England, Feb. 25, 1988.
68. *Daily Mail*, Hull, England, Feb. 26, 1988.
69. *Free Press*, Bury, England, March 4, 1988.
70. *Lichfield Mercury*, Staffordshire, England, March 11, 1988.
    Sun, Bremerton, WA, March 2, 1988.
71. *Star-Ledger*, Newark, NJ, March 3, 1988.
    New Jersey Press, Asbury Park, NJ, March 4, 1988.
72. *Daily News Leader*, Staunton, VA, March 5, 1988.
73. *Pierce Co. Herald*, Ellsworth, WI, March 9, 1988.
74. *Dorking & Leatherhead Advertiser*, Surrey, England, March 24, 1988.
75. *North Wales Weekly*, Conway, Wales, March 10, 1988.
76. *Wallsall Observer*, Staffordshire, England, March 11, 1988.
77. *Times*, Salisbury, MD, April 11, 1988.
78. *Hitchin Gazette*, Hertfordshire, England, March 16, 1988.
79. *Reporter Dispatch*, White Plains, NY, Feb. 21 & March 16, 1988.
    Hudson Dispatch, White Plains, NY, March 18, 1988.
    Post, New York City, NY, March 18, 1988.
    Daily News, New York City, NY, March 18, 1988.
80. *Ledger*, Gaffney, SC, March 23, 1988.
81. *Chase Post*, Cannock, England, March 24, 1988.
82. *Daily News Leader*, Staunton, VA, March 25, 1988.
    Sunday News Leader, Staunton, VA, March 27, 1988.
83. *McCurtain Co. Gazette*, Idabel, OK, March 31, 1988.
84. *Dispatch*, Columbus, OH, March 29, 1988.
85. *Evening Mail*, Birmingham, England, March 31, 1988.
86. *Daily Telegraph*, Bluefields WV, April 1, 1988.
87. *Leigh Journal*, Lancashire, England, April 7, 1988.
88. *Virginian-Pilot*, Norfolk, VA, April 26, 1988.
89. *Herald*, Morris, IL, April 12, 1988.
    Star, Oxford, England, April 14, 1988.
90. *Crow*, Royston, England, April 15, 1988.
91. *Evening Press*, Guernsey, England, April 15, 1988.
92. *Southend Evening Echo*, Essex, England, May 9, 1988.
93. *Sun*, London, England, April 16, 1988.
94. *Var Matin*, Toulon, France, April 17, 1988.
95. *Berkshire Eagle*, Pittsfield, MA, April 22, 1988.

96. *Barnsley Chronicle*, Yorkshire, England, May 13, 1988.
97. *Pierce Co. Herald*, Ellsworth, WI, April 27, 1988.
98. *Le Provencal*, Marseilles, France, April 25, 1988.
99. *Evening Mail*, Birmingham, England, April 24, 1988.
100. *Tribune-Democrat*, Johnstown, PA, April 25, 1988.
101. *Leader*, Aberdare Wales, April 28, 1988.
102. *Journal*, River Falls, WI, May 5, 1988.
103. *Inner-County Leader*, Frederick, WI, May 4, 1988.
104. *Press & Journal*, Aberdeen, Scotland, May 7, 1988.
105. *Sevenoaks Chronicle*, Kent, England, May 20, 1988.
106. *Dorking & Leatherhead Advertiser*, Surrey, England, May 19, 1988.
107. *Newsletter*, Stafford, England, May 20 & 27, 1988.
108. *Mercury*, Leicester, England, May 18, 1988.
109. *Sun*, Jonesboro, AR, May 19, 1988.
    Northeast Arkansas Town Crier, Manila, AR, May 24, 1988.
110. *Times-News*, King, NC, June 1, 1988.
111. *Enterprise*, Simi Valley, CA, May 27, 1988.
112. *News & Advertiser*, Lynn, England, June 10, 1988.
    Tennessean, Nashville, TN, June 7 & 9, 1988.

All the French cases in the above list were forwarded to me through the courtesy of Rene Voarino, Centre d'Etudes OVNI France, Bt. 5, Square Monaco, 13170 La Gavotte, France.

Details concerning the handwriting analysis of the Majestic-12 documents summarized from *UFO*, vol. 3, No. 2, 1988; Box 355, 1800 South Robertson Boulevard, Los Angeles, CA 90035.

The material concerning Major Coleman Von Keviczky was summarized from correspondence with him, as well as from *Gray Barker's Newsletter*, issue no. 12, July, 1980; Box 2228, Clarksburg, WV, 26301. The address of Major Von Keviczky's research group is: ICUFON, Suite 40, 35-40 75th. St., Jackson Heights, NY 11372.

The material concerning Dr. Hynek and the OSI is summarized from *Above Top Secret* by Timothy Good (Morrow, 1988). Mr. Good in turn credits it to "UFOs and the CIA Cover-Up" by B. Ann Slate and Ann Druffel in *UFO Report*, vol. 2, no. 4, New York, 1975. Concerning the early association of Jacques Vallee with Dr. Hynek, the review of Vallee's *Dimensions* (Contemporary, 1988) by John White in New Realities, July/August, 1988.

An edited and rewritten version of my research proposal was printed in *California UFO*, vol. 2, no. 3, 1987; Box 355, 1800 South Robertson Boulevard, Los Angeles, CA, 90035. The original version was published in the

Proceedings of the 1987 Rocky Mountain Conference on UFO Investigation, 1425 Steele Street, Laramie, WY, 82070.

CHAPTER TWO

The quote from Gray Barker is from *Gray Barker's Newsletter*, Box 2228, Clarksburg, WV 26301 (March, 1976).

The documentation on the Mundrabilla incident is number 50 on the list of credits for Chapter One.

CHAPTER FOUR

The material concerning Lake Tahoe is from the *Gazette Journal* of Reno, NV, issues of Jan. 29, Feb. 18, 19 & 23, March 26 & 27, 19B7, as summarized in *Light-Net Prosperity Newsletter*, 207 Birch Street SE, Topeka, KS 66609.

CHAPTER FIVE

The material concerning the vitrified prehistoric forts is summarized from *Needles of Stone* by Tom Graves (Turnstone, London, 1978)

The reference to L & L Research's Ra channel concerns the book *The Ra Material*, by Don Elkins, Carla Rueckert, James Allen McCarty, published by Donning in Virginia Beach, VA, in 1984.

CHAPTER SIX

A different version of Dr. Jean Mundy's article "Abduction: Was it all a Dream?" appeared in *UFO Universe,* Spring 1989. That version was entitled "Do Your Dreams Reveal a Hidden Alien Abduction?"

CHAPTER NINE

The Riley Crabb material is summarized from *Sky Crash: The Best UFO Story in Years*, which was published in 1986 by Mark Moeller, P.O. Box 115, Pea Ridge, AR 71751, as an overseas publication of the Borderland Sciences Research Foundation, 161 A Centreway Road, Orewa, Hibiscus Coast, New Zealand. The reason for this exotic address is to be found in an interview that appeared in *The Auckland Sun* of Feb. 22, 1988: "After what he believes were a couple of bungled attempts on his life, Riley Crabb packed his files and an overnight bag and headed for Godzone. Just out of San Diego, California, the Director of Borderland Sciences tells me he left a house, regularly spied on from helicopters, and where the phones were bugged — both done by shadowy organizations who like to keep their fingers on the pulse of the UFO business, and anything else Riley and his worldwide Borderland Science followers dug into."

The details concerning the Federal Reserve are from the Jan. 1983 issue of *Acres. U.S.A.*, P.O. Box 9547, Kansas City, MO, 64133.

The statement by John Lear originally appeared in *The Matrix* by Valdamar Valerian, published in 1988 by Arcturus.

CHAPTER TWELVE

The material concerning the U.S. Army report from the 352nd Civil Affairs Command on the New Kuwait is based on the excerpts from that report in *After Hussein's Military Defeat* by Craig B. Hulet, published in 1991 by KC & Associates, 13510-A Aurora Ave. North, Suite 108, Seattle, WA 98133.

APPENDICES

Excerpts from the article "The Control Factor in UFO Investigation" by Eugenia Macer-Story were published in the proceedings of the International Forum on New Science 1992, Fort Collins, CO.

Watch for the sequel to *Extra-terrestrial Friends and Foes*, entitled *Other Worlds in This One*, written in collaboration with abduction specialist Barbara Bartholic.

Index